Praise

'Every new book by Peter an... ...ration and *Extreme Eiger* is no except... ...ssion, intellectual rigor, and the sor... ...es their books well beyond the genre of mountaineering literature. *Extreme Eiger* is a story of courage and competition, triumph and tragedy, that will appeal to anyone keen to know just what happens to those who risk everything to achieve their dreams.' Wade Davis – author *Into The Silence: The Great War, Mallory, and the Conquest of Everest*

'Peter and Leni Gillman have given a detailed, human and absorbing account of this extraordinary story. It is utterly compelling and in places so vivid that it is vertigo-inducing. Several times I found myself involuntarily leaning back in my chair. It says far more about the human condition than most mountaineering accounts and is all the more fabulous for being told even-handedly from both German and British/American perspectives. A tour de force.' Julie Summers – author *Fearless on Everest; Jambusters; When the Children Came Home*

'Expertly assembled, marvellous telling detail, with fine photos and route-diagrams. Layton Kor, who I partnered on several first ascents, would have been thrilled to read his story and those of the two Eiger Direct teams.' Ed Webster – mountaineer and author *Snow in the Kingdom, My Storm Years on Everest*

'I'm fascinated that the story of the Eiger Direct half a century ago continues to ripen and touch our lives – and that as Peter Gillman peers back through his retrospectroscope, he sees, among much else, a half-a-century younger Peter Gillman watching the plot unfold in real time. *Extreme Eiger* combines imaginative new inquiry with fine storytelling to do justice to this historic ascent. This new telling reveals how what began as a competition between German and Anglo-American teams to be first, ended as a collaboration – an outcome that captures humankind at its best. The Gillmans' tale is moving, gripping and exhausting. I'm hooked.' Tom Hornbein – mountaineer and author *Everest, the West Ridge*

'*Extreme Eiger* ... ...e right balance of hum... ...such a meticulous day... ...to pull

off the trick of hooking casual readers as well as mountaineers. It stands as the definitive account of a tragic but ultimately record-breaking ascent of Europe's most unforgiving mountain, and the best possible memorial to those who took part.' Richard Girling – author *Sea Change – Britain's Coastal Catastrophe; Greed; The Hunt for the Golden Mole*

'I loved it, a real page-turner. Peter and Leni Gillman have done a superb job. Bringing in the recollections of the German teams makes it a gripping read and adds real poignancy as well.' Steve Dean – author *Hands of a Climber: A life of Colin Kirkus;* secretary and trustee, Boardman Tasker Charitable Trust.

'An impressive work, meticulously researched and, as far as I can see, scrupulously accurate. The Gillmans have tracked down the surviving Germans and their accounts are every bit as gripping as the better-known one of Haston. This is an important contribution to Eiger history, and the Gillmans deserve congratulation on such a compelling and well-written book.' Jim Curran – author *K2 – The Story of the Savage Mountain; High Achiever – the Life and Climbs of Chris Bonington*

'One of the greatest strengths of this book is its empathetic telling of so many powerful stories. It will, in my opinion, became a mountaineering classic. It is a skilfully written and sensitive account of a group of ambitious, seemingly invincible young men who, like so many before them, were lured into the spider's lair.' Noel Dawson, *Climb* Magazine

ALSO BY PETER AND LENI GILLMAN

'Collar The Lot!'

Alias David Bowie

The Wildest Dream

Everest: Eighty Years Of Triumph And Tragedy (Eds)

The Plumbat Affair (with Paul Eddy and Elaine Davenport)

ALSO BY PETER GILLMAN

Fitness On Foot

Eiger Direct (with Dougal Haston)

Siege! (with *Sunday Times* Insight team)

The Falklands War (with Paul Eddy and Magnus Linklater)

EXTREME EIGER

Triumph and Tragedy
on the North Face

PETER &
LENI GILLMAN

WITH JOCHEN HEMMLEB

**SIMON &
SCHUSTER**

London · New York · Sydney · Toronto · New Delhi

A CBS COMPANY

First published in Great Britain by Simon & Schuster UK Ltd, 2015
This paperback edition first published in Great Britain by Simon & Schuster UK Ltd, 2016
A CBS COMPANY

1 3 5 7 9 10 8 6 4 2

Simon & Schuster UK Ltd
1st Floor
222 Gray's Inn Road
London WC1X 8HB

www.simonandschuster.co.uk

Simon & Schuster Australia, Sydney
Simon & Schuster India, New Delhi

A CIP catalogue record for this book
is available from the British Library

Paperback ISBN: 978-1-47113-461-6
Ebook ISBN: 978-1-47113-462-3

Map in plate ... Hemmleb
Prin ...

Si ...
that is mad ... Forest
Stewardship ... sation.
Our bo ... er.

Contents

Prologue

THE SEARCH

Grindelwald was larger than I remembered. We arrived after dark and found ourselves in a busy tourist resort, with a stretch of hotels and cafés near the railway station and the lights from the shop fronts spilling across the street. It was nothing like the homely Alpine village I had somehow imagined from forty-eight years before. Our hotel, the Gletschergarten, was on a road winding up out of town in the direction of the Eiger. We did not know it until we arrived, but the hotel has history, for this is where Heinrich Harrer often stayed after he and his three comrades made the first ascent of the Eiger's North Face in 1938.

A papier mâché model of the mountain stands on a table in a room near the reception desk, and the guest book contains a photograph of Harrer, relaxed and distinguished with his receding grey hair, which was taken at the hotel on the fiftieth anniversary of the first ascent. Our bedroom was on the top floor and looked west, towards where I knew the Eiger should be. All we could see of it from our window that night was a brooding mass, inky black against the velvet sky, with a distant, solitary light that I knew to be the climbers' hut on the crest of the Mittellegi Ridge.

As always when coming to the Eiger, the weather was a concern. Which aspect would the mountain present to us the next day? Would it be hidden behind its habitual curtain of cloud, a token of the storms that rage in the amphitheatre of the North Face? Or would it be clear, revealing the terrible beauty that has lured climbers to its heart? In the morning the Mittellegi Ridge was sparkling in the early sun. The face was still beyond our view and even though the sky was clear, with a few wisps of cloud suspended in the valley, I was anxious to move up to Kleine Scheidegg in case the weather turned against us and the vision was gone.

We caught the train at Grindelwald soon after ten, competing for seats with the skiers who crowded on board. As the train climbed out of the valley the North Face slid into sight, rising so steeply above the track that it was hard to pick out its individual features, leaving the impression of a monumental ziggurat towering into the azure sky. Kleine Scheidegg was unquestionably larger than I had known, with a cluster of new buildings beside the station and an incongruous red and white wigwam bearing the Coca-Cola logo a few metres from the platform. The face was mostly obscured from our sight by the Hotel Bellevue des Alpes as we walked up the slope to its entrance.

Above a flight of stone steps, swing doors opened into the hotel, the largest and oldest in Kleine Scheidegg. Once inside, I tried to orientate myself. Some things had changed. All that remained of the reception desk was a nest of pigeon holes where guests could leave their keys; the reception staff had moved to a large, airy room to its right. Facing the old reception desk was the telephone cabin where I had dictated my nightly news reports; there was no telephone inside, only the shelf where it had rested. There was an aroma in the air that I thought I recognised: maybe it was from the polished parquet floor, mingling with the scent of a vase of lilies that stood on a table beside the entrance.

We had been allocated a room on the top floor. The hotel still had no lift, so we headed for the flight of stairs beside the lobby. There was a familiar wooden creak underfoot as I started on the first flight, a sound that reassured me that my memory could be trusted on some details at least. When we reached the first floor we had to pause to catch our breath: for a moment I felt dizzy and steadied myself on the banister. This was something I had not expected. Then I remembered that we were at an altitude of 2000 metres and were feeling the effects of the thinner atmosphere. I did not recall that from forty-eight years before, but I was a young man then – implausibly young, it seemed to me – and had spent the best part of a month at Kleine Scheidegg, giving me ample time to acclimatise.

Our bedroom was where I had hoped, looking towards the Eiger on two sides. The North Face was framed by the window, thrown into relief by the scintillating light on the West Flank and the glacier beside the neighbouring Mönch. Even in shadow the face's mythic landmarks were clear: the Second Icefield, the Traverse of the Gods, the white streak of the Spider with its legs radiating into the black rock around it, the Exit Cracks that led to the sanctuary of the Summit Icefield, where the angle relented at last and there was a gleam of sunlight across its crest. I gazed at the face, trying to absorb all that it meant to me, but after a while I felt overwhelmed and had to turn away.

We descended the creaking stairs and explored the ground floor. I remembered the bar, of course, but two other rooms were harder to place. There was a spacious restaurant with ornate chairs and a parquet floor, but I could not picture myself there. Nor did I recall a lavishly furnished sitting room, crowded with armchairs and ornaments. But I did remember the Gaststube, the 'guest room', with its bench seats and long communal tables, which we found down a further flight of stairs. In 1966 I had spent most of my evenings there, as often as not in the company of the climbers, becoming acquainted with the varieties of fondue on offer, and with an enticing range of beer and wine. Those were the days when journalists could spend their employer's money without inhibition or fear of retribution.

Leni and I returned to the railway station and had lunch in the café on the main platform. We crossed the tracks to the Restaurant Hotel Eigernordwand – also new since 1966 – and drank coffee on a terrace with a grandstand view of the North Face. As the afternoon passed, the rays of the sun slid over the edge of the West Flank, spreading across the face and somehow reducing its menace. We were tempted to watch the light show unfold but there was still one item we wanted to locate.

At first I thought we had found it beside a souvenir store next to our hotel, where a grey twin-barrel telescope sat on a plinth. It resembled a giant pair of binoculars and was directed towards the face. I posed for photographs beside it, but it did not fit my memories and I had to accept it was not the one we were looking for.

We returned to the hotel and asked for the proprietor, Andreas von Almen – a surname legendary in the history of the hotel and the North Face. His uncle, Fritz von Almen, bought the hotel in 1925 and thereafter occupied centre stage as attempts and ascents on the face were played out, hosting climbers, coordinating rescues and providing a running commentary for the media. He was still there in 1966 and I remembered him from my stay, a tall, patrician figure who was a stickler for formality when it came to his guests' dress codes – which was why I had so rarely eaten in his restaurant. He died in 1974 and the hotel went into decline until Andreas, an architect, and his wife Sylvia took it over in 1998 and began restoring it to its former grandeur. Andreas arrived in the lobby, a far less formal figure than his uncle, with raffishly long hair framing his face. I had intended to lead into the question gently but instinctively blurted it out: 'Where is the telescope?'

Von Almen led us along a corridor to an apartment beyond the guest bedrooms on the first floor. He showed us into his office and there, standing against the far wall, was the telescope. It had twin silvery barrels and rested on an elaborate tripod with two control wheels to adjust the height and spread of the legs. It was marked with its maker's name: Zeiss of Jena.

Von Almen had unearthed the telescope from among a jumble of furniture and ornaments in the hotel attic when he embarked on his restoration project. He now carried it to the centre of the room and we photographed it against the light flooding in through the windows. Still something jarred. I asked where the telescope used to stand and he opened a door on to a snow-covered terrace, where the North Face came into full view. The terrace was smaller than I remembered but von Almen explained that he had extended the hotel across one end to accommodate his office, thus reducing its length. Now everything fitted. This was where I had come to peer at the Eiger, searching for the two teams competing to climb the North Face by an audacious new route, measuring their progress as they vied to take the lead.

The climb took more than a month, and one day stood out. After four weeks the climbers were poised to push for the summit. One team was ahead, the other was attempting to catch up. A merger between the teams had been mooted, but nothing had been decided. The climbers were ascending ropes they had fixed on the face in order to carry supplies and return to the high-point of the ascent. That afternoon a rope broke. I was watching through the telescope at that very moment and what I saw became etched in my memory.

Soon afterwards I wrote a book, *Eiger Direct*, with the climber Dougal Haston my co-author. It told the story of the climb in a spare and restrained fashion, reflecting the viewpoint of a 24-year-old reporter, as I then was. It focused on one of the teams, an international partnership led by the American climber John Harlin.

While the book included what we knew about the rival German team, it reflected little of their experiences or point of view. Since then, the climb has never been far from my mind. I have considered its impact, its aftermath, its meaning. I have especially pondered what I saw in that moment I happened to be at the telescope. Was it a random event, the outcome of a game of existential roulette? Or was it foreseeable, predictable, even inevitable? I had still not reached a conclusion when I resolved that I should write this book.

Leni and I went to Kleine Scheidegg in March 2014. In March 1966, when I was reporting the climb for the *Daily Telegraph*, we had been married for a little more than three years and had two young children. For a time we pursued separate careers: Leni as a teacher, me as a journalist. Since the 1980s, when Leni gave up teaching, we have been writing books and articles under our shared by-line. We undertake our research and frame our story together; when we reach the writing stage, mine are the fingers on the keyboard and Leni is the editor. Even though this book is mostly written in the first person singular, it is no different. We conducted the research in Switzerland together and made a further research trip to the US.

We were also fortunate in having the assistance of the mountaineering writer and historian Jochen Hemmleb. We have known each other and worked together on a range of projects for twenty-five years, after we discovered a shared passion for the history of Mount Everest. Jochen secured the help of the five surviving German climbers, whom we met during visits in October 2013 and February 2014, and he remained in touch with them as we continued our researches. Jochen was tireless in handling the further questions that inevitably arose and his knowledge and expertise have been vital in shaping the book, which could not have been written without him.

It is said that it is usually only when you finish a story that you know where you should have started. For once that was not so: we knew we had to start in Kleine Scheidegg. But we were certain that we would learn things that would surprise us, even though we could not predict what they would be. That proved to be true. Much of our account offers a new perspective on what we thought we knew; some of it has never been told before.

We had an invaluable record of the climb in the two books written within months of the climb: *Eiger Direct*, by myself and Haston, which was published in several languages, but not German; and *Eiger: Kampf um die Direttissima*, written by the two leaders of the German team, Peter Haag and Jörg Lehne, which was published in German and French, but not English. Each naturally favoured the experiences and points of view of their respective teams and so our book marries these for the first time. But there was much more to add, above all from our interviews with the five German climbers; with the one survivor of the international team, Chris Bonington, Britain's best-known mountaineer; and with the family of John Harlin, whose name became indelibly linked with the climb. From all of this we have constructed an account which astonished even us for the levels of endurance and comradeship that it reveals; a story of loss, suffering and survival to which no previous accounts had done full justice.

Our story also became an inquiry into the nature of human memory and how it influences narratives. Some of the stories we unearthed contradict the earlier published accounts – and sometimes each other. We have presented these for the insights they offer into the nature of human experience as mediated by memory. Where we have been unable to resolve the inconsistencies, we have presented them to illuminate the differing perceptions of those involved. Our researches also led me to confront my own memory and prejudices and sometimes to revise judgements I had made

Chapter One

WELL MET IN TRENTO

The Saracini Cresseri palace in the Italian mountain town of Trento is a fitting venue for Europe's foremost gathering of mountaineers. The palace was built in the sixteenth century and was occupied by a succession of aristocratic families, including the Saracini and the Cresseri, distinguished enough for the Duke of Gloucester, brother of King George III, to have stayed there in 1777. It has an imposing arched front doorway, with a double door of walnut, a matching pair of balconies above the doorway and two storeys of recessed windows looking out over the Via Giannantonio Manci – named for an anti-Fascist partisan who died at the hands of the Gestapo in 1944.

The palace, which became the headquarters of the Trento Alpine Association in 1954, is one of the locations where Trento's annual international mountaineering film festival is staged. The festival, first held in 1952, is an uninhibited celebration of mountaineering and exploration, subsidised by city and regional authorities who are determined to consolidate Trento's reputation as the pre-eminent centre of Alpinism in Europe. Since 1972, when Trento became part of a self-governing province alongside South Tyrol, the festival has had the further purpose of underscoring the region's autonomy. It has always attracted the finest climbers of the time, paying for their fares and their hotels, and laying on lavish buffets of hams and salamis, mountain cheeses, stews of goat and boar, copious quantities of beer and the robust and fruity red wines of the Trentino region. (The buffets became less extravagant in the austere climate of recent years.)

When the festival was held in 1965, almost all who attended were from the principal Alpine countries: France, Germany, Austria, Switzerland and Italy. There were a few from Britain, re-establishing itself in the mountaineering rankings after turning its back on the Alps in the period between the two world wars. Implausibly, most of the climbers were conservatively dressed, with jackets and ties, whereas today the dress code would be a range of open-necked shirts and fleece jackets. Even so, one delegate was particularly noticeable, not only for his distinctive blond hair and his intense brown eyes, but for a muscular physique that stood out even in this assembly of the super-fit. His name was John Harlin, and he was the only American among the invited speakers.

Harlin was no upstart. At thirty, he had won a reputation for climbing the toughest, most challenging routes in the Alps. Three months before, he and fellow American Royal Robbins had become the first to climb a new *direttissima*, or super-direct route, on the West Face of the Dru, an *aiguille* or pinnacle in the Mont Blanc massif. It had been a test of fortitude as well as technical prowess, for a falling rock had hit Harlin on the right thigh on the first day, injuring his sciatic nerve and causing internal bleeding which persisted to the time of Trento. Harlin had climbed through intense pain during the two days it took to complete the ascent, then made a treacherous descent with Robbins through electrical storms and blizzards. That topped a list of ascents which included the first by an American of the North Face of the Eiger. To that point Harlin had won far less acclaim in the US, but his renown in Europe was secure. This was the fourth time he had attended the festival.

The most prestigious event of the festival consisted of the film awards which took place in the nearby Teatro Sociale. One was given for a documentary about the American expedition that had climbed Everest in 1963. The overall prize went to a short Polish film telling the winsome story of a teacher who has to walk to her school along a narrow mountain path. That led to muttering that the judging panel could be swayed by the politics of Europe in the 1960s, in this case the desire to award a prize to an Eastern European country then still part of the Soviet hegemony; perhaps to help loosen the grip of the Cold War, whose front line, in the shape of a high metal fence fortified with barbed wire, alarms and anti-tank ditches, ran through a divided Germany, ending 250 miles from Trento.

Happily such considerations did not apply to the set-piece debate staged at the Palazzo Saracini Cresseri on 1 October 1965. The title was beguilingly simple: *Perchè l'Alpinismo?* Which translates as Why Alpinism? Or, more simply, Why Climb?

It is the question to which climbers respond with varying degrees of impatience. The most succinct answer remains that of George Mallory, the Everest pioneer who made three attempts on Everest in the early 1920s, disappearing high on the mountain in 1924 and leaving the perpetual mystery of whether he and his partner Andrew Irvine reached the summit. In 1923, during a lecture tour of the US, Mallory was asked why he wanted to climb Everest. His celebrated three-word answer, 'Because it's there', has a Zen-like simplicity which can be interpreted to mean everything or nothing.

Prompted by the journalist Guido Tonella, who was chairing the discussion at Trento, the climbers served up a range of answers. Michel Vaucher, a Swiss Alpinist with a formidable list of summer and winter first ascents, said that mountaineering was the best way to know yourself. Toni Hiebeler, who made the first winter ascent of the Eiger North Face in 1961, said it was a need 'that became more and more acute over time'. René Dittert, a leader of the Swiss expedition that so nearly pulled off the first ascent of Everest in 1952, said, echoing Mallory, that he climbed the mountains 'because they were in front of him'.

When Harlin's turn came, he delivered not one but three reasons. 'I climb because I like it; because my father climbed; and for some reason I cannot define.'

The first part of Harlin's answer seemed reasonable, if verging on the banal. The third hinted at hidden depths, a psychological mystery which even Harlin himself could not plumb, and was perhaps more accurate than Harlin cared to admit. The second was the most intriguing, as it was not true. Harlin's father was an airline pilot and administrator, whom Harlin both admired and sought to emulate, having just spent five years as a pilot with the USAF, stationed for most of that time in what was West Germany. His father had helped imbue him with a love of the outdoors, taking him boating and fishing in Minnesota, where he grew up. But Harlin's father, who was fifty-nine at the time of Trento, had never been a climber.

No one at Trento was in a position to challenge Harlin's falsehood. And it was characteristic of him that he should spin an engaging myth about his reasons for climbing and his relationship with his father. He had previously made a range of similar claims which turned out to be exaggerations or untruths. He claimed that he had climbed the North Face of the Matterhorn when he was twenty – even sending his future wife a postcard to that effect. Not true. He claimed to have been apprenticed as a dress designer to the renowned Pierre Balmain in Paris. Not true either. This carelessness with the truth was something his son, John Harlin III, had to come to terms with later in life. 'Charitable friends say that he wanted these successes so badly that he probably came to believe in them himself,' John Harlin Jr wrote. 'I didn't think that such self-deception was possible, but now I'm learning that it is.' For his father, he added, 'failure simply didn't register'.

The reasons for Harlin's dissimulation form one aspect of a complex and controversial character who divided opinions among mountaineers. Harlin's supporters praised him for the inspiration he provided both on the mountain and in their lives. He was considered a dreamer and visionary, with interests and talents going far beyond the confines of the mountains. He was an idealist, a sceptic and a radical who, after spending a year on a duty roster that entailed sleeping beside his nuclear fighter-bomber, ready to go into action against the USSR and its Communist allies, told the USAF he was no longer prepared to unleash bombs on his allotted target, the historic city of Prague. He was a writer, a painter, a poet, experimenting with a range of styles and displaying an emotional intelligence in his mountaineering writing to match that of Mallory, who sought to explore his feelings and motivations and those of his fellow mountaineers.

Harlin's detractors recoiled from what they saw as an overpowering personality, manipulative and controlling. They considered him a fantasist whose dreams far outstripped his ability to carry them out. He could be harsh towards those he disagreed with and prone to bursts of anger and violence. He was married with two children but in the perennial battle between mountaineering and family responsibilities, mountaineering usually won. His critics included climbers who had partnered him on challenging routes: Robbins wrote that Harlin 'would have risked his life ten times over if he could have done it in a grand and heroic way'.

On one thing both sides agree: as a climber, Harlin was single-minded and competitive, driven to the point of obsession – key qualities for the next mountaineering project Harlin had in mind.

ened that another climber who took part in the debate at
ared some of those qualities, as well as Harlin's objective.

Peter Haag, a 28-year-old climber from Stuttgart in southern
Germany, was at his first Trento festival. His climbing CV,
although substantial, was less spectacular than Harlin's. When his
turn came to explain why he climbed, he was less enigmatic, more
open than Harlin. He had started climbing because he had fallen in
love with the sister of a mountaineer and used to meet her at the
foot of a climb. 'One day I realised I did not love her any more –
but by then I had a passion for mountains.'

Like Harlin, Haag had delivered a characteristic answer. Haag,
said his wife Barbara in 2014, was a mountaineering romantic.
They met while they were camping at the Mer de Glace, the glacier
below Mont Blanc. For their very first trip together he took her to
Switzerland to show her the North Face of the Eiger, and they
were married a few weeks after the Trento festival. She was
attracted by his spirited personality and a range of interests beyond
climbing. He was a poet, a jazz pianist and a comic who once
wrote a mountaineering cabaret poking gentle fun at his contemporaries and peers. His answer at Trento, belying stereotypes about
Germans lacking a sense of humour, was the wittiest contribution
to the debate. However, his story may have been no more accurate
than Harlin's. Barbara Haag had no knowledge of it, even though
they had a close and loving relationship, raising the possibility that
Haag too – a storyteller and troubadour – may have been expressing a poetic truth.

In the story of the Eiger Direct, what transpired in the public discussion at the Palazzo Saracini Cresseri was less significant than
what happened offstage. At some point during the festival, Harlin
and Haag – who spoke excellent English – met over beers. By then,
both knew that the other wanted to climb the route known, in a
mix of languages, as the Eiger-Nordwand Direttissima, or more

simply as the Eiger Direct. It was one of the hottest topics in mountaineering and would mark the first new route on one of the most dramatic and dangerous mountain faces in Europe.

To many climbers of that era, the North Face of the Eiger remained the ultimate test. It is one of a trio of mountains in the front rank of the Bernese Oberland, the Highlands of the Swiss canton of Berne, so that it is the first to be hit by storms sweeping in from the north. Massive geological forces have hollowed out a mile-wide amphitheatre rising from the sloping green meadows of Alpiglen to the apex of a dauntingly exposed ridge that comprises its 3970-metre summit.

The Eiger was first climbed in 1858 by an Irish adventurer named Charles Barrington, who approached the summit via its gentler West Flank, pausing to look in awe at the expanses of the North Face. An English Alpinist, Adolphus Moore, who made the third ascent of the Eiger in 1864, wrote of the face's 'rugged and precipitous character – a stone dropped from its edge would have fallen hundreds of feet before encountering any obstacle to its progress'. With its crumbling rock and its vast icefields and buttresses, swept by stone fall, torrents of water and avalanches, the face was considered so difficult and dangerous that not until the 1930s did any climbers venture on to it. In the space of three years, eight climbers died in successive attempts, succumbing to cold or exhaustion, in falls and in one hideous case being garrotted by the climber's own rope. It was finally climbed in 1938 by a four-man team of Germans and Austrians who overcame the storms and avalanches to reach the summit four days after leaving their tents at Alpiglen.

Further attempts and ascents of the North Face continued after the Second World War. In fifteen years, 109 climbers succeeded and fifteen died. John Harlin was number 86 on the list when he became the first American to reach the summit – one week ahead of the first British climbers to succeed, Chris Bonington and Ian

Clough. But that did not satisfy Harlin. Almost from the moment he descended from the face he was formulating a plan to climb it again, but by a different route.

The 1938 route was ingenious and distinctive for the way it snaked its way up the face as the climbers probed for the line of least resistance: slanting across the icefields, following the faultlines in the strata systems that led on a zigzag path to the Summit Icefield. By the early 1960s a new imperative was gripping climbers: to eschew the elegant lines of the first ascents in favour of routes that slashed their way up the great Alpine faces like scalpels. Their inspiration was said to come from the Italian Emilio Comici, who pronounced that the ideal route was one that followed the line of a drop of water falling from the summit.

By October 1965, when he met Haag at Trento, Harlin had been on the North Face in quest of the Direct half a dozen times. Some of those forays were for reconnaissance, as he searched for a line of ascent. Twice he had made full attempts, in partnership with leading French and Italian Alpinists, and he had reached mid-height on the face. Without question, said his son John, the Direct had become his obsession. That was also the term used by Peter Haag's wife Barbara, who recalled their visit to the face in the summer of 1965, when he pointed out the possible routes he might take. 'He didn't have a camera or a map,' she said. 'It was all in his head.'

Now, in Trento, over wine and schnapps, warily at first, they discussed their plans. Both intended to make their attempt that winter when the loose rock is frozen into place and the face is no longer swept by torrents of water – although the storms can also be at their most intense, bringing winds of 120 kph or more and temperatures plunging below minus 20°C. But they soon learned of one major difference in their approach. Harlin intended to make his attempt in a team of three: himself; Chris Bonington, Britain's most successful Alpinist; and a leading figure in a new generation of US rock-climbers, Layton Kor. Haag planned to climb with a team of eight, led jointly by himself and Jörg Lehne, a German climber who had taken part in the first great Alpine *direttissima* seven years before. Their six colleagues were all drawn, like Haag, from the southern German region of Swabia. They had no international reputation to match that of Harlin's team but were respected in climbing circles for their resilience and determination to see things through.

A photograph taken at Trento shows Harlin, with his distinctive blond hair neatly combed back, his jacket unbuttoned to reveal his tie, in a group that includes the British climber Bev Clark, later to play a small but significant part in the Eiger Direct. At the other end of the group is Peter Haag, with boyish looks that belie his twenty-eight years, his hand raised in a curious posture as if to block Harlin from his sight. It is a misleading image, since by Barbara Haag's account he struck a rapport with Harlin that had him bubbling with enthusiasm when he described their meeting to Barbara. 'They were sitting together at nights, drinking and smoking and talking and planning,' she related in 2014. 'He said it was wonderful.' In a letter to Barbara, Haag told her that Harlin and Clark had drunk two litres of schnapps between them. Haag plied his songs and 'played the piano for half the night'. After Haag took a rest, Clark dragged him back to the piano to continue playing – dislodging a journalist who had taken over the keyboard. It was all in character for Haag, who was sociable, made friends easily and disliked conflict and competition. Although Haag did not say so explicitly, Barbara believes that he would have preferred to form a combined enterprise with Harlin whereby the two teams would make one shared attempt on the Eiger Direct.

There are no equivalent reports from the Harlin side. He did not go home and excitedly report his meeting with Haag. His wife Marilyn could not remember him mentioning the Germans at all after Trento. Nor did he tell his fellow team members, who were shocked when they eventually learned that a German team had started on the route they considered their territory. Harlin's son John Jr believed his father would not have mentioned the Germans 'until he had to'. His father, he added, was intensely competitive and would have kept his cards close to his chest. He had secured a lucrative deal with the *Daily Telegraph* and would not have wanted to share it. In addition, he would have opposed a unified attempt on several grounds. As the respective team sizes indicated, he had a radically different concept of how the climb should be attempted. Having been on the route half a dozen times, he had a proprietary attitude towards it which most climbers would understand. The Germans, by contrast, were newcomers, perhaps even interlopers or carpetbaggers. When I first met Harlin in November 1965, a month after Trento, he told me he would not be upset if another team climbed the Direct first. I was unsure whether to believe him then. Now, that looks like another Harlin fiction.

In short, two driven men were pitched against each other to reach the same goal. The stakes were enormous: the climb would be played out, as climbs on the Eiger have always been, in a media glare. Ever since the first attempts of the 1930s, watchers at the telescopes at Alpiglen and Kleine Scheidegg have gazed at the ant-like figures acting out life-and-death dramas on the face. Reporters were invariably out in force, avid for snippets of news and ready to resort to fabrication if the truth proved elusive. The leaders' decisions would be scrutinised, mistakes magnified, success or failure rendered in melodramatic terms that could undermine their belief in what they were doing.

There was a further dimension to the rivalry, freighting it with historical significance. Here were teams from countries that had been adversaries in the Second World War, which had ended just twenty years before. On one side were climbers from two of the victor nations, Britain and the US. On the other were climbers who came from a country devastated by defeat, who had contended with hardship in the post-war period, and were living in a divided nation that was decades away from assuming its economic mastery of Europe. Both Harlin and Kor had spent the war years in the US, remote from any conflict; Bonington, by contrast, had been in London when V2 rockets were falling in 1945 and experienced the rigours of food rationing during and after the war. As for the German climbers, their memories included seeing Allied bombers pounding the cities of Swabia, sheltering in cellars, watching the arrival of American tanks, and fleeing from the Red Army as it neared Berlin. They had known rationing and deprivation during the Allied occupation and its aftermath and believed that these hardening experiences served them well on the Eiger.

The Trento festival ended on 2 October. Harlin returned to Leysin in Vaud, Haag to Swabia. There were three months to go before the attempts were likely to start. Both had to plan their strategies and draw up their equipment lists. Harlin had the financial advantage: while he had secured backing from the *Daily Telegraph*, Haag was wondering how much he should ask his climbers to contribute to the team kitty. Both would encounter setbacks as they prepared for the climb. Both knew that they were facing a formidable challenge, but both felt ready for anything that came. Harlin described it as the culmination of his climbing experience: 'I feel that everything I have done in the mountains leads to this.'

For Haag, the romantic, the Eiger had become 'a very great love', as he told Barbara in a letter shortly after Trento. 'I have to think of her every free minute, to woo her, to plan.' He wrote that he was about to go to Grindelwald, equipped with a telephoto lens, 'to take pictures of my great love in winter dress'.

'The Eiger,' Barbara said, 'was his dream.'

Chapter Two

THE REDOUBTABLE BEAUFOYS

Even the name is the subject of myth and speculation. It is often written that Eiger is German for Ogre and that the mountain thus occupies an appropriate position alongside its two more benign neighbours, the Mönch, or Monk, with its cowl of ice and snow, and the Jungfrau, or Maiden, with its demure yet alluring appearance. Sadly, this is not so. The German for ogre is *Ungeheuer*, and if you look for Eiger in a German dictionary it is not there. The name first appeared as 'mons Egere' in a document in 1252 and is a contentious topic among philologists and etymologists. One argues that since the document was a land deed, the name was that of the farmer who first settled the meadows below the face, one Agiger or Aiger, which was later shaded into Eiger. Another proposes that Eiger is based on Latin and/or Greek words meaning sharp, pinnacle or peak. A third suggests that it derives from a Germanic dialect phrase *dr hej Ger* – a *ger* being a sharp spear used in warfare. It looks like one of those disputes that will happily remain unresolved. But it says something of the mountain's aura that people persist in believing that Eiger means a monster that consumes human beings.

It is likely that Herr Aiger or Agiger moved up into the meadows below the mountain from Grindelwald, the village that sits at the northern approach to the Eiger and constitutes the principal gateway to the mountain. (In view of the Eiger's sombre history, it seems appropriate that J.K. Rowling gave the name Grindelwald to her second most powerful Dark Wizard, the murderer and practitioner of the dark arts.) The village was first mentioned by name, Grindelwalt, in documents in 1146, half a century or so before Herr Aiger/Agiger was staking his claim to the grazing meadows. Over the ensuing centuries the people of Grindelwald were caught up in a series of lethal battles as rival barons and abbots fought for territory and the villagers were pressed into fighting for one side or the other. In the sixteenth century, following the Reformation, the village was forcibly converted to Protestantism, and then took a back seat in European history.

That lasted until it was discovered by the pioneers of European tourism who preceded the first mountain climbers. It fired their imagination, inspiring a sense of awe that was common to all who came to gaze at the mountain. But while the tourists were content to explore its surroundings, the climbers wanted to engage with it, tackling it by ever harder routes – a progression that led eventually to the Eiger Direct.

Among the earliest English visitors, and typical of the character of the age, were the redoubtable Beaufoys. Mark Beaufoy, who was born in 1764, came from a Quaker family in Bristol that became prosperous from brewing and selling vinegar. As a young man he conducted important early experiments into the resistance of solids in water and later made measurements of the degrees of magnetic variation in Britain. He also spent fifteen years in the British Army, rising to the rank of colonel. There was a hint of scandal in his early life, for in 1784 he eloped with his sixteen-year old cousin Margaretta and they were married at Gretna Green. They went to live in Neuchâtel, Switzerland, and had two children. In 1787 they rode the seventy-five miles to the Swiss Oberland in a horse-drawn wagon, a journey assiduously recorded by Margaretta in a diary which was later published in the *Alpine Journal*. First they visited Lauterbrunnen, to the west of the Eiger, then she and Mr B, as she called him, rode on to 'the Valley of Grindenwalt'. There they 'beheld with astonishment the amazing fertility and populousness of this place ... Stupendous rocks whos [sic] impending summits threaten each moment to overwhelm the passenger necessarily strick one with horror.' They lodged with a farming family and were impressed with the 'honest integrity' of the villagers.

The Beaufoys first made a six-mile walk around the Lower Grindelwald Glacier, which flanks the eastern end of the Eiger. Margaretta found that glaciers 'did not at all fulfil the idea I had formed of them ... They appeard like a parcel of dirty Snow heaped together, but on a nearer view I must own there was nothing wanting to complete the horrid beauty of the scene.' She marvelled at the pyramids of ice on the glacier surface and an ice arch that Mr B would not allow her to climb.

After dining at their lodgings, they and a guide set off for another walk below the semi-circle of peaks formed by the Schreckhorn, Fiescherhorn and Eiger. Margaretta noted the 'dazzling whiteness of the Summits' and was then startled by what she took to be thunder. She looked up at the glacier to see 'a large piece of ice rolling down with a horrid noise'. Later she related the miraculous escape of their farmer host following 'an accident occasioned by one of these pieces of falling Ice, called Avelenches [sic]'. The farmer had been steering his cows to pasturage across a glacier when he was hit by falling ice. He fell through a hole in the glacier, landed in a torrent of meltwater sixty feet below and was disgorged lower down the glacier. 'In short the poor fellow escaped the treble danger of being crushed by the Avelanche [sic], of dashing his brains out in a fall of 60 feet, and 3d of being drowned' – all, she adds, 'with the trifling remembrance (in comparison) of a broken arm.'

Margaretta clearly had a relish for danger. Mr B was even more adventurous, as he left at four the next morning to inspect the Upper Grindelwald Glacier, where their host had his triple brush with death. To Margaretta's relief, Mr B returned unharmed and they left Grindelwald the same day. Later that year the Beaufoys travelled to Chamonix where Mr B had his sights on nothing less than Mont Blanc, first climbed by two Frenchmen the previous year. He set off with ten guides and provisions for three days, wearing only loose-fitting white trousers and jacket. The party battled intense cold and mountain sickness to bring Mr B the first British ascent. He descended in distress, having rejected his guides' advice to protect his face and eyes, and was both snow-blind and sunburned.

At nineteen, Margaretta was evidently a well-read woman, steeped in the culture of her class and age. Later she assisted her husband in his experiments and observations, winning praise for her mathematical skills. Her take on the wild landscape around Grindelwald is in keeping with the Romantic writers and poets who were discovering the mountains and imbuing them with a wild and forbidding beauty that proved part of their attraction. Her liking of the word 'horrid' was of its time, when it meant awesome and scary (Milton wrote in *L'Allegro* of 'horrid shapes, and shrieks, and sights unholy'). In addition, there is something about the confident spirit of this intrepid couple which foreshadows the stories to come. At times Margaretta felt ambivalent about her husband's exploits, admiring his courage but unable to suppress her anxieties – a theme that, until recently, has been less prevalent in mountaineering narratives. Sadly, Margaretta died in 1800, when she was thirty-two; Mr B outlived her by twenty-seven years.

The Beaufoys were pioneers in another respect. They were among the first tourists to Switzerland, helping to pave the way for an activity and industry that has become a key factor in the country's enviable prosperity. It took the Beaufoys several days to reach Grindelwald in their horse-drawn wagon, but before long Switzerland was building the roads, railways and tunnels that rapidly multiplied the flow of tourists. The people of Grindelwald were quick to spot the business opportunities that came their way. Early visitors such as the Beaufoys were accustomed to rewarding their hosts with presents. The villagers began charging tourists for occupying beds in farmhouses and the cheese-makers' chalets which dotted the meadows. The men who knew the mountains from herding sheep or hunting chamois set themselves up as guides, taking tourists to inspect the glaciers and venturing on to the heights above. In 1811 two local chamois hunters guided two wealthy Swiss merchants on the first ascent of the Eiger's southwestern neighbour, the Jungfrau. In 1844 two Grindelwald guides, Hans Jaun and Melchior Bannholzer, made the first ascent of the Wetterhorn, to the north-east of the Eiger.

These ascents were the prelude to what became known as the golden age of Alpinism, in which the British played the most important part. It was heralded by the ascent of the Wetterhorn by a London barrister named Alfred Wills in 1854. In the next decade, the British made the first ascent of dozens of Alpine peaks. In 1857 they formed the Alpine Club. Its members were university academics, barristers, solicitors, clergymen, bankers, City financiers and civil servants, thus illustrating the social composition of the new climbing world. All were men (the club finally voted to admit women in 1974). Most had attended English public schools, and many were graduates of Oxford and Cambridge universities. But it would be wrong to cast them as totemic members of the governing classes: many were non-conformists, atheists, radicals, scientists, who found in climbing a fulfilment all the more rewarding because it proved so challenging and intense.

The golden age is considered to have finished on 14 July 1865, the day four members of a party led by Edward Whymper, an Alpine Club member, fell to their deaths after making the first ascent of the Matterhorn. These were the first deaths in action of any club members and are reckoned to have ended not only the golden age but also the Alpine Club's age of innocence.

The man who made the first ascent of the Eiger came from outside this gilded group, and had no background in mountaineering. In 1858 Charles Barrington made his only trip to the Alps. Aged twenty-four, he came from Dublin and had an intriguing provenance. His ancestors were Protestant settlers implanted in Ireland by Oliver Cromwell to subjugate the Catholic majority in the seventeenth century. The Barringtons became Quakers at about the time they set up a soap-manufacturing company which made the family wealthy enough to send its children on European tours. Charles Barrington was a man of leisure. He enjoyed yachting, hunting and shooting, and later rode his own horse to victory in the Irish Grand National. That summer he arrived in Grindelwald where he hired the two best local guides, Christian Almer and Peter Bohren. Almer, a former shepherd, cheese-maker and chamois hunter, had guided Alfred Wills and his party on the Wetterhorn in 1854. He guided three ascents of the Jungfrau in 1856, and in 1857 made the first ascent of the Mönch with a doctor from Vienna, Sigismund Porges. Bohren was known as the *Gletscherwolf* – the glacier wolf – for his skills on icy ground. They first climbed the Jungfrau together then supposedly sought the advice of 'some Alpine men' in Grindelwald on what to climb next. They told Barrington to try the Eiger or the Matterhorn. Since the Eiger was closer, it was the obvious choice.

By then, hotels were being built in the most dramatic and

picturesque Alpine vantage points. In 1840 the first inn was opened at the crest of the col between Grindelwald and Lauterbrunnen, a location known as Kleine Scheidegg, or Little Watershed. A second hotel was opened at the nearby resort of Wengernalp the following year. On the afternoon of 10 August 1858, Barrington and his guides walked up to the hotel at Wengernalp and snatched a few hours' sleep. At 3.30 a.m. they set off up the Eiger's West Flank, the easiest-angled of all its faces and ridges, which rises around 1650 metres to the summit at 3970 metres. Almer had previously attempted the West Flank with Dr Porges and had turned back at a steep section of rock at mid-height. When they reached this point the guides wanted to look for an alternative route, but Barrington insisted on tackling the rock head-on. He led the steepest section, 'sticking like a cat to the rock', and then dropped a rope for the two guides to follow. After veering to the very edge of the North Face, with views across the vastness down to Grindelwald, they reached the summit at midday.

The guides gave Barrington the honour of stepping on to the summit first and they planted a flag which they had purloined from the hotel at Wengernalp. As clouds rolled in to shroud the summit, they started their descent, bypassing the steep rock section via a couloir where they narrowly escaped an avalanche. News of the attempt had spread and some thirty people were waiting for them when they reached the foot of the West Flank four hours after leaving the summit. They were escorted to the hotel at Kleine Scheidegg, then known as the Kurhaus Bellevue, where some residents doubted their account. But that evening the clouds around the summit cleared, revealing the flag they had planted. The hotel proprietor had installed a cannon to celebrate his guests' feats and he fired it in Barrington's honour. 'Thus ended my first and only visit to Switzerland,' Barrington wrote.

Barrington's ascent went almost entirely unrecorded, and it was only when his brother forwarded an account to the Alpine Club in 1878 that it was reported in the *Alpine Journal*. It was inscribed on his gravestone in Mount Jerome Cemetery, Dublin, in 2013, when the Irish climber and historian Frank Nugent, who was researching a book about Irish mountaineers, alerted Barrington's descendants to his achievement.

It may now be necessary to explain why the story of Eiger climbing does not end there. It is a mistake that even someone as eminent as Edmund Hillary could commit. In 1953, having made the first ascent of Everest with Tenzing Norgay, Hillary said that he could not imagine anyone wanting to repeat the climb. By 2014 there had been nearly 7000 ascents of Everest by twenty different routes, and that was the pattern on the Eiger. In 1861 the good doctor Porges made the second ascent, having replaced Christian Almer with three other guides. In 1864 Lucy Walker was the first woman to reach the summit. Walker, a lead merchant's daughter from Liverpool, was the first woman to climb regularly in the Alps. She reached the summit of the Eiger with her regular guide, Melchior Anderegg, and her father and brother, both members of the Alpine Club. Having been excluded from the club, Walker was a founding member of the rival Ladies' Alpine Club, formed in 1909 (it merged with the male Alpine Club in 1975). She was also the first woman to climb the Matterhorn, in 1871.

By then climbers were looking for new ways of reaching the summit. The most obvious alternative to Barrington's route lay up the South-west Ridge, which avoided the problematic rocks of the West Flank and ascended more ice and snow. The first ascent, in 1871, was led by three guides: Christian Almer, his brother Ulrich and Peter Bohren. Their clients were William Coolidge, a New Yorker who settled in Britain and joined the Alpine Club, his aunt Meta Brevoort and their dog Tschingel, which is said to have been a gift from Almer. In 1876, Alpine Club member George Foster and two guides climbed the South Ridge from the Eigerjoch, the saddle below the summit on the long ridge between the Eiger and the Mönch.

For almost fifty years, these three remained the only established routes to the summit. The next objective was the Mittellegi Ridge, a long, sharp crest which rises close to Grindelwald and twists its way over several kilometres to the summit. The first attempt was in 1874 and many followed, mostly made by the customary mix of guides and British clients. The sticking point was a steep buttress known as the Great Tower, which proved beyond the technical capabilities of the time. Two parties who had reached the summit via one of the established routes descended the ridge, using their ropes to abseil down the Great Tower.

This period brought a new influx of tourists, lured by a railway line running from Grindelwald to Lauterbrunnen via Kleine Scheidegg which was opened in 1893. It was complemented in the most dramatic fashion in 1912 by a further railway from Kleine Scheidegg to Jungfraujoch, the saddle between the Mönch and Jungfrau, taking passengers to within 700 metres of the Jungfrau's summit. The line snaked its way through tunnels excavated into the Eiger itself, with a station named Eigerwand and several tunnel windows that were to be used by climbers looking for a quick exit from the face.

The Mittellegi Ridge was finally climbed in 1921 by a law student from Tokyo, Yuko Maki. He arrived in Grindelwald in 1919 and spent the best part of two years studying the route through telescopes. He hired a guide, Samuel Brawand, who taught him to speak German and introduced him to the delights of Oberland beer (Brawand said later that he was impressed by how much Maki could drink). After climbing the Matterhorn, they made their attempt with two other Grindelwald guides, Fritz Amatter, who had already descended the ridge and Fritz Steuri. Amatter was equipped with a long pole with a hook at one end and spikes at the other, and they used it to overcome the Great Tower. They reached the summit at 7.15 p.m. and drove a makeshift flag, made of Amatter's climbing pole with a handkerchief attached, into the summit as proof of their success.

As a token of his gratitude to Grindelwald, Maki funded the construction of a climbing hut halfway up the ridge. He went on to a distinguished mountaineering career and led the Japanese expedition which made the first ascent of Manaslu in the Himalayas in 1956. However, his ascent presented the climbing world with an ethical dilemma. Strictly speaking, Maki and his guides had cheated by using Amatter's pole. But the editor of the *Alpine Journal*, Percy Farrar, normally a stern guardian of the Alpine purity, took a forgiving view. 'Most mountaineers will certainly deprecate all such artificial aids,' Farrar wrote. 'But in the case of the Mittellegi nearly fifty years had elapsed since the first attempt had taken place, and many a good climber had taken his shot without hitting the bull.'

In 1932, one more new route was climbed – the fifth – to the right of the Mittellegi Ridge, following the line of buttresses that form the left-hand edge of the North Face. It was accomplished on 20 August by two Swiss mountaineers, Hans Lauper and Alfred Zürcher, both members of the Alpine Club, and the guides Joseph Knubel and Alexander Graven. Lauper, a dentist, had been as obsessional in his quest for the route as Maki, spending weeks in Grindelwald scanning the face through telescopes and waiting several years for it to come into the best condition. Even so, the party had to contend with dripping or iced-up rock, loose snow, and long stretches of steep ice. They took thirteen hours to reach the summit, where they shared a flask of spirits and the two guides smoked a cigar. In honour of the lead client, the line was called the Lauper Route.

By then the *Alpine Journal* had a new editor, the idiosyncratic

figure of Colonel Edward Lisle Strutt. Of classic upper-class background, Strutt was a graduate of Christ Church, Oxford, and a
devout Roman Catholic. He fought with distinction in the First
World War, was wounded four times and was awarded the DSO.
He was an ardent monarchist and, in a daring episode in 1919, led
a squad of British soldiers who spirited the Austrian royal family to
safety from under the noses of republican forces, who had seized
power in Vienna in the aftermath of the war. He was deputy leader
of the 1922 British Everest expedition, proving to be arrogant and
bad-tempered and, in the words of one climber, the most outra-
geous snob he had ever met. He became editor of the *Alpine
Journal* in 1927.

To Strutt, the ascent of the Lauper Route marked the end of the
Eiger story, and he wrote this epitaph on climbing in the Oberland.
'We must congratulate our members on a superb expedition, by far
the most important of the 1932 season. We might add that it is a
source of gratification to us that the N. face of the Eiger, the last
important problem of the Bernese Oberland, should have been
solved by this unsurpassed all-Swiss party.' A photograph of the
route, with the 1932 route marked with the usual dotted line, was
captioned 'Eiger N.Face'. Clearly, the vast expanse of the face that
occupied most of the photo to the right of the dotted line counted
for nothing. Job done, as far as Strutt was concerned.

Strutt was ignoring the elephant in the room, that great sweep of
the North Face that Lauper and his colleagues had spent thirteen
hours skirting. But the Alpine Club, once in the vanguard of mountaineering developments, was now being left behind. Its greatest
preoccupation was Everest, scene of the successive failures of the
1920s, culminating in the deaths of Mallory and Irvine, commemo-
rated at a service at St Paul's Cathedral which was attended by King
George V and the entire British Cabinet. Now the club was concentrating on launching further attempts on Everest in partnership with

the Royal Geographical Society, which considered itself custodian of British global exploration. After failure in 1933, further attempts were made in 1935, 1936 and 1938, though none reached as high as Edward Norton – or possibly Mallory and Irvine – climbed in 1924. Just two Alpine Club members climbed new routes in the Alps of any significance between the two world wars.

In the Alps, meanwhile, climbers from Germany, Austria and Italy were leading the way in what was, after all, their home territory. In contrast to the middle-class and professional gentlemen of the Alpine Club, most were working-class climbers seeking escape from the economic depression and unemployment that gripped Germany and Austria following the punitive settlement of the First World War. Most had no work or earned pittances from seasonal jobs on farms or in the forests, and they sustained themselves while climbing on little more than bread, sausage and apples. Somehow, out of this background, came a drive to climb the great north faces of the Alps. Where previously the faces had been dismissed as unthinkable, that was justification enough for the new generation of climbers. Many came from Munich in southern Germany, and it was from there in July 1931 that four climbers travelled the 300 miles to Zermatt intent on climbing the North Face of the Matterhorn. After camping beneath the face for a week of rain and snow, two gave up. The remaining pair, brothers Franz and Toni Schmid, both in their early twenties, stayed on and climbed the face in two days, with a bivouac in the upper part of the face.

The next target was the North Face of the Grandes Jorasses in the Mont Blanc range, and it extracted a high price. Leo Rittler and Hans Brehm, both from Munich, died on the face in the summer of 1931. In 1934 Rudolf Haringer, another Munich climber, died in a fall while retreating during the second day of an attempt. His partner, Rudolf Peters, survived and returned to the face in 1935, reaching the summit despite rockfall which injured his partner,

Martin Meier. Climbing north faces was clearly a dangerous game and death appeared to resemble a baton, being passed from hand to hand, but there was still one major north face left.

In August 1935, five weeks after Peters and Meier climbed the Grandes Jorasses, two more young men from Munich arrived at the meadows at Alpiglen. Their names were Max Sedlmayr and Karl Mehringer, and they had more money than most other Munich climbers. They travelled to Grindelwald in Mehringer's trim two-seater BMW Dixi and wore stylish check shirts and patterned socks. Seventy years later they were remembered by the daughter of the hoteliers at the Hotel des Alpes at Alpiglen as friendly, personable and helpful young men. As she told the assiduous Eiger historian Rainer Rettner, they stayed in a bunkhouse adjoining the hotel and in the evenings, as they waited to make their attempt, they joined in singing with the hotel's guests.

Sedlmayr and Mehringer had a strong pedigree. Sedlmayr had climbed many of the toughest routes in the Dolomites. After teaming up that winter, the two men climbed a range of demanding summer routes in the eastern Alps before turning their attention to the Eiger. They were in no doubt about the challenge facing them. A year before, three fellow Germans had started an attempt but gave up after climbing the first third of the face. This is an easier-angled section that rises 600 metres to the point where the face abruptly steepens. (There is no accepted simple name in English for this lower section of the face, but in German it is known as the Vorbau – translated in dictionaries as a porch or balcony – and we have used the word in our account.) A senior German climber who had reconnoitred the face from the West Flank estimated it could take five days to climb, and warned Sedlmayr and Mehringer that if bad weather hit the mountain a retreat from high up would prove immensely difficult. The hotelkeeper at Alpiglen alerted them to the stonefall that raked the face in warm weather.

The media were on their case, for a reporter from the *Oberländischen Volksblattes* asked them how they judged their chances. They guardedly told him that the weather prospects were against them and they were thinking of postponing their attempt to the following year. That may have been a ruse to put the reporter off the track, as they placed a cache of supplies at the foot of the route and then Mehringer climbed the West Flank to place a second cache at the summit. They set off from Alpiglen at 2 a.m. on Wednesday, 21 August.

Sedlmayr and Mehringer spent that day climbing the Vorbau. That night they bivouacked at the foot of a cliff rising some 100 metres above the Vorbau that is now known as the First Band. The cliff is mostly vertical and in some places overhanging, and was subsequently accorded a difficulty of Grade V–VI, which put it close to the technical limit for climbers of the time. It took Sedlmayr and Mehringer the whole of 22 August to climb it, and they were compelled to remove their rucksacks and haul them up behind them. That night they reached a band of snow and ice that became known as the First Icefield. They made their second bivouac at its crest, as testified by watchers from Alpiglen who saw a light there at around 9 p.m.

So far, including the easier Vorbau, it had taken Sedlmayr and Mehringer two days to climb 800 metres; 1000 metres remained. From this juncture, their progress slowed. They had less experience of ice than of rock, and they spent most of the next day crossing the expanse of what became known as the Second Icefield. Then the weather broke, shrouding the face in cloud. Two days later the clouds briefly parted, allowing a glimpse of the two men edging their way towards the top of a giant rock buttress that became known as the *Bügeleisen*, or Flatiron. They were never seen alive again.

A group of Munich climbers, including Sedlmayr's brother

Heinrich, dashed to the Eiger in a fruitless bid to mount a rescue. Four weeks later a German pilot flying close to the face spotted the body of one of the climbers in the snow at the Flatiron. The later discovery of two pitons hammered into the rock at a ledge on top of the Flatiron suggested they had tried to shelter there – giving the site the name Death Bivouac. For a long time the two men were thought to have died there but Rettner has made a strong case for believing that they succumbed to cold and exhaustion or a fall while attempting to descend.

In July 1936, four more climbers – two from southern Bavaria, two from Vienna – arrived at Alpiglen. What ensued was one of the greatest dramas in the Eiger's spectacular and lurid history – and one in which the First Band was to be a major factor.

First to venture on to the face, on 6 July, were the Austrians, Willy Angerer and Edi Rainer. Troubled by how long Sedlmayr and Mehringer had spent on the First Band, they searched for a line to the right which led them to the foot of a giant red cliff known as the Rote Fluh. After climbing a feature known as the Difficult Crack, they intended to traverse leftwards across a 40-metre stretch of rock that led to the First Icefield. The face was in bad condition, coursing with meltwater and stonefall, and the two retreated. On 18 July, they returned to the face and met the German pair, Andreas Hinterstoisser and Toni Kurz, below the Rote Fluh. They joined forces and Hinterstoisser embarked on the traverse towards the First Icefield, gaining traction by pulling against the climbing rope as it extended behind him – a manoeuvre known as a tension traverse. After the other three climbers had followed, they retrieved the rope and continued across the First Icefield. By 20 July they had reached the Flatiron and were close to the site of Sedlmayr and Mehringer's final bivouac.

On 21 July, the four men started to descend the face, most likely because Angerer had been injured by stonefall. When they reached the horizontal rock section leading off the First Icefield they found that it was covered with ice. If they had left their rope in place during the ascent, reversing the tension traverse would have been straight-forward, but the ice had rendered it impassable. They attempted to bypass it by descending directly down the First Band. Then came catastrophe. Hinterstoisser slipped and fell to his death. The climbing rope caught around Angerer's neck and he was strangled. Rainer was jammed tight against his belay point and froze to death. Only Kurz was left alive. He spent a nightmare twenty-four hours trying to reach safety before he too died of cold and exhaustion after a knot jammed in his abseil karabiner just a few metres above a group of rescuers. It was the most publicised Alpine accident since the Whymper disaster on the Matterhorn seventy-one years before.

As these dramas unfolded, the elders of the Alpine Club had been watching, transfixed with horror. The European press had been critical, one newspaper railing against young climbers seeking 'honour and glory', but that was mild in comparison to the invec-tive dispensed by Colonel Strutt, who by then was both the editor of the *Alpine Journal* and the club president. The deaths of Sedlmayr and Mehringer, Strutt wrote, demonstrated the 'crass incompetence, complete ignorance or neglect of the first principles of mountaineering' sweeping the Alps and were a 'flagrant example of the neglect of every sane principle in the attempt to gain cheap notoriety by accomplishing mechanical variants to former routes'.

Following the deaths in 1936, Strutt approvingly cited remarks in a Basle newspaper by a Swiss member, Dr Oskar Hug. 'The forc-ing of the Eigerwand is principally a matter of luck – at least 90 per cent of the latter is required ... This face climbing lies completely outside the pale of mountaineering, belonging far more to a degen-erate form of the Children's Crusade of the Middle Ages.' Strutt added that 'modern German methods of what is misnamed "moun-taineering" are, but too often, thoroughly unsound, and in every way destructive to the first principles of that pastime as known to every beginner throughout the remainder of Europe'.

In December 1937, when he finally quit as both journal editor and club president, Strutt delivered a valedictory address to club members. 'The Eigerwand, still unscaled, continues to be an obsession for the mentally deranged of almost every nation,' he raged. 'He who first succeeds may rest assured that he has accomplished the most imbecile variant since mountaineering first began.' Strutt's outrage can only have deepened when two Italians fell to their deaths from the First Band in June 1938. So it must have been with some chagrin that his successor as editor, H.E.G. Tyndale, had to carry a report of the first ascent of the North Face in the very issue that contained Strutt's speech of farewell.

The climbers who succeeded were another German-Austrian foursome: Anderl Heckmair and Ludwig Vörg from Munich, Heinrich Harrer from Graz and Fritz Kasparek from Vienna. The year before, Vörg had been one of two climbers who were the first to return alive from a North Face attempt when he and Matthias Rebitsch retreated safely from the top of the Flatiron. Learning from that experience and their predecessors' mistakes, the 1938 group left a rope in place across what was now termed the Hinterstoisser Traverse, and stashed ropes and equipment at a bivouac site known as the Swallow's Nest as further safeguards in case of a retreat. Over the best part of four days they negotiated the great landmarks whose names became totemic in the Eiger's history. There was the Ramp, the great slanting crack system that led leftwards above the Death Bivouac. Then the climbers crossed the slender ledge known as the Traverse of the Gods, which led them back to the centre of the face and the Spider, a steep, narrow ice-field which acted as a funnel for avalanches and debris falling from the upper part of the face.

Above the Spider came the Exit Cracks, a rising diagonal line presenting further technical demands on the way to the Summit Icefield, where the angle eased at last. They survived a series of mishaps and storms on their way to the summit. Kasparek slipped near the foot of the Ramp, and was held on the rope by Harrer. They battled through avalanches and a storm at the Spider. Heckmair fell in the Exit Cracks, injuring Vörg when one of Heckmair's crampons impaled his hand. They endured an exhausting descent of the West Flank, losing their way in another storm, before stumbling into Kleine Scheidegg.

The four men's triumph was celebrated in the European press. But the report in the *Alpine Journal*, which had devoted pages to the Hinterstoisser disaster, was decidedly spare. The new editor, Tyndale, could not restrain himself from adding that in comparison with other recent north face ascents, such as those on the Matterhorn and the Grandes Jorasses, 'the Eigerwand may be said to possess little or no "mountaineering" value. While bearing ungrudging tribute to the skill, endurance and modesty of the 1938 party, we see no reason to dissent from the opinion expressed on p.9 of the present volume' – namely that of Colonel Strutt.

Across the Atlantic, the American *Alpine Journal* was inclined to a similar view, although expressed in a more temperate way. The editor was an urbane ophthalmologist named J. Monroe Thorington, who made numerous first ascents in the Canadian Rockies in the 1910s and 1920s. He also wrote guidebooks and ghosted the autobiography of a leading Canadian guide, Conrad Kain. In 1938, Thorington observed that to write about the Eiger meant to relate a tale of 'disaster, injury and death', adding that it was 'encouraging to note that even the German press is turning against these senseless exhibitions of heroics'.

In 1939, Thorington reported only briefly on the previous year's ascent. 'The N. wall of the Eiger was finally ascended this past summer by an Austrian party composed of H. Harrer and

F. Kasparek, and a German party composed of L. Vörg and A. Heckmaier [sic], the two parties combining their forces and making the climb together. The ascent took three days and was finished under extremely bad conditions with sleet, hail and fresh snow making the climbing more difficult and menacing the climbers. Perhaps, now that it has been demonstrated that this face can be climbed without the climbers meeting an untimely end, we shall have an end to attempts and accidents on this face.'

In retrospect, the Alpine Club resembles a beached whale, stranded by the tide of mountaineering history and reduced to grumbling about the unfathomable behaviour of new generations of climbers. Yet it has to be said that the choleric Strutt had a point. At times the activities of the European climbers, with the incessant toll of casualties, must have resembled a death cult, enabling Strutt to observe that in his three years as club president not one member had died on a mountain. Strutt also regarded with distaste the alacrity with which official bodies in Germany and Austria had moved in to oversee climbing – anathema to the libertarian ambience of climbing in Britain, where any official oversight was unthinkable. Strutt may have been closer to the truth than anyone realised.

In contrast to climbing in Britain, Alpinism in Germany and Austria was an organised affair which also provided a vehicle for an increasingly strident and sinister nationalism. In 1919, the combined German and Austrian Alpine union – the DuÖAV – had more than 250,000 members, organised into 400 sections. Before long its youth leader, Ernst Enzensperger, was celebrating its potential for achieving a 'new, greater, more masterful, all-encompassing German Fatherland'. When the Nazis came to power they had a ready-made organisation and ideology at their disposal, and their propaganda machine was quick to seize the opportunities the Eiger presented. Before the Berlin Olympics of 1936, Hitler promised that anyone climbing the Eiger would receive a gold medal. A week after reaching the summit in 1938, the four climbers were presented to Hitler at a sports festival in Breslau. They were photographed with Hitler, who gave them a signed photograph of himself and pointed out that the alliance of the Austrian and German climbers symbolised Germany's annexation of Austria four months before. An SS officer escorted the four on a holiday to Norway and the Nazis published a book about German attempts on the Eiger, culminating in the success in 1938.

It can be argued that the four young climbers did not necessarily support the Nazis but merely went with the flow of predictable nationalist celebration of their success. Later, Harrer liked to say that meeting Hitler was the equivalent, for a British climber, of being introduced to the Queen – an honour that you could not turn down. But information about Harrer's true allegiances was revealed during the 1990s. As a student teacher, Harrer joined the Nazi teachers' organisation in Austria in January 1933 and the illegal Austrian paramilitary SA the same year. He joined the Nazi Party in 1938, became an adjutant in the SS and had dealings with its leader, Heinrich Himmler. In 1939, following an expedition to the Himalayan peak Nanga Parbat, Harrer was interned by the British in India. Later, a fellow internee testified that Harrer was a virulent Nazi. In 1944, he escaped to Tibet where he eventually became a tutor to the Dalai Lama. He returned to Austria in 1952 and wrote the bestselling *Seven Years in Tibet*. He died in 2006 at the age of ninety-three.

Among the other three climbers, Fritz Kasparek had entirely different sympathies. As a socialist, he assisted Austrians seeking to enlist in the Republican forces who were fighting Franco in the Spanish Civil War. In 1938, after he was congratulated by Hitler at the sports rally at Breslau, Himmler personally asked him to join the SS – a request Kasparek felt he could not turn down. He became an instructor at an SS school for Alpine troops, and during the war fought in both France and the USSR. He died at the age of forty-four when he fell through a cornice during an expedition to the Peruvian Andes in 1954.

Anderl Heckmair stayed as far away as possible from involvement with the Nazis. He joined a mountain regiment at the start of the Second World War, but an SS member denounced him as unreliable and he was sent to the Eastern Front. A fellow Alpinist, Rudolf Peters – who made the first ascent of the North Face of the Grandes Jorasses in 1935 – secured his transfer to an Alpine brigade. He survived the war and became a professional mountain guide, dying in 2005 at the age of ninety-eight. Ludwig Vörg also steered clear of the Nazis. He volunteered to join an Alpine regiment which was sent to the Eastern Front, and he was killed by a sniper on 22 June 1941 – the first day of Operation Barbarossa, the German invasion of the USSR. He was twenty-nine.

After the war, as if the recent past had been cleansed away, activities on the North Face of the Eiger resumed. In July 1947, two stellar French climbers, Lionel Terray and Louis Lachenal, braved heavy stonefall and severe storms to make the second ascent in three days. There were twelve ascents by a total of thirty-five climbers, and six more deaths, before a new drama beset the face in 1957. Two German climbers who reached the summit died of exhaustion while attempting to descend the West Flank. Two Italians, Stefano Longhi and Claudio Corti, were marooned after Longhi was injured in a fall above the Traverse of the Gods. Corti was rescued by a climber who was lowered from the summit on a 300-metre steel cable. He strapped Corti to his back and they were hauled to safety. Longhi was out of reach and died of cold and exhaustion, haunting his would-be rescuers with his shouts of '*Fame! Freddo!*' – 'Hungry! Cold!'

In March 1961 three Germans and one Austrian made the first

winter ascent, enduring sub-zero temperatures for much of the six days they spent on the face. They had clear weather throughout and had the further advantage that the face was frozen, far reducing the risk of stonefall and waterfalls. In July 1962 came the first British attempt, by Barry Brewster, a chemistry and maths graduate from London, and Brian Nally, a painter and decorator. On the second day they had reached the top of the Second Icefield but Brewster was hit by falling stones and slid sixty metres down the icefield before being held on his rope. Nally climbed down to him and hauled him on to a ledge that he hacked out of the ice. The next morning Brewster was swept to his death by an avalanche.

Nally was fortunate that two of Britain's most accomplished climbers, Chris Bonington and Don Whillans, were a short distance behind. They escorted Nally across the Second Icefield, surviving a storm and further volleys of stones before they reached the Stollenloch, one of the railway tunnel windows that provided an escape route from the face. A month later, Bonington returned with a new partner, Ian Clough, to make the first British ascent. They were still on the face when a British climber and his Austrian partner fell to their deaths from the Second Icefield. The British climber, Tom Carruthers, had climbed the North Face of the Matterhorn with Nally the previous year.

Despite the death toll, climbers continued to arrive at Alpiglen. In the next three weeks, twelve more reached the summit, and a Swiss climber attempting the first solo ascent died in a fall from low down on the face. The only previous attempt at a solo ascent had ended the same way. On 19 August, eight more climbers set off up the face. One was a German law student named Konrad Kirch. His partner was an American air force flying officer named John Harlin.

Chapter Three

FALLING IN LOVE

John Harlin first saw the Eiger when he was nineteen. It was 1954, and he was making a pilgrimage to the Alps from his home in California, where he was about to start his second year at Stanford University. He had started climbing as a freshman and was already steeped in the legends of the North Face. He spent a long time at the Kleine Scheidegg telescopes, scanning the face for the mythic locations of its spectacular history: the Death Bivouac, the Ramp, the Traverse of the Gods, the Spider.

Harlin was in distinguished company at Kleine Scheidegg. Another visitor was none other than Tenzing Norgay, the Sherpa climber who had made the first ascent of Everest with the New Zealand beekeeper Edmund Hillary the previous year. Tenzing had numerous friends in Switzerland, having come tantalisingly close to making the first ascent of Everest with a Swiss expedition in May 1952. He had spent two weeks in Switzerland after Everest, and in 1954 was taking a course to qualify as a mountain guide at a training school at the Oberland resort of Rosenlaui. As part of his training, he and his Sherpa colleagues were to climb to the summit of the Jungfrau, 2100 metres above Kleine Scheidegg.

As Harlin related to his girlfriend – and future wife – Marilyn Miler, he introduced himself to Tenzing and spent some time in his company. He told her that he had attached himself to Tenzing's party and joined them in the climb to the summit of the Jungfrau. His story was amplified in the biography of Harlin by Jim Ullman, who noted that the route to the Jungfrau passes along the West Ridge of the Eiger, where Harlin and Tenzing 'studied at close hand the complexities of the bordering face'. They even did some exploratory scrambling on the lower part of the face itself, 'but turned back at the point where the real difficulties began'.

There is a problem with these stories. Not everything Harlin said about himself, even to his wife, turned out to be true. What is more, Ullman sometimes added imaginative details to his narrative. Ed Douglas, the British writer who is Tenzing's most recent biographer, considers it plausible that Harlin should have met Tenzing at Kleine Scheidegg, but is sceptical about whether the training school director, Arnold Glatthard, would have allowed a nineteen-year-old American to tag along. Even so, Marilyn Harlin, who was well aware of her husband's tendency to exaggerate and falsify, was inclined – sixty years on – to believe the Tenzing story, principally because of the detail it contained.

Besides confirming that stories about Harlin need to be carefully examined, the episode says much about him. According to Ullman, it was during that visit that Harlin first formed the ambition to climb the Eiger, one that would shape the rest of his life. Assuming that the core of the story is true, it also demonstrates an ability to make important friends and forge useful relationships. Even at nineteen, this handsome Californian, with his blond hair and athletic physique, had a personable, outward-going charm. It also reveals someone who was no insular American but a confirmed Europhile. He had spent four years living in Europe after the war, as his father, an airline executive with TWA, was posted to Ireland

and Paris, where the family lived in an eighteenth-century château close to the Palace of Versailles. He was a devoted traveller, a cosmopolitan who relished the sense of discovery that comes from exploring new places. But then, as his father liked to say, a love of both travelling and high places may have been in his son's blood. He was conceived in La Paz, Bolivia, which at 4000 metres is almost exactly the height of the Eiger. His father – also called John Harlin – was flying planes for a mining company operating in the Amazon basin. He had previously been a TWA pilot but lost his job when the company went bankrupt. Nine months later, after TWA had been reconstituted, he was working at its headquarters in Kansas City, Missouri, which is where, on 30 June 1935, his son was born.

As his mother described them, the first years of Harlin's life were 'so wonderful, almost too much so to be true'. Genevieve Sussenbach, known from her maiden name as Sue, came from Illinois and married John Harlin I in 1930. John Harlin II was an only child and, she told Ullman, 'a joy to be around and a joy to take anywhere'. She was quick to add: 'That is not to be construed to mean that he was a goody good, sitting around polishing his halo. He was all boy, he played hard, he laughed, he was angry, he cried ... He had home, he had dogs, he had freedom.' His father had resumed flying and was away for much of the time, but the family made trips that whetted Harlin's appetite for the great outdoors: boating and fishing on the lakes of Minnesota, shooting pheasants in South Dakota, trekking into the Black Hills, the Tetons and Yellowstone. For Sue Harlin, the memories were so pure and powerful that she told Ullman: 'John's childhood is sacred to us.'

Harlin was seven when the idyll came to an end. When the US and Japan went to war in December 1941, John Harlin Sr, then thirty-five, became a pilot for the US Navy. He was based first in

Kansas and then in Hawaii, flying transport planes in the Pacific, while Sue and John Harlin II moved to Oakland, California. Harlin Sr returned to TWA in 1945 and spent the next four years working in management for the company in Europe. It was an exciting and glamorous time, not only because the family lived in a château in Versailles. Harlin Sr used his flight privileges to take his family on excursions to Spain, Italy, Greece and Egypt, Warsaw and Prague. The Harlins returned to the US in 1949 and settled in Redwood City, California, where Harlin Sr left management and returned to flying.

California was home for the next six years of the young Harlin's life. He attended Sequoia Union High School at Redwood City, where he shone in arts subjects such as English and history. He was intellectually curious and questioning, interested in politics and current affairs. He was also developing artistic talents. He liked to draw and later took up painting. His interests included nature, interior design, women's clothing and fashion. He excelled at sports, playing on the school American football team, sprinting and jumping in the track team. He was also a keen wrestler, gymnast and swimmer, all of which helped him develop from a skinny pre-adolescent into a muscular athlete – and one who was well aware of his powerful physique.

Harlin took to wearing brief shorts and tight tee-shirts, and liked to pose, both for his schoolmates and for the camera, presenting one of a number of parallels between him and George Mallory. The English writer and historian Lytton Strachey said that Mallory had the body of an athlete carved by the Greek sculptor Praxiteles; a school friend of Harlin said he had a 'Greek god body'. One of the most celebrated images of Mallory consists of a nude photograph taken by the Bloomsbury artist Duncan Grant, with Mallory commenting, 'I like the nude me.' Harlin posed for muscle magazines and on one occasion, like Mallory, was persuaded to remove all his clothes, which led to the magazine publishers being arrested (though not Harlin). When Ullman used the word 'homosexual' in a draft account of this phase of Harlin's life, lawyers acting for his parents demanded that it be excised. Ullman agreed, spelling out that 'in the actual living of his life, there is no slightest suggestion that he was ever anything but sexually normal'. Yet Harlin's absorption with his own image led Ullman to use the term 'narcissistic', which survived the lawyer's demands for excisions.

There are signs of unresolved conflicts within Harlin, which gave rise to bursts of violence and anger that persisted into his adult life. They became so disturbing that when he was nineteen his mother wrote to him, setting out her anxieties: 'My dear John,' she began. 'For some long time I have hoped for a heart to heart talk with you but the time never seems right. I hope you will read this letter thru without a hot flare of temper and ponder it over and over. I sense a terrific chip on your shoulder and it seems very definitely to be me.'

Sue Harlin devoted the rest of her letter to searching for faults that could have contributed to her son's anger. She confessed to feeling 'terribly tired' as she grew old (she was in her mid-forties). She was likely to magnify minor irritations, and said that as her husband was doing his best to hold down several jobs, her son's assistance would be appreciated. 'I need your help, I can only hope that you need mine. Together we could make Dad unmeasurably happy.' It was a poignant testimony from a mother who later sought to protect the memories of her son's childhood, listing for Ullman the positive qualities he had displayed as a teenager: 'With John's vitality and beautifully wonderful inquiring mind, unafraid, it was necessary to probe into everything, no matter how far out ... He was a crusader, a converter, a bringer-home of new ideas ...'

By the time his mother wrote to him, Harlin was completing his first year at Stanford. His father had hoped he would join the US Navy and Harlin attended a preparatory naval academy, but disliked the discipline and regimentation. At Stanford he studied English, French, history, geology and art, later majoring in art and dress design. He continued to explore radical ideas, moving politically to the left of his parents and also declaring himself – unlike them – an atheist. He signed up for the university American football squad and also played a few games of rugby.

Soon after arriving at Stanford, Harlin had two crucial new encounters. The first was with climbing, the second with Marilyn Miler, a science student from the north-west US. A friend from the Stanford football squad, Paul Revak, took Harlin climbing on crags and outcrops in the hills nearby. He joined the Stanford Alpine Club and ventured further afield, to the granite walls of Yosemite, fast becoming the proving ground for aspirant American climbers. In short order he was hooked. Later, he would explore his reasons for climbing and the challenges and rewards it brought. For the moment he contented himself with constantly pushing his standards, climbing with a raw natural energy that compensated for a lack of the highest climbing techniques.

It was through climbing that he met Marilyn Miler. She went to a Sunday climbing meet where he was instructing and they were soon dating. She was twenty, pretty, slim, with blue eyes, a scholarship student majoring in biology, and he called her Mara. She came from near Olympia, the capital city of the state of Washington, where her parents had withdrawn from the urban rat race to subsist on farming and earnings from her father's work as a carpenter.

Harlin brought excitement to her life. 'I had grown up as a recluse without travel or excitement,' she related in a memoir, *Making Waves*, published in 2014. 'His life was one of adventure.' He enthralled her with his stories of living in a Versailles

château, visiting Prague after the war, and making a reconnaissance of the North Face of the Eiger with Everest hero Tenzing
Norgay. 'Not all of his stories held up under scrutiny,' she conceded, even though she considered the Tenzing anecdote sound.

In the summer of 1955, Harlin made a second trip to Europe,
from which two of his more fanciful stories emerged. Together with
an American law student named Richard Collins, whom he had met
by chance in Geneva, he travelled to Zermatt with the intention of
climbing the North Face of the Matterhorn. But after setting out
they were unable to find the foot of the route and switched to the
Hörnli Ridge, the easiest route to the summit, taken by thousands of
climbers every year. They were turned back by bad weather 300
metres below the summit and had a narrow escape when Collins
slipped on a patch of ice. Harlin was struggling to hold him on their
rope when three guides came to their rescue. Harlin nonetheless sent
Marilyn a postcard inscribed: 'I climbed the N. face of the
Matterhorn.' He also listed the supposed ascent on his application
form when he eventually joined the American Alpine Club (AAC).

The second story emanated from his hope of becoming a dress
designer. He was looking for jobs when his father's Paris connections brought an introduction to Pierre Balmain, the French
couturier and fashion-house head. Balmain invited him to a weekend house party where, Balmain related, he appeared on the lawn
'wearing the briefest of red shorts'. Balmain said that he and his
companions 'greatly admired both his physique and his noncha-
lance at displaying it'. If this was a ploy by Harlin, conscious or
otherwise, to persuade Balmain to employ him, it failed. But Harlin
later reversed the truth to claim that he had worked for a time as
an apprentice in Balmain's design studio. It was no more accurate
than his claim to have climbed the North Face of the Matterhorn.

These are among the fictions that his son, John Harlin Jr, had to
confront as he learned more about his father's habit of exaggerating

his achievements. The fault was in part mine, as I had credulously recycled the Matterhorn and Balmain stories, among others, when writing about Harlin at the time of the Direct. In his biography, Ullman gently debunked these stories. But John Harlin Jr has related another story arising from the 1955 trip that Ullman shied away from. Harlin was prone to intense jealousy in respect of Marilyn – another irony of his life, given that he had at least one major affair during his marriage and did not pass up opportunities for casual sex. John Harlin Jr told how his father wrongly believed that Marilyn was 'over- friendly' with another man while he was away in Europe. When he returned to Stanford they had a furious row. Marilyn finally convinced him she had remained faithful and they had make-up sex on the lawn of the house where she was lodging. John Harlin Jr was conceived that night and Marilyn and Harlin were married three months later (Ullman glosses over the dates).

The nearest thing the Harlins had to a honeymoon was to join the Stanford Alpine Club's visit to the local crags during the week-end following Thanksgiving Day. There were just two tents among seven people, and Marilyn slept in one between her husband and another club member, occupying the gap between the two men's inflatable mattresses. The weather was abysmal, no climbing was done, and – as the only woman on the trip – Marilyn had to roast the traditional Thanksgiving turkey during a snowstorm. The Harlins' son was born on 14 May 1956. As a placatory gesture to Harlin's parents, he was named John Harlin III – thus sowing confusion for anyone attempting to follow the family story.

After their son was born, Marilyn went to stay with her parents near Olympia. Although Harlin joined her there, Marilyn discovered that being married to a mountaineer entailed having an absentee husband. Harlin first went climbing in the nearby Cascade and Olympic ranges. He and Marilyn went hiking together, carrying their baby son in a papoose, before Harlin departed for several weeks climbing in the Canadian Rockies. In the autumn they moved in with Harlin's parents at Stanford, where they stayed in an annexe built by Marilyn's father. Harlin became president of the Stanford Alpine Club and was away climbing most weekends. Marilyn sometimes went with him to Yosemite, walking along the trails with their son on her back while Harlin climbed. With childcare assistance from Harlin's parents, she was able to resume her university studies.

In 1957, with graduation looming, Harlin faced a decision over his career. Dress design was no longer an option and he joined the United States Air Force. It seems an unlikely choice for a questioning young man who had disliked the routines of a naval academy. But Harlin's father was still keen for him to become a pilot and Harlin had trained with Stanford's officer programme, the Reserve Officers' Training Corps (ROTC). He enlisted in November 1957 and qualified as a fighter pilot the following summer. He was one of the best pilots of his unit and loved to match his skills in mock duels with his peers. He took illicit pleasure from flying low over Marilyn and their friends, an activity known as buzzing, and on one occasion in Nevada brought down a line of telephone wires. Later, he described the delights of 'rolling the plane in sheer joy of freedom and movement. The aircraft was my body and the sky the dimensions of my youth. Whether flying or mountain climbing, the sky had become more than a playground. It was my life.'

In summer 1959 Harlin was offered a choice of posting: Japan or Germany. Since Germany bordered the European Alps, it was no contest. He and Marilyn, together with John Jr and their newborn daughter Andréa, arrived at Hahn Air Base in the central Rhineland in December. Hahn was home of the 10th Tactical Fighter Squadron of the USAF's 50th Tactical Fighter Wing – also known as the Hahn Hawks. The Cold War was at its height, and the US forces which had originally occupied Germany at the end of the Second World War were in the front line of the confrontation with the USSR. As tensions increased, the US multiplied its stockpile of nuclear warheads, which soared from 1000 in 1953 to 18,000 in 1961. Some were to be delivered by the F-100 fighter-bombers that were stationed at Hahn. The pilots were on permanent alert, sleeping near their planes so that they could be airborne within three minutes. Their mission was to bomb cities in Eastern Europe and then, as they ran out of fuel, bail out and hope for the best. Harlin's target was the city of Prague, capital of Czechoslovakia and home to one million people, which he had visited with his father.

The Harlins were one of the few families who opted not to live on the base, with its facsimile of US small-town life, its cinema, café, the roads named Main Street and Broadway, and the PX, the store selling US goods. They rented an apartment in the town of Bernkastel-Kues on the river Moselle. Marilyn learned German and made friends with their neighbours. Harlin was less sociable, appearing to resent the German family living in an apartment in the same building, and Marilyn found herself subjected to the angry rages that his mother had witnessed.

Harlin, she had soon discovered, had a controlling personality that she found difficult to live with. She told Ullman: 'From the beginning, John censored my speech, my movements, my dress, my letters ... He controlled what I ate and with whom I associated. When John censored my speech and my movements, it was the reflection upon himself with which he was worried.' Even before they were posted to Hahn, he had chafed at marriage, pacing the room, picking fights with Marilyn and their friends, and sleeping with a gun beneath his pillow for no good reason that Marilyn could discern.

At Hahn matters worsened, and Marilyn later accounted this the worst period of their marriage. Harlin was ever more irked by USAF discipline and looked for exit routes, once asking Swissair if he could qualify for them as a pilot. At times he was like a caged beast and there were frequent rows, often arising from trivial causes. He would shout at Marilyn and sometimes hit her before storming out. He would return contrite, and as often as not they sought solace in sex. If she remonstrated with him over his anger and violence, he would apologise and say he didn't mean it.

The tensions deepened when Harlin had a full-blown affair with the wife of a fellow pilot which ended when her husband attempted suicide. Marilyn took the forgiving view that her husband was 'an awfully attractive man if you didn't have to live with him every day'. She was aware that she fell short in his eyes, but that was because, as she once memorably put it, 'all John wanted of a wife was that she be a Balmain model, an Eiger climber and a perfect housekeeper, have shining hair (without curlers), get a Ph.D (in her spare time), be a devoted mother (with invisible children), plus a reader, mixer, camp director, secretary-treasurer, and also (in her spare time) do anything else she wants'.

When Ullman asked why she didn't leave Harlin, she replied: 'John was the most interesting person I have known. He never lacked for ideas, for stimulating discussions. He had a wide range of interests and could talk at the frontiers of nearly every field he put any research into. There was his vitality, his strength, his enjoyment of life.'

As Marilyn recognised, Harlin's principal escape from his frustrations lay in the mountains, where she believed he was 'more at one with himself'. Although the USAF was supposedly banned from Swiss airspace, Harlin went close enough in his F-100 to see the Eiger rising darkly among its snow-covered Oberland neighbours, confirming its hold on his ambitions. In February 1960, he and Marilyn spent a weekend at Grindelwald – his first visit since 1954. By then, the North Face had been climbed seventeen times by a total of forty-seven climbers, none of them British or American. There had also been seventeen deaths.

That summer Harlin resolved to make his first attempt with

Jerry Robertson, an air force friend who was visiting Europe. They first went to Chamonix, together with Marilyn and Robertson's brother Gary, leaving John Jr and Andréa in the care of Harlin's mother, who had come to Hahn for a month. Harlin and Robertson intended to warm up with some climbs around Mont Blanc, but there was an unpropitious start. They failed on the three routes they attempted and then, as they prepared to spend the night in a mountain hut together, Harlin accused Marilyn and Robertson of having an affair. Although he and Marilyn made up, it was hardly the ideal preparation for a testing partnership on the Eiger. Once at the mountain they climbed a short distance on the Vorbau but the weather was against them and they turned back.

In November 1960, there was a decisive change in Harlin's air force career. He told his superior officers that he was morally opposed to nuclear weapons and asked to be removed from the F-100 squad. The USAF reassigned Harlin as an instructor and examiner, flying T-33 trainers instead of the supersonic F-100. Since he was no longer tied to the pilots' nuclear roster, he was able to finagle more time for mountaineering.

Harlin returned to the Eiger in June 1961. His partner was Gary Hemming, whom Harlin had first met in Yosemite in 1954. Hemming was an unsettled, anarchic figure, a climbing bum who was given to railing at Harlin in Marilyn's presence for having succumbed to marriage. He pitched up in Bernkastel just as Harlin was enjoying his new-found freedom. When they arrived at the Eiger they found it awash with melting snow and stonefall. They diverted to Mont Blanc, intending to return to the Eiger at the end of the summer, but were caught up in one of the most lethal episodes of Alpine history.

Seven climbers, including the peerless Walter Bonatti, were trapped in a storm on the unclimbed Central Pillar of Frêney. Two more, the Swiss Henri Briquet and the German Konrad Kirch, were marooned on the Peuterey Ridge. Four of the Frêney climbers died during their attempt to descend, while Hemming and Harlin helped to lead Briquet and Kirch to safety. Harlin and Hemming returned to Kleine Scheidegg but the weather was once again against them and they made only token progress on the Vorbau. To Harlin's chagrin, the weather delivered perfect conditions after he returned to Hahn and a further sixteen climbers reached the summit in the space of four weeks.

Soon afterwards, Harlin found a new partner for the Eiger. His relationship with Hemming was always volatile and they frequently squabbled, on one occasion coming close to blows. Harlin turned to Kirch, the German climber he had assisted on his retreat from the Peuterey Ridge. A law student from Munich, Kirch was a stable and methodical character, especially in contrast to the bohemian Hemming. That winter they climbed in the Austrian Alps and Dolomites, then teamed up again with Hemming and a Yugoslav climber, Aleš Kunaver, in a failed attempt on the Walker Spur on the Grandes Jorasses. In the summer they climbed in the Kaisergebirge and the Dolomites, and failed again on the Walker. On 18 August 1962, they pitched their tent in the Alpiglen meadows.

They started the climb the next day. At first it followed a familiar pattern, which is not to diminish its difficulties. Often climbing on crumbling, friable rock or loose ice, they had to dodge the customary bombardment of falling stones and ice. Then came a series of setbacks. Harlin was supposed to lead across the Second Icefield but he had forgotten to sharpen his crampons, so Kirch had to take over. Harlin dropped his ice hammer and between them they dropped their stove. When they reached the Spider it was swept by avalanches which they dodged by timing the intervals and dashing to the next stance. They were held up by a group of climbers at the Exit Cracks and had to wait for several hours, their hands and feet beginning to freeze, as a

Swiss climber fell three times from an overhanging bulge of ice. Kirch moved into the lead and passed the overhang but they were forced to spend a fourth night on the face, perched on a tiny stance and endeavouring to stay awake in case they fell off. They reached the summit the next morning and exchanged the mountaineers' greeting, '*Berg heil!*'

Harlin suffered mild frostbite and spent a week in hospital back at Hahn. Apart from Kirch, all the other climbers had serious frostbite injuries and two spent two months in hospital. It served as a salutary reminder, if one were needed, of the penalties exacted by the Eiger for delays and mistakes.

Harlin once told Marilyn that the Eiger could be the last climb he ever did – a seemingly ambiguous statement, but implying that he might renounce mountaineering. If – as Ullman put it – Marilyn believed it for even five minutes, it proved a frail hope. By then the satisfaction Harlin found in meeting the challenges of mountaineering was too intense to be set aside for a conventional life, as he was revealing in his writings.

His son John believes he valued climbing as a route to self-validation, testing himself in the most extreme circumstances. Harlin himself was keen to explore his motivations, writing: 'By subjecting oneself to the pure and focused experience of survival, accompanied by introspection, one can approach an ultimate in self-control.' He developed the same thoughts in the introduction to a book he planned to write: 'It is not for power, money or glory that men risk hardship or death in the mountains. They climb to control their own weakness and fear. From this control comes [sic] strength and the ability to enjoy the incredible harmony of human action among elements of beauty.' The theme common to both passages is that of self-control. The man who succumbed to displays of frustration and anger had found the antidote. Even in the most extreme circumstances, the mountains brought peace.

In was in this context that some were to accuse him of narcissism, of playing out melodramatic roles as if life were a permanent stage – the charge laid by Royal Robbins after their ascent of the West Face of the Dru. Harlin himself referred to climbing as a performance, but went further when he wrote in an essay about a solo climb that 'he yearned for that ultimate experience'. If that looked like a coded flirtation with death, he expressed it explicitly when he described how he and Kirch watched an approaching storm during their second bivouac on the Eiger. 'Melodramatic as it may seem in retrospect, I felt strongly that if this was going to be the beginning of the end, I wanted to absorb all of the visual stimulus [sic] that I could aesthetically enjoy.'

In another essay, he explored the reasons that spectators find climbers' struggles so alluring, seeing them as totemic figures who act out the eternal conflict between life and death. 'As the warmth of life rushes out, his body reacts in a spasm of the animal's desperation to live.' And when the climber proves to have survived, 'an awe emerges for the simplicity required to endure.'

Harlin once linked the two most powerful themes of all when he wrote to Marilyn proposing 'that we climb together something so interesting and so romantic that returning from it was unimportant'. In other words, love and death would combine to form the perfect narrative. Then he pulled back. In his essay about a solo climb in which he yearned for the ultimate experience, he said it would enable him to 'physically transcend the personal ... to find a vivid moment of truth'. He added the caveat: 'But not quite yet.'

Within weeks of coming down from the Eiger in August 1962, Harlin asked his Eiger partner, Konrad Kirch, to join him in an attempt on the Direct.

possible lines of a direct ascent. Brown later wrote that there was 'passion' in Harlin's eyes.

From that juncture, the quest for the Direct became a given in Harlin's life: an objective that did not need exploring or questioning and one that merited the term obsession. Ullman wrote that Harlin was motivated by a desire to gain recognition in the US, where his Alpine achievements were almost unnoticed. His ascent of the 1938 route had been reported in the European press, but to Harlin that was cold comfort. Competitive and ambitious, he 'wanted his excellence to be known'. If so, that would have strengthened the compulsions that fed his drive to climb: the self-validation, the search for peace. Over the next two years, Harlin's quest drew him back to the Eiger time and again. He had most success when he attached himself to other climbing teams, but these attempts were marked by friction and disagreement, sometimes followed by aspersions about his temperament and ability. By the end of 1964 Harlin was searching for new partners once more.

The man who inspired aspirants to the Direct was originally a stevedore from the Adriatic city of Trieste in north-eastern Italy. Emilio Comici was born in 1901 and was first employed shifting cargoes in the city's docks. After an initiation as a caver, he took up climbing and pioneered the techniques required for tackling the vertical or overhanging and often loose cliffs of the Dolomites. These included intricate new belay and rope systems and the use of short portable rope ladders known as étriers. Such equipment has always been the focus of ethical debate and was heavily disapproved of by the traditionalists of the English Alpine Club who strongly believed in the ethic of free climbing, where climbers use only the natural features of the rock for holds. The traditionalists were especially unhappy at what they saw as the overuse of pitons. In free climbing, these may be hammered into the rock to create belays which protect the climber in the event of a fall. Now, in what was termed artificial or aid climbing, pitons were being used to create hand- and footholds as well. While this was anathema to the old guard, the new climbers saw it as the only way to overcome the great faces of the Dolomites. In 1931, Comici and a partner used these methods to climb a new route on the 1200-metre North-west Face of the Civetta. In 1933, he and two new partners made the first ascent of the overhanging North Face of the Cima Grande, his most famous route and the toughest climb of its time. It was after climbing the Civetta that Comici made his epic and often-quoted declaration: 'I wish some day to make a route and from the summit let fall a drop of water and this is where my route will have gone.'

Comici's declamatory style raises an issue parallel to that swirling around the Eiger climbers of the 1930s. After making a solo ascent of his route on the North Face of the Cima Grande in 1937, he described his feelings during a moment of peril. 'What possessed me? Was it some sort of madness or alpinistic sadism? I don't know. Yes I was intoxicated, but fully aware because I felt in myself the physical power to overcome the overhanging and the moral security to master the empty space. I recognise from the outset that solitary mountaineering on difficult rock walls is the most dangerous thing anyone can do ... but the feeling in that moment is so sublime that it's worth the risk.' His declaration chimes uneasily with the heroic rhetoric of Italy's leader, Benito Mussolini, the country's dictator through the 1930s. Mussolini's black-shirted Fascists had been strong in Trieste, helping to drive out the Slavic-speakers who had been marooned there when the city was annexed from Slovenia after the First World War.

Comici supported Mussolini and became a Fascist town official in 1938, benefiting from commercial favours from the party. It can be argued that joining the Fascist Party was all but essential for anyone in public life – at its height, it had 13 million members – yet there were still many who resisted its call, among them Comici's contemporary, Attilio Tissi, a climber who opposed Mussolini and joined the anti-Fascist resistance in the Second World War. Ironically, Comici – the great technician – died when his abseiling sling broke during a training session in 1940. The circumstances were suppressed by the Fascist authorities, embarrassed that one of their own should die in such a banal manner.

The first great direct ascent of the post-war era was also in the Dolomites. A number of German climbers were eyeing the North Face of the Cima Grande for a *direttissima* and several made attempts in 1957. In 1958 four of them teamed up for a new attempt: Dietrich Hasse, Lothar Brandler, Siegfried Löw and Jörg Lehne, all of them from a new generation of climbers whose childhoods and upbringings had been scarred by the Second World War. Hasse, Brandler and Löw were from Dresden, where Löw had survived the devastating Allied bombing raid of February 1945; Lehne lived in the Bavarian town of Rosenheim, which was bombed a dozen times in 1944 and 1945. They reached the summit after five days on the face, using 180 pitons, sleeping in hammocks and hauling their supplies on ropes.

Four years later the North Face of the Eiger came into focus as the target for a direct. In the 1930s, the face had yawned open in the *Alpine Journal* photograph asserting that it had been climbed. Now, the single zigzag line across the face was an open temptation to establish a new route to reflect the modern era. To some climbers, the 1938 line was the perfect route for the way it probed the mountain's lines of weakness. The incomparable Scottish climber Tom Patey, who failed on the North Face with Don Whillans in 1963, told me that he considered the 1938 route the finest in the Alps for its elegance and ingenuity. Patey was still hoping to climb it in 1970 and had even bought some new crampons for an attempt, but he died in an abseiling accident on a sea stack in northern Scotland. By contrast, the potential line of the Direct had a brutalist feel, slashing its way up the mountain and expressing the imperatives of a new age of mountaineering. Just as the young radicals of the 1920s and 1930s had resolved to climb the great north faces traditional climbers had shunned, the next generation was going to assert its presence, and Harlin was in the vanguard.

In the winter of 1962-63, Harlin found a new potential partner while training over several weekends with the US forces biathlon ski team at an American base at Garmisch-Partenkirchen, in the Bavarian Alps. His trainer, Sandy Bill, was a keen climber and Harlin suggested they attempt the Direct. In February 1963 they visited the Eiger to look at possible routes, but Bill's interest went no further.

Two months later two Polish climbers made the first serious attempt. Jan Mostowski and Czeslaw Momatiuk had strong records, and Mostowski had already climbed three of the great Alpine north faces. Their attempt ended at the top of the Vorbau, where Mostowski slipped and fell most of the way to the foot of the face, escaping with minor injuries. The next attempt was made in July by four Italian climbers from a group named the Cortina Squirrels. They reached the top of the Vorbau and started up the First Band to the left of the line taken by Sedlmayr and Mehringer in 1935. The climbing proved exceptionally steep and they turned back at some fierce overhangs. The two failures offered a warning of the scale of the climb and the difficulties that even experienced teams could face. They also signified that the race for the Direct was on.

In the spring of 1963, Harlin was approaching another major decision in his life. His five-year stint with the USAF had ended in December 1962, but he had been given a six-month extension to allow him time to consider his options. These included staying in the USAF, applying to train as an astronaut, joining the Peace Corps, and becoming a commercial pilot, but he rejected them all. Instead, he and Marilyn drew up plans to open a college in Chamonix, to be named the International Institute of Mont Blanc. Harlin went as far as to try to secure backing from Dwight Eisenhower, the former US president who was travelling in Europe. But several opportunities to meet Eisenhower fell through and he and Marilyn were unable to raise the finance they needed. Meanwhile, Marilyn had been applying for teaching posts throughout western Europe and was finally offered a job as a science teacher at the American School in the Swiss mountain town of Leysin. There was one condition: Harlin was to become the school's sports director. Leysin was just three hours' drive from Grindelwald and the Eiger. They accepted.

The Harlins left Hahn in June 1963. With three months to fill before they were due in Leysin, they spent the summer in a series of climbers' campsites. The first was in Chamonix, where Harlin had convened a group of talented climbers who included Hemming, the Scottish climber Stewart Fulton and Tom Frost, a fellow Stanford man who was one of an elite group making new climbs at Yosemite, beginning with the breakthrough ascent of the Salathé Wall on El Capitan in 1961. After a number of false starts, the four made the first ascent of the South Face of the Aiguille du Fou; soon afterwards, Harlin and Frost made the first ascent of the remote Hidden Pillar of Frêney.

For all her husband's successes, Marilyn was still feeling disenchanted. She had found that Harlin wanted her to watch him climbing through binoculars, while she preferred to hike among the glaciers with her children. For her son John, however, this was a magical time. In March the family had been camping in the Calanques, a stretch of cliffs and inlets on the Mediterranean near Marseille. The trip provided him with some of his most scintillating memories: the evening chorus of cicadas, the ripple of waves as they slept on the beach, the salty aromas of the early morning. At Chamonix his father took him on to a glacier for the first time, strapping on his crampons, handing him an ice axe and attaching him to the middle of a rope with Marilyn at the far end. Forty years on, he remembered the ice sparkling in the sun, the colours of a crevasse as they faded from blue to indigo to black, the sound of a torrent of meltwater somewhere in the darkness below. Whenever he stepped on to a glacier as an adult and heard the crunch of ice beneath his feet he was transported to his hike up the Mer de Glace with his father. 'It's a magical feeling, one of the strongest and most visceral I have, and it surges through me like a rush of joy,' he later wrote.

In early August both family and climbers moved on to Alpiglen. While in Grindelwald Harlin met the president of the AAC, Carlton Fuller, and asked if the club would help fund an attempt on the Direct. Fuller said the club could not, but gave Harlin a personal cheque. The group set up camp in the Alpiglen meadows and Harlin's parents, who were visiting from the US, stayed at the Alpiglen hotel for a time. This being the 1960s, the heady aroma of marijuana, drug of choice of the era, frequently overlay the sweet scents of the meadows.

Among the climbers, Hemming and Fulton declared that they were ready for a direct attempt. Frost said he was not. Kirch turned up, still insisting he did not want to take part. Another climber to arrive was Pierre Mazeaud, a senior French Alpinist and a survivor of the Frêney disaster in 1961, whom Harlin was hoping to enlist. Harlin had asked Mazeaud to approach Walter Bonatti on his behalf. However, although Bonatti came to Alpiglen he was intent on making a solo attempt on the 1938 route.

There were other contenders for the Direct at Alpiglen. Already in residence were two Italian climbers, Roberto Sorgato and Ignazio Piussi, who had been interested in the Eiger Direct for almost as long as Harlin. Piussi, aged twenty-eight, was one of ten children, many of them professional guides, from a peasant family in the Julian Alps in north-eastern Italy. Sorgato, twenty-six, came from a professional family in Milan and was studying business administration. Piussi had racked up a long list of first ascents before teaming up with Sorgato in the early 1960s. In March 1963 they took part in the first winter ascent of the classic Solleder-Lettenbauer Route on the Civetta, made by a group who included German climber Toni Hiebeler and three other Italian climbers. Afterwards Sorgato and Piussi agreed to team up with Hiebeler to attempt the Eiger Direct. The Italians had arrived a few days before Harlin and were there to witness two solo attempts on the 1938 route. Bonatti withdrew after one night on the face. Two days later the Swiss climber Michel Darbellay reached the top after just eighteen hours' climbing spread over two days. Sorgato was in touch with Hiebeler but, according to Piussi's subsequent account, the German was not prepared to start until there was a guarantee of good weather.

There were, in fact, several spells of clear weather lasting a couple of days, but that was not enough for either Harlin or Hiebeler. Among Harlin's group, all but Fulton grew tired of waiting and left Alpiglen. Then Hiebeler called Sorgato and told him he was pulling out on the grounds that he had already done enough on the Eiger. A day or so later the weather improved and Sorgato and Piussi started an attempt. They made swift progress up the 1935 Sedlmayr-Mehringer route and bivouacked near the top of the First Band. Harlin, who had not been prepared to start without a clear weather forecast, was watching from Alpiglen and was doubtless relieved when a storm drove Piussi and Sorgato off the face.

The storm was the prelude to yet another Eiger drama. A Japanese team retreated from the 1938 route but two Spanish climbers, Ernesto Navarro and Alberto Rabadá, pressed on. On the fifth day the storm pinned them down at the Traverse of the Gods. Sensing a disaster, a group of the climbers at Alpiglen, including Harlin, Fulton, Sorgato and Piussi, set off up the West Flank in a bid to stage a rescue. But the two Spanish climbers were beyond help and died that night. The next day the Alpine rescue pilot Hermann Geiger flew over the face in a helicopter and spotted two bodies in the Spider.

By then, the rescue team had descended the West Flank. What transpired between Piussi and Harlin is the subject of conflicting accounts. As Sorgato told it, the descent developed into a race. The two men were keeping level until Piussi stepped up a gear and plunged down a steep ice gully with a speed and bravado that Harlin could not match. By the time Sorgato and Harlin reached the campsite at Alpiglen, Piussi had already finished eating his meal. Sorgato felt that 'the defeat of Harlin was like blowing a raspberry in his face – he really didn't like it at all'.

Sorgato's account reveals his own competitive state of mind as much as that of Harlin, who in fact described Piussi in generous terms: Harlin admired his 'speed and skill' and reckoned it was his way of throwing off the frustrations of the previous days. It was also clear that he saw Piussi and Sorgato as potential allies for the Direct. 'We discussed route possibilities and our different ideas of equipment and food,' Harlin wrote. But nothing had been settled by the time the three concluded that the season was over and quit Alpiglen.

Marilyn and the children, who had left Alpiglen ahead of Harlin, were already installed in Leysin. Their new home was a comfortable three-storey house named the Chalet Pollux. There was an unpropitious start to their new life, for when their removal van arrived outside the chalet the van crew refused to unload the Harlins' furniture. That was because – this being chauvinist Switzerland, where women were still not allowed to vote or stand for parliament in federal elections – they needed a man's signature and Marilyn did not qualify. After several days waiting with the furniture stacked up in the van, Marilyn persuaded the crew's boss to allow the director of the Leysin American School to sign. The chalet was a short walk from the school, which was housed in a former sanatorium dating from the days when Leysin was a busy spa town for tuberculosis patients. From their balcony, the Harlins could look across the Rhône valley to the Dents du Midi, a spectacular serrated line of summits rising to more than 3200 metres. A nearby chairlift gave access to distant views of the Matterhorn, Mont Blanc and the Oberland trio – Jungfrau, Mönch and Eiger.

The school, together with its partner, the American College, had around 200 pupils on their rolls, mostly Americans from expatriate families in Europe. Marilyn was soon teaching biology and chemistry, while Harlin found that his role as sports director allowed plenty of flexibility for climbing. It also enabled him to attract prominent climbers to Leysin by offering them teaching posts on his staff. Among those who accepted his offers were Stewart Fulton and his brother Robert, Don Whillans, and the gritty Lancashire climber Mick Burke. As well as providing potential climbing partners, Harlin's recruiting policy advanced his aim of making Leysin a focus of European Alpinism, and climbers from Britain and the US came to see it as the place to be. Most lodged at a glorified bunkhouse known as the Vagabond, or the Club Vag, and the club gained repute from having climbing celebrities in its ambit, boosting its appeal among the backpackers, hitchhikers, hippies, folk singers and others making the sixties equivalent of the Grand Tour.

It is from this disparate group of students and visitors that some of the most reverential and antagonistic views of Harlin were to be heard. Some were inspired by his ambition, his intellectual breadth and his physical presence. His son John Jr cited a range of adulatory website comments posted by some of his former students. 'The force of his character was amazing – he brought the best out of all of us,' one wrote. Another commented: 'He taught us to climb, and to extend our personal limits like no one I ever met before or since.' A third listed the lessons Harlin imparted: 'Be aware. Persist. Look inside for the strength you need. Above all, trust in yourself.'

The American climber Larry Ware, who first met Harlin as a student in Leysin when he was nineteen, witnessed the power of his charisma. 'People followed him almost like a god, they deified him – he was like a Greek hero to a lot of them,' Ware said in 2014; others, Ware observed, resisted being caught in Harlin's aura. Ware himself benefited from Harlin's tutoring. 'He introduced me to climbing and the climbing world and it helped give me an identity and a sense of worth.' Ware, who later became a teacher at Leysin, was not blind to Harlin's faults. 'I saw the weaknesses as well. He had an overbearing personality, he could crush someone, make them feel zero. I witnessed that. He was essentially very selfish. But most ambitious and successful people are.'

For Marilyn, Leysin represented a sea change from Hahn. Harlin was more relaxed away from military discipline, making the most of his freedom to climb and to dream. His anger and his jealousy were moderated. The family did more together, sitting and watching the rain from the chalet balcony, hiking among the hills, collecting mushrooms, swimming at the local pool. John Jr believed that living in the mountains 'had a calming effect – and brought out the best of him at home'. He could still be a stern taskmaster to his son, who long recalled two episodes where his father judged him to have failed: once when he did badly in a ski race, and his 'contempt was palpable'; and again when he was attacked by a school bully, and his father showed 'the rage of disappointment' that he came out worse in the fight.

At times, Harlin succumbed to the temptations of the Club Vag, drinking to all hours with the students and travellers, and returning to the chalet just as Marilyn was getting up to go to work. Even so, he showed marked improvement as a parent, leading the family on forest walks as his own father had done, picking flowers, having picnics and introducing the children to caving. Here, Marilyn said, 'he cared not a damn for his public image in this respect, so the public did not see him in these roles'. It was the happiest she had ever seen him. She particularly remembers him brushing Andréa's long fair hair – one of Andréa's few memories of her father more than fifty years on. 'In Leysin I was happy with John,' Marilyn said in 2014. At the time she wrote and told her parents: 'I am happier than I have ever known myself' – and the core of her happiness, she added, lay in being 'so very much in love'.

By mid-September 1963 Harlin was laying plans for an attempt on the Direct that winter. Invoking his understanding with Sorgato, Harlin wrote to propose that they attempt the climb together. Sorgato replied from Florence on 22 September. 'Dear John,' he wrote. 'I was happy to receive your letter. Half hour later I got a letter from Piussi, and the reasons was the same of yours. The idea is wonderful and I think we should try this stupid Eiger once more.'

Sorgato proposed that they discuss the idea at the Trento film festival in two weeks' time, and suggested adding two more Italians to the team. Harlin did not go to Trento and Sorgato wrote again, naming the two extra climbers: Natalino Menegus and Marcello Bonafede, both of whom had taken part in the first winter ascent of the Solleder-Lettenbauer Route on the Civetta in March 1963. 'They are very good climbers and companions,' Sorgato assured Harlin. 'I hope you will agree with us for the number of the team. It will be surer and we'll carry much more material.'

Harlin appeared unimpressed, as he did not reply. On 27 November Sorgato wrote again. There were evidently doubts among his own team, as Piussi had been talking to Menegus and Bonafede, who were now unsure whether they wanted to take part. Sorgato asked Harlin in turn if he still wanted to join them – otherwise 'we should find somebody else'.

Sorgato's implicit threat spurred Harlin and he responded with two long letters that revealed uncertainties of his own. How fit were Menegus and Bonafede? What languages did they speak?

What insurance cover would they have? What should they eat and who would organise the food? What bivouac equipment should they carry? Who would take photographs? What hardware did the Italians have? Would there be any rescue back-up?

Harlin seemed sceptical about the need for two more climbers and was uneasy that Sorgato appeared to be assuming leadership of the attempt. Sorgato replied to each of his questions and then dealt with two further points. The first was about the logistics of the attempt. Two climbers would lead the way, fixing ropes in place. The remaining three would haul the rucksacks, set up the bivouac sites and prepare food and drink. All five climbers would rotate between leading and supporting roles. To provide additional shelter at the bivouac sites, Sorgato proposed taking a lightweight tent. He added, unconvincingly: 'I'll try to borrow a wonderful one from my friend but I'm not sure to get it.'

The second point, and a vital question for Harlin, concerned timing. Harlin believed that they could only make the attempt if they had a guarantee of good weather. He recalled that Hiebeler had made his winter ascent during a week of good weather in March 1961 and reckoned that a similar spell occurred every winter. He told Sorgato that he would monitor the weather at the Eiger and would summon the Italians as soon as the forecasts promised the sustained clear weather they needed.

But there was a problem. Sorgato told Harlin he was sitting an examination in Milan at the end of January, which meant that he would not be available until the first week of February. Sorgato added that his three colleagues were willing to start without him, but his assurance lacked conviction.

For Harlin, the outcome was bitterly disappointing. The weather at the Eiger cleared in January but the Italians were not prepared to come, with or without Sorgato. Then four German climbers arrived at the Eiger, intent on the Direct. The four, all from

Saxony, were Peter Siegert, Rainer Kauschke, Werner Bittner and Gerd Uhner and they had form, as all but Bittner had spent seventeen days climbing a new *direttissima* line on the Cima Grande the previous winter. On 12 January 1964 they started up the Vorbau but took two days to reach the First Band. They spent 14 January sheltering from a storm and, although fine weather returned on the 15th, they retreated through the Stollenloch on the grounds that the face was in poor condition.

The Germans were further discomfited when they came across the leg of one of the Spanish climbers who had died on the 1938 route the previous summer (it was later identified as belonging to Ernesto Navarro). In December a Swiss team had descended from the summit in a bid to retrieve the two bodies. They found them in the Spider and lowered them to the Death Bivouac, where they secured them with pitons. The pitons pulled free during the night and the frozen bodies were dismembered as they fell, scattering body parts across the Vorbau.

The failure of yet another strong team to make any significant progress confirmed the immense challenge that the Direct posed. It also offered salutary lessons over dealing with the media, as the Germans had sold their story to the tabloid magazine *Bild* for 6000 Deutschmarks – to be paid if they climbed 800 metres of the route. *Bild* dispatched a representative to Kleine Scheidegg to field questions from a sizeable press pack, and she was able to reassure them that the climbers would have paused to say prayers when they found Navarro's leg. In the event, *Bild* did not have to pay up, as the Germans climbed only 580 metres, and there were caustic reports in rival newspapers about the media hype which the attempt had generated.

Following the German failure, a high-pressure system developed over the Alps, heralding three weeks of settled weather. Harlin hurried to Kleine Scheidegg but the Italians were still unable or unwilling to come. In his frustration, Harlin embarked on an impromptu bid to make the second winter ascent of the 1938 route. His partner was a friend of Konrad Kirch, a ski instructor at the Leysin American School named Hans Mayer-Hasselwander, known as Hansl. Conditions were ideal, with the temperature hovering around zero, clear skies and a good forecast. Harlin reckoned they could climb the face in three days, but they hit problems from the start. Hansl led up the Difficult Crack but Harlin, who was carrying a heavy rucksack, was unable to follow. They spent both time and energy hauling Harlin's pack and were forced into an early and uncomfortable bivouac. Hansl was not comfortable in his boots, which he had borrowed from Harlin, and they struggled to light their stove.

In the morning they retreated through the Stollenloch. 'I was impressed by his fanaticism and his physical strength,' Hansl said of Harlin in 2014. But he blamed Harlin for their equipment failures, adding ruefully: 'Never again such perfect conditions.'

The next day the weather was still perfect and Harlin teamed up with a local climber and guide, Martin Epp, to make the second winter ascent of the North Face of the neighbouring Mönch. It was a mark of the ideal conditions that they reached the summit in ten hours, three days faster than the first ascent. Harlin sent further telegrams to the Italians urging them to come, but Sorgato was still preoccupied with this exams. Ruing his luck, Harlin departed for Chamonix, where he made the first winter ascent of the West Face of the Aiguille de Blaitière.

The Italians were finally ready to depart in the second week of February. But the good weather had ended and the Eiger was battered by storms. Sorgato and Piussi came to Leysin, where they sorted out their equipment in the Harlins' basement and carried out training routines in the nearby quarry. The Italians were alarmed when Harlin impaled his thigh with the four-inch tip of his ski pole while skiing, but Harlin simply pulled it out and continued skiing to prevent his leg from stiffening up. The next day, the three moved on to Kleine Scheidegg, where they were joined by Menegus and Bonafede, who had apparently overcome their reservations about climbing with Harlin. The same could not be said for Piussi, who was at odds with Harlin from the start. He considered that Harlin was gate-crashing the Italians' party, and had also become convinced that he would be accompanied by at least one other American, and so felt misled when he discovered that only Harlin would be taking part.

There were more problems when the climbers started. They climbed most of the Vorbau on the first day, and Harlin and Sorgato led up the First Band the next day. But they were weighed down by their packs and had to scrape ice out of the cracks with their bare hands before they could place pitons. Harlin was irritated that the Italians had not prepared, as he had, by carrying snow in their bare hands to toughen them against the cold. Piussi felt in turn that Harlin was climbing too slowly. He and Bonafede took over on the third day, reaching the top of the First Band and pressing on up the First Icefield. But they returned with a gloomy estimate of their prospects on the rocky section above the icefield. After an uncomfortable bivouac it was clear that momentum was seeping away, and when they learned that bad weather was approaching they retreated through one of the railway tunnels.

There was a bizarre postscript to the attempt. Like the German team in January, they came across Navarro's body parts on the Vorbau. Harlin later wrote that he had been told that the Grindelwald police needed physical evidence in order to issue death certificates. He abseiled down to Navarro's leg and returned with it protruding from his rucksack.

Piussi told the story differently, writing that Harlin had fetched the leg on his own initiative and said he would deliver it to the police. Piussi told him to 'leave it' but Harlin insisted. 'Perhaps it was for show,' Piussi speculated. Piussi's gloss on the incident is consistent with the harsh judgement he and Sorgato made of Harlin. They considered him 'arrogant and presumptuous' and although he was agile and strong, with an athletic physique, 'he didn't really have the habits, practice and understanding of mountains that every good mountaineer should have'.

The disagreements with the Italians most likely contributed to Harlin's own sour conclusion. 'The deep feeling of emptiness in me,' he wrote, 'could only be removed by another attempt at the Eiger Direct.'

Harlin had only four months to wait. Once again he was to be plunged into anxiety on learning that two more top Alpinists had designs on the Direct, and once again there were tensions as he joined their attempt. In early June, Harlin heard that René Desmaison and André Bertrand were about to set off from Alpiglen. Desmaison and Bertrand, both professional guides, were leading figures of French climbing with a host of notable ascents to their names. Desmaison in particular had a high profile, the outcome of relentless self-publicity that was to win him acclaim and notoriety in equal measure. His reputation among British climbers was especially low in light of what happened when a four-man team, including Bonington and Whillans, snatched the coveted first ascent of the Central Pillar of Frêney. Desmaison was following close behind and accepted help from the British to overcome the crux pitch, which Bonington had led – and then claimed that he and not the British had made the first ascent.

Undeterred, Harlin hurried to Kleine Scheidegg to find that Desmaison and Bertrand had already set off. After reaching the foot of the First Band they examined a line 150 metres to the left of the Sedlmayr-Mehringer 1935 route, but concluded that it was too difficult. They returned to the 1935 route and bivouacked in a hollow at its foot. The First Band was plated with ice and they made slow progress, bivouacking for the second night on a ledge under an overhang forty metres below the top. In the morning they reached the top of the First Icefield but were hit by a storm and retreated, fixing a rope on the First Band for use on a possible return.

By Desmaison's account, Harlin was unable to conceal his relief when he and Bertrand returned to Kleine Scheidegg. When they said they intended to try again as soon as the weather improved, Harlin became 'silent and thoughtful'. Harlin told them he had stashed supplies at the foot of the First Band during his attempt with the Italians – and that he intended to make a new attempt with a partner as soon as the weather improved.

Eight days later, with good weather in prospect, Desmaison and Bertrand returned to Kleine Scheidegg. Harlin was already there – by himself and looking 'infinitely sad', Desmaison related. Harlin told them that his partner had dropped out 'for professional reasons' at the last minute. If this was another of Harlin's convenient fictions, it had the desired effect. Desmaison and Bertrand took pity on Harlin and asked him to join them in their attempt, even though a team of three would inevitably be slower than a pair.

They set off the next day and climbed the Vorbau, bivouacking in the hollow below the 1935 route. They made swift progress the next day, using the rope that Desmaison and Bertrand had left in place a week before. By the afternoon they had crossed the First Icefield, climbed the wall at its top and set off up the Second Icefield.

There was now a crisis and a disagreement. Some 200 metres above them a massive cornice looked ready to break away. There was a thaw in the air and fragments of ice were slithering down Second Icefield. Desmaison set off warily on an ascending traverse, placing ice pitons for belays. Harlin urged him to climb without protection and when Desmaison protested that it was too danger-ous, Harlin told him he wasn't climbing with one of his clients. In that case, Desmaison replied, they might as well climb unroped. The argument was terminated when the cornice smashed into the ice fifty metres above them, deluging them with snow and ice that threatened to sweep them from their holds. Desmaison hammered in a piton just in time and held all three of them on his rope. Desmaison – who always liked to have the last word – recorded that Harlin congratulated him on placing the peg that saved their lives.

The three continued and reached the top of the Second Icefield at 4.30 p.m., where they stopped at a rock outcrop that offered some protection from stonefall. They had climbed further on the direct route than any previous attempt, save only for Sedlmayr and Mehringer themselves. That night they received conflicting fore-casts from two Swiss weather stations, which led to a new dispute. Desmaison favoured an optimistic forecast from Geneva while Harlin – invoking his experience with the USAF – was inclined towards a pessimistic one from Zürich. Harlin won the argument and in the morning the three decided to retreat. This time Harlin was proved right, as the face was soon awash with rain and stone-fall. At the foot of the First Band they met Sorgato and Piussi, who had just abandoned a new attempt of their own, and all five left the face through one of the railway windows.

By the time Harlin returned to Leysin, Marilyn was no longer there. She had gone to the US, taking the children with her. With another summer's climbing in prospect, she had grown tired of waiting at the foot of her husband's climbs. She wrote that 'he liked to have me at the base of his mountains' – but he had no idea of 'the tension and agony' she went through. Rather than remain in Leysin, she had decided to stay with her parents on their farm in Olympia. Marilyn spent some time at a campus in Washington where she obtained another academic qualification, while the children played on the farm, driving their grandfather's tractor, fishing from his rowing boat and firing his rifle. Although his grandfather was fifty-seven, John Jr wrote 'he felt like an older brother'.

When Marilyn and the children returned to Europe in September she was flattered that Harlin came to meet them at Luxembourg airport rather than go climbing. Then he explained that he was only there because a climb he was planning had been called off. Marilyn felt belittled and was in tears. 'But that was life with John – highs and lows.'

Two years had passed since Harlin had descended from the Eiger with thoughts and dreams of the Direct. He had visited the face at least six times, including two serious attempts with accomplished climbers from France and Italy, and he had reached the highest point of any attempt. The First Band was now familiar and he knew what techniques and risks the First and Second Icefields entailed. Above, if he was to forge a true direct, lay expanses of virgin territory. Most of the great landmarks of the 1938 route – the Ramp, the Traverse of the Gods, the Exit Cracks – were off-limits. Only the Spider, the great slab of ice swept by stonefall and avalanches, was common to both.

Harlin was learning other lessons. His attempts to forge partnerships with leading Alpinists had not proved satisfactory: there had been tensions between them and several had made caustic judgements about his character and abilities. The leadership of the teams had been blurred and Harlin had been uneasy in a subordinate role. So who should he turn to next? Potential American partners were hearing stories of his fiery relationship with Hemming and were wary. It was now that a new set of climbers came into the story, brought together by a mix of serendipity and their own ambitions.

Enter the Brits.

Chapter Five

THE KILLER EIGER

Chris Bonington made his first attempt on the North Face of the Eiger in 1957. He was twenty-two and a tank commander with a regiment stationed in Münster in northern Germany. Bonington had a rising reputation as a climber in Britain and had received a letter from the Scottish climber Hamish MacInnes, proposing that they attempt the first British ascent of the North Face. It was a typically audacious venture on the part of MacInnes, who had attempted to make a two-man ascent of Everest a few months before the official British expedition succeeded in 1953. He and Bonington had last climbed together three years before, but while MacInnes had previously climbed in the Alps, it would be Bonington's first Alpine trip.

Bonington hitchhiked to Grindelwald from Münster and MacInnes drove there from Scotland on his Manx Norton motorbike. They had minimal bivouac equipment, Bonington was wearing a light nylon jacket, and their route map consisted of a tourist postcard MacInnes bought in Grindelwald the day he arrived. They set off the next afternoon, taking the train to Alpiglen and heading up the Vorbau. Bonington, who was weighed down by almost twenty kilos of equipment, had never previously climbed while carrying a rucksack. They bivouacked at mid-height on the Vorbau and, as MacInnes prepared their meal, Bonington was relieved to see clouds creeping up the valley, giving him an excuse to insist they retreat. They made a perilous descent in the darkness to Alpiglen and returned to Grindelwald in the morning. It was, Bonington later commented, an astonishingly naive attempt, made with inadequate equipment and insufficient regard for the reputation of the face. He swore that he would never set foot on the Eiger again.

The Eiger proved to be the defining mountain of Bonington's early career, an important stepping stone to his pre-eminent position in British climbing, culminating in a knighthood at the age of sixty-two. It also provided vital lessons as he searched for ways to become a professional climber, learning how to negotiate the pitfalls involved in selling stories to the media, with their need for melodrama and their urge to reduce climbing to a series of sensationalist constructs. Bonington – full name Christian John Storey Bonington – was born in north London in August 1934. His parents separated soon after he was born and he was brought up by his mother, assisted by his grandmother. He spent part of the war at a boarding school but was back in London when it was under siege from V2 rockets in 1945 – his mother described their explosions as 'what must be the most awful sound that human beings have ever heard'. In 1946, she had a breakdown and Bonington was cared for by his grandmother.

Despite his manifest intelligence, Bonington performed poorly at school. Then, at the age of sixteen, he discovered climbing. After seeing the mountains of Snowdonia from a train, he and a school friend hitchhiked to North Wales where they blundered around on Snowdon in a snowstorm – 'the most exciting and enjoyable day I had ever had', Bonington later wrote. He went climbing at

Harrison's Rocks, the sandstone outcrop south of London, and was absorbed by the physical and mental challenge it posed. 'I was conscious of feelings of confidence and immense enjoyment I had never known before.'

In 1953, Bonington started two years of military service, then compulsory for men aged eighteen (it was abolished in Britain in 1960). For those who joined the ranks, national service, as it was known, brought two years of numbing drudgery with only periodic bursts of action. Those who joined as officers served for three years, bringing a range of privileges and benefits. Bonington was deemed officer material because he had attended a public school (such were the selection criteria of the time) and he began in the RAF. After failing his pilot's test he transferred to the army and attended its officer training college at Sandhurst. In 1955, he joined a tank regiment and was posted to Münster – one of the bases of the British Army of the Rhine, which began life as the post-war occupying army and evolved into its Cold War role as part of the Western forces confronting the USSR. In 1956, Bonington signed on for another five years. He wrote that tank exercises were 'a magnificent game, the best I have ever played', but his biographer, Jim Curran, believes that Bonington found in the army a surrogate family of the kind he had lacked in his disturbed and often lonely childhood.

Although Bonington's climbing was limited to his periods of army leave, he was already recognised as part of a generation of climbers advancing standards in the years after the Second World War. The sport's social base broadened, with climbers such as Joe Brown and Don Whillans, both building trade workers from Manchester, leading the way. The British rediscovered their zest for the Alps and their success on Everest in 1953 boosted their international reputation, particularly in Switzerland, whose climbers so nearly made the first ascent the year before. That was the year

Bonington first climbed with MacInnes and they made several important first winter ascents in Glencoe. It was enough to commend Bonington to MacInnes, leading to their Eiger attempt in 1957. MacInnes later disputed the view that it had been a foolhardy venture, saying that he and Bonington had been 'pretty fit and technically competent'.

Bonington scored some notable successes in the Alps in 1958 and 1959. These included the first British ascent of the famed Hasse-Brandler Route on the North Face of the Cima Grande, and an epic first ascent of the South-west Pillar of the Dru, made with MacInnes, Whillans and Paul Ross. MacInnes suffered a head injury from a falling stone during their first bivouac but they completed the climb two days later. In 1959, Bonington became an army climbing instructor and made his first visit to the Himalayas with a services expedition which climbed Annapurna II. He left the army in 1961. After taking part in a second Himalayan expedition, which accomplished the first ascent of Nuptse, he made the five-week overland journey from Kathmandu to Chamonix, where he had arranged to meet Whillans. Their relationship, which lasted for fifteen years, was another of the intriguing partnerships of climbing. Bonington, who was tall and lean, talked at that time with the convoluted officer-class accent he had acquired at Sandhurst; Whillans, short and stocky, spoke with elongated Manchester vowels and a dry, irreverent wit that led him to claim that Bonington sounded as if he had a plum in his mouth. Once on the mountain they overcame any apparent class differences and became 'a single smooth-functioning regime', as Bonington wrote.

The first climb they attempted together – Bonington having discarded his pledge never to return – was the North Face of the Eiger. They arrived in Alpiglen in early July 1961 and spent a month waiting for good weather. When they finally set off they reached the Hinterstoisser Traverse but turned back because it was plastered with ice. They had their first media encounter when a freelance journalist working for the *Daily Mail* joined them at Alpiglen. Bonington recalled that he looked like a smoother version of Spencer Tracy, with rugged good looks and grey hair, and wearing an immaculate pair of climbing breeches. When he offered to help them they regarded him 'with the deepest suspicion' – although Bonington was more inclined than Whillans to extract a price for their story if they climbed the face.

Bonington and Whillans returned to Chamonix, where they made their celebrated ascent of the Central Pillar of Frêney together with Ian Clough and Polish climber Jan Długosz. After Whillans fell, Bonington led the crux overhanging pitch. He then had the satisfaction of lowering a rope to assist a chasing pack of French climbers headed by René Desmaison.

From Chamonix, Bonington and Whillans went back to the Eiger. They crossed the Hinterstoisser Traverse but the weather was against them once again and they turned back. The *Daily Mail* had signed them up in return for their expenses and a plane ticket to London, but published little more than a photograph of Bonington kissing a friendly American who had become a camp follower while they were at Alpiglen.

Back in London Bonington started his first job in civvy street as a margarine salesman for the Van den Bergh food company. It was not a success. After six months he had closed five accounts and failed to open a single new one, and when the company refused Bonington leave to go on an expedition to Patagonia he quit. In May 1962 he married a freelance book illustrator, Wendy Marchant, who had decided at an early age that she wanted to marry an explorer.

For the Boningtons, it was a difficult and uncertain time. Bonington was hoping to follow the path taken by figures such as

Edward Whymper and Frank Smythe, climbers who had lectured
and written about mountaineering. Others had failed to make it
pay, most notably George Mallory, a superb writer, with his fine
emotional intelligence and acute eye for detail. The qualities were
shown at their best in the 20,000 words he wrote for the official
account of the 1922 Everest expedition but, in an act of spectacular meanness, the Mount Everest Committee refused to pay him for
his contribution. In 1923 he made a lecture tour to the US, where
a packed New York audience heard him utter the three most
famous words in mountaineering – 'Because it's there.' But atten-
dances elsewhere were disappointing and on his return Mallory
took up a teaching job attached to Cambridge University, touring
the towns and villages of the East Anglia fens to lecture about
English constitutional and political history.

Bonington and Whillans made their next attempt on the Eiger in
July 1962. This time they had sold the rights to their attempt to the
Daily Express, who photographed them on Whillans's motorbike
before they set out: in an improbable pose, Whillans is wearing a
flat cap with a rope coiled around his shoulders, while Bonington
sits astride the pillion adorned with a climbing helmet and a massive rucksack. Their attempt barely got off the ground and on 17
July the *Express* ran a short, regretful story from Donald Seaman,
its reporter in Kleine Scheidegg, to the effect that the 'killer mountain' had become 'an angry giant, spitting out rocks and stones . . .
Any attempt to scale the pitiless North Face of the Eiger – it means
"The Ogre" – under these conditions would be suicidal.'

Bonington and Whillans returned ten days later, making the
attempt that ended when Barry Brewster was killed and they led
Brian Nally to safety. A pack of journalists had hired a train to take
all three down to Kleine Scheidegg, but they delayed its departure
until they had extracted Nally's account. Nally was presented with
a bill both for the train and for the guides who had done little more

than fetch Brewster's body while Whillans and Bonington brought Nally to safety. It was a salutary lesson in media exploitation but the *Daily Express* behaved honourably. It had a new reporter in Kleine Scheidegg, Martin Page, who ghosted an account of the rescue by Bonington and Whillans that was headlined 'Rescue on the Eiger' and was, in the circumstances, notably factual and sober.

A month later – a week after Harlin climbed the north face – Bonington returned with a new partner, Ian Clough. Whillans had gone home to Manchester and Bonington met Clough, one of his partners on the Central Pillar of Frêney, in Chamonix. It was Bonington's sixth attempt. The weather was stable, the face was in good condition, and they made an accomplished three-day ascent. Their only crisis came when they took the wrong line above the Spider and found themselves on steep, compact rock alternating with shattered sections where it was impossible to place pitons. Watchers at Kleine Scheidegg debated whether Bonington and Clough were attempting a direct finish, but the two climbers soon realised they were off route, abseiled back to the foot of the Exit Cracks and climbed steadily to the summit from there.

There was an all-too-familiar postscript when Bonington and Clough learned that two other climbers – one Scottish, one Austrian – had been swept to their deaths from the Second Icefield by a massive rock avalanche which they had witnessed from the Spider.

Bonington wrote that his strongest feelings afterwards were of relief that they had succeeded, and gratitude for their good fortune with the weather. This time there was no reporter on the spot, so Bonington telephoned the story to the *Daily Express* himself. The *Express* editors must have been disappointed to hear that the climb 'passed without any major incident – we never felt any danger at any time'. The most colourful remark came from Ian Clough's mother Jessie, who told an *Express* reporter: 'I did not think he would be so stupid.' The *Express* extracted its due with the head-line: 'Britons beat killer Eiger.'

The following week, after Bonington and Clough returned to Britain, the *Express* gave the climb more expansive coverage. It opened with a photograph of Bonington hugging Wendy and pro-claimed the story of his 'inch-by-inch struggle up the mountain'. Over the next two days it published a verbatim account headlined: 'How I got to the top of the Eiger – Chris Bonington who beat the killer peak tells his own story'. The shock headlines apart, it was a restrained and literate piece, showing that even though Bonington had supped with the devil through his deal with the *Express*, he had emerged with his honour intact.

The ascent brought Bonington public acclaim, which included a telegram of congratulations from the prime minister, Harold Macmillan. The publishers Gollancz paid him an advance of £500 for his autobiography, and he found that he could earn up to £70 a time from lecturing about the Eiger. He and Wendy moved from a room they had been renting above a garage on a farm near Ambleside in the Lake District, with an outside tap and an earth closet at the back of a pigsty, to a more salubrious furnished house which they rented for £3 a week. Their first son, Conrad, was born on 1 January 1964.

Even so, Bonington remained uncertain about his career. His new responsibilities were weighing on him and he felt that he was climbing at a less intense level. At times, Wendy had to nurse him through bouts of depression. Writing was not coming easily and he was several months past the date for delivering his autobiography. 'I wasn't quite sure how I was going to make a living as a climber and I was still struggling to write the book,' he said in 2014. It was then, Bonington said, 'that the idea of doing a new route on the Eiger germinated'. It would renew his relationship with the Eiger and would meet his demand for new routes – and, in light of his experiences with the *Daily Express*, Bonington reckoned he could turn the inevitable media interest to his advantage.

That summer, Bonington went to the Alps with Joe Brown and Tom Patey. They made just one worthwhile climb, the first ascent of the North Face of the Pointe Migot on the Aiguille des Pélerins. Bonington teamed up with Jim McCarthy, an American climber equipped with a selection of the new American hardware popular among Yosemite climbers. Bonington found it difficult to adjust to the complex rope management the Yosemite techniques required, and he and McCarthy only completed one climb. From Chamonix, Bonington travelled to Grindelwald, where he had agreed to be interviewed for a BBC documentary about the Eiger. It was presented by the former athlete Chris Brasher – he won a gold medal in the 3000 metres steeplechase at Melbourne in 1956 – who had moved into journalism and television. Even in 2014, Bonington was embarrassed that Brasher lured him into talking about the Direct when his ideas were still at an embryonic stage. 'I thought they had got me over to talk about our ascent of the ordinary route and they got me to talk as if I was preparing for an attempt – which was no more than an idea at that stage.' Bonington wrote afterwards that he felt cheapened by what he had done. 'It emphasised my vulnerability and made me doubt my integrity.' He returned to Chamonix 'washed out and depressed'.

Back in Britain, Bonington resumed his struggles with his autobiography, carried out a round of lectures and climbed with friends in the Lake District and Scotland. A television producer, Ned Kelly, enlisted him for a climb in the Cheddar Gorge, near Bristol, which was broadcast in May 1965. In July, he and Patey returned to Chamonix as guests at an international climbing convention known as the Rassemblement International. It was an occasion of both rivalry and conviviality, enabling them to meet and climb with their European peers. Bonington spotted Roberto Sorgato who, rather than compete with his fellow guests, 'was happy to eat, drink and flirt with the girls down in Chamonix'.

On 18 July two more of Bonington's climbing friends, Rusty Baillie and John Cleare, arrived in Chamonix. Baillie first met Bonington in July 1963, soon after climbing the 1938 route on the Eiger with the Scotsman Dougal Haston. (This was usually described as the second British ascent, leaving Baillie aggrieved since he came from what was then Rhodesia.) Cleare was a climber and photographer who had worked as camera operator on the Cheddar Gorge broadcast with Bonington, and was making his name with breathtaking and innovative climbing photography. His book, *Rock Climbers in Action in Snowdonia*, with Baillie photographed on many of the climbs, was published the following year. He and Cleare had driven to Chamonix from Zermatt, where they had taken part in a televised commemoration of the first ascent of the Matterhorn in July 1865, and met Bonington a day or so later.

For Baillie, the encounter with Bonington came at an opportune time. He too was hoping to earn a living from climbing and they discussed how this could be achieved. Even though Bonington could have viewed him as a rival, Baillie recalled in 2014, he was generous with his advice. They also confronted the risks involved in accepting sponsorship and perhaps distorting the values of mountaineering. 'I was fascinated by his mentorship in professional climbing. We discussed it a lot and I was impressed with his honesty and integrity.'

Out of these discussions came the idea that they attempt the Eiger Direct. They debated both the feasibility and the ethics of the route. How far should they deviate from the perfect plumb line in order to use the natural features of the mountain? Baillie felt that the concept carried some latitude and that there were natural lines that they could use, just as Sedlmayr and Mehringer had done. Equally important, it looked like a promising business venture:

'media-worthy, eminently fundable and good for a career', Baillie said in 2014. Cleare was equally enthusiastic, sensing there was a good chance of selling media coverage, ideally to the BBC. 'There seemed to be a media appetite for climbing, so we had our eyes open for possibilities,' he said in 2014. As Bonington observed, they had a ready-made slogan for the climb: The Last Great Problem of the Alps.

No one now is sure who proposed that they go to meet Harlin in Leysin; Bonington wrote that the idea came from Patey. They knew of him by reputation, both for his Alpine routes and for 'a flamboyance and drive', in Bonington's words, that 'had made enemies as well as friends'. Harlin's interest in the Direct was well known, and Cleare recalled that Hemming was talking about him in Chamonix. They had also heard the story about him delivering a Spanish climber's leg to the Grindelwald police. The question that arose was whether they should make an attempt themselves; or whether they should, at the very least, talk to the climber who had been on the Direct more times than anyone else.

They decided to go to Leysin.

Chapter Six

COMINGS AND GOINGS

Before the British/Rhodesian contingent arrived in Leysin, Harlin had already been talking to another British climber about attempting the Eiger Direct. His name was Dougal Haston – Rusty Baillie's partner on the 1938 North Face route just two years before. Baillie had a high regard for Haston's abilities: 'I liked and trusted him and could think of no one better for the Eiger.'

Almost as much as Harlin, Haston provokes a wide range of opinions. His advocates are as generous in their praise as Baillie, seeing him as intelligent, considerate, sensitive and loyal. His critics call him selfish, self-centred, arrogant and intolerant, with a dark side that could never be plumbed. His supporters include Britain's two most successful mountaineers – Bonington and Doug Scott. Haston, said Bonington in 2014, 'had a reputation for arrogance, but he wasn't an arrogant man. He knew exactly what he wanted, he didn't suffer fools gladly, he had a complete focus on where he wanted to get and he just quietly went out and got there. That's not arrogance, that's determination and self-understanding.' Both sides agree that he became a supremely accomplished mountaineer and those who have taken against him nonetheless believe that it was his 'dark side' qualities that helped propel him to the highest ranks.

Haston was born in Currie, a small farming town to the south-west of Edinburgh, in April 1940. As a baker, his father was in a reserved occupation and was not called up to fight during the war. There were sporadic German raids on the Edinburgh docks but they did not touch Currie. Haston proved himself bright at school and was showing promise as a goalkeeper when he discovered climbing, first on a moss-covered railway bridge and then on the rocky ridges of Glencoe. It was, he wrote, the 'only thing which gave me more than momentary satisfaction'.

Haston's long, lean frame was ideal for rock climbing, and he also acquired stamina by embarking on long walking days among the Munros, the term for the 282 Scottish peaks measured at more than 3000 feet (914 metres) high. He progressed to winter walking, which demands fast movement and accurate navigation to combat ferocious weather and dangerously short days, and then to full winter climbing, where he developed the specialist skills required in the bewitching realms of Scottish snow and ice.

In 1957, after mostly climbing with school friends, Haston found a new partner, an Edinburgh philosophy student named Robin Smith. Renowned for the new standards he was setting, Smith found it hard to attract partners because he was so disorganised and badly prepared. Haston bought into all that for the tutoring Smith provided, even if it meant climbing in atrocious conditions, with poor equipment, and often being benighted because they made such late starts, and they racked up ascents of many of the test pieces of Scottish mountaineering.

Smith also inducted Haston into a near-criminal subculture that featured fighting, vandalism, breaking and entering, and theft, above all from other climbers who found that their rucksacks, ropes or trousers could be missing when they returned to climbing huts where Haston and his colleagues had stayed – sometimes by breaking in. Later, they became notorious for stealing from shops and cafés in Alpine resorts, above all in Chamonix where they perfected the practice known as 'dine and dash', which entailed rushing out of a café or restaurant without paying for their meal. Americans called this behaviour 'mooching'. In Standard English, to mooch means to hang about or hang out without much purpose; in American English it means to parasite off other people. 'Dougal belonged to that way of thinking,' said Larry Ware, who came to know Haston in Leysin.

Haston hoped to become a physical training instructor, but was unable to start the course after dislocating a shoulder in a motorcycle crash. He enrolled on the Edinburgh University philosophy course, aware from Smith that its lax requirements allowed generous scope for climbing. He became enamoured of the writings of Friedrich Nietzsche, the nineteenth-century German philosopher whose *Übermensch* – by one reading – espouses notions of superiority and rejects the restrictions of conventional morality. In a journal, Haston later employed similar language to describe how climbing was making him 'more complete . . . A great hardness is setting in, and I am increasingly able to treat the petty and mundane with utter contempt.' He praised the notion of selfishness – 'a sin in the eyes of the masses', some of whom 'deserved to be trampled on' – and ended each entry: 'Thus spake DH', in the style of Nietzsche's philosophical novel *Also sprach Zarathustra – Thus Spoke Zarathustra*. Nietzsche, it seemed, had provided a philosophical underpinning for his ruthless approach to climbing and to life.

Haston first contemplated climbing the Eiger in 1959, when he was nineteen. He went to the Alps in a group led by Jimmy Marshall, a senior Scottish climber who had been mentoring promising young climbers, including Smith and Haston. Haston had

The North Face of the Eiger and the West Flank seen from Kleine Scheidegg in 2014 (the hotel is right foreground).

The face is in shadow for much of the day, but sometimes shows itself by the light of sunset – as it did this evening in 1966.

John and Marilyn Harlin on their wedding day, 25 October 1955, in Los Altos Hills, California.

Andréa (3) and John Jr (5) in Germany, 1961.

John (in USAF uniform), Marilyn and John Jr in California, 1956.

Barbara Haag

Peter Haag, the troubadour, with Barbara in 1965.

Barbara Haag

Barbara and Peter Haag on their
wedding day, 18 December 1965, in
Ehingen, Germany.

Chris Bonington, Chris Bonington Picture Library

Jörg Lehne on the Eiger.

Haston and Kor with Harlin at the Kleine Scheidegg telescope.

Kor, Haston and Harlin pose with their equipment for the *Weekend Telegraph* on 4 February.

Gillman calls the face.

Harlin, Kor and Haston examine route photographs at Kleine Scheidegg.

German climbers at a staging-post halfway up the Vorbau. From left: Strobel, Golikow, Rosenzopf, Haag, Hupfauer.

Golikow carries a supply 'bomb' on the Second Icefield.

Bonington and camera below the face.

When Bonington first photographed German climbers at the Vorbau on 19 February, Hupfauer threw a snowball at him.

Kor (left) and Haston at work on the First Band on 28 February.

Haston disentangles a crampon while Jumaring on the First Band.

Rosenzopf looks up the German line on the First Band.

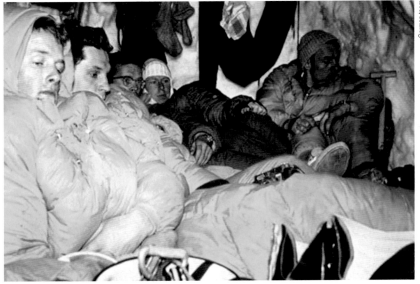

Inside the German *Eispalast* below the First Band. From left: Strobel, Golikow, Rosenzopf, Haag, Lehne.

Schnaidt looks into the Germans' ice cave at the Death Bivouac.

Kor stands in his team's first snow hole below the First Band.

Kor climbs the gully in the Second Band just below the Germans' *Kristallsalon*.

Harlin watches as Haston climbs the Second Icefield on 9 March.

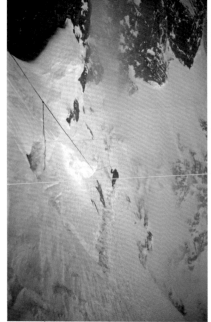

Strobel braves bad weather somewhere below the Death Bivouac.

A German climber makes the exposed traverse from the Death Bivouac to the Rulaman cave.

been devouring *The White Spider*, Heinrich Harrer's history of the Eiger, first published in English that year, and arranged to meet Smith in Switzerland after climbing in the Dolomites and at Chamonix. But Haston failed to make the rendezvous, ironically because his wallet was stolen while he was hitchhiking from Chamonix.

Haston saw the Eiger for the first time in 1960, this time in the company of one of his earliest climbing partners, Jim Moriarty, known as Big Eley. They arrived in Grindelwald after climbing in the Dolomites, including an ascent of the Cassin Route on the North Face of the Cima Ovest in the Dolomites. Haston later described their shock on seeing the sheer scale of the Eiger's North Face. 'We didn't speak but I could see Eley was feeling the same. What were we in for?' After climbing the first half of the Vorbau they retreated in the face of dismal weather.

Haston climbed in the Dolomites with Smith in 1961, then made plans to attempt the Eiger with him in 1962. They agreed to meet up in the Alps when Smith returned from an expedition to the Russian Pamirs led by Sir John Hunt. But on 24 July, Smith was killed while descending a snow slope with Wilfrid Noyce, the scholar-mountaineer who had been on the Everest expedition in 1953. One of them slipped – it was never clear who – and they fell 1300 metres to their deaths.

In his autobiography, *In High Places*, Haston describes Smith's death with a marked lack of feeling or affect. Maybe he was still in denial, or maybe even the loss of his closest climbing partner was not going to penetrate the 'great hardness' he considered so desirable. He paid Smith one implicit tribute by developing a writing style that owed much to stream-of-consciousness techniques that Smith had borrowed in turn from James Joyce. From comments Haston made to me, it was evident that he was angered by Smith's death. He made it clear that he blamed Noyce for the accident on the grounds that he was both older and an inferior climber and so was more likely to have made the fatal mistake. From other remarks, I deduced that Haston had hoped to assuage his grief by climbing the North Face as soon as possible.

Haston arrived at Alpiglen with Andy Wightman, a fellow student from Edinburgh, at the beginning of August. The meadows were abuzz with news. Barely a week had passed since Barry Brewster had died and his partner, Brian Nally, was rescued by Bonington and Whillans. A Swiss party of four, including the first two women to attempt the climb, had withdrawn from high on the face in a storm. Another Swiss climber had fallen to his death while attempting the first solo ascent. Two more climbers had just endured three bivouacs in order to reach the summit, and there had still been no British ascent. 'The time felt right,' Haston wrote.

At first Haston and Wightman enjoyed good conditions, 'dancing' over the Hinterstoisser Traverse. But they had forgotten to sharpen their crampons and had to chip out steps on the Second Icefield. They were slowed by a party of Italians and after being hit by a storm decided to retreat. Halfway down the Vorbau, Wightman fell and broke his ankle. After a tricky rescue, Wightman made a slow recovery in hospital. Haston, who later admitted to feeling 'depressed', returned to Scotland. Three weeks later Bonington and Clough made the first British ascent.

Haston returned to the Eiger in 1963. He met his new partner, Rusty Baillie, in Glencoe the previous winter, when both were working on training courses run out of the Glencoe Youth Hostel. Baillie, an affable, articulate character sometimes given to making gnomic utterances that his friends were required to decode, was both a talented and a methodical climber, offering a counterpoint to the disorganised improvisations of Smith. Baillie saw similar qualities in Haston, describing him in 2014 as 'very careful, rational, patient and painstaking in his preparations'. In short,

Baillie added with a hint of parody, 'a good man in a tight spot'. Like Haston, Baillie was thoroughly versed in Harrer's history of the Eiger, and his pulse quickened when he saw it for the first time. 'I knew *The White Spider* by heart.'

Conditions appeared perfect as the two set off at dawn on 31 July. The biggest problem proved to be verglas, a veneer of ice that covered the holds, requiring delicate balance on crampon points. They benefited from Haston's long Scottish apprenticeship as they cut steps across the Second Icefield. Above there they made swift progress, Haston singing and shouting as they encountered the historic locations of the face. They were delayed when they stopped to assist two Austrian climbers who were stuck beneath an icy overhang. They reached the summit on the fourth morning, carefully negotiating the Summit Icefield, which was turning mushy in the sun.

Like Bonington and Harlin before him, Haston's thoughts soon turned to the Direct. Baillie has pondered whether Haston was already considering an attempt while they were climbing the 1938 route. But even after sharing such an intense experience, he was still unable to plumb Haston's thoughts or 'his mystic thousand-yard stare'. Baillie added: 'Who knows what Dougal was thinking? He may have been dreaming.'

Haston alluded to his dreams in *In High Places*. Other climbers, he suggested, may have experienced 'a great sense of relief' on reaching the summit, but he did not succumb to anything so banal. Having seen the wide-open spaces of the North Face, 'ideas for a new route began to form'.

Haston was now looking for a new partner. After spending the winter of 1963–64 teaching in Glasgow, Baillie had gone to work in Kenya. Haston, by his reckoning, had outstripped the ambition and abilities of most of his Scottish colleagues and for a time he climbed in the Alps with his girlfriend, Joy Heron, who he considered competent for 'lesser things'. Then he met an engaging Londoner named Bev Clark, who was not only a strong climber but also had money, in the shape of an inheritance from his father, a fashionable mews home near Marble Arch, and a taste which he readily indulged for fast and expensive cars – the most spectacular of which was an orange Lotus Elan.

Haston was introduced to Clark in the urinal of the Biolay campsite near Chamonix in the summer of 1964. They agreed to climb together, lining up the South Ridge of the Aiguille des Pélerins, followed by the West Face of the Dru. 'We got on well,' said Clark in 2014, though adding that he found Haston 'always a bit of an enigma. He was an introverted, private person and it was difficult to have an intimate relationship with him.'

Or any relationship, it seemed. Even by the promiscuous standards of the mountaineering world, Clark's partnership with Haston proved short-lived. Their next climb was to be the Walker Spur on the Grandes Jorasses, and they were discussing their plans in a café near the Biolay campsite when Harlin came in. Harlin already knew Clark, having met him by chance at the Pen-y-Gwryd, the hallowed climbers' inn in Snowdonia, when Harlin was visiting Britain in 1960. Harlin approached their table and Clark introduced him to Haston, who was aware of Harlin's Alpine record. After the two had briefly sized each other up, Harlin proposed that they attempt the Shroud, an unclimbed 750-metre icefield to the left of the Walker.

'You're on,' Haston replied.

They spent the rest of the meal planning their attempt. Clark, although fuming at having his plan to climb the Walker so casually tossed aside, agreed to help carry their supplies. There was an inauspicious start when Harlin succumbed to a gastric upset and they set off a day later than planned. They climbed fast and were above halfway when they were forced back by a storm. 'We were happy in defeat,' Haston wrote afterwards. 'We seemed to make a good team.'

It is not clear precisely when Haston and Harlin first discussed attempting the Eiger Direct together. Certainly, it was uppermost in Harlin's mind that autumn, as he was invited to address the American Alpine Club about the Direct at its annual dinner in December, to be held that year in Boston. In his invitation, the club president, Carlton Fuller, encouraged Harlin to range beyond the Eiger to 'your general experiences climbing in Europe and your observations of international climbing habits'. The club would pay Harlin's airfare and help him rent a tuxedo, but it was not offering a fee. For Harlin the invitation was reward enough, as it marked his first appearance among his peers in the US, bringing the recognition he desired. (He did receive a second invitation, to talk to the Appalachian Mountain Club in Boston a day or so later, for which the fee was $150.)

Harlin, duly attired in a tuxedo, gave his talk on 'The Problem of the Eiger Direct and the Mood of Alpine Climbing' at the AAC dinner in Boston on 5 December. He presented photographs of possible routes for the Direct and ranged into the field of international relations, dispensing an optimistic take that contrasted with the Cold War rhetoric dominating US political discourse. He conceded that it was hard for Americans to comprehend the importance of mountaineering in Europe. But, he told his audience, 'because of the connotations of fellowship, non-competition, mutual understanding and enjoyment, it becomes a vehicle for the sustenance of peace'.

There were ironies in the highly competitive Harlin talking of the value of non-competition. Yet this was also the former nuclear bomber pilot praising European values and the quest for peace. Even that was a loaded word in the 1960s, since the peace movement, so-called, was staging demonstrations and marches opposing nuclear weapons and an arms race that risked impelling the world towards catastrophe, just as in 1914.

Harlin returned to Leysin with a new business scheme in mind. He intended to resign from the American School, where he was finding the teaching obligations increasingly irksome, and set up a climbing school of his own. It was to be called the International School of Modern Mountaineering (later the 'Modern' was dropped, and it became the ISM) and would be financed by Clark, who was prepared to overlook his slight over the Shroud. They produced a brochure setting out the school's ideals, which included enabling 'the individual to introspect into his [sic] character and then build upon it through analysis and adventure'.

The brochure promised more than it delivered. It said that the instructors would include elite climbers from Europe and the US, but while Don Whillans and Mick Burke – both already in Leysin – were enlisted, others did not materialise. The school was less grand than it sounded, since it had no actual premises. Students would be lodged at the Vagabond, whose secretary handled the paperwork for the school. Harlin devoted his motivational gifts to the experienced pupils but displayed less patience with the novices, and even Clark had reservations about the qualities of some big-name tutors. 'Whillans was the worst climbing instructor I had seen.'

At this point Harlin remained on the staff of the American School but still found time to climb. Haston had returned to Leysin, where he camped in the basement of the Harlins' chalet and lived on food that Marilyn smuggled out of the American School. In January 1965, Haston and Harlin made the first winter ascent of the North Face of the Tour d'Aï, a peak near Leysin, leaving Haston impressed with the bitter cold – more intense than anything he had known in Scotland.

In February they revived their plans for the Eiger Direct. They were strongly inclined to make an attempt in winter, when the freezing temperatures reduced the dangers of stonefall and cascading water. Harlin was still ruing his missed opportunity the previous winter, when he had been forced to wait for the Italians while the best conditions in decades had persisted for the best part of a month. They also hoped to find a line to the left of the customary Sedlmayr-Mehringer route of 1935, which would make theirs more obviously direct. They took the train to the Eigergletscher station and walked through the railway tunnel to the second gallery window, to the left of the better-known Stollenloch. (The window is coded as Km 4.1 – the distance from Kleine Scheidegg.) They climbed out on to the face and worked their way along the top of the Vorbau in cloying waist-deep powder snow until they could examine the First Band. It ranged from vertical to overhanging and they could find no continuous cracks or flaws to provide a natural line of ascent. After a night in the tunnel, Haston led most of the way up the 1935 line to obtain a taste of winter climbing on the Eiger. He returned with renewed respect for the abilities and resolve of Sedlmayr and Mehringer in climbing the line on sight almost thirty years before.

Back in Leysin, Harlin and Haston discussed their findings. Their first estimate was that the climb would take three weeks. Since that was out of the question, they revised their estimate downwards and came up with a new figure of ten to fourteen days. Even that was an intimidating prospect. They would need to carry around twenty kilos of equipment and supplies each. It meant pushing their luck in terms of the weather, as they would be in maximum danger if they were hit by a storm when they were high on the face. 'It would be a formidable problem,' Haston wrote – drily adding: 'We planned to make an attempt the next winter.'

At the end of February, Haston returned to Britain. By then he had dropped out of his philosophy course and had plans to become a professional climber. Clark proposed that they open a climbing school similar to Harlin's. Clark, who had ambitions of becoming

Cairngorms near Newtonmore. He was with a group including his friend Jim Moriarty, who was a partner in the climbing school and was driving the Transit van. The weather was abysmal so they returned to Glencoe, where they drank in the venerable Kings House Hotel and then moved on to the Clachaig Inn. At closing time, having consumed the proverbial skinful, they decided to drive to Glencoe Village. Haston, who was still a learner driver, insisted on taking the wheel. At least one person was so troubled that she refused to get into the van. It was a miserable night, the road was wet and unlit, and Haston drove into a group of students who were walking to the Glencoe Youth Hostel.

Haston and several passengers fled the scene. Three who stayed – Moriarty, the climber Fred Harper, and a nurse – did their best to help the injured walkers. One, an eighteen-year-old student named James Orr, died in hospital a week later. At Moriarty's insistence, Haston turned himself in to the police the day after the crash. He eventually pleaded guilty to driving without due care and attention and to driving while unfit through drink or drugs. A third charge of leaving the scene of an accident was dropped, possibly as the result of a plea bargain. Haston was sentenced to sixty days in prison, a remarkably lenient punishment by today's standards; if he had been prosecuted under more serious charges, such as causing death by dangerous or drunken driving, he could have gone to prison for years rather than months. On 5 July he started his sentence at Glasgow's Barlinnie Prison, a grim Victorian jail where Scotland's last-but-one judicial hanging had been carried out four years before.

The question of how far this catastrophe affected Haston's behaviour and personality would become another major issue in the persistent debates over his character. What is clear is that by the time Bonington, Baillie and Cleare met Harlin to talk about the Direct, Haston no longer featured.

When Harlin's visitors arrived at his chalet, he and Marilyn could not have been more welcoming and showed them into their living room, hung with a selection of Harlin's own abstract paintings. Bonington was struck by Harlin's 'Tarzan-style physique', his blond hair and 'thigh-sized biceps'. Before long, the discussion turned to the Direct. As Baillie recalled, there was the usual preliminary poker play, with each side reluctant to reveal its hand. But he and Bonington were disarmed by Harlin's frankness and enthusiasm and concluded that they should make an attempt together. As for Haston, Baillie recalled, 'he wasn't even mentioned'.

Harlin must have been delighted at the trio who turned up on his doorstep. If he had indeed already dropped Haston from his plans, he had no team left at all. Now he had the chance to recruit two Eiger veterans and, in Cleare, someone with strong media connections who could help secure financial backing. In approaching Harlin, the three had a far better hand than they had realised. Bonington later spelled this out when he said, in 2014, that Harlin – 'a good climber, but not a star' – had the skill of 'recruiting the right people to make successful his dreams'. The further truth was that, whether or not Harlin knew about Haston's imprisonment, he was surplus to Harlin's requirements.

The new team, Cleare recalled, would consist of Harlin and Bonington in the 'nose-cone' role, with himself and Baillie climbing in support. The new dispositions also meant that Harlin shelved the plans he had made for a winter attempt. Instead, it would take place in late August or September, and Harlin was newly optimistic about their prospects. The nights would be longer and colder, reducing the risk of stonefall – and there had been sustained clear spells in late summer before, notably in 1962 when both Harlin and Bonington had made their ascents of the 1938 route.

Bonington and Baillie settled down to wait in Leysin. Both camped in the quarry near Harlin's chalet: Bonington with Wendy and

Conrad, who had driven out to join him; Baillie with his girlfriend Pat, who had arrived from Kenya. Cleare returned to Britain, where he had other assignments to work on, and made the first approaches to the BBC. At first things looked promising. He had a good contact in Chris Brasher, the former Olympic athlete who had acted as commentator and producer on several of the BBC's climbing broadcasts.

Cleare proposed that the BBC film the attempt (this was not to be a live outside broadcast) and said that Harlin was looking for £1500 for the rights, including an upfront payment of £100, plus repeat fees calculated at 80 per cent of the original. Cleare listed the camera operators: himself, Ian Clough – Bonington's partner on the 1938 ascent – and Martin Boysen, another young climber building a reputation on British rock and in the Alps. 'I was on the phone a lot to Harlin, Brasher and the BBC, discussing various offers and ideas,' Cleare said in 2014. But the complications were formidable, not least the scale of the operation and the difficulties of pinning down a date. 'Brasher was sceptical,' Cleare recalled.

At around this time, Bonington took a hand. On learning that negotiations with the BBC were foundering, he called the *Weekend Telegraph*, the magazine published every Friday with the *Daily Telegraph* newspaper. It had been launched in 1963, in a bid to emulate the success of the *Sunday Times Magazine*, first published the year before. They and the *Observer Magazine*, launched in same month as the *Weekend Telegraph*, were products of their time, sponsoring a brave new era of photojournalism which ranged, sometimes uneasily, from trends in fashion, entertainment and the arts to coverage of far more edgy and dangerous subjects. These included reportage from the Third World and the front lines in wars and conflicts such as Vietnam, Biafra and Northern Ireland. At the same time they attracted a tidal flow of advertising revenue that cashed in on the expanding consumerism of the 1960s.

The editor of the *Weekend Telegraph*, John Anstey, had developed a liking for adventure stories, continuing in a tradition established in the nineteenth century. In 1874, the newspaper had funded the journey made by Henry Stanley, the journalist and adventurer who found David Livingstone, to trace the course of the Congo from its source to the sea; a pair of Livingstone's pistols were still displayed in the *Daily Telegraph*'s offices in Fleet Street. Bonington had previously written a short article about the Alps to accompany a photograph for the magazine. It had caused him much angst – he rewrote the article endlessly on his portable typewriter, missed his deadline for posting it by an embarrassing margin, and finished up driving to Manchester airport so that it could be air-freighted to the *Weekend Telegraph*. Bonington nonetheless felt that his article gave him a toe in the door and he asked Anstey if he was interested.

Anstey was, to say the least, a controversial figure, one who became notorious for his bullying, paranoia, financial chicanery and sexual impropriety. Bonington's dealings with him were relatively straightforward by comparison. For a time, Anstey considered making a joint deal with the BBC, but it would have been hard to coordinate their coverage and the BBC was becoming less enthusiastic anyway. Anstey in fact struck an internal deal whereby he shared the costs with the *Sunday Telegraph*. He offered Harlin and his team £1500, to be delivered on a sliding scale: £500 as a down payment, £500 for making what was termed 'substantial progress' on the face, £500 for reaching the summit. It was a tempting sum, matching what Harlin had hoped for from the BBC, and worth almost £20,000 in the values of 2014. Harlin accepted.

These negotiations were still under way when Harlin told his new partners that he wanted to take them on a training climb to initiate them into a climbing technique he hoped to use on the attempt. It had been developed in Yosemite and involved the use of metal clamps known as Jumars, which were invented by a Swiss climbing manufacturer. After one climber had led a pitch, the second would use Jumars to ascend the climbing rope. The second clamped one Jumar on to the rope, pushed it up and closed a line of metal teeth to lock it into place. He (and it was almost invariably 'he' in those early days in Yosemite) then put one foot into a sling attached to the Jumar and stood up. He repeated the procedure with the other Jumar, and in that way gradually made progress up the rope. Later, a slightly more comfortable procedure was developed. The second Jumar was clipped into a seat harness and the push-up was performed with both legs on the first Jumar. In between push-ups, the climber would rest on the seat harness.

Jumars were known generically as ascenders, and were markedly better than another form that came into use around the same time. These were Hiebler clamps, which were developed by the German climber Toni Hiebeler after making the first winter ascent of the North Face of the Eiger in 1961. They were supposedly better suited to ascending frozen ropes, as they locked in place by kinking the rope rather than gripping it with metal teeth, but had an alarming tendency to slip off sideways. Both Jumars and Hieblers represented a notable improvement on the original prusik knots, loops that were knotted around the climbing rope to achieve the same purpose, and which were hideously difficult to use. (The verb 'to prusik' was still used to describe ascending a rope by whatever means, and was applied in that context during the Eiger Direct.)

Bonington and Baillie had heard about the American 'big-wall' technique, as they termed it, but had never tried it out. Harlin proposed that they do precisely that on an unclimbed section of the North Ridge of the Dents du Midi. Bonington and Baillie dutifully started up the climb where, after Baillie had led an overhanging pitch, Harlin instructed Bonington to attach the clamps and swing out on to the rope.

'I stepped off the ledge and went spiralling into space,' Bonington wrote. 'The rope dropped with a sickening jerk – it had caught round a flake. My heart, already pounding, seemed to plummet down into my stomach.' After 'a murderous struggle', Bonington reached the top of the pitch. The rest of the climb was straightforward by comparison and Bonington felt reasonably confident that he had mastered the technique.

As Harlin's new team waited for good weather to arrive, they had other projects to keep them occupied. Newly arrived in Leysin was Royal Robbins, one of the pioneers of big-wall technique, who had succeeded Harlin as sports director at the American School. He and Harlin took the opportunity to attempt a new direct route on the West Face of the Dru. It would be the first time they had climbed together and marked a formidable partnership between two leading figures of American climbing. They had barely started when Harlin was hit on the leg by a falling rock. He was in intense pain and suspected the rock had fractured a bone, although it later proved to have damaged his sciatic nerve. He climbed on through the pain and the two men completed a route which became a new set piece for Alpine climbers.

There was a bitter aftermath. Although Robbins had done most of the leading, Harlin attracted the lion's share of the media attention. 'I talked to Royal after the Dru,' said Larry Ware in 2014. 'He said [John] took everything for himself.' Robbins later imparted the view that he considered Harlin 'disorganised, careless of the truth, bemused by his image of himself as a grand-design hero'. Harlin, always willing to give as good as he got, saw Robbins as 'plodding, unimaginative and a bit of a cold fish'. Harlin had once considered Robbins a potential partner for the Eiger Direct, but this was the first and last time they climbed together.

Meanwhile, Bonington and Baillie attempted a new route of their own, and they too survived an epic in what proved an eventful ten days. Their goal was the Right-hand Pillar of Brouillard, an unclimbed face in one of the most remote areas of Mont Blanc. They gambled on making a fast ascent with minimal equipment but were hit by a storm and made a difficult and dangerous retreat. They returned to Leysin where Baillie and Pat, who was pregnant, got married. The ceremony was staged in the Leysin mayor's office then progressed to the Protestant church nearby. Harlin gave away the bride, Bonington was best man, and Marilyn and Wendy laid on a splendid spread at the Harlins' chalet.

There was no time for such niceties as a honeymoon. A day or so later Baillie and Bonington returned to the Brouillard, this time with Harlin and a Scottish climber, Brian Robertson. They climbed the Right-Hand Pillar in a day and descended through the inevitable storm, leaving Bonington impressed with Harlin's speed and confidence. 'We were supremely fit and ready for the Eiger Direct,' he wrote.

It was not to be. Back in Leysin the weather declined to deliver the good spell Harlin had predicted. Harlin talked to Bonington and Baillie about other projects, which included a grandiose scheme to climb a succession of great faces down the length of North and South America (how the trip would be financed was never made clear). As September wore on, Bonington became increasingly uneasy: he was not earning any money, a new round of lectures awaited him, and he had still to finish his autobiography. In the last week of September he, Wendy and Conrad headed for the Channel ports in their minivan. Once on the road, Bonington was relieved to be free of 'the demanding, all-embracing presence of John Harlin – for eight weeks I had been caught up in his dreams and plans'. Even so, he was still committed to attempting the Direct with Harlin, who had reverted to the plan of doing so in winter. They told the *Weekend Telegraph* that the climb had been postponed, and were reassured that their deal still held.

Baillie left Leysin too – but, unlike Bonington, he was out of the Direct. A summer attempt was one thing; one during the winter, with its increased length and commitment, was different. Pat's pregnancy was taking its course and a career as a professional climber was looking uncertain. He returned to Britain to start work with the Outward Bound Trust, which ran outdoor courses for young people. Like Bonington, he was feeling increasing doubts about Harlin, for all that he had been so hospitable. 'I never really knew if he was for real,' he said in 2014. 'He was so culturally different, not just Yank but with some noble savage in there. Very macho and deep. I didn't buy in.'

At around the time Baillie and Bonington departed, there was a new arrival in Leysin. Layton Kor was revered as one of the most naturally talented rock-climbers ever to emerge in the US. He was tall, long limbed, with light brown hair and blue-grey eyes. He spoke in a slow, considered manner that belied his instinctive intelligence. At ground level he could appear restless and ill at ease, as if itching to climb. Once on the rock he climbed with an effortless fluidity that left his colleagues open-mouthed in envy. He was refreshingly untainted by the jousting and manoeuvring, the backbiting and gossip, that prevailed in the elite climbing world. He was direct and decisive and not prone to existential doubts and discussion about the routes he intended to climb. He had also been inspired by tales of Alpine pioneers such as Buhl, Cassin and Comici, and saw the Alps as climbing's spiritual home.

Kor, who was born in Minnesota in 1938, did his early climbing out of the US mainstream. His father was a bricklayer of Dutch ancestry, who led a nomadic life chasing work across the Midwest. Kor grew up variously in Minnesota, North and South Dakota, then Colorado, mostly staying in trailer parks. When he was in his mid-teens he saw a mountaineering movie called *High Conquest*, which was based on a novel by Jim Ullman. The very next day he tried climbing an outcrop in a nearby sandstone canyon. The movie characters had used ice axes to hack steps across a glacier; Kor attempted to follow suit by chipping steps up a slab with a geology pick he had borrowed from his father. Shortly afterwards the family moved on to Wichita Falls, Texas. Kor had acquired a handful of ex-army pitons and a short hemp rope, but when he used these to try abseiling from a canyon wall he fell into the river at its foot. He overcame these setbacks to display a precocious rock-climbing talent and was delighted when, in 1956, the family moved to Boulder, Colorado, on the edge of the Rockies. This time he told his parents that if they were planning on moving from Boulder any time soon, they would have to leave him behind. 'I was more excited by climbing than anything I had done before.'

From that moment Kor's path was set. Over the next three years, he pushed his climbing standards ever higher, regularly leaving his peers in his wake, and setting new levels of difficulty. He and a handful of colleagues established Colorado as a rival to Yosemite, hitherto considered the fount of American climbing. But whereas many of his partners were looking to the standards of California to measure their achievements, Kor had his eyes set on Europe and the Alps.

Kor had been reading about Alpine climbing almost from the start – Hermann Buhl's *Nanga Parbat Pilgrimage* was a key text – and grasped the importance of moving fast and mastering the use of technical aids. In 1960, when he was twenty-two, Kor made a pilgrimage to Europe, where he hoped to climb some of the classic routes in the Dolomites. The trip did not fulfil his expectations. His climbing partner dropped out at a late stage, leaving Kor to travel alone. When he arrived at the Dolomites they were covered in snow. He was ill at ease over his first exposure to European culture and legend has it that his diet consisted of beer and cream buns, as they were the only items he knew how to order. 'Layton was shocked to discover that Europeans did not speak American,' said Jim McCarthy, then a trainee lawyer and rising star of US climbing, who climbed with him later that year. 'Given his family background, he was naive about a great many things, except climbing.'

Kor made a similar journey of discovery when he returned to the US, climbing first in the Shawangunks in the north-east, then in Yosemite. Kor was impressed by the level of climbing that so far he only knew by renown. The Yosemite climbers were equally impressed when Kor proved adept at tackling their most challenging routes. Gradually, as the two climbing centres lost their insularity and climbed in each other's territory, respect for Kor's abilities grew. McCarthy, who partnered him in the Shawangunks, was astonished by his speed, as well as his 'sheer energy, joy and fun'. Others came to admire his drive and determination, his ingenuity and imagination – and a phenomenal reach which meant that when he placed pitons, his partners were hard-pressed to follow him. He was as competitive as other climbers and intent on adding to his roster of new routes – yet he was never heard to disparage his rivals' efforts. I remember him as a gentle giant: thoughtful and considerate, with the old-fashioned courtesy that can be found outside the frenetic cities of the US north-east.

Over the next three years, Kor was voracious in climbing new routes. He had an eye for the great monuments of the US southwest, such as Shiprock, the spectacular volcanic plug in the north-west corner of New Mexico. He was chased out of Monument Valley by a Navajo patrol but compensated with climbs on Titan, Standing Rock, Cleopatra's Needle and Spider Rock, desert towers and spires that had the additional relish of being prohibited to climbers. His partners accepted that they were living on the edge, both on the rock and during wild desert drives with Kor barrelling his car one-handed at up to 80 mph. Kor also appreciated the talismanic rewards of the early sixties, unabashed in his liking for easy sex and even easier drugs.

Still Kor's thoughts kept turning to the Alps. He attended Harlin's Boston talk in December 1964, listening intently to his account of the challenges the Alps offered, headed by the Eiger Direct. He was impressed by Harlin's photographs of possible routes and talked to him afterwards – it was the first time they had met. Most previous accounts relate that Kor providentially arrived in Leysin at the very moment Harlin needed him. In fact, Harlin had been wooing Kor for most of that year. In March he wrote to McCarthy proposing that he come to Europe to tackle a range of possible routes which (to McCarthy's recollection) did not include the Eiger Direct. He also asked McCarthy to forward a letter to Kor urging him to come too. McCarthy replied that Kor was likely to arrive in Leysin in July, although it now appears that he did so in late September, just as Bonington was preparing to leave.

By Kor's account, which he delivered in a long interview with John Harlin Jr in March 1983, Harlin's invitation to attempt the Direct came out of the blue. 'When I went to Europe I wasn't thinking about the Eiger Direct. I wanted to climb the Eiger, it was one of the climbs I was really keen on doing over there – the Walker, the Matterhorn . . .' He had no thoughts of attempting the Eiger Direct until Harlin 'just came right up and asked me point blank. He made my mind up right on the spot. That was a great classic and there weren't many of those things around. I figured I ought to go up and give it a shot. You're never going to get another chance, they're going to do the thing obviously quite soon.'

In another account by Kor, his conversation with Harlin was brief and to the point. Harlin asked if he was interested in taking part in the Direct, warning that it was a complex and dangerous project and suggesting he take his time before coming to a decision. Kor said he didn't need time to think about it. He was in.

By the last week of September, Harlin had secured the dream team. In Bonington he had Britain's most accomplished Alpinist, who knew the Eiger almost as well as he did and was keen to attempt the Direct. In Kor he had a supreme rock technician from the US, who was in love with the history and ambience of the Alps and equalled Harlin in his drive for new routes. He had a lucrative media deal in place. The attempt would begin, at the earliest, in January 1966, leaving three months for detailed planning. Meanwhile, Harlin had a date in Italy, where he had been invited to attend Trento's mountaineering film festival. There he would be able to mix with his peers, savour being the only American in a group of top-flight Alpinists, absorb the gossip and find out what everyone else was up to.

Chapter Seven

THE UNKNOWNS

For their very first date, Peter Haag took his future wife to the Eiger. Their visit came as the culmination of a dramatic encounter on the Mer de Glace and an eventful journey from Chamonix to Grindelwald.

Barbara Morlok, then twenty-four, had known Haag for several years when she went on a trip to Chamonix with the *Alpenverein*, a walking and climbing group from their home town of Reutlingen in south-west Germany, in the summer of 1965. Haag joined the group in Chamonix after climbing the North Face of the Matterhorn with a climber from Czechoslovakia, Karl Hauschke. The group was camping at the Mer de Glace and Haag went out with a guide, who was hit by stonefall that broke his leg. The group retreated to its tents and spent twenty-four hours sheltering from a storm. 'Peter was talking all the time about the Eiger,' Barbara said in 2014.

When the storm lifted, a rescue team arrived to fetch the injured guide. Most of the group decided to return to Reutlingen but Haag proposed to Barbara that instead they should visit the Eiger. They had little equipment or money and so they started hitchhiking.

One night they slept in a railway carriage in a siding on the French–Swiss border and had to jump out when it started moving in the morning. They finally reached Grindelwald and walked to a point where they could see the North Face. 'He showed me everything he had planned. He showed me the route and said, this is what he wanted to do. It was his big challenge and I was just amazed.'

It was Haag's passion and enthusiasm which won Barbara's affection. 'He was a very interesting, intelligent, talented, entertaining and companionable person,' she said in 2014. 'I loved to spend time with him and we could talk about everything.'

Haag, who was twenty-eight when he first showed Barbara the Eiger, was born in Munich in August 1937. His grandfather owned a construction business and his father, Adolf, was an engineer who had fought in the First World War and then worked on the network of Autobahns as they were extended across Germany in the 1930s – resisting all pressure, as Nazism took hold, to join the Nazi Party. During the Second World War he was an officer in a pioneer corps, which first constructed bridges to help the advancing German Army and then, when the German Army went into retreat, was tasked with demolishing them. When he returned from the war, said Barbara, he did his best to make it sound like fun – 'like playing cowboys and Indians'.

At the start of the war, Haag's mother took him to live with her parents in the town of Auingen in Swabia. His father's return in 1945 required a period of adjustment that occurred in many families' lives. While his father was away, Haag had his mother to himself, winning her full attention and sharing her bed at night. That ended when his father came back, creating tensions that were never fully resolved. Throughout his life he did his best to avoid confrontations and search for compromise where possible. In so doing he developed social skills that brought him a large group of friends and even more acquaintances. He was quick to like people and to empathise with them, and also to convince them of his own arguments. 'Peter was very diplomatic and usually ended up with what he wanted,' Barbara said in 2014. 'He was a complete individualist but he got on with everyone.'

Haag's father found work as an engineer in Reutlingen after the war and the family joined him there. As Haag grew up he displayed myriad talents. He acquired a love of singing and writing poetry from his mother, who came from a musical family and provided him with piano lessons. He followed his father in becoming an accomplished gymnast and they both won awards in national championships. When Haag was seventeen a group of friends took him climbing on the rocks of the Swabian Jura near his home. Haag was hooked, and also found that he preferred the sport's libertarian ethos to the organised aspects of gymnastics and the officious figures who ran it.

When Haag announced that he was giving up gymnastics for climbing, his father was furious and there was an unseemly row. Haag hid his climbing kit under his bed and there was another row when his mother found it while she was cleaning his room. Haag handled the next conflict differently. He wanted to be a geologist, reflecting his new-found love of the mountains, but his father wanted him to follow the family tradition and train as an engineer. Haag consented and enrolled on a technical course in Stuttgart. But after finding that engineering was not to his taste, he went through the motions of attending university without actually doing so. He finally confessed to his mother on the day his father died in 1967. She told him that they had suspected for some time that he was bunking off, but decided not to say anything about it.

From his first ventures in the Swabian Jura, Haag progressed through a roster of climbs that would take him to the highest levels. In 1958 he climbed the Spigolo Giallo on the Cima Piccola and the North Face of the Cima Grande in the Dolomites, both Grade VI. In 1962, he climbed the West Face of the Dru and the Walker Spur on the Grandes Jorasses. In 1964, he was tackling serious routes in winter. The only pause in his climbing came in 1959, when he joined a travelling circus and spent five months in Sweden, working as a kitchen hand and assistant rigger. Afterwards he went on a hitchhiking odyssey from Sweden through Denmark, Belgium, France, Spain and Morocco. His enjoyment of travelling and exploration spoke of his other interests. With his mother's example before him, he became a versatile musician, play-ing jazz piano and folk guitar and learning an extensive repertoire of songs, in French, Spanish and English as well as German. He formed a group which played at mountaineers' gigs and dances in Stuttgart. He also wrote and recorded his own songs, in a variety of styles. 'He was obsessed with jazz,' said Barbara. 'But he was obsessed about everything he did.'

Barbara was born in Bad Saulgau in southern Germany in 1941. She grew up in the Swabian town of Ehingen, where her father ran a company selling heating systems. After leaving school she trained to become a dietician in Stuttgart, and for a time worked in med-ical clinics in Munich. She became a keen walker and skier and met Haag when she joined the Reutlingen branch of the *Alpenverein*. On their first outing, she and Haag, together with Haag's girl-friend of the time, were caught in an avalanche but dug themselves out. That was two years before the visit to the Mer de Glace and the trip to inspect the route on the Eiger Direct, which so imprinted itself on her memory. 'He had it totally in his head, precisely what he wanted to do – but not when, and not who with …'

No one is quite sure when Haag first met Jörg Lehne or asked him to become co-leader of the team. Although Lehne's fellow climbers respected his abilities, they found him more serious, less communicative than Haag. Harlin's team tended to view him through the prism of wartime stereotypes: grim, unyielding, humourless; Bonington even described him during the climb as 'looking like a storm trooper'. He was, in fact, thoughtful and articulate in his attitudes towards climbing and as strong a writer as Haag, although without the poetic flourishes. As a climber, Lehne was keen to succeed at the highest levels, and he had ambitions towards the Eiger that preceded even Haag's. He compensated for a lack of technical skills with a willingness to take risks that sometimes surprised even his colleagues – a quality that was to prove itself at a decisive stage in the Eiger Direct.

To Barbara Haag, Lehne's relationship with Peter is a closed book; she knew only that they were very close friends, and she found Lehne 'strange'. His demeanour spoke of hidden hurts, a protective shell against revealing too much about himself. The mysteries may reflect an obdurate character that was shaped in childhood and a profound loss he suffered when his most important climbing partner died four years before the Eiger Direct.

Jörg Lehne was born in Berlin in May 1936. He was the second of three children: his parents had a daughter in 1933 who died in infancy. His younger brother, Peter, was born in 1938 – and in 2014 was living in the Munich suburb of Lochham-Gräfelfing, with strong memories of Jörg. Their father had been a Prussian officer and a pilot in the Great War. Afterwards, he worked in advertising and was successful enough, said Peter in 2014, 'that he always had a good chair in his office'.

Soon after Jörg was born, the family moved from Berlin to Rosenheim, close to where their father had grown up. Peter was born there shortly afterwards. Life changed for the family at the start of the Second World War. At forty-three, their father was considered too old for the army, so was conscripted as a security guard at the giant BMW plant at Eisenach in central Germany. The plant made motorcycles for the Wehrmacht and aircraft engines for the Luftwaffe and he was supposed to prevent internal sabotage, but most of his work consisted of fighting the fires caused by Allied bombing (the factory was 60 per cent destroyed by the end of the war). In southern Germany, Allied bombers were pounding the cities of Bavaria and Swabia, and the Lehnes would watch them passing overhead on their way to Munich and Stuttgart. When the bombers headed on, Peter recalled, 'We said "thanks to God".'

Rosenheim was not spared, suffering a dozen or more attacks on the railway station and tracks in the last year of hostilities. 'You could tell from the whistles of the bombs whether you had to run fast or not. If the bombs fell, people said, well, if they hit us then it is soon over – and if they do not, one has to move on. People said, it will be as it will be, we cannot change it and somehow it will go on. The main thing was not to get desperate, that did not help.'

The Lehne children suffered sleepless nights because of the air-raid alarms. In the morning they had to walk several kilometres across the countryside to school as there were no buses. They were taught by retired teachers who had been pressed back into service. 'They did not really want to do it and they were very strict.'

When their father returned to Rosenheim there was no advertising industry left. Instead, he worked as a farm labourer, cleaning out stables and performing a range of other tasks. In his spare time he made paintings of local scenery and hawked them around the bars where the American soldiers in the occupying forces drank. He distilled hooch liquor and sold it to GIs who called at their home. Food was always in short supply and Peter remembered the day his mother told them there was nothing to eat. When they seemed sceptical she opened the larder door to show that it was bare. But their father had contacts in the black market. 'Someone would throw a sack of oats over the fence at night and we would have porridge for six weeks in the morning, at lunchtime and in the evening.'

Peter Lehne remembered his father and mother fondly. They had a strong, harmonious marriage and were positive and encouraging. Their father eventually found work again as an advertising consultant specialising in economics, and had his own office in Rosenheim; at one point he ran a wholesale wool business. 'He was moderately successful and we weren't badly off.' Their mother was an adventurous person who had climbed before the war and taught her sons to ski. But somehow his older brother grew into a stubborn character, argumentative and uncompromising. 'For him, even as a child, there was only black and white. Our parents used to say, if he gets something into his head, you cannot change his mind.' His obstinacy was such, Peter related, that he would 'bang his head against the same wall thirty times over – and on the thirty-first time he would take a run-up as well'.

Peter speculated that his brother's personality was moulded by the family dynamics during the war. When their father came home on leave, he told Jörg: 'You are the big one, you are a boy and a man, you have to look after your brother and your mother.' Although Jörg looked out for his mother, 'he could not care less for his little brother ... If somebody entered his space, he just reacted, he was like a dog who just bit.' He too had to adjust when his father returned from the war and resumed his place in the family.

As the brothers grew up, their mother encouraged them to be adventurous and explore their surroundings. 'She used to say, if you want to go into the wide world, just go.' In their early teens they cycled 250 kilometres to Lake Constance. 'There were no mobiles or telephones and we were away for three weeks. She said, come back soon and if you have time, send us a card to let us know where you are.'

By then Jörg had discovered climbing. He found that his mother's battered climbing boots fitted him and unearthed an ancient hemp rope from their cellar. He started a climbing log and recorded his first climbs – Christaturm-Ostwand, Fleischbank-Ostwand, Totenkirchl-Ostwand – in the Wilder Kaiser, the mountains some forty kilometres from Rosenheim across the German border into Austria.

His father and mother issued due parental cautions over taking up a risk sport. 'Our parents rarely said no. They said, if you really want to do this, you must be careful and you must accept the consequences of your actions yourself.' Jörg had an early scare when one of his climbing friends fell 600 metres to his death from a mountain peak. 'This really affected him,' said Peter. 'He was about fourteen years old at the time. Then he found himself new friends.'

The closest friend and climbing partner he ever had was Siegfried Löw. They first teamed up in 1951, the year after his school friend fell to his death, and over the next ten years forged one of the most important and productive partnerships of German Alpine climbing of that era. Of all the climbers of that generation with wartime stories to tell, Löw's was among the most dramatic. He was born in Dresden in 1933. His family was in the city when much of it was obliterated by a devastating – and deeply controversial – Allied bombing raid, in February 1945, when Löw was twelve. Löw's father was among the 25,000 people who died in the bombing and the firestorm it caused.

In the chaos Löw was unable to find his mother and was certain that she was dead. He set off to walk to Munich, covering the 450 kilometres in three weeks. He was taken in by childcare officials, who assigned him to foster parents in Rosenheim – which is where he met Lehne. They went walking and scrambling together and then began climbing, starting with the routes that Lehne recorded in his climbing log in 1951. In five years they progressed to top routes such as the North-east Face of the Piz Badile and the West Face of the Dru. At the same time Lehne won a reputation as a wild child, driving a BMW motorbike at high speed, undertaking extreme climbs in worn-out jeans and wrecking the sleep of climbers in mountain huts – qualities reminiscent of another character in the story of the Eiger Direct, Dougal Haston. Lehne was the dominant figure in the partnership with Löw, given to teasing him and displaying his superior intellect. Löw was a compliant figure, soft and sensitive beneath a tough exterior, who gave unconditional support to his climbing partners.

The renowned German mountain filmmaker Lothar Brandler, who climbed with both men on two significant occasions, offered this judgement on their respective personalities. Löw, he said in 2014, 'was always calm and quiet and also very pleasant to talk with. He got his points across easily. But Jörg was always talking big, always had the last word, and always knew better.'

In 1957, the greatest challenge in the Alps was held to be the direct route on the North Face of the Cima Grande. It was conceived by the Saxon climber Dietrich Hasse, who made the first attempt that year. With remarkable aplomb, Lehne and Löw also made an attempt: they spent a month waiting for the face to come into condition and then turned back after two days because of the cold and bad weather. All three climbers returned in 1958 and, with Brandler as fourth man, teamed up to make the first ascent in five days. The partnership brought together two pairs with complementary skills: Hasse and Brandler were steeped in the free climbing of Saxony, while Lehne and Löw had always mixed free and aid climbing. Even so, Brandler judged Lehne's aid climbing as rather inept – 'from the Stone Age' – but what struck him most was that Lehne was a risk-taker who sometimes jumped to reach holds. 'Seldom have I seen such a reckless bird in climbing,' said Brandler, adding that Löw's main role in his partnership with Lehne appeared to be to hold his frequent falls.

There was a poignant postscript for Löw: his mother, who had survived the Dresden bombing, recognised her son from the media reports on the climb and the two were eventually reunited.

By then, Lehne was establishing a career in the printing industry. He had learned typesetting in Rosenheim and then undertook a two-year apprenticeship in Munich. In 1959 he got married: his wife, Gertraud, was an accountant and their daughter Marina was born in 1960, followed by a son, Klaus-Peter, the following year.

Neither marriage nor fatherhood had a visible effect on Lehne's climbing, and he continued to climb at the highest standard with Löw. In February 1960 they teamed up again with Brandler in a bid to make the first winter ascent of the 1938 route on the North Face of the Eiger. A winter ascent had become the new talking point among Alpinists but this was the first serious attempt. On the first day they reached the Shattered Pillar, a rock spur in the upper Vorbau that is the prelude to the serious difficulties, and during their bivouac endured temperatures of minus 20°C and constant powder-snow avalanches. Brandler's principal memory was of Lehne's casual approach to safety and protection. Brandler arrived at a stance to find that he could pull out Lehne's belay piton with his hands. 'I said, "Are you crazy? We are all hanging from this." He replied, "He who doesn't dare to climb on bad pitons doesn't belong in the mountains."'

In the morning, Brandler insisted that they retreat. He told Lehne that their equipment was unsuitable – Lehne was wearing heavy Himalayan boots – but also that he was not to be trusted. 'You lead until you drop – and I am not willing to take the risk.'

In 1961, Lehne and Löw joined an expedition to Nanga Parbat in Pakistan, the ninth highest mountain in the world. Led by Karl Herrligkoffer, a figure controversial in the climbing world for his autocratic style of leadership, the expedition attempted the unclimbed 3500-metre Diamir Face. The lead climbers of Lehne, Löw and Toni Kinshofer reached around 950 metres below the summit, where they were turned back by exhaustion and bad weather. Lehne lost one of his crampons but they survived a perilous descent on dangerous avalanche-prone slopes.

Herrligkoffer invited Löw and Lehne to return to Nanga Parbat in 1962. Löw accepted; Lehne turned him down. He was now the only wage-earner in his family and was starting a new job with the Belser Verlag, a publishing company in Stuttgart that had specialised in religious books and was looking to expand into illustrated books about culture and art. On Nanga Parbat, Löw and four other climbers passed the 1961 high-point and spent a bitterly cold night in a flimsy tent 925 metres below the summit. In the morning two climbers turned back but Löw, who was suffering from frostbite, joined Kinshofer and Anderl Mannhardt in going to the summit. It took them sixteen hours and they were forced to bivouac shortly afterwards. The next day an exhausted Löw was injured in a fall and died in Kinshofer's arms. Both Kinshofer and Mannhardt suffered severe frostbite. Mannhardt lost all his toes and part of his feet, leaving him with little more than stumps; Kinshofer lost all his toes.

Those who knew Lehne were in little doubt that he was profoundly affected by Löw's death; they also agree that this is a surmise, as Lehne gave almost nothing away. Lehne visited Mannhardt in hospital, as did Löw's widow, Hilde. 'It was hard to know what was really going on inside Jörg,' Mannhardt said in 2014. Hasse later wrote of his sadness that Lehne 'could never entirely overcome his reserve to express himself'.

Paying tribute to Löw, Lehne described him as 'one of the best and most consistent climbers after the war and I know no one who had his class and was yet so modest and made so little of his achievements ... He was cheerful, amiable, modest and always in for a joke.' The closest Lehne came to revealing himself after Löw's death was when he met the climber Helmut Dumler on a route and muttered the two words: '*Scheiss Bergsteigerei*' – 'Shit mountaineering'.

It may be no coincidence that Lehne's climbing suffered a decline. Hasse observed a 'dip in form' when he and Lehne had to retreat from the Philipp-Flamm Route on the North-west Face of the Civetta, one of the toughest climbs in the Dolomites. Lehne climbed far below his best and Hasse attributed this to Löw's death. At the same time, Lehne was finding his job at Belser ever more demanding. Having begun as a progress chaser, he became assistant to the company's managing director, and was leaving home in the morning before his children got up and returning after they went to bed. At this stage his climbing CV, previously packed with routes of the highest standard, peters out, with almost nothing listed for the years 1963–65.

It is this hiatus that makes Haag's decision to recruit Lehne to his enterprise all the more intriguing. Lehne had a supreme track record, both as technician and mountaineer, and had been tested in the most demanding circumstances. He had also been on the North Face of the Eiger. Haag may have spotted that someone so accomplished would likely be frustrated by his inactivity – and guessed that the Eiger Direct would prove a powerful temptation. Haag may also have seen Lehne as a foil to himself: Haag, the sociable extravert allied to the introspective, unyielding Lehne, thus illuminating Haag's qualities – or bringing strengths to the team that Haag lacked.

There is a further reason for believing that Haag was exceptionally keen to enlist Lehne – namely, that he was the only member of the team who did not grow up in Swabia. Most distinctively, he did not speak with the pronounced Swabian accent or dialect that even many Germans find impenetrable. In an English context, it parallels the Geordie accent and dialect to be heard, with many variations, in Newcastle and nearby areas of north-east England. Swabian speakers reverse word endings, soften consonants and add diminutive endings – producing a dialect that is softer and more fluent than Standard German or *Hochdeutsch*, which Lehne spoke. It is said to go alongside a range of characteristics that were praised by Angela Merkel during the depths of the financial meltdown of 2008, which she said would have been averted if everyone had behaved like Swabians, who worked hard, spent cautiously and hated getting into debt.

Although it came close to stereotyping, Swabians were delighted at Merkel's compliment, particularly as it reversed the traditional typecasting of them as penny-pinching Scrooges who needed to get a life. Swabians have a strong sense of themselves, reflected in their pride in a regional peasant cuisine of soups and stews, dishes of potato and pasta, and the imaginative use of offal. They are given to a self-deprecating humour that mocks the stereotypes, referring to Swabian intelligence, Swabian humour and Swabian workmanship. They delight in confusing non-Swabians with the formulation '*Janoi*' – which means 'yes' and 'no' at the same time. In 2009 the word '*Muggeseggele*' was chosen by a group of Stuttgart newspaper readers as the most beautiful Swabian word. It denotes a tiny unit of measurement and means, literally, the scrotum of a male housefly.

The Swabian landscape is another of their totemic pleasures. The Swabian Jura is a long, low mountain range that offers a variety of hill walking and rock climbing. It produced a stable of climbers sufficiently distinctive for the writer Nicholas Mailänder to produce a book about them, *Hart am Trauf*. In English, this means climbing near the edge – and so alludes both to the climbers' technical daring and to the escarpments or edges where they performed. Climbing in Swabia, he wrote, is no fashionable sport of the moment but a way of life and tradition stretching back more than one hundred years. Its climbers have avoided the limelight but have demonstrated a tenacity and determination allied with technical skills and ingenuity to rank them with those performing on an international stage.

There is another element which links the German team, I believe, shaping their personal histories and adding steel to the Swabian resolve. All, like Haag and Lehne, were born shortly before or during the Second World War. In Britain the war has remained an obsession, reflecting a victor's narrative where good triumphs over evil and individual heroism is validated. In Germany there is no parallel narrative, leaving the dwindling generation which remembers the war to contend with embarrassment and humiliation. It is a far harder subject to broach in Germany, with the result that many personal stories remain untold. Yet that generation's experiences illustrate the drama and trauma of conflict in a way that converts the shifts of history and strategy into something personal and tangible. The climbers' memories help to account for the resilience, determination and solidarity that proved vital on the Eiger Direct.

That autumn Haag recruited six more climbers, all of them Swabians. The oldest was Günter Schnaidt, who was born in December 1933 and was thirty-two at the time of the climb – earning him the nickname Papa Schnaidt. His father was a carpenter and he grew up in the small town of Rommelshausen, close to Stuttgart, which is both the capital of the state of Baden-Württemberg and the largest city in Swabia (Swabians pronounce it *Schtugert* or *Schtuagerd*). His father was thirty-six when the war started and was conscripted in 1943, when he was forty. Schnaidt suspects his father had been denounced for having made an incautious remark in a bar. However, conscription was working its way up through the age levels as Germany's military defeats demanded ever more manpower, so it may simply have been his father's turn. As his father was considered too old to fight, he was sent to work as a carpenter at a mental hospital in the town of Stetten im Remstal, many of whose patients were sent to the gas chamber at the nearby Schloss Grafeneck. The victims included one of his father's aunts. Later, his father was transferred to a security brigade, one of the *Landesschützen* battalions, and was assigned to guard Russian prisoners working at a limestone quarry near Stuttgart.

On 23 February 1945, he was on a train at Pforzheim, a small town north-west of Stuttgart. Just after the train left, RAF bombers destroyed the town, supposedly because its watchmakers and jewellers could have been making precision instruments for military purposes. The raid killed 17,000 people. He was transferred to German-occupied Czechoslovakia where he guarded railway tracks. At the end of the war he was taken prisoner by the Americans but was transferred into Soviet hands and was compelled to walk some 2000 kilometres to a prisoner-of-war camp in Rostov. He was sent home in 1947, one of the first German prisoners to be released, after developing oedema which caused his legs and ankles to swell. He told his son that he had survived by eating raw onions and making tea from sage bushes collected from the nearby fields. Schnaidt's father lived to the age of ninety-two.

Schnaidt's own dominant memories are of being evacuated with his mother and five brothers away from Stuttgart, a principal Allied objective because of its Daimler and Porsche factories and railway network. The family was moved to a farming community in the Allgäu region of Swabia. His mother was allowed to keep her two youngest children but the other four, Günter among them, were split up. He helped to make hay and did forestry work, but what sticks in his mind most is the moment he was riding on a timber truck and caught a sudden glimpse of distant snow-covered mountains. 'There was a spark,' he said in 2014.

Schnaidt resolved one day he would see the mountains close at hand. After the war he joined a nature group, the *Naturfreunde*, in Waiblingen, and took part in walks into the Swabian Jura. He did his first rock climb on the massive East Face of the Watzmann, a popular peak near Berchtesgaden in south-east Bavaria in 1952. He climbed steadily through the 1950s and was undeterred when he suffered frostbite on a high-level walking trail in the Allgäu in 1955. He had a series of painful spinal injections of the frostbite drug Ronicol at a hospital in Waiblingen and was left with three fingers that remained susceptible to frostbite for the rest of his life.

By then Schnaidt was working as a carpenter, first at the same firm as his father, later setting up a business with his father and brother. In 1960, he took the summer off and climbed thirty or more routes that represented a decisive advance in his technical prowess and a commitment to climbing at a higher level. In 1962, he suffered a head injury from stonefall while climbing a tough route on the Piz Roseg in the Bernina Alps in Switzerland. He was back climbing after two weeks, with ascents of the East Face of the Grépon and the North Face of the Grands Charmoz in the Mont Blanc range. Also that year he climbed the West Face of the Dru and the Walker. In 1964, he got married. He met his wife Margret, a keen walker since her childhood, in the local *Naturfreunde*. She was drawn to him, she related in 2014, when a friend told her 'about a certain Günter Schnaidt, who could climb so well'. Although his climbing tailed off for a while, Margret was clear that she did not want to hold him back. 'Why should he stay at home when we had children? In the war, the wives also had their children while the men were away.'

Schnaidt's partner during his breakthrough summer of 1960 was Karl Golikow, a friend from the *Naturfreunde*, and the only one able to take enough time off from work. Golikow, who became known as Katastrophen-Karle – Catastrophe Charlie – because of an easy-going nature that included a propensity for carelessness and making mistakes, was born in Silesia in March 1935. He was adopted and grew up in Bremen, a city in Germany's industrial north. His experiences during the war, when Bremen's port factories and U-boat pens were continually bombed, are lost. Golikow did not get on with his adoptive parents and in 1952, when he was seventeen, he moved to Stuttgart.

In Stuttgart, Golikow trained and worked as a mechanical fitter. He also developed radical political views, inspired in part by the writings of Wolfgang Borchert, a young anti-Nazi who described his experiences as a soldier, mostly on the Eastern Front, where he was denounced and arrested several times for making allegedly subversive statements. Golikow became a committed socialist and joined the protest movement against nuclear weapons that took hold in Germany in the late 1950s, paralleling its development in Britain. He was a devoted trade unionist and when his union called a strike at his engineering plant he stood on picket duty – impressing climbing friends, who thought that he should use his free time to head for the Jura.

A highlight of Golikow's climbing in 1960 was his ascent with Schnaidt of the Hasse-Brandler Route on the North Face of the Cima Grande. They tackled it on the spur of the moment, after a sudden improvement in the weather, even though they were carrying nothing to drink. Golikow took an eight-metre fall but they reached the summit in eleven hours, a record at the time, and marking the second one-day ascent. He set another record by climbing the Bonatti Pillar on the Dru in 1963 in eight hours, also the fastest at that time. He started making winter ascents in the Mont Blanc massif in 1964 and was staging further top-grade climbs at Mont Blanc and in the Dolomites in 1965.

Sigi Hupfauer, a sociable, easy-going character with a sense of humour that came close to matching Haag's, was born in February 1941 and grew up on a farm near the village of Balmertshofen, some ten miles outside the city of Ulm. Ulm was heavily bombed and by the end of the war most of the city centre had been destroyed. Among Hupfauer's memories is the air-raid shelter his father constructed among the rocks of an ancient glacier moraine in the forest near their home. When Allied bombers flew overhead on their way to Ulm the family took refuge there, emerging once the planes had passed to watch the bombing. Later, when he was older, Hupfauer cycled into Ulm with a friend to inspect the rubble and ash. As his parents were farmers, they were able to cater for themselves, and Hupfauer recalled in 2013 that villagers would call and ask to buy food. His mother listened to illegal Swiss news broadcasts and warned him not to open the front door in case the Gestapo came to arrest them. 'The thought of that still makes me shiver,' he said in 2013. He remembered the arrival of American tanks and the story of an SS officer who hid in the woods and was determined to fight on – and was shot, possibly by another villager who did not want to attract US fire.

Hupfauer acquired a love of nature living on his parents' farm, walking for hours in the nearby fields and forests as a child. He first climbed in the Allgäu at the age of thirteen and then spent as much time as possible hill walking and scrambling – bringing him 'the deepest fulfilment'. He started rock climbing at sixteen and went winter mountaineering at eighteen. At twenty, he began a two-year spell of military service, which was introduced in Germany in 1956. He joined a mountain regiment, the *Gebirgsjäger*, based at Mittenwald near the border between Bavaria and Austria. Afterwards, having trained as a tool-maker, he worked at a watch factory in Senden, a town twenty kilometres from Balmertshofen. His mountaineering gained in intensity as he racked up first winter ascents in the Rätikon group of the Vorarlberg range. He developed a liking for arduous winter traverses, testing himself with multi-day trips in the Mont Blanc range in 1963–64. By 1965 he had done many early repeats of the hardest routes in the Dolomites, such as the Philipp-Flamm on the Civetta, and was climbing at the highest levels, which included free climbing at Grade VII ten years before the grade was formally introduced.

Rolf Rosenzopf – the 'quiet man' of the German team – was born in Berlin on 22 June 1941. It is one of the most potent dates in history, for it marked the opening of Operation Barbarossa, Germany's invasion of the Soviet Union. It signified both the launching of Hitler's overriding war aim and Germany's eventual defeat. (My father was among those who believed that Hitler was doomed to lose the war from that moment. He persuaded my mother that it was safe to have a child, and I was conceived that night.)

Rosenzopf's father was an engineer and he was one of four children. The family remained in Berlin throughout the war, surviving the massive bombing raids of 1943 and 1944. In early 1945, as raids by American and Soviet air forces intensified and the Red Army advanced from the east, Rosenzopf's mother fled from Berlin with her four children. They made a 48-hour train journey to Ulm, surviving bombings en route, where they stayed with her mother. As Ulm was devastated in turn, the family was evacuated into the countryside, sleeping in school halls and then on a farm. Rosenzopf's father escaped from Berlin during the final Red Army assault in April 1945 and cycled the 600 kilometres to join his family, purloining and fighting for food during the journey.

The family lived in a fortress that also housed German refugees from Bohemia and Moravia until 1953, when they were allocated a municipal house in Ulm. In 2013, Rosenzopf retained positive memories of the farm where he had been lodged in 1945. After the war, he and a brother returned there for holidays, helping to make hay, looking after the cows and eating sumptuous farm suppers.

He left school in 1959 and qualified to become a tool-maker and later an engineering technician. He first went climbing in 1961 in the Wilder Kaiser, becoming a strong rock climber and by 1965 was climbing set-piece routes in the Dolomites and around Mont Blanc.

Günther Strobel, reckoned the technically most accomplished climber in the team, was born in Stuttgart in December 1941. During the war he lived in the countryside, away from the city and the bombing. Of the war, he would say only: 'It did not affect me very much – and what I think about it now is another matter.' His family were carpenters and Strobel joined the family business when he left school. He came to notice when, at the age of seventeen, he and a fellow climber were seen standing at the foot of a tough route with apparently no idea how to attach their rope. A mountain-rescue team member showed them how to do so and within a few weeks Strobel and his partner were climbing at a precociously high level. As he became more proficient, Strobel faced hostility from his family – 'my brother hated climbing,' he said in 2014 – and at one stage his mother resorted to hiding his equipment. Strobel did some of his most notable ascents with other members of the future Eiger Direct team: he was with Schnaidt when he was injured on the Piz Roseg in 1962, taking over the lead to see them to the top; and he made the record eight-hour ascent of the Bonatti Pillar with Golikow in 1963. By his team-mates' reckoning, Strobel combined his technical expertise with a fierce ambition to excel at the highest levels.

Roland Votteler was born in Mainz in November 1942. As the youngest member of the team, just two and a half when the war ended, his memories are of deprivation and hardship as Germany contended with the aftermath of defeat. 'It was a time when everyone was poor,' Votteler said in 2014. His father worked in manufacturing as a master moulder and he was one of a family of six who occupied just ten square metres between them. He slept on the floor for ten years before the family was finally allocated an apartment in Reutlingen. In the summers he worked on a farm and was paid in food for his family. In the autumn he collected firewood in the forest, an activity that was controlled by official permits. He occasionally truanted from school and came to love the outdoors. 'It was much better than sitting in a classroom in good weather.' He displayed early entrepreneurial skills when he constructed a raft from telegraph poles and charged his friends a few pfennigs for rides on the local stream. He trained to become a moulder like his father and worked in Reutlingen.

Votteler's climbing followed a familiar trajectory, starting on the nursery faces of the Swabian Jura and moving through an increasingly serious roster of routes in the Dolomites and Western Alps. Like Hupfauer, he did military service in an Alpine brigade, and it was during that time that they formed a deep and enduring friendship that persisted throughout their lives. Hupfauer, the older by nine months, took the lead in deciding what routes they should climb – often doing so on aesthetic grounds, according to Votteler. (For Hupfauer, he said in 2014, '*Schönheit ging voraus*'– beauty came first.) Votteler acquired a reputation as a joker and was given the nickname Donald, after Donald Duck. 'He had an endearing laugh and could keep up the spirits of an entire group,' said Hupfauer in 2014. 'He could see the lighter side of everything.'

A key link among the six climbers, besides their experiences of the war and its aftermath, is that all were expert manual workers and in occupations that were vital as a divided nation struggled to construct a new economy. All were practical men with important technical skills. Unlike Lehne or Haag, they were not given to philosophising about climbing, and preferred doing it to writing about it. All had impressive climbing CVs and a commitment to advancing to the highest levels. Among their strengths was a good-natured rivalry that spurred them to new challenges. By 1965 most had climbed Alpine routes that were standard-setters for the time – taking them to a position where, as Mailänder observes, an attempt on the Eiger Direct was a realistic objective. Yet, in contrast to the climbers Harlin was recruiting, none apart from Lehne had anything like an international reputation. 'We weren't prominent climbers but we were good climbers,' said Schnaidt in 2013. That in itself was to prove an advantage, in so far as this team of relative unknowns, from the unfashionable German region of Swabia, would be consistently underestimated until it reached high enough on the Eiger Direct to be taken seriously.

In recruiting his team, Haag took advantage of a network of partnerships and friendships among them, with Papa Schnaidt occupying a central position. Schnaidt first climbed with Golikow in 1960. Schnaidt met Haag the following year, when he cycled to the Rutschenfelsen, a crag near Bad Urach-Bleichstetten to the east of Reutlingen. Schnaidt was sunning himself on a rock when Haag, sociable as ever, approached and asked what he was doing. Schnaidt replied: 'Enjoying the sun, as you can see.' They swapped addresses and met a week later at the home of Haag's parents in Reutlingen. The two men started climbing together, as did Strobel and Golikow. Schnaidt climbed with Strobel in 1962 and Strobel climbed with Golikow, the various pairings often competing to put up the best routes. Haag met Votteler and introduced him to the group; that brought in Votteler's climbing partner Hupfauer, who introduced Rosenzopf. Although Schnaidt considered it a loose network, since none of them had telephones – let alone mobiles – to assist communication, that in itself helped cement its links. 'When you went climbing one weekend you knew what you were doing the next,' Schnaidt said in 2013. 'Because nobody had a telephone you made plans on the spot and stuck to them.'

That autumn – around the time he attended the Trento festival –

Haag started assembling his team. What is striking about his recruits' responses is both their ingenuousness towards the North Face's lurid history and the alacrity with which they accepted. 'I had never been to the Eiger, knew nothing about it, had seen a few pictures maybe,' recalled Votteler in 2014. Haag approached him after Trento and said: 'You are going really well. Do you feel like coming along?' Votteler replied: 'OK, I will come along.'

Votteler in fact first consulted Hupfauer, his long-standing climbing partner. 'We had our short way of communicating,' Hupfauer said. 'He said, "Sigi, we will do something." I had to take a deep breath. I was a winter climber anyway, I had done a lot of difficult climbs already and I really enjoyed winter climbing. It was my cup of tea.'

Votteler himself was partly motivated out of loyalty to Haag. 'The Saxons who climbed the Direct on the Cima Grande in 1963 later tried the Eiger. This didn't work, so we thought, "If Peter is looking for someone, let's give it a try."'

Schnaidt had considered climbing the 1938 route with Golikow at the end of their successful summer in 1960, but the weather had been against them. When Haag approached him, he recalled, 'I thought, "What the heck – why shouldn't we give it a try?" I said to Peter, "Let's give it a try. We will do it somehow."'

The hardest to persuade was Strobel, potentially the fastest and most proficient climber in the team. Because his family so disliked him climbing, he told them: 'It's impossible – I can't go.' His brother insisted he could not be spared from the family carpentry business. But Haag and Lehne, said Strobel in 2014, 'gave me no peace' and he agreed – telling his brother he would be away for two weeks. He felt flattered at being invited to take part alongside climbers he admired, especially Golikow and Lehne. 'I felt really honoured that they wanted me to join them.'

Most of the other team members were promised similar amounts of time off work. An unexpected snag arose when Belser refused Lehne's request for three weeks' leave. Lehne and Haag suggested that Belser should publish a book about the attempt. Their proposal came at an opportune moment, as Belser was trying to broaden its appeal by publishing books about sport. But although Belser gave Lehne leave, the company imposed miserly terms on the climbers which still rankled forty-eight years later. Lehne and Haag were to write the book without being paid and the team members had to hand over all their photographs and diaries of the ascent. The climbers' reward would be one Deutschmark – out of a likely cover price of 24DM – for each copy that Belser sold. That was to be split eight ways, giving them 12.5 pfennigs each – around 3p.

At the end of October, Haag wrote to Barbara to report that the team was now complete. He had 'a perfect expedition ... and a yet unfinished plan of battle'. He also reported on a practice climb that four of them – himself, Hupfauer, Votteler and Rosenzopf – had undertaken on the North Face of the Ortler, an imposing 3905-metre peak in the Eastern Alps. It was first climbed by Hans Ertl and Franz Schmid in 1931, the same year that Schmid made the first ascent of the North Face of the Matterhorn with his brother Toni. Considered one of the most dangerous faces in the Alps, it replicated the mix of ice and rock they would encounter on the Eiger, with 'a grim and threatening' gully that Haag called 'a really steep death chute'. They spent most of the climb in shadow, leading Haag to write: 'I have never experienced anything as glorious as poking my head into the sun afterwards – good training for the Eiger.'

Haag was evidently concerned that Barbara might feel he was devoting too much of his attention to the Eiger instead of to her. 'In case you think I have forgotten you, let me reassure you. But for now I am totally living for the moment, and for one very great love I have right now' – namely, the Eiger. He added: 'Imagine my love were the landscape of the Eiger. You would then be lying beneath the Eiger Nordwand on the pastures in the sun.' He signed himself: 'Your Pierrot'.

In November, Haag and Lehne worked on finishing their plan of battle. They had reckoned that the climb would take ten to twelve days (similar to the estimate made by Harlin and Haston), a figure which dictated both the tactics and the team size. Two climbers would take the lead, fixing ropes in place as they did so. The remaining six would haul supplies and establish a series of bivouac sites as the climb progressed. The climbers would not leave the fixed ropes in place, but would continually recycle them, returning them to the lead climbers so that they could be used again.

This approach became known as capsule-style climbing, a term that was adopted in the 1970s. The mountaineer and writer Stephen Venables believes that it was coined by Pete Boardman, after he and Joe Tasker used the method to climb the bewitching Himalayan peak Changabang in 1976. It represents a compromise between two principal styles. Climbers making an Alpine-style ascent carry their supplies with them and bivouac where they stop each night – the method used on the classic 1938 North Face route. At the other end of the scale is expeditionary or Himalayan style, where climbers set up a series of camps which they return to each night. At the same time they establish a route, often with fixed ropes, for carrying loads up the mountain. This was the method used on the first ascent of Everest in 1953, as well as on most first ascents of the thirteen other 8000-metre Himalayan peaks, all made in the period from 1950 to 1964. (The principal exceptions were Cho Oyu in 1954 and Broad Peak in 1957, which were both climbed by small teams – in the case of Broad Peak, without even the help of local porters on the mountain.)

The Germans' strategy gave rise to multiple misunderstandings, not least during the climb itself, when I was among those who misread – and misrepresented – their intentions. In doing so, I now feel, I was the victim of collateral damage in an initial propaganda war during which Harlin claimed that his bid to climb the route was tactically and morally superior to that of the Germans. He portrayed the German strategy as Himalayan-style in contrast to the Alpine style he intended to pursue, and in *Eiger Direct* I wrote: 'John felt that his concept of the climb was more in keeping with the spirit of Alpinism, and he wanted to see his concept justified.' In fact, both Harlin and the Germans modified their approach under the pressure of events and adopted the best parts of each other's approach.

In November, Haag sent each climber two lists of equipment. One showed the personal items they should bring, the other the collective equipment that was required. He asked each climber to tell him what items they could contribute and what they needed. The personal list included one or two sets of woollen underwear, one pair of silk socks, three pairs of long socks, one knee-stocking, one woollen shirt, two thin pullovers, one pair of down trousers, one down jacket, one oversuit combining jacket and trousers, one pair of silk gloves, one pair of woollen gloves, two pairs of mittens, two pairs of overgloves, one pair of wrist-warmers, one balaclava, one pair of Lowa climbing boots, one down sleeping bag, one foam pillow and one climbing helmet.

The collective list included four bivvy bags, four headlights with eight spare batteries and four spare bulbs, four stoves, four pots with handles, four spoons, four boxes of storm matches, eight lighters, twenty candles, two or three Thermos flasks, four spoons, nine pocket knives, and a single roll of toilet paper. 'When that was finished, we were supposed to use snow,' Hupfauer observed.

The collective climbing equipment consisted of eight ice axes, four rock hammers, eight climbing harnesses, eight pairs of crampons, three double slings, three étriers, four screw-gate karabiners, sixty light alloy karabiners, one hundred rock pitons, twenty-five ice pitons, twenty ice screws, two drill handles, six drilling bits, four replacement expansion wedges, and twenty-five bolts. There were seven ropes of different lengths and thickness, three 15-metre rope ladders, and four ascenders. In addition, each person was to carry a first-aid kit ('contents to be decided') and there would be one team first-aid kit as well.

The climbers replied, telling Haag what items they had and what they needed. Rosenzopf appeared to need the most: among a dozen items he listed a pair of down trousers (75cm long), one oversuit (to fit 172cm), one climbing belt (100cm), one pair of silk socks, and three sets of gloves. Against that he could contribute a number of items to the collective pool: a bivouac sack, a lamp, an ice axe, crampons and twelve karabiners. Hupfauer needed a pair of size ten Lowa boots but he could contribute a pair of size elevens. Schnaidt needed down trousers and jacket, the special oversuit, a down sleeping bag and the Lowa boots; he could contribute towards most of the team items that were needed. Lehne's list of missing items was the shortest: he needed only silk socks and gloves, felt mittens and overgloves.

On 17 November Schnaidt, Haag and Lehne embarked on a shopping expedition to Munich, reporting the next day that it had been a 'prima' experience. Haag had evidently been using his diplomatic skills, for they had obtained some good discounts and had even persuaded some manufacturers to supply equipment for free. They included Edelrid, who contributed ropes, and Salewa, who provided crampons. Lowa were talking about donating four pairs of boots.

These were vital contributions to the project, for the costs were tight. In contrast to Harlin and his £1500 deal with the *Weekend Telegraph*, the Germans had no direct financial support, and each climber was asked to contribute 2000DM to the team's funds. As

Hupfauer pointed out in 2014, that was a sizeable amount – for him, the equivalent of around three months' wages.

Haag also issued detailed nutritional charts for the climb. He worked on them with Barbara, who used her dietician's expertise to list each item together with its value in terms of protein, fat, carbohydrates, calories and vitamins. Twenty grams of milk powder contained 5g protein, 5g fat, 8g carbohydrates, 100 calories and vitamin A. One hundred grams of hazelnuts contained 17g protein, 63g fat, 7g carbohydrates, 685 calories and vitamin A. Among the principal items were dried meat, cheese and *Soldatenbrot* – soldiers' bread, a form of hard and very bland cookie, sometimes known derisively as *Panzerplatten*, which means armour plating or sheet iron. They looked for items that would be the lightest and easiest to carry, but including one luxury: each climber was allowed fifty grams of cognac a day.

The list, Barbara said in 2014, would look very different today, and would include cereal bars and electrolyte drinks. It was, however, a considerable improvement on the traditional diet for Alpine trips in the 1950s, when – she joked – climbers' rations typically consisted of half a pig and a bag of potatoes.

In December Haag and Barbara had a new matter to attend to. Barbara was three months pregnant and they got married. Hupfauer, Votteler and Rosenzopf were among the team members who attended the ceremony at Barbara's home town of Ehingen on 18 December, where climbers created an arch of ice axes as the newlyweds emerged from the church. Two of Barbara's sisters were pregnant when they too got married that year. 'That was the way it was in those days,' Barbara said in 2014. Previously, she added, 'we hadn't thought about marrying. But we talked about it – and Peter was very happy that we were having a child.'

In the first week of January, four of the climbers did a second training climb, this time on the Eiger itself. They were Lehne,

Haag, Schnaidt and Rosenzopf and they climbed the Lauper Route bordering the left-hand edge of the North Face. Their aim was to take a closer look at the face, particularly the headwall above the Spider, and they climbed much of it unroped – 'it was not so easy,' commented Rosenzopf in 2014. They exited from the Lauper Route on to the Mittellegi Ridge and spent the night in the hut there before going on to the summit.

What was especially notable was that out of all eight climbers, only Haag and Lehne had seen the face before. Were they deterred by what they saw? No, said Rosenzopf in 2013. 'We all thought, we can do that.'

Chapter Eight

THE OPPOSITION HAS STARTED

While Haag and Lehne were assembling their team of Swabian unknowns, Harlin was in trouble – and it was partly my fault. At the start of November 1965, I telephoned Bonington to ask if I could interview him about his part in the Eiger Direct attempt. I told him that I was a feature writer on the staff of the *Weekend Telegraph*, and was preparing an article that was scheduled to appear at the time of the attempt. John Cleare had been commissioned to take the photographs, and I asked Bonington, who by then had moved to a house in Ennerdale on the western edge of the Lake District, if we could meet in two days' time.

Bonington agreed, although his words – 'I suppose so' – hinted at reservations. Once Bonington put down the phone, his growing doubts about taking part built towards critical mass. Having escaped the aura around Harlin in Leysin, he was beginning to lose confidence in his abilities as organiser and leader. He was also uneasy that he was approaching a point of no return where – as he wrote later in his autobiography – he would be committed to performing as a gladiator in a very public arena. In part he had brought that on himself, as he helped secure backing from the

Weekend Telegraph for the attempt. He amplified his doubts in 2014 when he said that, after climbing with Harlin that summer, he had become troubled by Harlin's 'overbearing control – we didn't have any empathy and it was that more than anything'.

Harlin may have discerned that Bonington was less than fully committed when he left Leysin, as he wrote to him soon afterwards to tell him the climb would be 'the culmination of our climbing experience'. His grandiose language may only have exacerbated Bonington's qualms and after discussing them further with Wendy, who expressed her own doubts, he telephoned me back to call off the interview. He then wrote to Harlin saying he was pulling out.

Reporters often find themselves becoming agents in stories, rather than mere describers of events. So who was I, and how had I got myself into a position where my telephone call could lead Bonington to question his commitment to the project and thus disrupt Harlin's plans? I was all of twenty-three; I had been a journalist for little more than a year, and had joined the staff of the *Weekend Telegraph* that summer. I was married; my wife Leni and I had one child and Leni was expecting our second in two months' time. We had left university eighteen months before and lived in south London. Although I was a walker and rock-climber, I had never written about mountaineering before.

Looking back, I feel fortunate to be part of the generation who grew up during a time of optimism and renewal that characterised Britain in the post-war years. I was born in Bromley, then a town fringing south London, in March 1942. I was an only child and lived with my parents in the commuter suburb of West Wickham. My father was a civil servant who had served throughout the First World War, surviving two spells on the Western Front and action in the Balkans, Egypt and Palestine. My mother was a teacher and linguist and a widely travelled and independent woman, having had to contend with the deaths of both her parents by the time she was thirteen. My mother and I spent part of the war away from London, staying with her sister in Birmingham. My father remained in London, working as a customs officer at Croydon airport and acting as a firewatcher from office rooftops when London was bombed. My parents disliked being separated and so my mother and I returned to London. In January 1945, I was visiting aunts in Beckenham when a German V2 rocket crashed to earth in playing fields near their house, shattering glass in their windows and leaving a scar on my nose which is visible today.

We lived through the rationing that extended beyond the war to 1953. At the same time we benefited from the reforms in health and education that were the crowning achievements of the post-war Labour government and helped create new meritocratic openings for people like me. In 1953, the year my father died, I passed exams to go to Dulwich College, a public school which had opened its doors to pupils funded by the local education authorities – something it termed the Dulwich Experiment, which ended in the 1970s. In 1961, I won a scholarship to University College, Oxford, where I studied philosophy and psychology and was editor of Oxford's left-wing student magazine *Isis*. My mother died the following year.

It was also in 1962 that Leni and I were married. A year younger than me, she came from a radical family in Croydon. We met at the inaugural meeting of the Croydon branch of the Campaign for Nuclear Disarmament and first held hands on the CND protest march from the Aldermaston atomic weapons research plant to London in 1960. Leni was generous, committed and passionate, with a keen intellect and a sceptical curiosity. She had mysterious grey-green eyes and long shapely legs, which she put to good use with the London Dancers, a group organised by Jean MacColl, wife of the folk singer Ewan MacColl – their daughter Kirsty MacColl was born in 1959. In 1961, the year I started at Oxford, Leni began a three-year course in psychology thirty miles away at Reading. The only way the authorities would allow us to live together was if we got married and so we did, renting a flat during term time in the market town of Watlington, midway between the two universities. By a mishap of planning – the same kind that affected at least three of the climbers in this story – Leni was eight months pregnant when she took her final degree exams. Our first son, Danny, was born in July 1964.

That was a few days before I started working on *Town*, a glossy magazine that for a time captured the liberating spirit of the 1960s, commissioning talented young writers and photographers who were themselves part of a cultural new wave. Later, it became fashionable to decry the sixties as a time of self-indulgence and hedonism which contributed to the financial and economic crises of the new millennium. I reject that utterly and insist it was a decade that emancipated a generation from the stultifying conservatism and consumerism of the fifties. Leni and I enjoyed it all. We marched and demonstrated against nuclear weapons and the Vietnam War. We attended jazz and folk clubs and were enraptured by the new popular music of the Beatles and the Stones. Leni showed off her legs in miniskirts and I acquired a kaftan and a Mexican moustache. As for drugs, we discovered cannabis, although we only consumed it on an experimental basis and – of course – did not inhale.

On *Town*, I wrote articles about politics, the cinema, fashion, sport and travel – the highlight being a trip to Hawaii to write about surfing. For this I was paid a salary of £850 and was sacked at the end of my first year. The publisher said he was 'letting me go' because I was not developing fast enough as a writer; later, an editor told me that the magazine was losing so much money it had to get rid of someone, and I was dispensed with on the traditional last in, first out basis. By great good fortune, I was recommended to the editor of the *Weekend Telegraph* by a literary agent who had taken an interest in my work, and in July 1965 I was given a job as a feature writer on a salary of £1400. I moved into an office occupied by three other writers in the magazine's offices close to Fleet Street, putting me within a two-minute walk of the fabled headquarters of Britain's national newspaper industry.

At the time I joined the magazine I had resolved not to write about climbing or mountaineering. I had started climbing in 1964, when Leni encouraged me to go to Snowdonia for a weekend with a Dulwich College friend named Dave Condict, who was experienced enough for her to consign me into his hands. Leni and I already shared a love of the wild places: we had driven to northern Scotland in my mother's Renault Dauphine on our very first holiday together in 1961, and we were keen walkers. I took to reading everything I could about climbing and was especially affected by Lionel Terray's *Conquistadors of the Useless*, Hermann Buhl's *Nanga Parbat Pilgrimage*, *The Last Blue Mountain* by Ralph Barker and – above all – Harrer's *The White Spider*. Having seen how crudely mountaineering was portrayed in the media, with their crass language and sensationalist constructs, I was unwilling to write about it until I understood it better. Then I learned that the *Weekend Telegraph* was sponsoring Harlin's attempt on the Direct. I broke my self-imposed embargo and grabbed the story before anyone else could do so. I was asked to write an article about Harlin's preparations, leading directly to my call to Bonington and the setback to Harlin's plans.

Bonington's withdrawal notwithstanding, Cleare and I flew to Zürich on 8 November. We spent several days in Grindelwald, listening to the complaints from guides and officials about the notoriety of the Eiger, the costs and difficulties of rescues, and the futility of attempting the Eiger Direct. It was clear that the Direct was the hot topic among mountaineers. The young Lauterbrunnen guide Hilti von Allmen, who had made a fast ascent of the classic route in 1961, told me: 'Everybody's been thinking about the *direttissima* – it will be done.' We visited Kleine Scheidegg where Fritz von Almen told us: 'The *direttissima* will certainly be done … but climbers must be well-prepared. It must not be a question of luck – it must be brainwork, not just muscles.'

We drove to Leysin, where we met Harlin and Marilyn as well as Harlin's parents, who were visiting from the US. He and Marilyn were welcoming and hospitable and appeared unconcerned that I was so young. Harlin talked the talk, telling me 'an extreme climb like that has to be the culmination of one's complete climbing experience'. He was skiing without gloves to condition his hands and making meticulous nutritional plans. He talked of the psychological training that was required, which meant making the most of his Alpine experience and 'considering just about all possibilities – what do we do here if something goes wrong?' I felt that he was emotionally articulate to the point of self-absorption, which I saw as a Californian trait. Harlin was keen to know how I would present him, turning the tables on me by asking why I had wanted to be a journalist. Marilyn told me: 'Just as long as he keeps coming back I'm happy.'

Because the *Weekend Telegraph* had an exceptionally long lead time, my article did not appear until 18 February 1966. Looking back, it is apparent that I had not known enough about Harlin's plans to enquire about his team. I did not ask how he intended to replace Bonington and I did not meet Kor. Harlin did reveal that 'eight German climbers and two Italians' had been preparing for an attempt. As far as I recall, I did not enquire further about them either. Nor apparently did I challenge him when he insisted: 'I wouldn't be upset if someone else does it first.'

It was an accomplished performance by Harlin, given the uncertainties he faced: he came across as thoughtful and methodical, as well as relaxed about potential rivals. I can only imagine that, once Cleare and I departed, he started a search for someone to replace Bonington. I know that he approached Don Whillans, Royal Robbins and Yvon Chouinard, but cannot be sure if this was before or after Bonington withdrew. All turned him down and Harlin had still not found a replacement by Christmas, when he visited London and stayed with Bev Clark. It was then that he called Haston to invite him back into the team. In his accounts of the conversation, Haston sustained the disingenuous air with which he described the 'trivial quarrel' that led Harlin to drop him from his plans. Now, Haston wrote, Harlin 'decided to patch up the quarrel and rang me up'. Haston forgivingly accepted the invitation and rejoined Harlin's team.

Harlin also visited the *Weekend Telegraph* during his stay in London, meeting Anstey and the magazine's picture editor, Alex Low. A hale and genial character who had been on the magazine's staff since before its first issue in September 1964, Low now appears like a figure from a golden, even fantastical, age of magazine journalism. When Low became picture editor, Anstey agreed that he could take his pick of the magazine's photographic assignments. He spent nine months of the year on commissions at remote and exotic locations around the globe, from movie stars' retreats in the Caribbean to sand-yacht races in the Sahara. During his periodic visits to the *Weekend Telegraph* office he commissioned enough stories from other photographers to keep Anstey happy, and entrusted the task of handling them to a loyal and discreet assistant named Susan Griggs.

Low did all this in the happy knowledge that the magazine had no budget so there were no financial restrictions to worry about. The main proprietor of the *Telegraph* newspapers, Michael Berry –

later Lord Hartwell – appeared to live in blissful ignorance of what his newspaper cost to run. He met the magazine's senior staff over lunch in the Fleet Street office every Tuesday, but was painfully shy which made meaningful conversation difficult. The proceedings, such as they were, were liable to be interrupted whenever Berry inadvertently put his foot on a bell housed under the dining table. His butler, a towering figure with an overpowering personality, would stride in and demand: 'You called, sir?' Berry would apologise and say it was an accident, and the conversation became even harder to resume.

The *Weekend Telegraph*, it should be said, was far from alone in its extravagance. The *Sunday Times Magazine* was equally renowned for its expenditure and the size of its staff. At one stage it had three staff writers (I was one of them) and a host of commissioning editors. Although some did little or nothing to earn their salaries, as far as I could tell, others commissioned as many articles as possible in competition with each other. The result was that two-thirds of the articles that were written (and paid for) never made it into print. According to Low, that wastage was surpassed by the *Weekend Telegraph*, where the kill ratio was around nine articles out of ten.

A few weeks before the meeting with Harlin, Low had returned from two months in the Caribbean where he had been stage-managing a somewhat dubious attempt by a writer and photographer to act out a Robinson Crusoe-style existence on a desert island. The writer was a staff member named Andrew Alexander, later to achieve prominence as a right-wing columnist and commentator; the photographer was Don McCullin, who must have wondered what he was doing on a desert island in the Caribbean instead of taking the war photographs for which he became renowned. Low had his next trip planned, an ambitious odyssey through Africa, taking in the return to power of the

Mahdi tribe in Khartoum; religious and tribal warfare in southern Sudan; the coronation of the king of Toro in Uganda; the East African motor safari in Kenya, Tanzania and Uganda; a story on Haile Selassie and the royal family in Ethiopia; and finally the secessionist war being waged in Ethiopia by the Eritrean Liberation Front.

Since Low was due to start his trip in mid-February, that left him free in January, and Anstey asked him to cover the Direct attempt. Low would not be able to photograph the climbers on the face itself – even he was not up for that – and so the *Weekend Telegraph* made a move that brought Bonington back into the story. Anstey wrote asking if he would like to cover the climb and for Bonington, who had been agonising over whether he had been right to withdraw from Harlin's team, the letter arrived at the perfect moment. He called it 'the very chance I had been waiting for' – an opportunity to pursue his skills as a mountaineering photographer and, he hoped, develop his career from there.

When the meeting with Harlin ended, Low was under the clear impression that the attempt would take place in January, and he made his preparations in keeping with the expansive approach that prevailed at that time. He equipped his racy rear-engined Hillman Imp with snow tyres paid for by the *Weekend Telegraph* and was accompanied by his wife, who was German and could act as an interpreter. They took the ferry across the English Channel on 1 or 2 January and drove to Wetzlar, a town in central Germany where the Leica camera manufacturers were based. Leica lent him an M2 camera that had been winterised by having its lubricating oil removed, so that it did not freeze up, and a set of lenses. Low had six cameras with him in all: the Leica M2, two Leica M3s, and three Nikon Fs. (Neither the M2 nor its lenses ever made it back to Leica – in 2014 Low was not sure where they ended up.)

From Wetzlar, Low drove to Leysin, where he photographed Harlin, who had returned from London, together with Marilyn and the two children. One of Low's principal memories, recalled in 2014, is of Harlin showing him the photographs he had taken of his rucksack with a Spanish climber's leg protruding from the top. 'The photographs were absolutely gruesome,' Low said. 'He seemed quite proud of them. He struck me as a very hard man.'

From Leysin Low moved on to Grindelwald, reserving hotel rooms both there and at Kleine Scheidegg. Over the next week he took photographs of the face from every conceivable vantage point, which included travelling to Männlichen, the peak opposite the Eiger, where he could take telephoto shots from head-on. Low also agreed to provide Harlin with prints of the face so that he could study possible routes which – in those pre-digital days – meant air-freighting the film to London to have it processed and then air-freighting the prints to Switzerland. 'I recall making numerous trips to Geneva airport to send film to London and to collect transparencies and prints sent back to help plan the route,' Low said. He estimated that he used 150 rolls of 36-exposure Ektachrome – more than 5000 shots in all.

There is a curious disconnect about these events. Harlin had said he required ten days of good weather for the climb and Low was under the impression that this was likely to occur in January. 'During the time I was there, there were repeated postponements of the start date because the weather forecast failed to predict the ten days of good weather Harlin said was essential.' What was more, two members of the enterprise were not even in Switzerland. The first was Haston, who was still in Scotland. Harlin called him on 14 January and asked him to be ready to come 'at short notice'. Haston agreed, and promptly departed on a climbing trip in Scotland with Bev Clark. The second was Bonington, who was patiently waiting for instructions to proceed to Kleine Scheidegg.

Meanwhile, it had not escaped Low's attention that a team of Germans were planning an attempt. Previous news of the Germans had been vague but their plans were no longer a secret following their reconnaissance on the Mittellegi Ridge. Low learned about this when he fielded calls at Kleine Scheidegg from news agencies asking if the Germans had arrived and when Harlin's team intended to start. When Low asked Harlin about the Germans he was scathing about their chances. 'He dismissed the Germans' plans on the basis that they were planning to climb using Himalayan methods, for which the North Face was unsuitable due to a lack of places to set up bivouacs and store supplies,' Low recalled in 2014. 'He said they were inexperienced and did not know the mountain, and he said that his team would climb much faster and would be the first to reach the top.' It was an accurate summary of the grounds Harlin would repeatedly advance for not taking the Germans seriously.

While Low was reassured about the Germans, he became increasingly uneasy as the end of January approached. Anstey was calling him repeatedly to ask when the climb was going to start and Low needed to return to London to prepare for his Africa trip. He was booked to fly to Khartoum on 19 February and had a host of arrangements to make, which included obtaining visas. Eventually Low accepted that he would be unable to cover the climb, but wanted to line up two more shots.

For the first, Low planned to hire a helicopter. Although he had given Harlin numerous photographs of the face, Harlin wanted more, and Low concluded that a helicopter flight would provide both another compelling image and the close-up shots Harlin had asked for. Low drove to Sion airfield, some fifty kilometres from Leysin, where he met Hermann Geiger, the pilot who had pioneered the use of light aircraft and helicopters to make daring Alpine rescues. Geiger agreed to make the flight as soon as the weather permitted. His customary charge was two pounds ten shillings a minute – around £40 a minute in 2015.

Low also needed a shot of Harlin with his team. Although he had taken photographs of Harlin and Kor, he had none of Haston, or of the three climbers together. Following a further conversation with Harlin, during which Low said that Anstey was anxious to know when the climb would start, Harlin said he would bring Haston to Switzerland.

On 30 January Haston and Clark came down from three days' climbing on Ben Nevis, having spent the nights in the Scottish Mountaineering Club hut beneath the North Face, to find a note on the windscreen of Clark's Mini Cooper. It read: 'Please ring at once. John.' To reach Haston, Harlin had called Clark's wife, Jan, in London. She called Haston's girlfriend, Joy Heron, who called Graham Tiso, a climber and equipment dealer in Edinburgh. Tiso called the climber Hamish MacInnes in Glencoe. MacInnes called a policeman he knew in Fort William who put the note on Clark's car. Harlin had got lucky, as Haston and Clark had come down from Ben Nevis earlier than expected in order to report a fatal accident. After reading Harlin's note, Haston called him from Fort William and discovered that he was required in Kleine Scheidegg. It is almost superfluous to point out that in more recent times the entire transaction could have been completed in seconds with mobile telephones.

Haston arrived in Leysin on 1 February. He took the rack railway that climbs to the town from the Rhône valley, and when he stepped on to the platform with his enormous rucksack Harlin reached out to grasp his hand and pull him through the crowd. They drove to the Chalet Pollux where Haston shook hands with Kor. It was the first time they had met: Haston's impression was of a 'nervous, dynamic character' constantly on the prowl. They spent some time discussing the route and then Harlin announced that he had arranged a helicopter reconnaissance for the very next day.

It was in fact Low who called Geiger from Kleine Scheidegg to report a clearing in the weather. Geiger confirmed this the next morning and flew in an Alouette III helicopter to a landing strip near Leysin. He picked up the three climbers and half an hour later they were over Kleine Scheidegg, where Geiger made a pass across the face before touching down near the hotel. For reasons of weight, Geiger could take only two passengers on the reconnaissance flight and so Low replaced Haston and Kor.

The flight, Low recalled with notable restraint in 2014, was 'an interesting experience'. Geiger made a dozen passes across the face, gaining height in small circles and doing his best to hold the Alouette steady as it was buffeted by turbulence which increased the higher it climbed. When Harlin urged Geiger to go as close as possible, Geiger pointed out that if the rotor blades touched the face, they would crash. 'Harlin was shouting, "Closer, closer" above the engine noise and Geiger was shouting back: "Too dangerous, too dangerous." I concentrated on taking pictures, but thought to myself, Harlin almost seems to have a death wish.'

Low's images show Harlin, who is holding some of Low's earlier photographs and a pen, peering thoughtfully at the face. Watching from Kleine Scheidegg, Haston thought the helicopter looked like a fly buzzing across the face. Kor, who was seeing the Eiger for the first time, admitted to feeling 'pretty impressed', particularly as the face appeared to be twice the height of El Cap. After the flight Geiger took the climbers back to Leysin, where they prepared to return to Kleine Scheidegg the following day.

On 3 February the three men made some hasty last-minute purchases in Leysin, then climbed aboard Harlin's Volkswagen Microbus. Harlin drove to Lauterbrunnen, the village to the west of the Eiger, where they caught the last train to Kleine Scheidegg. Fritz von Almen had agreed to rent them two rooms in the Villa Maria, an outpost of the Hotel Bellevue des Alpes on the far side of the railway tracks which was also used to accommodate hotel staff. They installed themselves on the top floor, colonising the landing as their overspill equipment store.

The next day, 4 February, Low took his shot of the team with their equipment. It is a classic colour magazine image. The three climbers are lined across the middle of the frame; Kor and Haston are wearing jackets while Harlin sports a pullover with rolled-up sleeves, leaving his forearms bare. Behind them glowers the Eiger, the top half of the face obscured by cloud. Spread out before them across the snow are rows of equipment. Their boots and inner boots are at the front. An array of hardware sits on a ground-sheet. Outer clothing is jumbled at the back. Three ice axes are impaled in the snow beside Harlin. The impression is of a team armed with the very latest hi-tech equipment, giving them a vital edge as they prepare to tackle the greatest challenge of Alpinism.

We listed the equipment in full in *Eiger Direct*. The boots were made by a specialist firm of French bootmakers, Le Phoque, who had worked with Harlin to produce a prototype winter boot with a leather outer and a suede inner. Harlin had added a second inner layer by cutting up an old fur coat that had belonged to Marilyn. They wore one pair of socks each and Millet gaiters with a side zip – a recent innovation. They wore traditional woollen climbing breeches and long woollen socks, although Harlin preferred ski trousers with short socks instead. Their undergarments consisted of all-wool long johns. Wool dominated the rest of their clothing: a cashmere undershirt, a woollen shirt and two woollen sweaters. They each had down jackets too, and their outer layer consisted of a polyurethane zip-up parka and overtrousers made of polyurethane and nylon.

There was a striking array of climbing hardware, much of it selected by Kor and imported from the US. It included sixty pitons of a variety of shapes and angles, mostly made of chromoly, a high-strength steel alloy used by the equipment manufacturer Yvon Chouinard. Haston selected the ice equipment, which consisted of three short ice axes, one traditional long-handled axe and three Asmü ice daggers, together with twenty Salewa and ten Marwa ice screws plus twenty-four assorted ice pegs.

It all sounds highly impressive – and so raises the question of just how good the equipment of the time was. What is significant, in retrospect, is how much of it would prove a handicap rather than a help. There were differences between the equipment of the two teams, but they are far less marked than the differences between what was available in 1966 and what climbers would wear and use now. As Sigi Hupfauer starkly observed in 2014: 'Nothing worked.' The climbing equipment historians Mike Parsons and Mary Rose offered a startling metaphor for the comparison between the two eras: it was as if the 1966 climbers were in a 'bare-knuckle fight'.

The most important development in outer clothing since 1966 has been the advent of breathable fabrics, which expel the moisture arising from perspiration while repelling water from the outside. Before it arrived in the 1970s, the lack of breathable clothing contributed to numerous deaths among mountain users, mostly from hypothermia. The Harlin team's outer garments, while waterproof, allowed condensation to gather inside. Harlin had attempted to reduce this by insisting on zip-up parkas instead of over-the-head cagoules, thus reducing condensation, but it was a second-best measure.

The Germans were far worse off. They were envious of Harlin's team as their own outer layer consisted of one-piece cotton overalls, custom-made by a tailor in Ulm. He had previously provided them with climbing anoraks made from a Perlon fabric, but these had proved too flimsy and did not resist abrasion. The specially woven Damast cotton was tear-resistant, and cotton is effective in dry, cold conditions; but it is decidedly ineffective when it is wet. The Germans' overalls had no waterproof coating and they became saturated and froze. 'Nothing dried, we were all iced-up,' commented Hupfauer. They had one advantage, however – the Harlin team's overtrousers were frequently punctured as they struggled to pull them on while wearing crampons.

The emphasis on wool was sensible for the time, since wool has some wicking properties and retains some heat when it is wet. Some of the German climbers wore angora underwear, but others could not afford it and made do with a less effective wool-cotton mix – cotton being notorious for retaining moisture. Harlin's team and some of the Germans had down jackets, which although warm when dry also become saturated. Hupfauer thought that the team's Loden breeches were the most effective item, but even they were heavy and uncomfortable, especially when they were wet.

Modern climbers would be appalled at this clothing. Instead, they would wear outers made of Gore-Tex or another breathable fabric; a mid-layer of insulating fabric, either down or synthetics such as Polarlight fleece or Primaloft; and wickable thermal underwear. Worn in what is known as the layer system, the combined clothing is lighter, easier to wear and adjust, and more robust.

The second great advance lies in the ice-climbing equipment. Haston's strength was his experience of Scottish techniques, using short ice axes and ice daggers; the Germans were similarly equipped. But the picks of the axes were straight or only slightly curved, which made them more suitable for step cutting than for direct ice climbing (known as 'piolet traction'). In 1970 the introduction of the Terrordactyl axe with its steeply angled pick, invented by Hamish MacInnes, made it far easier to climb steep ice, and winter climbing standards advanced rapidly as a result. More recently, drytooling, where climbers hook ice-axe picks in cracks and over edges, has made climbing on both rock and mixed ground both easier and faster, in comparison to some of the exposed and insecure climbing that would be encountered in 1966. As for crampons, the climbers had repeated struggles to strap theirs on: during the desperate final stages of the climb, Haston spent an hour replacing a broken strap. What was more, the straps compressed both boots and feet, restricting circulation and making frostbite more likely. By the 1980s, straps were replaced with heel-clamp bindings which were far easier to use.

Boots are another area of enormous improvement. The inner boots of the Germans' Lowa Triplex boots proved almost impossible to dry once they got wet. The Harlin team's Le Phoque boots were more effective, but still left them vulnerable to frostbite. Modern mountaineers use high-end boots made from synthetic fabrics like Kevlar, with a closed-cell foam inner for insulation. Boots have become lighter and less cumbersome, making them more suitable for difficult climbing.

In numerous other ways, the odds were tilted against the 1966 climbers. They had repeated problems with their stoves, reducing their opportunity to have hot drinks and sapping their energy when it most needed replenishing. The Germans had small 'Enders Baby' petrol stoves, Primus stoves and gas stoves. Harlin's team had a Primus stove and a gas stove. All proved increasingly fallible and difficult to light. Modern gas stoves function in cold conditions, thanks to a mix of butane and propane which evaporates at sub-zero temperatures and can therefore be lit, and there is a wide range of ingenious stove and pot combinations that transfer heat far more effectively. Bivouac sacks, used as substitute tents at night, were another problem. The Germans' consisted of nylon sacks with a non-breathable waterproof coating which became shredded by the constant use, and Harlin's team had repeated struggles to keep themselves dry too. The awe with which I described the team equipment in 1966 clearly needs revisiting. It is astonishing now just how far it magnified the obstacles they faced in tackling a climb that would test their strength, skills and resolve to the utmost.

After completing his equipment shot, Low called Anstey to tell him that he intended to return to London so that he could prepare for his Africa trip. He also told Anstey that he needed Bonington to replace him and asked Anstey to dispatch him to Kleine Scheidegg as soon as possible. That afternoon, a Friday, Bonington was in Snowdonia, where he and John Cleare were helping the BBC to prepare for its next climbing outside broadcast. I was at the *Weekend Telegraph* when the command reached me that I was to find Bonington and to instruct him to proceed to Switzerland at once – on the grounds, so I was falsely told, that the start of the climb was imminent.

Bonington had already booked to fly to Zürich on Monday, 7 February, but I was left in no doubt that this was too late. In a series of moves that matched the way Haston was tracked down and sent to Leysin, I located Bonington and Cleare in the Pen-y-Gwryd, the mountaineers' hotel in Snowdonia. Cleare drove Bonington to Holyhead in time to catch the night sleeper to London. On Sunday morning Bonington took the first flight to Zürich from Heathrow and arrived in Kleine Scheidegg that afternoon, having left half his climbing and photographic equipment scattered among locations from Snowdonia to Ennerdale (Wendy eventually shipped it out to him).

When Bonington met the climbers at the Villa Maria he was puzzled to discover that they were about to go skiing and that the start of the climb was very far from imminent. Until 2014 both Bonington and I believed that it was Harlin who had called him to Kleine Scheidegg. Only then did we learn that the summons emanated from Low. It turned out that Bonington could have flown to Zürich on 7 February as he had originally planned, as Low did not leave for London until the 9th. On the 8th, Low gave

Harlin prints of his helicopter photographs, which had arrived from London, and handed Bonington some of his lenses. Low had a farewell drink with the climbers at Kleine Scheidegg and headed home from Grindelwald the next day.

That morning, the four men studied Low's photographs of the face. Harlin, Haston and Kor had discussed the route on the day Haston arrived at Leysin, but the new photographs gave them far better detail to assist their planning. Once at the top of the Vorbau, they had already decided to search for a new line on the First Band to the left of the Sedlmayr-Mehringer Route. To the untutored eye it all looked equally unnerving, but Kor reckoned he could see a line that would give some 100 metres of technical climbing, ranging from vertical to overhanging, and appeared to give the quickest access to a series of snow-and-ice terraces where the angle eased. They led to a second cliff, provisionally called the Second Band, which appeared to be intersected with ice gullies and would be Haston's forte. Above that loomed the Flatiron, the 250-metre buttress that flanked the Second Icefield on the left. There they could either follow another gully system to its left, or climb up the edge of the Second Icefield to its right.

At that point the unknowns increased. Above the Flatiron the rock steepened further. The best prospect appeared to lie in climbing the first pitch of the Ramp on the 1938 route, then moving back into a network of gullies that Harlin had christened the White Pony. Further steep rock would take them to the foot of a massive pillar 100 metres below the Spider. Here there appeared to be two possibilities. They could follow a line to the left of the pillar and then, once at the top, could traverse into a secondary ramp leading to the Spider. Or they could traverse the foot of the pillar and approach the secondary ramp into the Spider from the right.

Above the Spider, further mixed ground led to a second, smaller icefield that had been named the Fly, as it appeared trapped in the web of gullies extending around the Spider. The headwall above there, avoided on the 1938 route by the diagonal Exit Cracks, looked especially problematic. Before the helicopter flight Harlin had traced a sequence of ice gullies, chimneys and cracks that would take them on to the summit ridge some eighty metres below and to the west of the summit itself. But now they reckoned there could be a more direct line that should exit close to the summit itself. Although chastened, they came to a firm conclusion: expressed in climbing parlance, the route would 'go'.

The largest remaining unknown was when the climb would start. It was always central to Harlin's strategy that they should not begin until they had a guaranteed spell of good weather like the one in January 1964, when he had been so frustrated that his Italian partners were unable to climb. At the time of the helicopter reconnaissance, the face appeared to be in close to ideal condition. The icefields seemed to have a firm crust while the rocks were largely free of snow. When Low took his equipment shot two days later, clouds obscured the headwall but the rest of the face was clear. By Harlin's reckoning, that was not good enough. He remained firmly of the view that the attempt should not start unless and until a high-pressure system developed that would bring the good weather they needed. Harlin began a routine of calling forecasting stations in Geneva, Zürich and sometimes London for the latest predictions, and also tapped into contacts from his USAF days.

In retrospect, it is striking how much faith Harlin placed in his strategy. Long-range forecasting was in its infancy, and the forecasters Harlin talked to were reluctant to commit themselves more than two days ahead. But Harlin was confident that he would know when the ten-day spell began and was insistent that the attempt should wait until it did. Somewhat tenuously, he argued that if they were forced to retreat after climbing for a couple of days, they could need several days to recuperate and would risk missing out on the ten-day spell when it did arrive. Later, under the pressure of competition, Harlin would be compelled to modify his waiting game. But even at a very late stage he persisted in believing that the long-awaited high-pressure system would bring the climbers the salvation they awaited.

On 9 February, the four men – Bonington included – climbed together for the first time. Partly to assuage the ever restless Kor, they decided to practise by tackling a steep pinnacle that rises from the foot of the West Flank. Harlin led up an icy groove while Haston prospected for a route up a gully to the right. Haston reached the top of his pitch first, whereupon Harlin retreated from his groove and followed him. Two more pitches took them to the top of the pinnacle, by which time it was snowing and they abseiled back down and retreated to Kleine Scheidegg.

The outing gave Bonington the chance to assess Harlin's two team members. He had met Haston only briefly before, and found him guarded, distant and self-contained. Kor was the opposite, brimming with nervous energy that suggested he would not be content until he was on the mountain. Bonington wondered how Kor would contend with his first foray into winter mountaineering: 'He knew even less about it than I did.' But he was impressed that all three men (unlike Bonington) had climbed without gloves.

By the time of their practice climb, the promising conditions on the face at the time of the helicopter reconnaissance no longer applied. The Vorbau was especially deep in snow, and this prompted Harlin to make a new and controversial proposal. On the most optimistic version of his climbing schedule, he had allocated one day to climbing the Vorbau. That was now looking unrealistic, particularly in view of the massive loads they would have to carry. As well as rucksacks weighing around twenty kilos, they would have seven or eight kilos of climbing hardware draped around their waists.

Harlin recalled that the Saxon climbers who attempted the

Direct in January 1965 had spent three days on the Vorbau. It was coated with ice; they consumed far too much time and energy hauling their rucksacks, and they gave up at the top of the Vorbau. It was in light of all this that Harlin proposed they use the Eigerwand station to dump their rucksacks at the top of the Vorbau.

The controversy rested in the fact that climbing ethics dictated that they should transport both themselves and their equipment for the entire length of the route – and when the Germans were presented with a similar temptation during the climb they turned it down. But Harlin argued there was a precedent. When Hiebeler led the first winter ascent of the face in 1961, he and his team had been hit by bad weather and forced to retreat. Instead of carrying their equipment back down the Vorbau, they stashed it in one of the railway tunnels. When the good weather returned, they climbed on to the face through the window, retrieved their equipment and resumed the climb.

Hiebeler had been criticised for his action, even though his team had in fact carried its equipment up the Vorbau at the start of the climb. Harlin argued, somewhat tenuously, that the criticism stemmed from the claim that Hiebeler had initially tried to conceal what he had done. Kor admitted to misgivings: 'In Alpine etiquette I don't know if that was considered right or not and we had a big debate over that.' Harlin's clinching argument, Kor remembered, was that 'this may be the difference between our making it and not making it – those were his words, I recall'.

Harlin secured permission from the railway to use the exit at the Eigerwand station and Haston and Bonington took the train there the next day. Haston abseiled on to the face and deposited three heavily laden rucksacks on a ledge ten metres below the station window. Bonington suppressed his own misgivings, telling himself that he was only the photographer, after all. 'It was their climb, not mine.'

Bonington was beginning to feel uneasy about his relationship with the climbing team in other ways. It was partly that he was being paid while they were not, partly that he was staying at the Kleine Scheidegg hotel while the others were slumming it in the servants' quarters on the wrong side of the railway track. The climbers were, in fact, able to enjoy the *Telegraph*'s largesse by eating in the Gaststube, where the meals (and drinks) were added to Bonington's ever mounting bill. More sensitively, Bonington found himself acting as intermediary in negotiations between Harlin and Anstey over such issues as syndication revenue from the *Telegraph*'s coverage. At one point Bonington was pressing Harlin's case with Anstey from the telephone cabin in the hotel lobby while Harlin – apparently suspecting that Bonington was selling him out – pounded on the glass from the outside. 'He was absolutely furious and I thought he was going to hit me,' Bonington said in 2014.

Bonington's contretemps with Harlin had a direct effect on me, as it helped to impel my arrival in Kleine Scheidegg. I had spent January going about my regular duties as a feature writer for the *Weekend Telegraph*, taking as much time as I could to help Leni with our second son, Seth, who was born on 22 December – this was long before there was any such concept as paternity leave. I had little contact with Alex Low, but assumed that at some point I would be returning to Kleine Scheidegg to write about the attempt for the magazine. Then I learned that the newspaper planned to cover the climb and needed someone to file daily reports from Kleine Scheidegg. Once again I grabbed my chance. When I called the news editor to press my claim he asked if I had done any reporting before. I had written precisely one news report in my life, a freelance piece for the *Observer* while I was working at *Town* magazine. I felt entitled to say 'yes', and the job was mine.

Once Bonington arrived in Kleine Scheidegg, I called him almost every day to ask whether I should join him. For a while he stalled, telling me that the weather was poor, the climb could start in a day or so, it was impossible to be sure. When I called on 14 February his tone had changed: the weather had improved and I should come at once. I suspect now that Bonington wanted to have a staff member in Kleine Scheidegg who could take the flak from Harlin over his dealings with the *Telegraph*. I flew to Zürich the next day, picked up a hire car and headed for Grindelwald.

My arrival in Kleine Scheidegg could hardly have been worse timed. It also served as the prelude to a sequence of accidents, misunderstandings, exits and entrances worthy of a theatrical farce.

As the three climbers continued their wait for settled weather, they made a habit of skiing each morning around Kleine Scheidegg. They became friendly with a group of young women from Interlaken, who joined them as they set off down the Lauberhorn run on 15 February. Harlin, both the most proficient skier and the one most inclined to show off, attempted to perform a manoeuvre known as a Royal Christiania, which entailed carrying out a turn on one ski while lifting the other as high as possible behind him. He crashed at high speed and lay in the snow clutching his shoulder. When Kor and Haston arrived and enquired after his health, he told them: 'It's fucking painful.'

They helped Harlin to his feet and escorted him back to Kleine Scheidegg, where he took the train to Grindelwald to look for a doctor. At almost precisely the time Harlin was descending, I parked my hire car at Grindelwald and caught a train to Kleine Scheidegg. I checked into the hotel and climbed the stairs to the room Bonington had booked for me. It offered a breathtaking view of the face, enabling me to pick out the features I knew from reading *The White Spider*. The face was clear and parts of it were gleaming in the late-afternoon sun slanting in from the south-west. I wondered if the climb was under way but could not see anyone on the face. An hour later I bumped into Bonington in the hotel lobby and asked if the climb had started.

'You're joking,' he replied. 'John's dislocated his shoulder.'

Harlin called from Grindelwald that evening with a gloomy prognosis. Although his shoulder was back in place, he had been ordered to rest it for five days. He was to avoid skiing for another ten days and climbing for three weeks. Harlin returned in the morning with the news that he had persuaded the doctor to reduce the climbing ban from three weeks to two. He recalled how quickly he had recovered from his thigh injury on the Dru and predicted that he would able to climb again in four or five days.

This was my first meeting with the full team. As far as I can remember, Kor and Haston were courteous but reserved towards me, presumably waiting to see if this journalist in their midst was worthy of their trust. I do not recall undue despondency on their part over Harlin's injury. The weather forecast was gloomy and Harlin reckoned that if the ten-day spell began while he was recovering, Haston and Kor could make a start and he would join them as soon as he was ready. Besides, they had found a new diversion. The director of a girls' school in Interlaken had invited them to a party, and it was with high hopes that they set off from Kleine Scheidegg. When they arrived in Interlaken they found it was not the sort of party they had expected. After drinking coffee and exchanging pleasantries with the director, they decided to cut their losses and drive to Leysin where Harlin's shoulder should recover all the more quickly with the benefit of Marilyn's home comforts.

Back at Kleine Scheidegg, the start of the climb appeared more distant than ever. Bonington and I resolved to hold the fort until the others returned, which in practice meant exploring the further possibilities of the menu at the Gaststube and sampling its range of wines and beers. We did not entirely neglect our duties, and that evening Bonington and I discussed our plans for covering the climb. I told Bonington that my ambition was to be at the summit to meet the climbers, which would mean climbing the West Flank. The next morning he took me up the practice climb he had undertaken with the climbers a week before. I climbed three pitches and was gratified when he told me I had done well.

That evening we met in the hotel bar and sat at a table over beers and a copy of *The White Spider*. We opened the fold-out photograph of the face and were discussing possible routes when we noticed two men sitting at the bar who were wearing red pullovers and talking in German. As they left, one paused by our table and looked down at the photograph. I looked up at him and he moved on.

At that time any notion that German climbers could be about to attempt the Direct was remote from my mind. I had included a passing reference to 'eight Germans' in my preview article for the *Weekend Telegraph* but had heard nothing more about them. Harlin had not mentioned them and although Low had some information about them he had not passed it on to me. That evening I called Leni to ask how she was managing with our two young sons. She said enough to persuade me to call the *Telegraph* office to propose that, in view of the continuing inactivity at Kleine Scheidegg, I should return to London and await events from there.

The *Telegraph* agreed and the next morning, 18 February, I departed for Zürich airport and home. My flight to London had already been called when I heard an announcement calling me to the information desk. There I was handed a note which read: 'Opposition has started. Please phone. Bonington.'

Chapter Nine

UNBEATABLE, IMMORTAL

The Germans had always planned to start their attempt in mid-February. Unlike Harlin, most were tied to jobs and had to arrange to take time off – either two weeks or three at most. They also hoped to complete the climb in the winter, bringing them the further prize of making the second winter ascent. For that they would have to be on the summit before 22 March – the first day of spring. As the attempt neared, they fixed on the date of Wednesday, 16 February. Hupfauer drove to Grindelwald with Rosenzopf and they met most of the group in the restaurant at the railway station at Grindelwald-Grund, the first stop down the line from the Grindelwald terminal.

As the team congregated, Haag felt apprehensive about the mounds of baggage waiting to be loaded on to the train. When the face came into view, he saw how thickly it was covered with snow – far more than he ever remembered. Once at Kleine Scheidegg the team carried the baggage up to the Stöckli, a chalet providing economy-rate rooms at the top of the cluster of buildings on the slope facing the main hotel. It had been recommended by the Schnaidts, who stayed there at Christmas 1962, when Margret was working as a medical technical assistant at a hospital in Interlaken. Haag had met the owner, Fritz Bohren, in November and the four climbers who did the January recce had stayed there afterwards.

That evening they celebrated their arrival with beers, inducing a sense of euphoria that Haag hoped was not merely the alcohol talking. It was not. That day four of the climbers – Strobel, Votteler, Hupfauer and Golikow – had seen the face for the very first time. Votteler, who had hardly even read about the face before, said that he felt 'totally slap-happy' on seeing it. Strobel recalled: 'We thought, it's a beautiful wall and we can do it. We felt unbeatable, immortal.'

Haag had a further reason to feel pleased: his 'biggest worry of the previous weeks' had been dispelled. Ever since the January reconnaissance, he had worried in case Harlin started the climb before his team arrived. At Grindelwald he had looked for Harlin's Microbus and was relieved that it was not there. Once at the Stöckli he scrutinised the lower part of the face and was reassured to see no signs of Harlin and his team.

It so happens that, by exquisite timing, the very day the Germans arrived was also the day the focus of their anxieties departed. For that was when, following Harlin's skiing accident, he, Haston and Kor went down to Lauterbrunnen, where Harlin – unusually – had parked his Microbus two weeks before. From there, after sampling the schoolgirls' party at Interlaken, they had driven to Leysin. Meanwhile, as Bonington and I stayed at our posts in Kleine Scheidegg, we saw nothing of the eight Germans decamping with their equipment at the station 200 metres away. The following morning, 17 February, dark clouds swirled around the Eiger. Bonington and I relaxed in the fond belief that there was no need to summon our team – with or without Harlin – from Leysin.

Despite the poor weather, Haag was determined that the German team should make a start by carrying equipment to the foot of the Vorbau. They walked down from the Stöckli and headed across the slopes from Kleine Scheidegg. They found it hard work ploughing through the knee-deep snow, but consoled themselves that the effort would improve their fitness. They found a suitable location at the foot of the Vorbau and, by the evening, had dumped most of their equipment there, ready to complete the carry the next day.

This was the day when, according to the respective published accounts, Bonington had tested my aim of going to the summit via the West Flank by leading me up the pillar at its foot. Either our dates are wrong – or somehow the Germans' activity below the Vorbau passed us by. Maybe, as if in a pantomime, we had our backs turned at the crucial moments. It was also that evening when we saw two Germans, who I now believe were Lehne and Haag, in the hotel bar. It was only the next day, 18 February, when the penny dropped.

The Germans made an early start that morning and carried the remaining loads to the foot of the Vorbau. They then started prospecting for a route up the Vorbau. At Kleine Scheidegg, I too had made an early start as I set off for Zürich airport and home. Bonington was enjoying a leisurely breakfast when a waiter asked him to go to Fritz von Almen's private terrace. When he arrived, Von Almen told him to look through the telescope. Bonington saw a group of climbers at the foot of the Vorbau. He counted seven in all, plus one who had climbed a short distance up the Vorbau.

Bonington dashed to the telephone cabin. In Leysin, Harlin, Haston and Kor were searching through equipment in the basement of the Harlins' chalet when a shaken Marilyn burst in and announced: 'A German team has started on the face. There are eight of them.'

Harlin went to the phone and spoke to Bonington. By Bonington's account, he affected a remarkable calm. He said that he and the team would return to Kleine Scheidegg the next day, and suggested that Bonington should 'have a look' at what the Germans were doing. By other accounts, his team was far less composed. Haston wrote that he was 'shattered' to hear Bonington's news. Harlin had apparently intimated that a German team was interested in making an attempt but Haston had no idea how serious they were or even that there were eight climbers involved. As for Bonington, he recalled in 2014 that he had known little or nothing about the Germans before that moment: 'I seem to remember that when the Germans arrived it was a surprise.'

It was after calling Leysin that Bonington tried to contact me at Zürich airport, leaving the dramatic message that 'the opposition' had started. Beyond what I had written in the preview article, I too knew nothing about a German team, and probably did not know who 'the opposition' were. Moments before I was due to board my flight, I called Kleine Scheidegg but Bonington was not to be found. I called the *Weekend Telegraph* who agreed that I should get on the flight and be ready to return to Switzerland after my weekend at home.

On Saturday, 19 February, the Germans began their climb in earnest. Golikow and Lehne led up the Vorbau to an iced-up section where the climbing proved unexpectedly difficult. Below them, Haag, Strobel and Schnaidt put the Germans' transport operation into effect. Their equipment included plastic canisters with the bottoms removed which they used to protect their equipment sacks as they were hauled up the face. The canisters were designed to be used in chemical laboratories and had a capacity of sixty litres. The German team called the canisters 'bombs' and, with their loads, they weighed thirty kilos each.

The Germans were hard at work when Bonington arrived on

skis. When he started taking photographs, Lehne and Hupfauer responded by throwing snowballs at him, and Hupfauer took Bonington's photograph in turn. Bonington retreated to a safe distance and used a zoom lens instead. He returned to Kleine Scheidegg impressed by how far the Germans had climbed and by their systematic approach to load-hauling. Lehne and Golikow eventually reached more than halfway up the Vorbau while the support team established a substantial cache of bombs a short distance below them. By mid-afternoon it was snowing so they returned to the Stöckli, content with a good day's work.

By a further chance of timing, Harlin, Haston and Kor, who had left Leysin that morning, were riding up in the train from Grindelwald as the Germans were descending from the Vorbau. They spotted the Germans on the slopes below the face and saw that they had fixed ropes halfway up the Vorbau. That evening Bonington passed on his verdict that – contrary to any previous impression he may have been given – the Germans appeared resolute and well organised. Harlin was not ready to revise his view that the Germans did not pose a serious threat; but since they were well established on the Vorbau they could hardly be ignored. He was particularly keen to stake his claim to what he and Kor considered the best line on the First Band – one where the rock seemed the least compact and offered the shortest route to the mixed ground above. He asked Haston and Kor to make an early start the next morning, adding that this should be considered a reconnaissance but one that could be converted into a full attempt if the weather allowed.

That evening it was the Germans' turn to be surprised. When they returned to the Stöckli, they were met by Harri Frey, a Swiss journalist in his early thirties, who had joined the German team in a role very similar to mine. Frey had worked with Lehne at Belser and had been assigned to the team to act as reporter and media coordinator. Belser also asked him to sell articles and photographs to newspapers and magazines, and paid him a salary for doing so. His role expanded, much as mine did, so that he was effectively the team's base camp manager and the man who handled the radio calls between the climbers and the Stöckli. Both the German team and ours had two-way radios, known endearingly as walkie-talkies, and they proved equally fallible. In addition, the Germans' radios were limited in the way they operated. The climbers had two radios on the face but were unable to use them to talk to each other. Instead, they had to relay information via a base set at the Stöckli, using the numeral call signs *Belser Eins* for the base and *Belser Zwei* and *Belser Drei* for the climbers' sets. (In contrast we had two radios and two call signs: Scheidegg and Eiger.)

Frey was once a boxer and had a reputation as a combative figure who was not to be tangled with, although I always found him straightforward and fair. He was also sociable and resourceful, and that afternoon, while the climbers were on the Vorbau, he had been putting himself about in Kleine Scheidegg. He greeted the climbers at the Stöckli with the news that Harlin and his team had arrived that afternoon – having previously spent three weeks at Kleine Scheidegg waiting for good weather. He also told them that Harlin had recruited three top climbers: Haston, Kor and Bonington. For the Germans, Hupfauer related in 2014, the news came as both a surprise and a shock which even inspired a touch of paranoia. 'Had the Americans been lying in wait for us? Did someone inform on us?'

In 1966, the main source of information about Alpine climbers and climbing was *Alpinismus*, the magazine founded by Toni Hiebeler three years before. From that, the Germans knew most about Harlin, and considered him, from his track record around Mont Blanc, an '*Überstar*'. They knew of Bonington and Haston but not Kor, as *Alpinismus* reported little of US climbing. They learned more about Kor, much of it from Frey, as the climb developed. At first they felt in awe of Harlin. But as the climb progressed, their overall judgement – allowing for the Americans' superior equipment – was that in technical ability the two teams were, in Hupfauer's words, '*Gleich, gleich*' – 'Equal, equal'.

It was a measure of Harlin's determination to catch up with the Germans that Haston and Kor got up at three the next morning, 20 February, and were on their way by four. Bonington, who had volunteered to show them the way, took the lead through the snow – Haston noticing his beery breath wafting back as a mark of how much they had drunk the previous night. Because they had stashed their rucksacks at the top of the Vorbau they could move fast and were at the foot of the Vorbau by first light. Bonington took his leave while Haston and Kor set off up the Germans' fixed ropes. They knew that was a little cheeky, but concluded after 200 metres that they could climb faster without them, which would also help them train for conditions on the face. They passed the Germans' high-point and reached the top of the Vorbau by late morning – an impressive feat, even without rucksacks. They traversed to the ledge below the Eigerwand station where they had left their rucksacks. They sat on the ledge and brewed a drink, doing their best to ignore the mystified rail passengers watching from the window above. Then they returned to the starting point of the line they had selected on the First Band.

At last, after so long waiting and hoping, the climbing was about to begin. Above them rose 100 metres of sheer, compact limestone, fractured by minute perforations that gave Kor his opportunity. He selected the thinnest pitons from his set, known as knifeblades, and hammered them into the holes and hairline cracks, sometimes only an inch deep. He suspended an étrier, a short rope ladder containing up to four rungs, from a piton and stood in it. Sometimes he attached the étrier to the eye of the piton; sometimes, to reduce the leverage, he tied a hero loop – a small tape loop – around the piton so that it was flat against the rock and hung the étrier from that. It was a supreme example of the skills of a climber schooled on the walls of Yosemite and Colorado who was operating for the first time in the winter environment of the Alps.

Even so, Kor considered it a close-run thing. 'We were just forcing our way up this blank wall. Fortunately, it was perforated to a degree – it had little holes and that's the only reason we were able to get up that wall.' In four hours Kor climbed ninety feet, almost one third of the First Band. By then it was late in the afternoon and dark clouds were welling up around the face. Kor called down to Haston that it was time to call a halt. He drilled a hole and inserted a bolt into the limestone, hung a rope from it and abseiled back down.

Kor's use of a bolt marked an important juncture in the climb. Pitons and bolts are used to create an anchor point in a rock face. Pitons are hammered into cracks in the rock; where there are no cracks, climbers drill a hole and hammer in a bolt. (In the 1960s, climbers used a hand-drill to make the hole; now, they use a power-drill.) The bolts are designed to expand when they are driven in, to give a stronger grip. The use of bolts raised a matter of ethical concern for Harlin's team, reminiscent of the controversy over climbing methods during the 1920s and 1930s. Climbers use pitons or bolts as 'protection', principally by establishing belay points to prevent or limit a fall. Where they are used to provide a hold, this is known as 'direct aid'. Kor and his team-mates made it a point of principle not to use bolts for direct aid throughout the climb, and they succeeded in that aim. The German team were to use a total of eight.

As darkness approached, Haston and Kor faced a choice: should they return to Kleine Scheidegg, or bivouac where they were? It was snowing, which made Kleine Scheidegg all the more tempting. But Harlin's game plan called for the team to bivouac on the face and continue if possible the following day. Also, descending the

Vorbau as the night and weather closed around them was an unappealing prospect. They unpacked their stove and fried two thick steaks that had been donated by the hotel's head waiter, a Sicilian named Mario. Then they snuggled into their two-man bivouac sack and settled down for the night.

That day, the Germans had been watching with surprise and unease. Haag had decided not to climb, reckoning that the weather was unsuitable and that the team deserved a rest. They were baffled to see Haston and Kor heading for the face in such poor conditions, having remained inactive during far better weather over the previous three weeks. They were also worried to see Haston and Kor traverse rightwards at the foot of the First Band and presumed they were heading for the line taken by Sedlmayr and Mehringer in 1935. Since the Germans intended to climb the First Band by a far harder new route, Haag feared that Harlin would quickly establish a lead.

At this point Fritz von Almen stepped in. He foresaw the pitfalls that could arise from competition between the two and proposed that they should at least talk to each other. That morning, at around the time Haston and Kor were brewing up below the Eigerwand station, the two sides convened in the hotel bar. Representing the Germans were Haag and Lehne; for the Americans, as the Germans called their rivals, Harlin and Bonington.

There was a polite opening to the meeting. Harlin, recalling his discussions with Haag in Trento, greeted him with the words: 'It's good to see you, Peter.' His next remark was less civil: 'You seem to have come here with a whole circus.' Haag conceded that this was how the team might appear to an outsider and then got down to business, asking if Harlin intended to use the Sedlmayr-Mehringer Route up the First Band. Harlin assured him that, like the Germans, he intended to climb a true direct.

Harlin and Haag outlined their respective strategies. Harlin confirmed that he had a three-man team – Bonington was there as photographer – and said that he planned to fix ropes for part of the route, perhaps as high as the Flatiron, where he would establish a camp as a base for launching his summit bid. In the event of bad weather his climbers could use the fixed ropes to return to Kleine Scheidegg. 'We can be down from the Flatiron in eight hours,' he said.

Haag and Lehne set out their plans in turn. They explained that the so-called 'circus' in fact intended to climb the face – like Harlin – in a single push. Two climbers would lead while the other six would haul equipment and establish bivouac sites. They were not intending to fix ropes up the entire route, only on the section they were engaged on at the time. In keeping with what became known as capsule-style, they would recycle the ropes as they moved up the face.

Although Harlin had talked about making an Alpine-style ascent, his strategy was a modification insofar as he planned to fix ropes up to the Flatiron. The change had been partly brought about by the arrival of the Germans, as he could no longer afford to wait for the full ten-day spell of good weather he was expecting. Instead, he would climb whenever he could, fixing ropes in place to safeguard a retreat – although always hoping to reinstate an Alpine-style ascent if the opportunity came. The Germans felt that if Harlin had adopted that approach before they arrived, his team would have been a long way ahead. But they too now altered their plans. They saw the wisdom of leaving fixed ropes in place and decided to order more. They also needed more clamps to ascend them: they already had some Hiebler clamps but would now buy more, together with four pairs of Jumar clamps, which they had never used before.

I knew nothing of this at the time. I was still in London and it was only when I returned to Kleine Scheidegg a week later that Harlin briefed me on his meeting with Lehne and Haag. It was from this that I somehow gained the impression that he had emerged with a moral advantage, stemming from the fact that his team intended to make a pure Alpine-style ascent, while the Germans planned a Himalayan-style siege – with the implication that this in some way cheapened their approach. I went on believing that for a very long time, and was only corrected when I met the German climbers while researching this book and grasped that they had planned to make a capsule-style ascent. In any case, both teams modified their strategies through force of events, so that the two styles gradually merged.

In the Kleine Scheidegg meeting, one issue was still hovering. How far should the teams cooperate? Should they combine to make a collective attempt? At that stage neither side wanted to broach the subject in case this was read as weakness. Harlin came closest when he said he expected a team of three to climb much faster than one of eight – which ruled out a combined attempt. But that raised a further sensitive topic. If the two teams were not going to climb together, how would they avoid getting in each other's way?

At this point Haag deployed his diplomatic skills. Frey had told him about the close-up photographs Harlin had obtained from the *Weekend Telegraph*'s helicopter reconnaissance. Haag had only a set of five small square photographs on which he had marked possible routes. The photographs were poor quality and lacking in detail, and Haag proposed that they should use Harlin's photographs to help decide which lines they should follow. Harlin appeared reluctant to reveal his photographs – presumably, Haag suspected, because he wanted to preserve one of his biggest assets. But Haag persisted and Harlin agreed.

The four men moved to the Villa Maria where Harlin spread the photographs across his bed. They first looked at the First Band, where Harlin knew he had an advantage. Thanks to their early departure, as he made clear, Haston and Kor would shortly be starting up the line they had previously selected. Haag had marked four possible lines on the First Band. Two were to the left of Harlin's line, one roughly coincided with it, and the fourth was some fifty metres to the right – the line that Haag and Lehne now chose. Above the First Band it was agreed that Harlin's team would follow mixed ground leading to the Second Band, while the Germans would mostly stay on rock to the right. At the Second Band Harlin hoped to push up a gully system to the left and the Germans would once again climb on rock to the right.

Above there the lines were less certain. But it followed that if there was only one obvious route, whoever got there first would have a major advantage. Even so, the two teams made one gesture towards cooperation: the first team to reach the top of the First Band would offer to drop a rope to the other. Haag, always ready to put an optimistic gloss on events, left the meeting with the feeling that although rivalry was in the air, it was to have limits. In other words, as Haag himself put it, it should be a fair fight.

Chapter Ten

PARALLEL LINES

That night, Haston and Kor were in trouble. Soon after they settled into their bivouac sack at the foot of the First Band, it began to snow. Before long powder snow was billowing down around them, funnelled by an avalanche chute directly above the sloping ledge they were perched on. Their bivouac sack was too small to cover their heads and it gradually filled with snow. If one of them drifted off to sleep he would slide off the ledge, dragging the other with him. Their breath was condensing inside the sack, insidiously soaking into their clothes and equipment. The wind was intensifying, leaving them to cling on grimly and wait for dawn.

Down at Kleine Scheidegg, where gusts of wind up to 120 kph were buffeting the hotel, Harlin and Bonington were concerned for their colleagues' safety. Early on 21 February Bonington hired an emergency train – at a cost of 100 Swiss francs, around £8 – to take him and a local ski instructor to the Eigerwand station. When they peered out of the station window they were relieved to see tracks in the snow, showing that Haston and Kor had already set off to descend. Bonington returned to Kleine Scheidegg in time to greet them as they walked in out of the storm.

As Haston and Kor described their night, it was clear that the strategy of bivouacking on the face in the hope of continuing the next morning had been severely tested. And the contrast in conditions with the long-awaited ten-day clear spell bordered on the ridiculous. Haag, meanwhile, had seen the two climbers arrive at the hotel. He detected no sign that they had been unduly affected by their ordeal and concluded that their rivals were 'tough guys'.

The retreat by Haston and Kor marked the prelude to a three-day storm during which both teams were forced to bide their time in Kleine Scheidegg. That was followed by two weeks of intermittent progress as the climbers grabbed their chances between spells of poor weather. This phase saw the two teams in open competition on the face, each determined to establish an advantage. The Germans referred to themselves as the steamroller, and more often their relentless team approach took them into the lead, leaving Harlin's team to catch up and sometimes forge ahead with bursts of individual determination and skill. While the rivalry was intense, it was mitigated by moments of cooperation and friendship.

The storm raged until 25 February, smothering the face and piling snow knee-deep around Kleine Scheidegg. With climbing out of the question, the two teams kept their distance. The Germans holed up in the Stöckli while Harlin and his group passed much of the time in the Gaststube and at the hotel bar. Back in Britain, the prospects for climbing seemed so remote that I had joined John Cleare on a winter survival course based at Glenmore Lodge, an outdoor sports centre in the Cairngorms in the Scottish Highlands. Our assignment required us to spend two nights in a snow hole, which somehow felt appropriate at the time.

On the 25th, a Friday, the weather eased enough for the Germans to consider returning to the face. Haag was reluctant, feeling that the conditions were still too poor, with an angry sky and a bitter west wind. In a testy conversation, Lehne insisted that they should make a start, and Haag gave in. As the eight Germans crossed the slopes below the face, Haag's misgivings appeared justified. Hupfauer was leading on skis, while the others – heavily laden – followed on foot. Slabs of snow broke away beneath Hupfauer's skis and slid down the slope, at one point even carrying him down for a few metres. These were classic avalanche warnings and Haag and Hupfauer exchanged glances as if to say they should turn back. Pride and the fear of losing face kept them going, and the party of eight reached the Vorbau without mishap.

Conditions at the Vorbau were savage, with violent updraughts bringing clouds of powder snow surging around them. The Germans had intended to collect the equipment they had stashed at mid-height and haul it to the top of the Vorbau but they modified their plans. Instead, they climbed with their rucksacks to an ice cave they had previously spotted near the Eigerwand station. They reached it by the evening and all eight squeezed in for the night.

At Kleine Scheidegg Harlin was watching the Germans with concern. He was impressed that they were prepared to return to the face in such challenging conditions and aware that they were gaining an advantage by doing so. In the morning of 26 February, although the weather was no better, he decided that his team should try to catch up. He, Haston and Kor set out for the face but were still some way short when they saw a massive avalanche sweep across their path ahead. Without further ado, they returned to Kleine Scheidegg, assuring themselves that the Germans would be unable to make any progress either.

In fact, the Germans spent the day enlarging their bivouac, hacking out a space that was ten metres long and two wide and high enough in places to stand up. They named it the *Eispalast*, the Ice Palace, and celebrated with two rounds of cognac. On 27 February the storms abated enough for the Germans to start up the First Band. Golikow led the first pitch, belayed by Haag, and found the rock smooth and compact, reminding them of the limestone walls of the Kaiser or Wetterstein, the popular rock-climbing areas along the German–Austrian border.

These were the same problems Kor and Haston had encountered. But whereas Kor had been able to take advantage of his Yosemite hardware, Golikow was using soft-steel pitons that bent as he attempted to hammer them into the narrow cracks. Golikow climbed fifteen metres and Haag took over, climbing a further fifteen metres before calling it a day. While Haag felt satisfied with what they had achieved, Strobel had been watching in frustration from below. He was impatient to climb, but Golikow and Haag had been occupied on the same pitch all day. In a disgruntled journal entry, he noted that this was not the speedy climbing he was accustomed to, and that he was feeling 'small and insignificant' at the foot of the face.

Meanwhile, the other five Germans descended to fetch the supplies that had been lodged halfway up the Vorbau and hauled them up to the Ice Palace. That night, in a significant shift of strategy for the Germans, all five returned to Kleine Scheidegg, leaving Haag, Strobel and Golikow on the face. Haag and Lehne recognised that it would take several more days to climb the First Band and decided it would be sensible for the support climbers to bide their time in comfort at the Stöckli instead of consuming valuable supplies on the face.

Although Harlin could see the Germans at work on the First Band that day, he still hesitated. He had been deterred by Haston and Kor's trials in their bivouac below the First Band and was reluctant to resume the climb until better weather returned. That afternoon there was a promising forecast and Harlin decided that they should return to the face the next day. From my point of view this was excellent timing, as I was on my way back to Kleine Scheidegg at last. I had stayed in touch with Bonington from the Cairngorms and it was clear, with the two teams on the face, that the story was taking off. I caught the sleeper train to London, leaving John Cleare to cover the two-night stay in a snow hole by himself. I arrived in Kleine Scheidegg that afternoon and went to look for Bonington in his bedroom. I opened the door to see the prostrate forms of Haston and Kor on his bed. They stirred and told me they were attempting to sleep before departing for the face at midnight. Their loaded rucksacks were leaning against the bed and I withdrew.

Haston and Kor, accompanied by Bonington, left at 2.30 a.m. on 28 February. The tracks made by the Germans the day before had been obliterated and they had to break trail afresh, alternating in the lead and navigating by the slender beam from their head torches. Once at the Vorbau, Haston led up the fixed ropes on his Jumars, finding a rhythm after an ungainly start. Dawn broke as they reached the top and Bonington held back to take photographs. It was fully light by the time they reached the foot of the First Band.

A short distance away was the Ice Palace. It seemed churlish to ignore the Germans, so Haston and Kor walked over to the entrance, to be greeted by the enticing aroma of coffee. Haag offered them a cup while beside him Golikow and Strobel were preparing to resume climbing on the First Band. Behind them stretched the ice cave, with equipment neatly stacked along the walls. Kor remembered the size of the cave and how the Germans 'had all the goodies imaginable – they had special little shovels, they looked like little kiddies' shovels, to use on a sand pile'. He and Haston finished their coffee and returned to the foot of their route up the First Band, where Bonington was just arriving. They told him about the Ice Palace so Bonington took a look for himself, telling Haag: 'Wonderful, wonderful.'

Bonington returned to the First Band, where Haston and Kor were already at work. After taking more photographs, Bonington set to work digging out a snow hole that would provide an improvement on the wretched bivouac Haston and Kor had endured. He did not have a shovel and spent half an hour hacking into a bank of compacted snow with his ice axe. He remembered the shovels in the German ice cave that Kor had seen and wondered whether he should ask to borrow one. He did not want to be in the Germans' debt, and he was uncertain how Harlin would react. But after another ten minutes' hard labour, common sense prevailed and he returned to the Germans' ice cave. (Harlin's team generally used the term 'snow hole' for their accommodation, the Germans used 'ice cave', and we have preserved that nomenclature.)

Golikow and Strobel had departed, leaving Haag there alone. When Bonington asked to borrow a shovel, the joker in Haag asserted itself. Haag affected surprise that Bonington's team had not thought of bringing a shovel, and insisted that he could not possibly lend him one without consulting his colleagues. 'I shall be talking to them on the walkie-talkie in an hour or so,' Bonington recalled him saying. 'I shall let you know.'

A discomfited Bonington withdrew. A few minutes later Haag arrived at the snow hole and handed Bonington a shovel, accompanied by a grin and an invitation to a coffee cognac when he had dug out his snow hole. They chatted for a while and Bonington returned to his task.

Thirty metres above him, Haston and Kor had returned to the high-point they had established eight days before. Kor was later to feel that somehow the Germans had obtained the better line up the First Band – but noted that whereas they eventually used eight bolts for direct aid, he used none. 'I just assumed they really weren't that good direct-aid climbers.'

It would in fact have been hard for any Alpine climbers to match Kor's skills, as he proved when he embarked on the next section of rock, a mosaic of shallow cracks that looked impassable. Haston watched in awe from a sling belay as Kor placed and moved his pitons with a precision bordering on artistry. After three hours Kor secured his belay with a bolt – one of two he used for protection on the First Band – and waited in his slings as Haston followed. As the second, it was Haston's task to remove Kor's pitons as he climbed the pitch, returning them to Kor so that he could use them again – a procedure followed throughout the climb. Haston was so absorbed in his work that he barely noticed when it started to snow. Then, as night follows day, a sprindrift (powder snow) avalanche enveloped them, followed by another and another. Both men hunched up in a bid to protect themselves but it was to no avail, and when Haston tried to call up to Kor his mouth filled with snow.

It was time to descend. Somehow, as they juggled their climbing and abseil ropes, Haston got into a muddle. He was halfway down his abseil when his rope jammed and he flipped upside down. With fresh avalanches pouring over him, he spent ten minutes trying to free himself, then called to ask Bonington if the Germans would lend him a knife. Bonington returned with a knife which he tied to Haston's rope. Haston had a further struggle to untie the knife with his freezing fingers and sever the correct rope. When he finally touched down beside Bonington both of them knew it had been a narrow escape. Of the three climbers, Kor appeared the most shaken and announced that he was returning to Scheidegg. With notable resilience, Haston and Bonington stayed to enlarge their snow hole.

Meanwhile, the Germans were making good progress. Strobel, delighted to be released from his ennui, took the lead, seconded by Golikow, and climbed a further twenty-five metres. At first they did their best to ignore the snow but finally returned to the Ice Palace, where Golikow – displaying the same homing instinct as Kor – announced that he too was descending to Kleine Scheidegg. Haag had been watching both pairs of climbers and shared Haston's admiration for Kor, whom he described as a cheerful and modest young man with a 'lanky charm'. But Haag remained alive to the competition between the teams, reckoning that whoever was first to the top of the First Band would have the choice of routes at the First Icefield.

Earlier in the day Harlin had hoped to carry a load of food to the foot of the First Band. He had a new partner for the trek: none other than Don Whillans, who had arrived from Leysin to assist Bonington in his photographic duties. Whillans had long been sceptical towards Harlin and his projects, considering him – in his typically forthright phrase – a bullshitter, but as he was being paid by the *Weekend Telegraph* he was able to put his doubts to one side. Harlin had hoped to tempt him into joining the climb, but Whillans did his best to restrict his help to a minimum. He did agree to assist Harlin that morning but when they encountered the powder snow pouring down the Vorbau they dumped their loads and headed back to Kleine Scheidegg. 'It wasn't really too good up there,' Harlin told me once he had returned.

I included Harlin's remark in a short report I wrote for the *Telegraph* that evening, beginning: 'Bad weather hampered the two attempts on the unclimbed "direct" route on the North Face of the Eiger today. Driving snow hit the face at two p.m. GMT . . .' It was my first report and brought me the experience of consigning my precious words to one of the copytakers who staffed Fleet Street, mostly men who would patiently type as I dictated to them from the hotel telephone cabin. The copytakers were gradually superseded by such hi-tech developments as telexes and fax machines; but the notion of keying your words on a laptop and pressing a button which transmitted it instantly to the newspaper was beyond imagination.

The next day, 1 March, climbing came to a halt. When Haston and Bonington peered out of their snow hole they were almost overwhelmed by spindrift avalanches. At Kleine Scheidegg, Harlin reckoned they were the largest he had ever seen. Haston and Bonington continued to work on the snow hole until midday, when it was large enough for three people and high enough for anyone but Kor to stand up. Avalanches were still tumbling down the face and it was snowing as well, and they decided to return to Kleine Scheidegg. From the foot of the Vorbau, they descended directly to Alpiglen to avoid the avalanche risk on the slopes below the face.

In the German snow hole, Haag and Strobel stayed put, doing their best to block the entrance and retreating to the back of the cave. Haag wrote that Harlin urged him in a radio call – of which I was previously unaware – to descend 'for the sake of your life and your health'. Haag resisted, later writing that he was forming a relationship with the face and his anxiety was receding, to be replaced with 'a curiosity to see how it played out'.

The Germans were thus in position to make an early start when the next day, 2 March, dawned fair. Haag and Strobel were climbing at 7 a.m. Haag, who was leading, encountered the same difficulties as his colleagues: hard, compact rock and ice-filled cracks that he had to clear with his fingers. At the top of the pitch loomed an ice-plastered corner capped by a massive overhang. Below him, out of sight under more overhangs, Strobel was once again nurturing dark thoughts about how slowly they were progressing – about as fast, he reckoned, as the small hand on a clock face. Above him Haag was finding the climbing more and more testing. When he reached the overhang he hammered a piton a few millimetres into a crack. He inserted a second piton higher up and was attaching a karabiner when the first piton flew out. He fell twelve metres before being held on his rope. As he dangled free, he saw that his hand was bleeding and felt a searing pain across his buttocks.

Below him, even though he had effectively saved Haag's life, Strobel had noticed only a slight tug on the rope. When Haag shouted that he had just taken a fall, Strobel – showing a distinct lack of sympathy – told him to hurry up and get on climbing as they still had an hour of daylight left. A shaken Haag ignored his advice and descended to the Ice Palace, to find that Lehne and Schnaidt had arrived from Kleine Scheidegg. The Germans had climbed another twenty-five metres in the day and reckoned they were forty metres from the top of the First Band.

While the Germans had made good progress, Harlin's team had not climbed at all. Harlin and Kor returned to the face at midday – Harlin's first visit of the climb, apart from the occasion when he had retreated because of the avalanche risk. Then Harlin decided on a change of strategy. Instead of climbing, he and Kor set about enlarging the snow hole at the foot of the First Band. Haston and Bonington had told Harlin about the Ice Palace and he had got the point. By remaining on the face the Germans were able to resume climbing as soon as the weather permitted, and Harlin – previously so disparaging about the German tactics – resolved to do likewise.

Harlin's new approach meant that he needed more bivouac equipment and he asked me to order this from an equipment store in Lucerne run by a Swiss Alpinist, Max Eiselin, who six years earlier had led the first ascent of Dhaulagiri, the seventh highest mountain. Harlin told me that he still intended to remain true to his original concept for the climb. If and when good weather arrived, he would revert to Alpine tactics 'and make a summit push from wherever our high-point is at that time'.

The change of tactics raised another problem. If Harlin's team was to emulate the Germans' approach, how could they do so with just three men? Here a transition was already under way. Bonington, officially the *Weekend Telegraph* photographer, had already been co-opted as a member of the climbing team when – at the cost to his self-esteem – he had borrowed the Germans' shovel and spent a day excavating a snow hole. Before long Bonington's role as climber would expand further. Bonington also gave a clue to his true feelings during his conversations with Haag, who later recorded that Bonington had praised the German strategy as 'better than Harlin's' and had said that it was sensible for the two teams to work together because the climb was so dangerous.

Harlin told me about the new tactics in a radio conversation later that day. Like the Germans, Harlin had equipped his team with walkie-talkies so that they could communicate between Kleine Scheidegg and the face. Ours were large, clunky affairs with a metre-long antenna which only worked in line of sight. They were powered by batteries and proved frustratingly unreliable, and were supplemented with new and equally unreliable models several times – on one occasion Harlin purchased a set from someone he met on a train to Interlaken. But they enabled the climbers to liaise with each other and Harlin to provide information for my daily reports. Harlin set a schedule for four calls a day, to be made at 7.45 a.m., 11.45 a.m., 3.45 p.m. and 7.45 p.m. We also started recording the calls on a cumbersome reel-to-reel tape recorder that predated even cassette machines; Harlin was shooting 8mm movie film on the face and hoped to combine film and recordings in a documentary about the climb. That evening, after talking to Harlin, I led my report with Haag's fall. I predicted that he was unlikely to climb the following day, and noted (in the fourth paragraph) that the Germans were now fifteen metres higher on the First Band than Harlin's team, who had spent the day at work on their bivouac site.

By that time, my duties were beginning to expand. I remember that Harlin appeared guarded towards me at first, as if weighing me up. But once he felt I had passed muster, I presume, he accepted me not merely as a reporter but also as a member of his team. He would ask my opinion on how to deal with the *Telegraph*, how to handle the other journalists who were beginning to assemble at Kleine Scheidegg, and how to deal with the German group. Eventually, I effectively became the base camp manager, coordinating communications and logistics, and was gratified that Harlin was willing to trust me in this way.

Another of my tasks was to ship Bonington's film to the *Daily Telegraph* in London. In the twenty-first century his images would be downloaded and dispatched by pressing the 'Send' button. In the 1960s, it meant driving with the film to Zürich airport – a three-hour journey – and freighting the film to London, just as Low had done. Harlin had recruited as courier a cheerful young Canadian woman, Joan Matthews, from Leysin. On 2 March, making her second trip to Zürich, she took the train to Grindelwald and picked up one of our hire cars. She stopped at Max Eiselin's store in Lucerne to collect the equipment I had ordered and continued to Zürich airport. On her way back she was overtaking another car at 60 mph when it pulled out and pushed her into a ditch. The hire car was a write-off but she emerged from the wreckage with nothing worse than a scratched finger. She told me all this in a telephone call at 7 p.m., adding that she hoped I had insured her to drive the car (I had).

My overriding reaction was relief that Joan had not been injured. Equally concerned was Haston, who had been taking what may be described as a romantic interest in Joan. She had telephoned me from Grindelwald and so, because the last train had departed, he skied down there in the dark to offer his consolation. Not long afterwards we decided to strengthen the courier team and Wendy Bonington arrived in Kleine Scheidegg, boosting her husband's morale and reducing the load on Joan, who came through her ordeal unscathed.

On 3 March, Harlin was able to put his new strategy to good use. He and Kor emerged from the enlarged snow hole to good weather and they started climbing at 7.30 a.m. Just fifteen metres of the First Band remained to be climbed and by 10 a.m. Kor was at the top.

The next obstacle, seventy-five metres above them, was the Second Band. It looked less problematic than the First Band and a gully system appeared to offer a route through it. Harlin took over the lead and started up a steep ice gully immediately above the First Band. He found the ice worryingly thin and after climbing twenty

metres fixed his rope in place and abseiled back down. He told Kor
that, rather than climb any more that day, they should safeguard
the 100-metre length of 7mm Perlon rope that stretched down the
First Band. It hung clear of the rock for much of the way and was
already showing signs of wear. They fixed a second length of 7mm
alongside it to provide a double rope for climbers who would be
ascending with their loads.

The Germans, climbing fifty metres to the right, reached the top
of the First Band that day too. Following their principle of rotating
their climbers, Lehne and Schnaidt had taken over the lead and by
8.30 a.m. Lehne had climbed the overhang where Haag had fallen.
The remaining forty metres to the top of the First Band took him
another nine hours of climbing. Lehne ignored the plan whereby
the team that reached the top of the First Band first would drop the
other a rope: he had been less inclined than Haag to cooperate with
the Americans and was not about to ask for their help. Above the
First Band, at the far side of a twenty-metre sheet of ice, Lehne
spotted a recess that could provide a bivouac site. But he did not
have his crampons and had to turn back. He and Schnaidt returned
to the Ice Palace where Haag and Strobel had been waiting all
day.

Having climbed alongside each other, intermittently, for the past
twelve days, the two teams had reached the top of the First Band
on the same day. If this was a race, honours were roughly even. In
2014, this was an important point, which addressed the question of
whether the American team had better climbers. Hupfauer considered the two teams equals and Rosenzopf added: 'The best
indication that we were similar in ability was that on the First
Band we went up parallel lines and arrived on top at approxi-
mately the same time.' In 1966, however, the statistics confronting
the teams were hardly encouraging. They had climbed just over one
hundred metres in twelve days – against Harlin's estimate that,

given good weather, the entire ascent could be done in ten days. Above them, a further one thousand metres waited to be climbed.

Both teams were keen to push on. The next morning – 4 March – the Germans were in a position to do so but Harlin's team was not, as the result of a series of misunderstandings the previous day. While Harlin and Kor were climbing, Bonington, Whillans and Haston – who had safely returned from Grindelwald – had carried loads to the foot of the Vorbau. Whillans headed back to Kleine Scheidegg, leaving Bonington and Haston to replace Harlin and Kor on the face. At least, that was the plan. But Harlin and Kor were out of earshot and Bonington somehow presumed that they would prefer to stay in the snow hole that night and resume in the lead the next morning. So he and Haston followed Whillans back to Kleine Scheidegg.

Above them, as dusk approached, Harlin finished fixing the ropes on the First Band and returned to the snow hole. Kor had gone ahead of him and was already packing his rucksack, clearly intent on returning to Kleine Scheidegg, irrespective of whether Bonington and Haston were going to take over on the face. Kor, it was evident, was developing a liking for the ambience of Kleine Scheidegg, which included courting the demure young postmistress at the railway post office. Harlin judged it futile to stand in his way and the two descended together. Once back at Kleine Scheidegg Harlin told me they had come down because there was 'a certain amount of high cirrus about' – a reliable sign of impending bad weather, he explained.

Meanwhile, the Germans had been watching the American comings and goings with some surprise. Haag had reported his meeting with Harlin on 20 February, relating how Harlin had claimed the moral high ground by saying that he intended to climb with a team of just three. 'And then, "Hoopla",' said Votteler in 2014. 'We see Harlin, Haston, Kor – then Bonington and Whillans.' Only later did they learn that Bonington and Whillans were supposedly there as a photographic team – and even then they were not fully convinced.

Now, on 4 March, there were further mishaps. So while there were four Germans on the face who were ready to climb (Golikow had returned to Kleine Scheidegg), there were none from Harlin's team. Burdened with guilt over their failure to replace Harlin and Kor, Bonington and Haston left Kleine Scheidegg with heavy rucksacks at 2.30 a.m. At 9 a.m. Haston reached the top of the First Band intent on climbing the ice gully where Harlin had turned back. He lowered a 100-metre rope and slid down a pair of Jumars for Bonington to use. But Bonington had neglected to secure the end of the rope and the clamps bounded past him, coming to rest halfway down the Vorbau. Then Haston dropped a camera he had borrowed from Wendy Bonington. Disheartened, he abseiled back to the foot of the First Band where Bonington had retrieved the Jumars and they retired to the snow cave to brew a drink.

Bonington and Haston decided to cut their losses and spend the rest of the day consolidating the team's position at the First Band. They were joined by Harlin and Kor and all four ferried the equipment stashed at the foot of the Vorbau to the ice cave. Then Kor hauled four rucksacks to the top of the First Band. That night they settled into the snow cave, ready to push on towards the Second Band in the morning. Kor particularly remembered Harlin's meticulous approach to snow-hole living. 'He was very organised as far as how you get in the cave, you take off your boots, brush them off, take your parka off and brush it off. Everything had a spot it had to go – he had all these things thought out.'

The Germans had mixed fortunes that day too. They hauled supplies to the top of the First Band and Strobel crossed the sheet of ice to the bivouac site Lehne had spotted. He and Haag hacked out enough space for them to lie down, while Lehne and Schnaidt returned to the Ice Palace. The Germans had difficulty communicating with each other as their radios had stopped working altogether, and they made themselves hoarse shouting to each other. Strobel, keen as ever to push ahead, lamented that he climbed just twenty metres horizontally during the day. But they now had an important lead. They had established their second bivouac site, the Villa Hammerschmidt, named after the residence of the German *Bundespräsident* in Bonn, then the West German capital (it also evoked the hammering required to carve out the cave). Harlin's team were still in their snow cave below the First Band, and Haag looked forward to consolidating the Germans' lead the next day.

Harlin's team had a miserable night. It snowed heavily, driving spindrift through gaps around the entrance, and they had to keep getting up to brush it off their clothes and equipment. In the morning fresh avalanches were pouring down. I radioed at 7.45 a.m. on 5 March to report that the snow was likely to continue for the next two days. Harlin proposed that Bonington and Kor should return to Kleine Scheidegg while he and Haston remained in the snow hole, ready – like the Germans – to continue as soon as the weather improved. Kor needed no second asking and was back at Kleine Scheidegg by midday, followed an hour later by Bonington. Haston and Harlin spent the rest of the day trying to block the entrance with the mail bags they had used to carry food and equipment.

In three days, Harlin's team had done no climbing at all – and the Germans took advantage. While Kor and Bonington were descending on 5 March, Golikow, Rosenzopf, Votteler and Hupfauer were carrying more loads from Kleine Scheidegg. They reached the foot of the First Band at lunchtime, pausing to greet Harlin and Haston in their snow hole – Rosenzopf, the last in line, doing so with the broadest grin. Above them their four colleagues – Haag, Lehne, Strobel and Schnaidt – had been enlarging the Villa

Hammerschmidt, while Haag found time to savour the avalanches pouring past: 'It was like sitting behind the Niagara Falls.' He and his three colleagues stayed in the Villa Hammerschmidt that night while the other four remained in the Ice Palace. The two groups amused themselves by exchanging messages tied to a nylon cord. The Villa Hammerschmidt four felt sufficiently buoyed to join Haag in singing an American song from his repertoire: 'You Are My Sunshine.'

That night, Haag wrote a letter to Barbara on a dismantled cig-arette pack that reflected his elation. He said he wanted to reassure her about the climb. 'The face is not black and gruesome, but glows in all colours in the evening sun. I like it very much here. Apart from the occasional frostnip on my toes, I am doing very well. We are marching up the wall ... and are getting along very well with the Americans. It is very good that they are here because otherwise we would be considered mad in mountaineering circles because we are taking so long. But believe me, this is one of the most difficult and beautiful things there is.'

Haag told Barbara that he and Strobel had climbed well the previous day and that they were 'halfway to the Spider ... The end is in sight and we will come through for sure.' He ended by saying he was looking forward to a pullover she was knitting for him, 'and to Danny, and to seeing you soon'. Danny was the name they had given to their unborn child, who was due in three months' time.

As usual when writing to Barbara, Haag signed himself: '*Dein Pierrot*' – 'Your Pierrot'. The letter reached Barbara at home about a week later – having been taken to Kleine Scheidegg by Golikow, who descended on 9 March, and posted to her by Frey.

For the Germans, their progress on 5 March demonstrated the effectiveness of the plan Haag had described to Harlin in the Kleine Scheidegg meeting, even if it did not fulfil all the criteria he had set out. He told Harlin that the German team was composed of equals who would share the leading and support work in equal measure. But some were proving more equal than others, as the team began to divide into the climbers and the carriers. 'We were finding out who was leading and who was bringing up the rear,' Hupfauer said in 2013. 'Some were hogging the lead and said they wanted to stay in front.'

Hupfauer was winning renown as the expert in creating bivouac sites and was acquiring some spectacular blisters from carving out ice caves. Lehne later praised his doggedness in chopping out water ice and even the underlying rock – 'we are altar boys by comparison'. Schnaidt, when not assisting Hupfauer, became the load master, usually supported by Rosenzopf and Votteler, who became collectively known as Transport Command.

The Germans clearly had an advantage over Harlin's team in numbers, which helped to shape their strategy in another way. Harlin's original plan overwhelmingly depended on his belief that a ten-day spell of clear weather would arrive, enabling him to make his Alpine-style ascent. The German attempt, in stark contrast, was not predicated on the weather. Hupfauer recalled that they had started out in bad weather and did not allow the forecasts to determine their decisions. Although Harri Frey was relaying them to the face – Hupfauer recalled 'a couple of forecasts from Zürich' – they were not a dominant factor. If the weather was good, they climbed: if it was poor, they didn't. In any case, the bivouac and transport teams were able to continue their work, even if the lead climbers couldn't, which meant that the steamroller kept on going.

On 6 March, Haston emerged from the snow hole to find that the weather forecast I had given – which had induced Bonington and Kor to return to Kleine Scheidegg – was wrong. It was a scintillating morning, with a flawless blue sky and wraiths of mist lingering over the Alpiglen meadows. Haston and Harlin ascended the rope to the top of the First Band and Haston started up the gully in which Harlin had turned back. The climbing was precarious and he found himself balancing on ice-plated slabs with the front points of his crampons and having to contend with the drag of his rope as well. He was relieved to find a stance where he could belay and bring Harlin up.

A short distance to his right the German team was hauling equipment up to the Villa Hammerschmidt. This time Golikow was acting as gangmaster, calling out to his team-mates so that they pulled in rhythm. Haston shouted a greeting and Golikow responded, 'It's a hard life' – four words in English that became his catchphrase. Haston pressed on, leading another fifteen metres over steep, thin ice with minimal protection, finally reaching a fifty-degree snow slope where he could relax. He called up Harlin who led through for another 140 feet, taking him close to the foot of the Second Band. Harlin plunged his axe into a bank of snow below an overhang and found a cave offering a perfect bivouac site. Ahead, the route through the Second Band looked easier than they had expected. Below them, Kor had returned to the face and bivouacked in the snow hole at the foot of the First Band.

The Germans were moving fast too. In two hours Haag and Strobel climbed eighty metres above the Villa Hammerschmidt, taking them to the foot of the Second Band. There they had to stop as they did not have any more ropes to fix in place. The support team spent the day hauling the equipment bombs up the First Band and from there towards the Villa Hammerschmidt. In the end, Haag and Strobel gave up waiting for the fixed ropes and descended to help with the hauling. That evening there was some complaining with six climbers squeezed into the Villa Hammerschmidt, while Votteler and Schnaidt descended to the Ice Palace and spent the night there.

Thanks largely to Haston's skill on the ice pitches, Harlin's team had all but caught up with the Germans. As the good weather continued, the two teams spent the next day, 7 March, climbing neck and neck. Haston led off again, climbing a crisp, firm snow slope that enabled him to savour the wild landscape of the face and the landmarks he knew from his previous visits. He reached the foot of the Second Band and saw that Golikow had started up a predominantly rock line to the right of the gully system that Harlin's team preferred. Haston was setting up his belay stance when Golikow, who had just called out 'It's a hard life', took a fall, slithering down the rock into a snow bank at the foot of the pitch. He stood up with a grin. After a discussion, he and Lehne crossed to the gully system where Harlin was about to set off.

The two teams were now climbing alongside each other, at times almost within touching distance. Then the two routes converged to the point where the four climbers jostled for space on the same stance. As Harlin led up a snow-filled chimney on the left, Lehne aid-climbed brittle overhanging rock to the right; Haag wrote later that he was impressed at Harlin's 'mastery' in overcoming the chimney. Meanwhile Haston and Golikow joshed over the race taking place above them. When Harlin arrived at the top of the pitch a few minutes ahead of Lehne, Haston told Golikow that he owed him a beer. They both followed up their respective pitches and when Haston arrived Lehne pushed a piece of chocolate into his mouth – a gesture of friendship that caught Haston unawares, particularly as it came from the customarily impassive Lehne.

I had been watching these events from Kleine Scheidegg and reckoned I had seen enough to compile my report for the *Daily Telegraph*. I noted that Harlin and Haston had advanced a few metres beyond Lehne and Golikow and wrote: 'British-American

team takes 15-foot lead in Eiger climb', deploying an irony that
may have been lost on some *Telegraph* readers. I was premature in
writing my report, as Haston was not finished. While Lehne and
Golikow abseiled back to the Villa Hammerschmidt, Haston was
not ready to stop. He led another pitch and reached the top of the
Second Band in the gathering darkness, to be rewarded with the
breathtaking vision of a crimson sun sinking into a cloud inversion
that filled the valley. Harlin joined him and they had a long and
frustrating search for somewhere to bivouac, finally scratching a
ledge into the ice and pulling their bivouac tent around them. They
had no food and instead brewed a succession of hot drinks, more
than content with what they had achieved and still savouring memories of the Eiger sunset. They were ahead of the Germans.

On the morning of 8 March, Haston and Harlin looked forward
to extending their lead. Below them, Haag and Strobel were determined to catch up. They had bivouacked in a small additional ice
cave, eighty metres above the Villa Hammerschmidt, which they
named the Wilhelm-Tell-Höhle – the William Tell Cave. After an
early start they reached the rope that Haston and Harlin had left
on their last pitch the previous night. As Haag saw it, the two
teams had a tacit agreement to use each other's fixed ropes.
Although this had not been voiced at the Kleine Scheidegg meeting
on 20 February, Haag felt that it was in the spirit of the occasion –
and, anyway, the Americans had used the Germans' ropes on their
first day on the Vorbau. Haag and Strobel now invoked that agreement, tacit or otherwise, and set off up the Americans' rope.

Haston and Harlin were still sorting out their equipment when
Strobel bid them 'Good morning' and headed for a gully they had
intended to follow themselves. To their further dismay, Golikow
arrived, plunged his ice axe into a bank of snow and discovered an
ice cave that they had missed during their search for a bivouac site
the previous night.

Rather than follow Strobel, Harlin and Haston examined an alternative route up a chimney to the left of the gully but it was clogged with snow. As the morning slipped away, they took stock. They still had no food, their equipment was in chaos and several important items were still in the snow hole below the First Band with Kor and Bonington, who had returned to the face the previous day. They decided to spend the rest of the day consolidating their position and their supplies. Bonington and Kor brought up loads from the First Band and joined them in hacking out a new snow hole at the top of the Second Band. By the evening they had divided their supplies into five loads, but found that they were still short of several important items, and Kor needed no second invitation to fetch them from Kleine Scheidegg.

Meanwhile, Strobel and Haag had made a crucial advance. The first pitch above the Americans' bivouac site looked daunting, to say the least. Forty-eight years on it was engrained in Strobel's memory. 'It was a steep rock wall, covered with water ice, in places hollow, leading in one pitch to the coveted Second Icefield. Peter Haag said that we had to risk this pitch. We exchanged a long, hard look. We decided to draw matchsticks to decide who was to lead it.' In fact, they tossed a karabiner, which had a number on one side and a letter on the other. Strobel lost.

'I had a terrible fear to lead but I had to do it,' Strobel recalled. Although he placed some pitons he felt they had only 'moral value'– a phrase climbers use when their protection is poor and illusory – and instead relied on 'iron will and fighting spirit' to claw his way to the top.

They were now on the easier ground of the Second Icefield. With the Flatiron to their left, they made rapid progress before halting at a steep buttress below the Flatiron's crest. Once again Haag and Strobel were ahead of their supply team and they prepared for an open bivouac, without sleeping bags, on a tiny platform with only a low ridge of rock to provide shelter from the wind. Haag, delighting in the canopy of stars that sparkled above them, reckoned the Germans were now a full day ahead of the Americans.

Two hundred metres below, the men of Transport Command were feeling elated too. They had been hauling supplies all day, doing their best to contain their anger when the bombs became stuck. As Hupfauer later wrote, those pulling from above blamed the ones below for not attaching the bombs properly, while those below thought the ones above should be pulling harder. 'I was the one who cursed the most because I spent so long waiting – and the bombs dislodged stones that it was hard to dodge.' Meanwhile, a digging team – this time excluding Hupfauer – had created a new snow hole in the location found by Golikow which they named the *Kristallsalon*, the Crystal Saloon. After the final load had been safely hauled, Hupfauer joined his team-mates there and was greeted with the news that Haag and Strobel were near the top of the Flatiron. His anger dissipated, Hupfauer fired a signal rocket in celebration. It soared away from the face in a cascade of sparks that momentarily outshone the stars.

On 9 March Harlin's team awoke to a sense of crisis. The Germans were now two hundred metres ahead and there was no time to be lost. The Germans had left a rope on Strobel's ice-pitch above their bivouac site which – in accordance with Haag's tacit agreement, and the fact that the Germans had used their rope the previous day – they felt licensed to use. Kor, who had left Kleine Scheidegg at 2 a.m., had joined them and the four were soon at the foot of the Second Icefield. Here they had originally considered following the line to the left of the Flatiron which Harlin had favoured, but the obvious route to the Death Bivouac, the one the Germans had taken, stretched up invitingly to the right. Haston led up it, front-pointing up the firm frozen snow, fixing ropes with Harlin as he went. He was now on the classic 1938 route and

Haston relished using the battered pitons that had been hammered into the rock by climbers over the years. He and Harlin swapped leads until, late in the afternoon, they came level with Haag and Strobel near the crest of the Flatiron. Shortly afterwards Golikow and Lehne joined them there, too.

After climbing eighty metres, the two Germans had another frustrating day, as they had once again outstripped their supply line and run out of rope. While Golikow descended to deliver Haag's film – and his letter to Barbara – to Harri Frey at the Stöckli, Haag, Lehne and Strobel started excavating yet another ice cave to the right of the top of the Flatiron. Haag named it the Rulaman Bivouac, after a caveman in a popular nineteenth-century novel written following the first Neanderthal finds and Darwin's exposition of the theory of evolution. Their clothes were saturated with sweat from the day's exertions and then froze as the temperature plummeted inside the cave. Alongside them, Lehne did not even have a sleeping bag but, as Haag observed, he was at least dry.

Harlin's team was not finished. It was almost dark and had started to snow. But Haston was determined to reach the site of the Death Bivouac, where he thought they could dig out a snow hole. He removed his rucksack and set off across a 100-metre stretch of steep crusted snow, cutting steps with his ice axe in his left hand and his ice dagger in the right, and placing just two pitons for protection – one sound chromoly piton and one weak ice screw. As soon as he reached the Death Bivouac he started hacking into a bank of snow. Harlin, Bonington and Kor followed him across and joined him in his efforts, illuminated by the two head torches they had among them. The wires of one had come loose and they took it in turns to hold them against the terminal with their bare hands. Kor remembered 'powder avalanches coming down, it was a bizarre place, it was wild'. Only at midnight was the snow hole large enough for all four to squeeze inside.

Their trials were not over. So far they had brought over two rucksacks, which meant that two were at the far end of the 100-metre traverse. The missing equipment included their stove. Neither Bonington nor Kor appeared keen to fetch it. Bonington pointed out that he was there to take photographs; Kor said his feet were cold and he was worried about frostbite. Without saying a word, Haston departed into the snowstorm with the one functioning head torch. He clipped into the rope but it dipped alarmingly and he was unable to follow the footsteps across the snow. Then he lost his footing and slid on his back towards the drop above the Second Icefield, only too aware how insecure the rope anchors were. The rope held. Haston climbed back up on a Hiebler clamp, used his ice dagger to replace the ice screw that had held his fall, and tightened the rope.

Once at the end of the traverse, Haston peered into the Germans' ice cave. Lehne, hunched over a stove, greeted him with a terse: '*Salut, Dougal.*' Haag – a smoker – gave him some cigarettes for Kor, the only member of Harlin's team who also smoked. Haston retrieved the rucksack containing the stove and set off on the return journey, feeling more confident now that the rope was secured. As he approached the snow hole he heard Harlin anxiously calling out to him. He had been gone for more than an hour and his colleagues' relief was clear when he arrived. He later described the traverse as the wildest he had ever done, all the more memorable for taking place on the North Face of the Eiger in darkness and a storm. 'As an experience it was total.'

Reassured by Haston that the traverse was safe, Harlin set off to fetch the second rucksack and returned an hour later, having paused to pay a social call on the Germans. The four settled into the snow hole to enjoy their hard-won drinks by the light of a candle. The legs of the stove were missing and so Haston held it between his knees; he, Harlin and Bonington sat with their backs against the wall while Kor curled into the remaining space.

1 EIGER NORTH FACE from Kleine Scheidegg

The main diagram shows the lines of the 1966 Eiger Direct, the 1935 Sedlmayr-Mehringer attempt (to Death Bivouac area), and the classic 1938 Heckmair route (see coding at foot of page). The inset diagrams appear on the following pages.

Rope broke here

EIGER DIRECT		classic route	— — — route out of sight
1966	1935 attempt	1938	···· failed attempts

VORBAU

Eigerwand Station ✳

FIRST BAND

Km 4.1 ✳

Stollenloch (Gallery Window) Km 3.8 ✳

SECOND BAND

FIRST ICEFIELD

SECOND ICEFIELD

FLATIRON

THIRD ICEFIELD DB

2

DB = Death Bivouac

CENTRAL PILLAR

SPIDER

FLY

HEADWALL

3

2

US-GB line
German line

Death Bivouac

4th Snow Cave

Rulaman Cave

THIRD ICEFIELD

German Death Bivouac Cave

FLATIRON

SECOND ICEFIELD

Strobel's Ice-pitch

3rd Snow Cave

Kristallsalon

US-GB line (ice chimney)

German line (aid wall)

Wilhelm Tell Cave

SECOND BAND

FIRST ICEFIELD

2nd Snow Cave

Villa Hammerschmidt

US-GB line

German line

FIRST BAND

1st Snow Cave

Eispalast

Eigerwand Station

Gallery Window
Km 4.1

The Lower Face

US-GB activities
German activities

The Upper Face

US-GB activities
German activities | Joint activities
--- route out of sight
.... failed attempts

FLATIRON

German Death Bivouac Cave

4th Snow Cave

Rulaman Cave

Death Bivouac

Kor's Traverse

German failed attempt

Central Pillar

Rope broke here

Bivouac Mar 21-23

SPIDER

4

Fixed ropes

Climbing route

Exit Cracks (1938 route)

Bivouac Mar 22 & 23

FLY

Lower Bivouac Mar 24 ?

Summit Dihedral

Higher bivouac Mar 24

HEADWALL

Summit Icefield

5

3

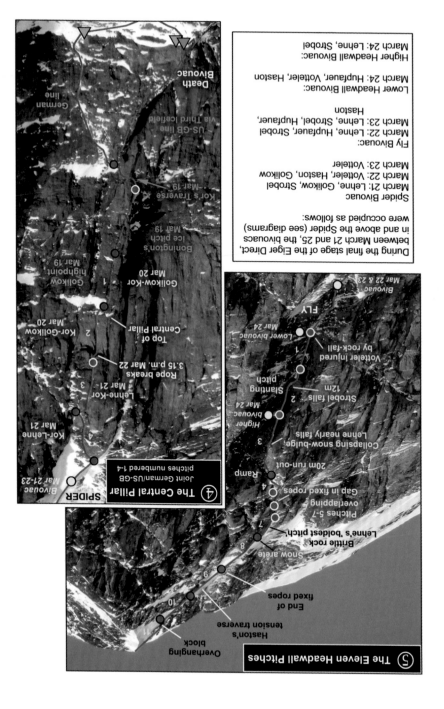

④ The Central Pillar
Joint German/US-GB pitches numbered 1-4

- Kor's Traverse Mar 19
- US-GB line via Third Icefield
- German line
- Death Bivouac
- Bonington's ice pitch Mar 19
- Golikow highpoint Mar 19
- Golikow-Kor Mar 20
- Kor-Golikow Mar 20
- Top of Central Pillar 2
- Rope breaks 3.15 p.m. Mar 22
- Lehne-Kor Mar 21 3
- Kor-Lehne Mar 21 4
- SPIDER
- Bivouac Mar 21-23

⑤ The Eleven Headwall Pitches

- Bivouac Mar 22 & 23
- FLY
- Lower bivouac Mar 24 1
- Votiteler injured by rock-fall
- Strobel falls 2 Slanting pitch 12m
- Higher bivouac Mar 24
- Collapsing snow-bulge; Lehne nearly falls 3
- Ramp
- 20m run-out
- Gap in fixed ropes 4
- Pitches 5-7 overlapping
- Brittle rock Lehne's boldest pitch
- Snow arête 8
- End of fixed ropes 6
- Haston's tension traverse
- Overhanging block 10 11

During the final stage of the Eiger Direct, between March 21 and 25, the bivouacs in and above the Spider (see diagrams) were occupied as follows:

Spider Bivouac
March 21: Lehne, Golikow, Strobel
March 22: Voiteler, Haston, Golikow

Fly Bivouac:
March 22: Lehne, Hupfauer, Strobel
March 23: Lehne, Strobel, Hupfauer, Haston

Lower Headwall Bivouac:
March 24: Hupfauer, Voiteler, Haston

Higher Headwall Bivouac:
March 24: Lehne, Strobel

There was more drama to come. When Haston unscrewed a gas cylinder in the belief that it was empty, a jet of escaping gas caught alight in the flame of the candle. Haston threw the blazing canister at the entrance but missed. Bonington dived for the entrance, then remembered that they were on the edge of a 3000-foot drop. Harlin grabbed the canister and hurled it out of the cave. He scowled at Bonington, muttering darkly about 'inappropriate behaviour'. Haston merely assumed that Bonington's tank-training had kicked in. They fell asleep somewhere between 3 and 4 a.m.

On 10 March both teams awoke to another fine morning. In the Harlin team's snow hole, light was gleaming through the walls. Harlin prodded a hole with his ice axe so that the team could urinate without leaving the cave and discovered that he could see the roofs of Grindelwald, more than two thousand metres below. They also realised that they were perched in the lip of a cornice on the crest of the Flatiron – probably the very location of the 1935 Death Bivouac. At 8.45 a.m. I radioed a promising forecast: a spell of snow followed by at least another day of good weather. Harlin was determined not to fall behind the Germans, but first the climbers needed to tidy the chaos in the snow hole, rehydrate themselves with brews, and redistribute the equipment in the four rucksacks.

Soon after 9 a.m., Strobel and Haag set off up a line of chimneys above and to the right of the Flatiron that led to a small rounded pillar head below a 100-metre rock obelisk known as the Central Pillar, which was the next prominent feature on the face. Strobel, delighted to be climbing at full throttle again, predicted they would bivouac in the Spider that night. But the climbing became harder as the day wore on, and it was afternoon before they reached the foot of the Central Pillar.

Harlin opted for a different route to the foot of the Central Pillar. He had always intended to climb to the left of the Flatiron, perhaps crossing the Third Icefield to follow the Ramp for a pitch before traversing back into a line of gullies that led to the foot of the pillar. Now that they could see the route up close, they reckoned they could climb directly up the Third Icefield alongside the Flatiron and reach the foot of the Central Pillar from there. It was a good call. Haston led up two long but straightforward pitches, his calves straining at the repeated front-pointing, which took him to the top of the Third Icefield. Kor took over up a pitch of steep mixed ground, arriving at the foot of the Central Pillar shortly after Haag and Strobel. Haag observed that Kor looked dishevelled, his anorak and shirt having pulled away from his trousers, exposing the skin of his back. Irrespective of any violations of the climbers' dress code, Kor and Haston had caught the Germans up.

Above the four climbers loomed the Central Pillar – the key to reaching the Spider, now just 250 metres above them. As they stood on the platform at the foot of the pillar, Haston asked Haag what route he intended to take. Haag pointed to a crack system to the right of the pillar which looked straightforward at the start but culminated in an overhanging chimney that was blocked at the top by snow. Haston nodded non-committally. He and Kor abseiled back to the Death Bivouac, fixing ropes as they did so. They arrived to find the snow hole in good order and Harlin already cooking.

Haston delivered his opinion of the German line. 'It looks way out,' he said. 'I wouldn't touch it.' Kor weighed in with a contribution of his own: while Haston was talking to the Germans, he had scrutinised the foot of the Central Pillar and reckoned there was a traverse line across its foot. On the far side, it looked as though a long ice chimney would lead to the top of the pillar. Harlin agreed to his proposal and reckoned it could open the way to a full summit push. It was in an optimistic mood that they tucked into their food.

By then, Bonington was back in Kleine Scheidegg. He reckoned he had taken enough photographs and was keen to dispatch them to the *Telegraph*. He wanted to resist being drawn any further into the role of climber and did not want to be distracted from taking the best photographs he could. He also reasoned that more than three climbers risked becoming a crowd, given the cramped conditions in the snow hole. He took some final shots of Haston and Kor setting off up the Third Icefield. He presumed that the next time he photographed the climbers would be as they approached the summit, maybe in just four days' time. On the way down he stopped to greet the German load-hauling team on the Second Icefield. Votteler persuaded him to help pull up one of the bombs, instructing him in Swabian: '*Komm' und ziag amol*' – 'Come and pull'. Since Bonington did so, Votteler liked to say afterwards that it proved that Swabian was an international language.

Otherwise it was the Germans who were feeling deflated. Strobel swiftly climbed forty metres up the crack system that Haag had pointed out to Haston, and then returned to the platform at the foot of the Central Pillar. From that moment, things began to go wrong. Strobel carved out a bivouac site while Haag hauled a bomb with Lehne, who had joined them. They had started to cook when it began to snow. They had no bivouac sacks and huddled together as the wind buffeted them with increasing force. At 10 p.m. Lehne declared that he had had enough and abseiled down into the night, promising that he would attach a bomb to their rope so that they could haul up their bivouac equipment. But when he signalled to Haag and Strobel to pull the rope, it became tangled and stuck. Haag and Strobel gave up and reached for a bag containing their sleeping bags and several days' rations of food. A clumsy movement by Strobel dislodged the bag and it disappeared into the void.

There was nothing for it but to descend. Haag was looking forward to joining his colleagues in the relative comfort of the Rulaman Bivouac. He was quickly disillusioned. Votteler and Rosenzopf, clearly not best pleased at being woken, indicated a cramped place by the entrance where Haag could sleep. Strobel departed to join Schnaidt and Hupfauer in a second ice cave which they had excavated near the Harlin team's cave at the Death Bivouac. It was Schnaidt's turn to be surprised when at some time after midnight Strobel arrived, covered in ice and with his clothing torn. There was no spare sleeping bag, so Schnaidt said that Strobel could share his. 'We were rather cramped but we managed to sleep,' Schnaidt said in 2013.

The morning of 11 March brought disappointment to both teams. Haag awoke to find he was covered in snow and his clothes frozen solid. In a rare moment of discord, Votteler complained that his colleagues had spent all day in the snow hole but had failed to secure the entrance against the snow. In addition, despite all their best efforts, the Germans were running out of food. They were reluctant to abandon their position but in the end decided that Lehne and Rosenzopf should descend to Kleine Scheidegg to fetch more supplies. Golikow was still there, which left five of the German team on the face.

In their snow hole a short distance away, Harlin, Haston and Kor were engaged in similar deliberations. Although it had stopped snowing, the sky was heavily overcast, confirming a gloomy forecast I had given them at 7.45 a.m. They decided that Kor should go down to Kleine Scheidegg to await the good weather from there. Harlin and Haston would stay in the snow hole, like the Germans, ready to resume climbing as soon as the bad weather ended. They were still in an upbeat mood and reckoned that once good weather returned, they could be at the summit in four days.

It was a forlorn hope. A storm that hit the Eiger proved to be one of the worst of the winter, pinning the eight climbers on the face, unable to move up and unwilling to come down. Both teams ran out of food and Harlin and Haag fell ill. The key question was which team would have the resilience to resume the climb once the bad weather passed.

Chapter Eleven

STORMS BATTER EIGER MEN

When Kor left the snow hole at the Death Bivouac to return to the delights of Kleine Scheidegg on 11 March, he stretched a tent bag over the entrance and fastened it in place with a selection of pitons. It was intended to protect Harlin and Haston from snow and spindrift, and it effectively sealed them in. The snow hole was just large enough for them to lie down side by side but there was no scope for enlarging it, as the walls were already wafer-thin while the rear of the cave consisted of the impenetrable black rock of the Eiger itself, scarred with icy grooves. In their confinement, their senses became attuned to cues and clues from the outside world. They heard Kor's muffled footsteps as he walked away from the snow hole, followed by the whipping of the fixed ropes as he set off down. Before long the storms resumed, bringing the hammering of the wind and the hissing of spindrift avalanches. Occasionally, they would be startled by creaks of the cornice shifting and settling, reminding them that it would eventually split away from the rock and tumble down the face – but not until the spring, they fervently hoped.

The worsening weather, while confirming that there was no immediate prospect of climbing, brought other consequences.

Despite Kor's efforts to block the entrance, every avalanche brought fresh clouds of spindrift bursting past the tent bag. The truth was that the entrance was too large, a consequence of the frenzy with which the snow hole had been dug out two days before. Haston and Harlin adjusted the tent bag and stuffed socks and gloves around it. But still the spindrift spurted in, both via the entrance and trickling down the rock at the rear. Each time Harlin insisted they brush the spindrift away for fear that it would saturate their clothing. On their first night, Haston was woken at 2 a.m. by Harlin calling: 'Christ, Dougal, we've got to get up.' They spent an hour clearing snow before Haston collapsed back into sleep. At 5 a.m. they went through the same routine again.

They faced other difficulties. In order to brew drinks, they had to fill a stove from an unwieldy yellow plastic canister that held a gallon of paraffin. But they had no funnel and it proved an awkward operation. The stove needed to be preheated, which normally required white powdery blocks known as Meta Fuel. They had none of those and Haston used a candle instead. As soon as he rested the stove on the snow its flame dwindled and died because the cold prevented the paraffin from vaporising. Instead, Haston had to hold a candle against the stove. Even finding snow to melt was a problem: apart from spindrift, there was none inside the snow hole, and they had to hack out ice from the floor below the rear wall.

Their drinks were made with two nutritional supplements, Minivit and Calcitonic, which were meant to replenish mineral loss. For food, they consumed the supplies that were intended for the summit push: mostly dried meat, bacon, peanuts and dried fruit. They spent the time alternately dozing and talking, the subject matter ranging as widely as their imaginations allowed. They laid plans to climb in the mountain ranges of the world, from the Himalayas to Alaska. Haston talked about his Celtic ancestry.

They talked about philosophy, women, the meaning of life – and food, including the steaks tartare and the chateaubriands they planned to eat once they were back at Kleine Scheidegg.

By Saturday evening they had to confront another bodily requirement, the need to defecate. Urinating was simple enough: they each used a hole in the ice next to their sleeping bags. Defecating in such a confined space was going to be more problematic, as they had to undo so many layers of clothing as well as find a suitable location in the snow hole. After due discussion they crouched by the entrance, which became gradually rimmed with excrement. They hoped it would not smell in the cold but they were wrong. Their nights were otherwise comfortable enough, even though the temperature touched minus 20°C. They swallowed Ronicol tablets, an anti-frostbite treatment intended to stimulate blood circulation, which Haston calculated would keep his feet warm for four hours. At night he sometimes dreamed there was a third person in the cave with them. He huddled closer against the wall to give him room; when he woke he shifted back into the space he had vacated.

This period of enforced proximity, with its discomfort and excess of intimacy, led Haston to re-evaluate his view of Harlin. He was a complex person, Haston later wrote, someone who liked to hold court to an attentive audience, a dreamer who sometimes believed his dreams were reality. They had some furious rows since first climbing together, leading Haston to suggest that until then 'the basis of our relationship was respect rather than friendship'. But during their incarceration at the Death Bivouac, when 'everything was laid bare', they learned enough about each other to start building a new relationship.

Down at Kleine Scheidegg, we did our best not to feel too guilty about the contrast between conditions in the snow hole and life at the hotel, where snow was driving past the windows and the Eiger was out of sight. Kor was succeeding in his pursuit of the Kleine Scheidegg postmistress, who proved less demure than she appeared. We greeted a range of visitors who included the British equipment dealers Frank Davies and Graham Tiso, Harlin's Leysin friend Larry Ware, and the distinguished figure of Norman Dyhrenfurth, leader of the successful American Everest expedition of 1963. These social duties apart, I had two principal tasks. The first was to write my dispatches for the *Daily Telegraph*. Given that the climbing had stalled, I did my best to keep the story alive with reports of life in a snow hole, but the *Telegraph* devoted less and less space to them each day, with headlines such as 'Eiger Climbers Bivouac in Snow Holes' and 'Storms Batter Eiger Men'. On 14 March the *Telegraph* carried no report at all.

My second duty was to gather weather forecasts and relay them to Harlin via radio calls, which we were making three times a day. By now a whole team was engaged in this: not only myself and Bonington but also several camp followers, who included Joan Matthews – Haston's paramour – and Marie-France Rivière, a journalist and filmmaker from Paris who had become entwined with the team. The group would gather in my room and transmit its findings to Harlin, trying to clarify the differences between the three principal weather centres we were using: London, Geneva and Zürich. Since Geneva was usually more optimistic than Zürich, we relayed its findings first. Of greatest interest to Harlin was a high-pressure system south of Ireland which was supposedly drifting eastward and so would bring the long spell of clear weather he still believed would arrive.

That, in turn, shaped his strategy for staying on the face. In the Germans' two snow caves to his right, the five climbers still on the face were also waiting for the weather to improve. There was a good case to be made for Harlin and Haston to descend and wait in the comfort of Kleine Scheidegg, but Harlin felt that risked losing more time to the Germans. Of crucial interest to Harlin was the location of the next bivouac site, most likely on top of the Central Pillar. He felt that whoever reached it first would not only choose the best position – even assuming there was space for more than one team – but would also get ahead on what looked like the natural line from there to the Spider. The team coming second, as Harlin graphically put it, 'could lose the whole ascent'.

On the morning of Sunday, 13 March, a new factor entered the equation. When I spoke to Harlin at 11.45 a.m., he asked me to hand the radio to Kor. 'Layton,' he said, 'I am not feeling well. I have sickness, I have fever, and I think a respiratory cold. I'd like some medicine when you come up. Could you see if there's a doctor at Scheidegg, please?'

Kor assigned the task of finding a doctor to Bonington and me. We discovered from the receptionist that no fewer than five doctors, all from Paris, were staying at the hotel. Two hours later all five gathered in my room. They asked Harlin about his pulse, his breathing, his temperature, his urine and whether he was vomiting. After going into a huddle to discuss his answers, they conveyed their collective diagnosis: Harlin probably had a cold, he could stay on the mountain, and they would consult again tomorrow.

Haston, otherwise so positive about sharing the snow hole with Harlin, later delivered a harsh verdict about this episode: Harlin was suffering from 'one of his attention-seeking fits'. At the time, Haston admitted, he had felt sympathetic in case Harlin really was ill. In retrospect, he wrote, Harlin had nothing worse than a cold – but then he 'was always prone to a little bit of drama'.

Later that day, some new visitors arrived at Kleine Scheidegg: Marilyn, John Jr and Andréa, who were driven from Leysin by an American couple, Sam and Sara Jane Elliot, who taught at the American School. It was, in fact, Marilyn's third time at Kleine

Scheidegg during the climb. She had visited with the Elliots two weeks before, at a time when Harlin was down from the face. John Jr recorded that she had been 'wildly excited' at the prospect of seeing him and had discarded the informal clothes she usually wore in favour of something more alluring. It proved effective. Harlin, so John Jr wrote, made a new commitment to her: having survived the difficulties of their marriage, he felt that they knew how to make it work and he wanted to grow old with her. Afterwards Marilyn wrote: 'Never before had he considered the future with me in it to the end.' Marilyn was there again on 6 March, when Harlin and Haston had made good progress above the First Band, and she had spent much of the day watching them through the hotel telescope. On this occasion, on 13 March, Marilyn and the children all spoke to Harlin by radio at the Death Bivouac. John Jr wrote later that it did not feel strange to be talking to his father 'behind the clouds', as he had spoken to him by radio on climbs before. 'He said he was fine, and I took him at his word.' Harlin, whatever Haston wrote later, was clearly determined to put on his best front for his children. When Marilyn took the radio, however, she was far from reassured. As she described later, her throat was tight and her eyes were moist. Harlin made day-to-day conversation: he hoped Marilyn had enjoyed some skiing and asked for news of his parents. But Marilyn – dismayed that her husband was 'freezing, hungry, sick' – seemed overwhelmed with a sense of premonition. 'It was as if I was talking with a trapped miner when there did not seem to be much chance,' she said. 'Hearing his voice made it so much worse.'

Barbara Haag visited Kleine Scheidegg, too. It was a ten-hour drive from Reutlingen and on one occasion she made the journey with Hupfauer's girlfriend, Gaby, in a Fiat 550. Even though Barbara was married, she was still living with her parents and found, contrary to expectations, that her mother admired Haag and was as caught up in the drama of the Direct as she was. 'Other people might find it terrible or dangerous but she was quite intrigued that he did these things. My father didn't say much but my mother was quite relaxed about it and she was a great help to me. It was a different life to what you might imagine for a pregnant wife. But life with Peter was never normal. It was always exciting, to the very end.'

Haag was, in fact, in trouble. The five Germans on the face were divided between their two caves. Hupfauer, Schnaidt and Strobel were in the newer one near the Death Bivouac; Haag and Votteler were in the original Rulaman cave to the right. Schnaidt and Strobel were still sharing a sleeping bag but they and Hupfauer kept up their spirits by chatting, singing and talking of their past exploits. In comparison, Haag and Votteler were suffering. They had one luxury item, a transistor radio belonging to Rosenzopf. They stuffed it under their duvets to try to preserve its batteries and listened to music and news broadcasts. They, too, fantasised about the meals they would eat as soon as they had finished the climb. But they had far less space in the Rulaman cave and were jammed together between rock and snow; Haag cursed under his breath whenever Votteler tried to find a more comfortable position and his bony elbow prodded him in the ribs.

The five Germans were less well-equipped than Haston and Harlin, who had groundsheets. The Germans were lying on bare snow and ice and were suffering from pains in their muscles and joints, the result of the damp, cold and enforced inactivity. As Hupfauer recalled in 2014, they were also afflicted by diarrhoea, perhaps caused by the cold, and there was a long tell-tale stain running down to the Second Icefield that was detectable in a photograph taken during the climb. For Haag, matters got worse when he developed a fever that appears to have been more severe than Harlin's. He shivered for the best part of four days, barely able to move, as Votteler testified. 'He couldn't stand up so I had to deal with his bodily needs. I had to catch it in a plastic bag and get rid of it.' When Haag tried to visit the second German snow hole, he collapsed and Votteler had to drag him back to his 'bed of pain'.

By 14 March, their fourth day on the face, both teams faced a new problem. They were running out of food. The five Germans had begun with five litres of fuel for cooking and enough food to make themselves what they called 'Eiger toast' – a sandwich of rye bread, cheese and smoked meat. But gradually their food had dwindled so that they were reduced to consuming soup and nuts, which they shared out one by one. But they found that the nuts were too dry and stuck in their throats, and as their food diminished they spent more and more time asleep. 'We were ailing,' said Votteler in 2014.

Harlin and Haston, too, had eaten most of the supplies intended for the summit push, and were left with a small amount of dried meat which they reckoned would last for another two days, plus enough of the drinking supplements for four days. This issue now dominated the discussions between Kleine Scheidegg and the face. A briefly optimistic forecast allowed the possibility that Kor could return to the face with fresh supplies, but it proved illusory.

In a long conversation, Bonington and Harlin considered whether they should meet the Germans with a view to pooling both their ideas and resources. Bonington had already agreed with Lehne that when the two teams finally returned to the face, they should break trail from Kleine Scheidegg together. Should they now propose a 'sit-down-and-talk-it-out conference', Harlin wondered? But he was still preoccupied with the risks of making a formal approach to the Germans, in case it became the thin end of a wedge leading to a 'coordinated ascent'. He told Bonington: 'We don't have this conception of a great group going to the summit. And we don't want to come up the third or fourth rope as though we were being pulled up by the Germans, because we are of course capable of doing the climb ourselves.'

Harlin insisted that his original concept of the climb held good. The Germans were still 'plodding on' – whereas, once good weather arrived, 'we can just drop all our gear and make the summit in three bivouacs'. But he had another concern. If Bonington and I did talk to the Germans it would be difficult to conceal Harlin's illness or the possibility that he might come down, which would further weaken his position in any negotiations. Bonington and Harlin decided to make no decision and postponed further discussion until the next morning.

In the morning of 15 March, the five French doctors reconvened in my room. Harlin had clearly improved overnight and the doctors said they would conduct another consultation later that day. Harlin and Haston said they would stay on the face, which meant that replenishing their supplies became the immediate priority. During the next call, at 11.45 a.m., Bonington told Harlin that he and Whillans would bring more food the next day. He added that because the slopes below the face were loaded with snow and liable to avalanche, they would take the train to Eigerwand station and exit on to the face from there.

Since Bonington had previously agreed that Harlin's team would go to the face with the Germans, he now had to ask them if they were willing to use the Eigerwand station. That afternoon Bonington and I met Lehne and Golikow, together with Frey and Toni Hiebeler, around a table in the hotel bar. Harlin had instructed us to limit our agenda to the proposal to use the Eigerwand station. Bonington accordingly outlined his plan, pointing out that it would reduce the risk of being caught in an avalanche.

The negotiations did not take long.

Bonington (to Germans): 'Do you want to come with us?'

Lehne: 'No.'

After some inconsequential chat, the meeting broke up. I cannot recall what judgement I made of Lehne at the time, but it is clear now that he was determined to maintain the purity of the ascent. A man who would not consider using the train to take rucksacks to the top of the Vorbau was not about to compromise. That evening Bonington told Harlin that they would revert to the plan of forming a party with the Germans which would cross to the Vorbau by foot. A delivery of Jumar clamps was due in the morning so the party would leave in the afternoon. It would bivouac in the respective snow holes below the First Band and would reach the Death Bivouac snow holes the following morning.

Harlin objected that this would leave him and Haston without food for twenty-four hours and suggested that Kor leave in the morning. Bonington agreed to the new time, with the startling proviso that I help Kor break trail to the foot of the Vorbau. I had heard the avalanche warnings but felt in no position to challenge the recommendation of Britain's foremost Alpinist, and declared that the *Telegraph*'s representative was ready and willing to assume this new role.

By the morning, to my profound relief, there had been a change of plans. As Bonington told Harlin in the 7.45 a.m. radio call, a combined team would leave for the face at 11 o'clock. It would consist of himself, Kor, Whillans, Lehne, Golikow, and would travel on skis, which meant that I could not take part. Bonington had been teaching me to ski on the nursery slopes above Kleine Scheidegg but my skills did not yet extend to tracking across deep powder snow at the foot of the Eiger.

The Germans, however, were having misgivings about crossing the slopes below the Eiger, as they were laden with snow and there was a clear avalanche risk, and both Von Almen and Hiebeler had warned them against making the trip. At 10 a.m., as the British-American trio were preparing their rucksacks, Lehne arrived at the hotel and proposed that they should wait another twenty-four hours. This time it was Bonington who displayed his fortitude, telling Lehne that he and his team-mates still intended to go, although without revealing that Haston and Harlin had run out of food.

'OK,' said Lehne. 'I will come too.'

The five men finally left at 3 p.m. They embarked on the ski traverse from the Eigergletscher station, hoping that they were crossing high enough to minimise the avalanche risk. They were swallowed up by swirling snow and mist for much of the way and were relieved when they reached the foot of the Vorbau, where it was snowing hard and avalanches were flowing down the face. Kor and Whillans dumped their loads and headed back to Kleine Scheidegg, followed shortly afterwards by Bonington, but Golikow and Lehne were determined to carry their supplies higher. Enduring a succession of avalanches that repeatedly engulfed them in powder snow, they reached the Ice Palace after dark. They dumped their rucksacks and battled their way back to the Stöckli, arriving at 9.30 p.m., just as Rosenzopf and Frey were wondering whether to prepare a search party. Lehne later wrote that their feat in taking supplies to the Ice Palace was of little importance in the overall scale of the attempt. 'But our struggle against the forces of nature ranked among the greatest pleasures accorded us in the whole expedition.'

By then I had dictated my daily report to the copytakers at the *Telegraph*, which published a terse, three-paragraph story on 15 March under the headline: 'Climbers leave with Eiger supplies today'. Maybe that understated the drama of what was happening; but there were other reporters at Kleine Scheidegg determined to extract its full value. Half a dozen journalists were now in residence at the hotel. They included the veteran Guido Tonella, who had chaired the discussion at Trento six months before, and was writing for the *Tribune de Genève*; several news agency reporters; and a reporter named Hugo Kuranda, who was covering events – under two different names – for the London newspapers the *Evening News* and the *Daily Sketch*, both owned by Associated Newspapers, which also owned the *Daily Mail*. He was almost certainly the same journalist who had attempted to groom Bonington and Whillans during their first North Face attempt in 1961: Bonington's description of rugged good looks and grey hair, and wearing an immaculate pair of climbing breeches, fitted him exactly.

My instinct would have been to socialise and swap gossip with my fellow journalists, but I felt constrained because the *Weekend Telegraph*'s deal with Harlin meant that I was required to keep my lips sealed about his attempt. The other reporters had to go on what they could see, assisted by tips and steers from Fritz von Almen. Kuranda himself had a colourful past. He came from a Jewish family in Vienna and had sought refuge in London as the Nazis took over Austria. During the war he worked for the Ministry of Information, the British propaganda department, where his duties included delivering morale-boosting talks to audiences such as the Ladies Luncheon Club in Hornsea, Yorkshire, and the Bradford Rotary Club. After the war he moved to Switzerland and became a stringer, as freelance correspondents were known, for a selection of British provincial newspapers. He also found the time to take part in the 1948 Winter Olympics at St Moritz, Switzerland. He represented Austria in the bobsled competition on the notorious Cresta Run, but sadly was placed last after he made a mistake at a turn and hurtled off the course.

A man of such a background and resourcefulness was clearly not going to be deterred by a shortage of facts when filing his story, as he demonstrated when writing a report which appeared in the *Daily Sketch* on 16 March, headlined: 'It started as a race ... now it's a rescue.'

'It began as a light-hearted race, almost in the mood of a boyish escapade. But there was no laughter on the Eiger today and no dancing in the valley below, where the wives and the sweethearts of the climbers wait ...'

According to Kuranda, Haston and Harlin had sent a 'walkie-talkie message' to their comrades in Kleine Scheidegg saying: 'It is terribly grim up here. Can't you help us?' There was more in this vein, culminating in the final thoughts: 'The happy hours seem so far away, when Marilyn Harlin, pig-tailed Wendy Bonington, and Audrey Whillans would take turns at the big telescope on their hotel roof and tell each other what grand chaps their husbands were.

'Today the adventure has gone sour ...'

It was probably fortunate for Kuranda that the subjects of his story did not hear about it for several days. When I finally obtained a copy I read it out to Harlin, Haston and Kor in a radio call with the face. Harlin asked me: 'Why don't you get a hold of that guy and rope him down and straighten him out?' Haston was even more forthright: 'I'd like to kill the fucker.' Later, Kuranda would display a talent for invention which surpassed even this.

At 3.45 p.m. on the 15th, just forty-five minutes after the five-man provisioning party left for the Eiger, I called Harlin and Haston to give them the news that reinforcements were on the way. Harlin seemed strangely untroubled when I said that the food would not reach them until the following morning and once again he focused on the latest weather forecast. I broke the news that the high-pressure system he was so keenly awaiting appeared to have got no further than Wales; what was more, it appeared to be weakening.

'Things don't look too good, Pete,' John said. I had to agree. Harlin announced that he and Haston were thinking of descending to Kleine Scheidegg – adding that if he had heard the latest forecast two hours earlier, they would already have started. That night, having returned from the face, Bonington told Harlin that conditions were so poor that climbing could be ruled out for at least two days. He added that climbers on the face were likely to have been weakened by their five days of inactivity and would need time to recover in Kleine Scheidegg. Harlin agreed. 'It would seem to me that the best thing would be to retreat until the weather turns good,' he said, adding that he would make the final decision in the morning.

When I called Harlin at 7.45 a.m. on 16 March he was clearly minded to descend. It was snowing all the way down to Kleine Scheidegg, the weather forecast was indeterminate, and he was still preoccupied with his illness which had 'gone into a certain amount of bronchitis'.

Bonington made a remarkable offer. Despite his previous insistence that he wanted to concentrate on taking photographs, he told Harlin he was willing to return to the face with Kor if the weather improved before Harlin felt ready to resume. Although Bonington had felt distanced from the attempt, he clearly did not want it to fail by default. Harlin accepted his offer and confirmed that he and Haston would come down.

Haston led the way out of the snow hole, clearing a path through the excrement that decorated the entrance. He felt dizzy from a rush of blood to his head as he stood up, and it took him five minutes to stabilise himself before making the traverse to the Germans' ice caves. There they paused to talk to Haag and Strobel, who told them that they and Votteler were staying put, while Hupfauer and Schnaidt were going down. Although Harlin and Haston were feeling light-headed from a lack of food, all went well until they reached the First Band where Haston's abseil rope snagged, slamming him into an overhang so hard that he almost lost his grip. He reached the foot of the cliff safely and in a further half-hour he and Harlin had shinned down the line of fixed ropes to the foot of the Vorbau.

Bonington and I had set out to meet them. Bonington travelled on skis while I took the train to Alpiglen and we headed up the slopes from the station. As we laboured up through the thigh-deep snow, I was struck by just how cold it was. Harlin had retrieved his skis from the cave below the Vorbau and came slicing towards us while Haston was glissading on his back, the snow piling up around him.

'Hi, man,' Haston shouted as he arrived.

'It's great to be back,' said Harlin. 'It was really cold up there this morning.'

Bonington and I were embarrassed to realise that we had brought them nothing to eat or drink. They were in a forgiving mood and we set off for Alpiglen station. There we met Hupfauer and Schnaidt, who seemed equally demob happy. As Schnaidt later said, they too had felt 'stiff and awkward' descending the fixed ropes and noticed how far they had been weakened by their enforced stay in the snow hole, but were relishing the prospect of rest and recuperation at the Stöckli.

As we waited for the train, the sky had all but cleared of cloud and the sun was beginning to slant across the face from the West Flank. The timing, to say the least, was unfortunate. Harlin and Haston had come down on the very morning that the weather had finally improved – and after fresh supplies and food had been carried to the face. What was more, just as Harlin and his team were heading for Kleine Scheidegg, the three Germans on the face were preparing to climb.

Chapter Twelve

THE TURNING POINT

It was I who gave the Central Pillar its name. At some early stage during the attempt, I was with Harlin and his team as they discussed their route, and the pillar became the focus of their attention. It looked tall, sheer and utterly daunting and was obviously going to be a crucial feature. The classic route, so elegant and ingenious, avoided it by slanting leftwards up the Ramp and striking back rightwards along the Traverse of the Gods to the Spider. If the attempt was going to be true to Comici's edict about a drop of water falling from the summit, it had to be tackled head-on. But what should it be called? I remember that we groped for ideas and then I came up with the obvious answer – so obvious that it appeared banal. But since no one could think of anything more imaginative, the name stuck.

The Central Pillar was to dominate the attempt for the next five days. The two teams were tackling it by different routes, and the outcome of their endeavours was to have a significant bearing both on the competition between them and on their leaders' continuing preoccupation with whether they should cooperate.

On 16 March, the Germans appeared to have the advantage.

Haag and Strobel were at the Flatiron and well placed to push on. But, as they reported to Lehne in Kleine Scheidegg, the weather was against them. Although the sky was clear, it was bitterly cold and the wind was strong; in addition, Haag was still recovering from his illness and both men were short of food. Below them, for almost the first time, the support effort was faltering. Hupfauer and Schnaidt were supposed to fetch the supplies that had been dumped at the Ice Palace by Lehne and Golikow the previous evening, but – after securing their colleagues' approval – had succumbed to the temptation of returning to the Stöckli.

Earlier in the day, Lehne had watched Harlin arrive at Kleine Scheidegg and judged that while he appeared physically fit, his spirits seemed low. Had Harlin known what Lehne thought, he would probably have argued that the opposite was true. He was still preoccupied with his health and planned to go to a hospital in Interlaken for a check-up. Meanwhile, Bonington and Kor were preparing to return to the face the next day, in keeping with Bonington's pledge to keep the climb going.

On 17 March, a five-man party left Kleine Scheidegg at 7.30 a.m. It consisted of Bonington and Kor, each carrying around twenty kilos of food and other supplies, together with Lehne, Rosenzopf and Golikow. Rosenzopf broke trail for much of the way, crossing fresh avalanche debris in several places. Once at the Vorbau, the Germans headed up the fixed ropes first, Golikow in the lead. By midday the two teams were at their respective staging posts at the foot of the First Band. But when Lehne attempted to follow Golikow up the long stretch of fixed ropes hanging clear of the First Band, he hit trouble. He was attempting to use Jumars – the Germans were equipped with Hiebler clamps but had ordered a batch of Jumars after seeing Harlin's team use them to such good effect. Lehne had experimented with them during his ascent to the First Band the previous day, but found that the fine teeth of the clamps iced up. Now he tried them again but, swinging free on the rope and using all his strength, it took him five minutes to climb just three metres.

Bonington and Kor were brewing tea in their snow hole as they waited for the Germans to climb the First Band. Seeing that Lehne was in trouble, Kor called him to descend and then explained how to make the Jumars work. Lehne carried out Kor's instructions and, although he found his energy was still sapped, he eventually reached the top of the First Band.

By 5 p.m. all three Germans – Golikow, Lehne and Rosenzopf – were at the Death Bivouac snow holes, where they were greeted by Votteler. One hundred and fifty metres above them, Haag and Strobel were at work in the gully system that led to the head of the pillar. They had passed their high-point of 10 March but were finding the climbing increasingly difficult as they grappled with loose, sloping rock where it was impossible to place pitons or even bolts. They were finally halted by the giant snow plug that over-hung the gully, with the top of the pillar just ten metres beyond.

'It was hell up there,' Haag reported when he and Strobel returned to the Death Bivouac. As they talked through the day's events, they reckoned that the ten metres separating them from the top of the Central Pillar looked like the hardest so far – and also held the key to the route to the summit.

Bonington and Kor spent the evening consolidating. They had reached the Death Bivouac at 6 p.m. and sorted out their equipment, ready for an early start. But their spirits were dented after Kor returned from a visit to the Germans to report, erroneously, that they had reached the top of the Central Pillar. Maybe it was a misunderstanding; maybe Kor was another victim of Haag's sense of humour. Either way, it left Bonington and Kor depressed in the belief that the Germans had obtained a decisive lead. Not only would they have secured perhaps the only bivouac site at the top of the Central Pillar, they would be out in front on the crucial section from there to the Spider.

Harlin and I missed much of these events. That morning we had taken the train to Lauterbrunnen, where we attended the funeral of Hilti von Allmen, the guide I had interviewed during my previous visit to Switzerland in November. Von Allmen had been caught in an avalanche while skiing on 14 March, the very day when climbers from both teams had crossed the unstable slopes beneath the Eiger. The funeral, which was attended by almost the entire population of Lauterbrunnen, was a reminder, if one were needed, of the part played by sheer chance in the lives and deaths of mountaineers. Afterwards Harlin and I discussed this very topic as we waited for our trains at Lauterbrunnen station – I to return to Kleine Scheidegg, Harlin to continue to his hospital appointment in Interlaken. In a concise summary of an attitude he had previously expressed in his writings, he told me: 'Climbing is dangerous, and there's no getting away from it. People do get killed. But death's just a part of it all.'

If that was so, I asked Harlin, what about the effect on his family?

'I reason it this way. Your family accept you and have accepted you for what you are. They wouldn't want you to change, which you would be doing if you gave up climbing.'

On that very day, as if by some presentiment, Marilyn wrote to Harlin from Leysin. She warned him: 'Don't play with the gods up there. It appears they are jealous of you and thus manifest their wrath in peculiar ways.' She finished with the words: 'We all give our support through this last stretch.' She enclosed notes from both children. John Jr reported that he had passed his college exams, and told him: 'Try to make it to the very top.' Andréa wrote: 'I hope you come back home pretty soon. I love you very much.'

I returned to Kleine Scheidegg that evening and met a new team member: the British climber Mick Burke, who had arrived from Leysin to replace Whillans as Bonington's photographic assistant. Burke now made a timely intervention. During the evening radio call, a despondent Bonington passed on the news that the Germans had reached the top of the Central Pillar. Shortly after the radio call, I told Burke what Bonington had said. Burke knew that Bonington was mistaken, as he had been watching through the hotel telescope while I was in Lauterbrunnen and had seen the Germans turn back from beneath the giant snow plug. But we were unable to put Bonington right until the scheduled radio call in the morning.

I could hear the relief in Bonington's voice when I called him at 7.45 a.m. the next day, 18 March. There was a reasonable forecast – weather fine but unsettled – and he told me that he and Kor intended to climb to the foot of the Central Pillar to examine the possible traverse line Kor had spotted ten days before. They climbed the fixed ropes and Kor started edging towards the foot of the pillar, but then the 'unsettled' part of the forecast kicked in. The wind intensified and spindrift avalanches were following their familiar path down the face.

'It's no bloody good,' Bonington called to Kor. 'How about coming back?' Kor accepted the inevitable and by early afternoon the two men were settled back into the snow hole.

The Germans had a similar experience. Lehne and Golikow took over the lead in an attempt to climb the final ten metres that had defeated Haag and Strobel. The sky was clouding over as they set out and by the time they reached their high-point they were being inundated with spindrift. There was nothing for it but to return to the snow holes at the Flatiron. There were now six Germans on the face and that afternoon, during a radio call, Schnaidt and Hupfauer, the two at the Stöckli, described with undisguised relish how much they were enjoying sitting in chairs, sleeping in beds, drinking beer and wearing ordinary clothes.

It all sounded very enticing, and after the call Lehne advised Haag, Strobel and Votteler to return to the Stöckli for a similar break. 'The weather isn't going to improve any time soon and our supplies are going down fast,' he told them. 'We will need new supplies soon, so you might as well go down now.' Haag and Strobel put up the strongest resistance to his arguments, saying that having spent twenty-two days on the face they were determined to see the climb through in one push.

Bonington and Kor proved equally resistant to temptation. Harlin returned from Interlaken that afternoon with the news that a doctor had told him he was suffering from bronchitis, although he was now on the mend. He was still following the weather forecasts and, during the evening radio call to the face, said he could explain why the customary period of settled winter weather had not arrived as predicted. A mass of cold air was moving south from Scandinavia, with the result that the high-pressure system over Wales was stationary. However, a new high-pressure system was in prospect and was likely to develop once the mass of cold air had passed, bringing good weather in about two days' time.

Harlin proposed that Bonington and Kor should return to Kleine Scheidegg in order to wait for the good weather he expected. Kor, as always vulnerable to the call of Kleine Scheidegg, was inclined to agree, but asked Harlin what the Germans were planning to do. Harlin told him: 'We could care less at this moment, Layton.' In American vernacular, this meant that Harlin could *not* care less – and if he had indeed stopped worrying about what the Germans were doing, it was a striking change of heart. Harlin added that if Kor and Bonington did descend to Kleine Scheidegg, they could return to the face as soon as the good weather came. He went as far as to recommend that they get up at 5.30 or 6 a.m., tidy up the bivouac and then descend – otherwise they would find themselves coming down 'later in the day when you have a lot of spindrift avalanches'.

It was Bonington who rejected Harlin's blandishments. Bonington told him that if the forecast was as good as Harlin promised, and fine weather was going to arrive in a maximum of two days, they might as well stay on the face. And if Harlin was inclined to disregard the Germans, Bonington was not, saying it would be disastrous to lose a day to the Germans if they stayed on the face – 'which I think they will'. Bonington proposed that they should review their options in the morning. Harlin, who said he would collect the latest forecasts before the morning call, agreed.

That night, Harlin called Marilyn in Leysin. In a conversation later described by their son, he told her that he was keen to finish the climb so that he could get back home. Marilyn went as far as to suggest he abandon the attempt, but Harlin said he did not think the family could sustain another attempt the following winter. He was confident that 'things would go smoothly' from that point – and said he was looking forward to taking care of John Jr and Andréa in April, when Marilyn was due to take her pupils on a field trip to Greece.

On 19 March we awoke at Kleine Scheidegg to a cold, crisp dawn; from my bedroom, I could see a few streaks of high cirrus above the Eiger in an otherwise clear sky. In keeping with his agreement with Bonington, Harlin made the round of the weather stations. 'The weather report confirms what I gave you last night,' he told Bonington at 7.45. 'Except, of course, that we have what seems to be beautiful weather.'

To Bonington, the weather appeared perfect for climbing. But as the conversation unfolded, it was clear that Harlin still wanted him and Kor to descend and await the new high-pressure system that was supposedly on its way. The mass of cold air that was heading south from Scandinavia would bring a period of snow showers, and then the high-pressure system would take over. 'It is so large [that] once it is here and in dominance there is no question about having five-plus days, five to shall we say ten or even fifteen days of good weather,' Harlin said. But in light of the bad weather that was likely to precede it, he added: 'I think the best decision is to come down.'

Once again Bonington resisted Harlin's proposals, arguing that it would be sensible if they at least examined conditions on the face before descending. Harlin responded that if they could find something useful to do, such as fixing more ropes in place, then he agreed. 'Otherwise it would be better to come down and then go back up when constructive work is possible again.'

'Yes, John,' Bonington said tolerantly. 'We'll go out today and see if any progress can be made. If progress can't be made, we'll come down.'

That morning the Germans were equally preoccupied with their team's dispositions, following the discussions the previous night about whether anyone should descend. Lehne was sorting out his climbing equipment when Haag, Strobel and Votteler arrived from the neighbouring snow hole and told him they were going to take him at his word and descend to the Stöckli. Lehne was baffled: if they had refused to go down the previous night, why were they doing so now? 'They could not give me any explanation,' Lehne wrote. 'For me, their decision was incomprehensible.'

Lehne assumed that their determination had finally been weakened by the twenty-two nights they had spent on the face, often in atrocious conditions. In the dynamics of the German team it was a crucial moment, as it saw Lehne emerging in place of Haag as the critical force. The Germans still viewed themselves as a democratic group, in contrast to what they saw as Harlin's autocratic style.

That in itself was misleading, given that at several junctures it was Haston and Bonington who showed the drive to take the team forward, while Harlin prevaricated. As for the Germans, while their collective spirit was vital in keeping the steamroller moving, it was Haag who had been making the important decisions – a role that would now be assumed by Lehne.

True to their agreement with Harlin, Bonington and Kor left the snow hole to consider the prospects for climbing. They could hardly have been better – and, what was more, the Germans were back on their route. Bonington and Kor arrived at the foot of the Central Pillar to find that Lehne was belaying Golikow as he approached the snow plug near the top of their gully system. Bonington chatted to Lehne but did not tell him he shared Haston's bleak verdict on the Germans' prospects of overcoming the snow plug. But when Bonington told Lehne that they intended to traverse the foot of the pillar, Lehne told him he thought it was impossible.

'To Layton, anything is possible,' Bonington assured Lehne, with as much confidence as he could muster.

Kor was already at work, deploying all his skill and artistry as he probed for a route. The limestone was as sheer and compact as the First Band but often more brittle and festooned with ice. Kor cleared the cracks with his bare hands as he searched for place-ments for his pitons, most if not all knifeblades. Bonington was in awe at the speed of his decision-making, selecting a crack and tapping in his piton at first sight. He hung his étrier from the piton and swung his weight on to it, with 1000 metres of space yawning below. As Kor approached the far side of the pillar, Bonington watched with increasing trepidation, aware that he would soon have to follow. After three hours, Kor completed the pitch and disappeared beyond the left-hand edge of the pillar, then yelled for Bonington to follow. Bonington had to contend with the effect of Kor's immense reach, which meant that he was at full stretch when he moved from one piton to another. He was immensely relieved when he joined Kor on his stance on the far side of the pillar.

Above them, fulfilling Haston's predictions of 10 March, an ice gully led directly to the top of the pillar almost 100 metres above. It was steeply angled – around seventy degrees, Bonington reckoned – and the ice looked thin, but the line was clear with no obstacles of the kind the Germans had met. Kor set off in the lead but Bonington soon saw that the man with such mastery of rock techniques did not have the same expertise on ice. Kor fumbled with his ice screws and became tangled with his crampons. He had climbed only a few metres when Bonington called up and offered to take his place.

'This just isn't my scene,' Kor confirmed.

Bonington took over and soon passed the point Kor had reached. He moved confidently and methodically at first, savouring the excitement of being in the lead. He cut holds with his ice axe for both his hands and his feet, chipping cautiously at a skin of ice that overlay the rock of the face, and placing a piton twenty feet above the start. But he could find nowhere to place any more pitons and the veneer of ice was becoming ever thinner, with an inch of clear space between it and the rock. Bonington imagined it shearing away, most likely carrying both him and Kor to the bottom of the face. Acutely aware of how far he had climbed without protection, Bonington finally reached a patch of firm snow some twenty-five metres above Kor's stance. From there he kicked his way up on his crampons to a ledge at the foot of a groove that formed the left-hand edge of the pillar, exhilaration mixing with relief in equal measure. 'It is the hairiest thing I have ever done,' Bonington said in 2014.

Kor readily confirmed Bonington's judgement. The pitch 'was

really spooky. Bonington did a long run-out; he'd put one piton in the middle that was no good at all – it wouldn't have held anything. It was a really bold pitch ... a real borderline thing.'

Bonington's boldness meant that the way to the top of the Central Pillar was secure – and, since there was no sign of the Germans from the other side of the pillar, Bonington presumed that he and Kor had taken the lead. No matter that he had switched from team photographer to lead climber. It was a good moment.

Their presumption was correct – and there was despondency in the German camp. Golikow had spent the best part of the day grappling with the problem of their chimney and its overhanging cap of snow. He could find nowhere to fix pitons in the loose snow, nor would it support his ice axe. He searched for a way on the rock to both right and left, but it was loose, friable and overhanging. He inserted one insecure piton and climbed two metres above it, bringing him almost level with the snow. But even Katastrophen-Karle, the risk-taker, had to admit defeat.

Then came a moment of crisis for Lehne. He had been getting colder and colder as he remained immobile on his belay stance. Suddenly, he was overcome by nausea and a violent headache. His arms and legs went numb and he was gripped with panic, fearing he was about to die. He managed to abseil to the foot of the pitch and reach the Death Bivouac. There he was seized with self-doubt: was he really up to the task? Gradually, the feeling returned to his arms and legs and his terror subsided, leaving him puzzled by what could have caused this panic attack. Later, his best guess was that he had returned too quickly and without proper acclimatisation to the team's high-point after six days' indolence at the Stöckli. But it may have been accentuated by the sense of isolation he felt after Haag departed, and a premonition that he would be assuming a full leadership role. That night, Lehne and Golikow slept in one of the ice caves, while Rosenzopf kept a lonely vigil in the other.

Lehne's discomfort accorded with the morale of his team-mates, who voiced their dismay on learning that he and Golikow had yet again failed to reach the top of the pillar. Lehne understood their frustration. Until that day they had been comfortably ahead of their rivals. Now the Americans had taken the lead. What was more, Bonington had offered to drop a rope for them if he and Kor climbed the pillar first. In a manifest blow to the Germans' pride, as Lehne saw it, this would be the first time they took their rivals' help in this way. 'But there was no other solution,' Lehne wrote. He consoled himself with the thought that the Americans had previously used the German ropes on Strobel's crucial ice pitch below the Second Icefield on 9 March – but also that the rivalry between the two teams was moderating and that the climbers were becoming friends.

The day had not finished for Bonington and Kor. After abseiling to the foot of the Central Pillar, Kor speedily reversed his traverse. But when Bonington set out, he became stuck at the point where the rope across the pitch sank to its lowest point. As he dangled over the void with night approaching, Bonington was acutely aware that one mistake could prove fatal. He freed himself by the desperate measure of untying from the rope and holding on to it with one hand while he reattached his Jumar with the other. When Bonington reached the Death Bivouac he met Lehne at the entrance of the main German ice cave. It was then that Lehne admitted that the Germans had been unable to climb their route and asked him to drop them a rope when they reached the top. Bonington agreed, with the proviso that the Germans waited until his team was at the top of the pillar before they followed.

These events had been hidden from Kleine Scheidegg by a cloud inversion that filled the valley. It was only when we talked to Bonington at 6.45 p.m. that we learned what had happened. Bonington explained that he and Kor had been above the cloud all day and that they were no more than one short pitch from the top of the Central Pillar. As for the Germans, Bonington told us, 'They're completely stuck. They just went up their chimney and came down.' He told Harlin that he had agreed to Lehne's request to drop him a rope.

Bonington's news left Haston content that the decision he and Kor had made about the respective routes at the Central Pillar had proved correct. Kor's supreme skills, followed by Bonington's determination and nerve, had opened up the top section of the route. Harlin felt gratified that their scrutiny of the face before the attempt was proving its worth. What was more, his team was out in front at last and held both a strategic and a moral advantage over the Germans. That night, as we celebrated in the Gaststube, he told me it was 'the turning point of the climb'.

Chapter Thirteen

A HAPPY SCENE

The morning of 20 March brought the second clear dawn in succession, further belying the gloomy forecast Harlin had given two days before. In their snow hole, Bonington and Kor prepared to return to the route and climb the final pitch to the top of the Central Pillar. It consisted of a steep gully and could be difficult to protect, but it looked as though it would be less nerve-racking than Bonington's dangerous lead the evening before. Above it lay perhaps another four pitches that would take them to the great landmark and staging post of the Spider.

Just as they were preparing to leave, Lehne arrived at the snow hole. Bonington presumed he was paying a social visit, but Lehne had come to make a proposition: the two teams should climb together. It was a startling suggestion, and in *Eiger Direct* I recorded that Lehne explained it as follows: 'It's we who are asking you whether we can join you. We're not stuck completely. If you don't agree we can go to the right or just follow you up. But it doesn't seem sensible to climb on separate routes a few metres apart.'

In the story of the Eiger Direct, it was a significant moment. To begin with the two teams had circled each other cautiously. Gradually, they showed small kindnesses to each other, lending equipment, sharing hospitality. Golikow always greeted Harlin's team cheerily, usually with his 'hard life' catchphrase, and they were drawn to him especially. Harlin appeared the most wary, leading Haag to write that the closeness they felt at Trento had been lost. Harlin's team in turn felt that Lehne was the German climber most inclined to keep his distance.

There had, in fact, been three occasions when the friendship had extended to cooperation on the route. Harlin's team had used the Germans' fixed rope when they started up the Vorbau. The Germans had used the Harlin team's rope to ascend to the top of the Second Band on 8 March, and the following day Harlin's team had climbed the rope on Strobel's vital lead to the Second Icefield. Ironically, both of those instances had enabled one team to catch up the lead the other had established, thus vitiating the supposed competition between them. But now Lehne was proposing something more formal: namely, that members from each team should climb together. The proposal was to cause consternation in Harlin's team.

It is first worth noting that if the account of Lehne's proposal is accurate, it was not entirely true: the Germans *were* stuck, having failed to reach the top of their pitch after two days of trying. Either way, Bonington quickly saw the advantages. It would put an end to each team's preoccupation with what the other was doing, and it accorded with his feelings about their rivalry which he had confided to Haag. More practically, it would resolve the ambiguities about his own role, enabling him to revert to taking photographs. Now that the Spider was within reach, he was keen to return to Kleine Scheidegg and prepare to climb the West Flank, enabling him to photograph the climbers as they approached the summit.

Bonington also grasped the politics of the proposal. He felt that

Lehne was making it from a position of weakness, but also suspected that Harlin might be wary of any permanent arrangement. He told Lehne that he agreed – but added that the arrangement was temporary until it was ratified by Harlin. Lehne agreed in turn, and before long Kor and Golikow set off on the fixed ropes, ready to return to Bonington and Kor's high-point and tackle the final pitch to the top of the Central Pillar.

Bonington gave two accounts of his conversation with Lehne. The first informed my description of the episode in *Eiger Direct*, including the quote I have cited above. The second appeared in Bonington's second volume of autobiography, *The Next Horizon*, published seven years later. It contains minor differences of detail and some extra verbatim conversation, but otherwise is consistent with the first.

There is, however, a radical discrepancy between these two accounts and the one provided by Lehne in the book that he wrote with Haag. He and Haag authored separate sections of the book: Haag takes us from the start of the attempt to 16 March, three days before he descended to Kleine Scheidegg after spending twenty-two nights on the face; Lehne picks up the story, with a small overlap, from there. His is thus the principal voice in the second part of the book. He is less inclined to the poetic than Haag, but discloses more of his feelings than would have been expected from his impassive exterior.

Lehne's account of the morning of 20 March, however, is notable for its terseness. He and Golikow left their ice cave at 8 a.m., determined to make one more attempt on their line to the right of the Central Pillar. 'It was unthinkable for us to remain inactive while the Americans overtook us on their apparently easier route,' Lehne wrote. He described how he retrieved some equipment from the second German ice cave, but does not mention visiting Bonington and Kor in their snow hole. By the time he arrived at the foot of the Central Pillar, Golikow and Kor had already teamed up: Kor had made the traverse across the foot of the pillar and Golikow was about to follow him.

'So there I was, out of work,' Lehne concluded, 'and I was not too unhappy about that.' He did not wait to see how Golikow and Kor fared, instead returning to his snow hole for coffee with Rosenzopf and was joined there by Bonington who had descended with him after taking his photographs.

As Lehne told it, the joining of the teams was a fait accompli, made by the likeable, impetuous Golikow; and the conversation described by Bonington did not take place. In 2014, Hupfauer inclined towards Lehne's version: his impression was that the two teams came together by agreement between Golikow and Kor. That is also the account given by Haston in his autobiography *In High Places*, even though it is at variance with *Eiger Direct*, which he co-authored. Suffice to say, Bonington stood by his account in 2014. If, between the two versions, Lehne is culpable by omission, the best explanation may be rooted in the politics that Bonington had identified – namely, that Lehne was reluctant to admit that he had proposed the amalgamation from what could be seen as a position of weakness.

Politics were to dominate that day's radio calls between Harlin's team. It was only when he spoke to Bonington at the scheduled call time of 11.45 a.m. that Harlin learned what had transpired. 'We've made rather a radical decision,' Bonington told him, adding swiftly that it was a temporary one, pending Harlin's ratification. 'Layton and Charlie Golikow are climbing together up the pillar. This seems quite a good compromise to me as it's inevitable that we're going to be following the same route. What do you think of this?'

'It's a lot to swallow at the moment,' Harlin replied. 'I'll have to think about it.'

As always, Harlin did his best to appear unconcerned by

Bonington's revelation; but he was undoubtedly caught off balance. The previous evening he, and the rest of us, had been celebrating the fact that Bonington and Kor had established a significant lead over the Germans. Once at the top of the Central Pillar, they would have the pick of bivouac sites and could establish themselves on the route to the Spider. Now, so it appeared to Harlin, all that had been compromised. With notable restraint, he told Bonington that his decision 'should have come a hair later' – that is to say, after he and Kor had reached the top of the pillar.

Harlin's first concern appeared to be the presentational aspects of Bonington's decision. If Bonington had waited until he and Kor were at the top of the Central Pillar before agreeing to climb with the Germans, it would have been clear that they had done so from a position of strength rather than because Harlin's team needed help. 'I don't want it to come out in the press that we were taken up the mountain,' he told Bonington. It was a measure of Harlin's anxiety that, following the radio call, he asked me to contact as many journalists as I could and tell them what had happened. It was a marked reversal of our policy of keeping our story to ourselves in order to preserve Harlin's exclusive deal with the *Telegraph*. In my new role as team spin doctor, I called Guido Tonella in Geneva, searched out the two German television teams at Kleine Scheidegg, and talked to several other journalists I met.

Blissfully unaware of these considerations, Kor and Golikow were approaching the top of the Central Pillar. After they had ascended on Jumars to the top of Bonington's long, unstable ice pitch, Kor improved the belay by placing a bolt and two pitons in the wall of the pillar to his right and Golikow set off up the narrow gully that led to the top. He climbed it using the classic bridging technique of placing his feet on each wall and, like Bonington the previous day, could only insert one piton for protection. Kor was watching apprehensively: 'Charlie only got one peg in on the whole pitch and that wasn't worth much,' he told me later. 'When he slid down a couple of feet I thought he was going to kill both of us.'

Golikow's final moves took him over a cluster of unstable ice blocks, where he belayed for Kor to follow. Ironically, in view of the importance both teams had attached to arriving at the top of the pillar first, there was only a narrow neck of snow on the head of the pillar, which made it useless as a location for a snow hole. More significantly, ten days after the climbers first stood at its foot, the Central Pillar had been climbed.

At that very moment, further political manoeuvres were taking place. Bonington, who was at one of the German ice caves, radioed Harlin to report that Golikow and Kor were nearing the top of the Central Pillar and that, once there, they would drop a rope for subsequent climbers to use. Then Bonington added that Lehne had made a new proposal – namely, that he and Kor should climb together the following day.

Having been so concerned at the link-up between the teams, Harlin now appeared to accept that he was in no position to contest it, particularly as he had not returned to the face that day. At least Kor would be in the lead rope, ensuring that Harlin's team was represented at the front end of the climb. He told Bonington: 'It's about the only thing we can do in as much as we don't have a complete climbing team there at the moment, and this enables us to keep in the progression of the lead.'

'Yes, John,' said Bonington, whose diplomatic skills were matching Haag's. 'I thoroughly agree.'

Lehne was listening to these exchanges in the snow hole with Bonington. He asked Bonington to send greetings to Harlin, but Bonington went further, suggesting that Harlin and Lehne talk to each other. Lehne took the radio set from Bonington. 'Hello, John. What do you want to talk to me?'

'Hello, George,' Harlin replied, using the Anglicised version of

Jörg. 'I wanted to say hello and tell you that I would see you tomorrow and good luck in progressing above the pillar.'

Lehne now attempted to broach the question of how far the teams should cooperate, but the call was interrupted by heavy interference. I have listened to the recording numerous times and the only words I could discern were: 'Thank you very much, John ... I don't understand ... when you ... of me. There are many different ... to this ... Over.'

The garbled call perhaps serves as a metaphor for the failure of Harlin and Lehne to communicate on the question of cooperation between the two teams. Harlin, who presumably cannot have understood any more of this than I did, made no attempt to continue the conversation. Instead, he said: 'Roger, George. Could you put Chris back on now, please?'

When Harlin spoke to Bonington, he did say that he intended to discuss 'the joining of the parties' with Lehne when he returned to the face. But he emphasised his concerns to Bonington. 'As far as a coordinated ascent is concerned for us, going to the summit, it doesn't mean the whole German group because this is just too many people and we don't have a provision for being third, fourth, fifth or sixth in a rope of that magnitude.' Bonington replied that Lehne was planning for two summit teams: the faster team would lead, the slower would follow. 'I imagine we could do it with three teams,' Bonington speculated. But Harlin would not be drawn, and repeated that he would discuss the issue with Lehne once he was back on the face. It proved a crucial interchange as events of the next forty-eight hours unfolded.

Back on the route, Kor and Golikow had reached the top of the Central Pillar. Their first move was to drop a rope down the right-hand side – the side the Germans had failed to climb – for both teams to use. The next pitch looked formidable: sheer, near-vertical rock leading to a groove that fed into an overhang about thirty metres above them. Kor set off with his customary confidence and was delighted that the cracks took his pitons securely. Once at the overhang he found that the groove formed enough of a corner for him to follow it without dangling clear of the rock. He was now within fifteen metres of the ice gully that formed a right-hand leg of the Spider, and he fashioned a belay stance there, just above the lip of the overhang.

Meanwhile, Bonington had left the snow hole and ascended the rope to the top of the Central Pillar so that he could photograph Kor. From there he used the team walkie-talkie to supply an on-the-spot description for my report for the *Daily Telegraph*. 'There's the most fantastic situation you could imagine,' he told me. 'The pillar is like a pedestal set from the rock and you can look down deep gullies on either side. You can see the whole face dropping away very steeply below you.' One of Bonington's photographs shows Golikow looking up at Kor just after he passed the overhang, an extraordinary testament to his ability to climb at the highest technical level in winter conditions. Other photographs show the face dropping away spectacularly into the void.

After reaching the top of his pitch, Kor secured the rope and abseiled back to the top of the Central Pillar. He and Bonington descended to the Death Bivouac while Golikow cleaned up Kor's pitch, removing all of Kor's pitons so that only the free-hanging 100-metre rope remained. When Bonington reached the Death Bivouac he met Lehne and told him he was returning to Kleine Scheidegg. Lehne wished him good luck and Bonington replied that he hoped to see him on the summit the next day.

At 7.45 p.m. Kor radioed to tell Harlin that Bonington was on his way down. Kor mistakenly thought his high-point was some sixty metres below the Spider but Harlin, who had been watching through the Kleine Scheidegg telescope, told him that no more than fifteen metres remained to the ice forming one of the Spider's legs.

Kor was delighted, and told Harlin that he would be setting out early the next morning with Golikow or Lehne; they hoped to 'perhaps get across the Spider with luck, to get a good cave set up there'. But Harlin was still troubled about climbing with the Germans. 'Be careful, Layton,' he said. 'This join-up is a little bit unfortunate that it was so early, in my opinion. We've got to be very, very careful in our commitment for a complete amalgamation of the teams. Do you understand?'

Kor assured him he did, but Harlin pressed the point: he did not want 'a forced amalgamation of the teams because this would commit ourselves to climbing with the complete German team which is not in our scheme of things'. If Lehne and Golikow wanted to join them in going to the summit, he told Kor, 'that's fine. But otherwise we'll find ourselves with maybe one man on the lead team'. Kor understood. But he doubted whether the Germans would accept Harlin's proposal, as they wanted to ensure that all eight of their team got to the summit. In that case, Kor told Harlin, 'taking off by yourself will be the only thing to do'.

Harlin told Kor that he and Haston planned to depart for the face that night; they would leave soon after midnight and hoped to join him 'bright and early'. By then, Harlin had been away from the face for five days. His remark looked like a belated recognition that he should have returned earlier, which would have enabled him to negotiate with Lehne instead of Bonington. But he was still anxious to safeguard his team's position, and told Kor: 'If we're not there by departure time, go ahead and climb with George or Charlie.' For all his concerns, Harlin wanted to ensure that Kor was part of the lead team into the Spider.

Following his abortive radio conversation with Harlin, most of this passed Lehne by. Bonington did tell him that Harlin intended to talk to him once he returned to the face, but otherwise Lehne was buoyed by the day's events. It no longer mattered that the

Americans had established a lead the previous day; the two teams were now effectively level again, and the Germans had been hard at work hauling their equipment and supplies. Lehne observed that Kor looked exhilarated as he returned from the Central Pillar with Golikow, and the three celebrated 'like children'. Lehne, noting that Kor was the only member of the American team on the face, invited him to eat with the Germans that evening.

Lehne was clearly drawn to Kor, describing him as 'the sympathetic giant American' as he joined them in what became a double celebration. They had almost reached the Spider; and it was Golikow's birthday (he was thirty-one). The five Germans in the Stöckli sang the climbers' anthem 'La Montanara' over the radio and dispatched a firework into the sky. The three Germans in the snow cave responded by firing off three of their signal rockets: green, red, green. It was a suitably euphoric ending to the evening. As Kor departed for his snow hole, Lehne promised to wake him in the morning so that they could set out early for the Spider.

Late that night, Haston and Harlin took over my room at Kleine Scheidegg to prepare for their departure for the face. Harlin had made the round of the weather centres and reported that the conditions looked good for the next three days. They ate a colossal high-protein breakfast in the hotel bar, munching their way through two steaks provided by their ally on the staff, head waiter Mario. At 2 a.m. they disappeared into the night and followed the familiar track through the snow towards the face. They hit difficulties halfway up the Vorbau, where a fixed rope had come adrift, leaving them to free-climb a steep section of ice in the darkness. Harlin was coughing badly by the time they reached the ice cave at the foot of the First Band.

After a brew, Haston went ahead and reached the top of the Second Icefield by late morning, where he wondered whether Kor had started climbing with the Germans. Looking up through a skein of cloud he saw Kor swinging gently on a belay on the pitch above the Central Pillar he had climbed the previous evening.

'How's it going, big daddy?' In the still air, Haston's shout reverberated around the great amphitheatre of the face.

'Just great, man!' Kor shouted back.

Kor was climbing with Lehne, who followed Kor up the rope when he reached the top of the pitch. Kor photographed Lehne halfway up, obtaining a breathtaking image of one of the most spectacular and exposed locations on the climb, with the face dropping away as if to infinity below the tiny figure of Lehne on the rope. When Lehne reached Kor's stance, Kor hung a new 100-metre length of blue 7mm rope from the piton at the stance, allowing them to retrieve the thicker rope they had ascended for use as a climbing rope.

Lehne took over in the lead, weighed down with an array of pitons, karabiners and slings that Kor had passed to him. Like Kor on previous rock pitches, he had to scrape snow away from the cracks and holds with his bare hands, which became painful with the cold. Near the top of the pitch he made a short traverse from the crack he had been following and gained a footing in an icy gully that formed one leg of the Spider. He fixed the rope and called for Kor – who later commented that he admired Lehne's perseverance more than his technique – to follow.

When Kor arrived he was all but overcome by the grandeur of the occasion, saying, 'Fantastic, fantastic, fantastic' over and over. Kor later remembered trying to manoeuvre so that he could lead into the Spider. But Lehne recalled that Kor first offered him the honour, only for Lehne to reciprocate, telling Kor: 'Go ahead – you shall be the first into the Spider.'

Kor led up the final pitch, following a brittle band of rock to the left of the ice. His lead was imprinted on his mind seventeen years later. 'There were no cracks to the side, it was a real steep thing, about seventy degrees. I remember just nicking little chunks out of the side where the rock came together with the ice and I just balanced on my crampon points. I was certain that I'd get a little higher and there'd be a crack but there wasn't. I remember saying, "Good grief, Layton, if you fall it's going to be serious."'

Kor reached the foot of the Spider and brought up Lehne, who noted that Kor had climbed with his 'customary virtuosity' – and that he had preferred to climb on rock, rather than the ice of the gully itself. When Lehne joined Kor they placed a bolt and fixed the rope to it. They were in the Spider at last.

From the Germans' start on 19 February, it had taken thirty-one days to climb the 1400 metres to the Spider. Already Lehne's eyes were drawn to the headwall above the Spider, rising a further 400 metres to the summit: 'a mountain in itself', Lehne reckoned. But Kor did not linger. He had seen Haston and Harlin arriving at the Death Bivouac and told Lehne he wanted to join them. Soon after he had disappeared down the rope, Golikow arrived with bivouac equipment. He and Lehne moved up the prominent ice rib running along the very centre of the Spider and hacked out a ledge wide enough for both of them. It was well after dark when they were able to settle down, gazing up at a star-studded sky with scarcely a breeze to disturb them. Then they heard a shout: it was Strobel, arriving after an arduous nine-hour climb with a massive rucksack from Kleine Scheidegg.

Lehne was both delighted and relieved, as he had been told in a radio call from the Stöckli that Strobel was suffering from frostbite and had dropped out. What was more, the five climbers who had been at the Stöckli had returned. All eight Germans were back on the face and three of the best climbers were in the Spider, eager to tackle the headwall at first light.

There was a different spirit among Harlin's team. He and Haston had arrived at the Death Bivouac snow hole in a confident mood. Although Harlin was still coughing, he was evidently on his way back to full fitness, having reached the snow hole only an hour behind Haston. The route to the Spider had been established and – so they thought – the weather was set fair for the next three days. Their aim, as Harlin told me in a radio call at 3.45 p.m., was clear. 'We're planning on prusiking up the ropes in the morning and blasting for the summit.' He added that they would pack food for three days. 'I hope you've got a good weather forecast for us.'

Sadly, I did not. I told Harlin that the forecast had changed once again, and that a cold front was expected to arrive in twenty-four hours, bringing an end to the good weather by the following night. 'It does not look good,' I admitted.

Assembled in my room was the full weather-reporting team, who included Joan Matthews and Marie-France Rivière, the Paris journalist who had joined our camp. Harlin pressed us for further details and we presented the verdicts from all three weather centres we had consulted: London, Geneva and Zürich. Although they disagreed over the precise timing, all three predicted that a cold front would arrive no later than the following night.

'We'd sure appreciate a triple and quadruple check on the weather report and all the specifics about this front,' Harlin said. We pointed out that the good weather was likely to last for another day. That was not enough for Harlin, who made clear that he intended to postpone the summit attempt. 'We'll just have to sit it out until we get a good forecast,' he told me – adding that if the forecast had altered again in the morning, they could revert to a summit push.

During the call the question of climbing with the Germans arose once again, this time following an intervention by Rivière, who had met Haag before he left for the face. Haag had asked if Harlin was still opposed to a combined ascent and she had replied that he might be prepared to climb with three of the Germans – 'but certainly not with the whole lot'. Haag told her he was still keen for the two teams to combine; he did not want to be in the first summit group, as he was enjoying taking photographs, 'but he was positive that Lehne wanted to be the first or at least the second' to reach the top. Rivière told Haag that he she knew Harlin 'didn't want to hang back'.

All of this she now related to Harlin. After he thanked her for the 'very valuable information', I took the opportunity to ask if he had yet spoken to Lehne about plans for a shared ascent.

'Jörg is in the Spider,' Harlin replied, closing down the discussion.

We ended the call with the promise to relay any updates on the weather forecasts we could obtain. Soon afterwards, Kor arrived at the snow hole, elated at having reached the Spider and at the prospects for the summit. Then Harlin told him of the change of plan; Kor's disappointment was clear. At Kleine Scheidegg, Bonington and Burke returned from a tough reconnaissance climb on the West Flank full of their plans for photographing the last phase of the climb. The West Flank had been deep in powder snow and they were still perhaps 300 metres below the summit when they turned back, arriving at Kleine Scheidegg two hours after dark. Bonington remained determined to descend from the summit on a 100-metre rope to photograph the climbers, and they too were clearly disappointed when I broke the news that the summit push had been postponed.

The next morning, 22 March, Bonington and I got up early in order to call the weather centres. When we radioed Harlin at 7.45 a.m., we told him there were some grounds for hope. Bonington admitted that there was no expectation of any high-pressure systems developing 'in the foreseeable future'. But there were now two cold fronts in prospect. The first was milder and was predicted to arrive that night, bringing light snowfall. It would be followed twenty-four hours later by a medium front and heavier snow. Bonington pointed out that the weather would be fine that day, which meant that it would be possible to climb.

Harlin remained reluctant to do so. 'We're not too happy about this bad weather,' he said. 'It's coming right at the wrong time and it's going to screw up conditions on the top of the face.' His inclination was to 'sort of make a leisurely day of it' – perhaps setting out later to reconnoitre the route up to and beyond the Spider.

Bonington suggested that he and Mick Burke could carry fresh supplies to the First Band which would help sustain Haston and Harlin during any further wait. Harlin said he needed time to think about the suggestion, then asked us again to 'keep hounding the weather people' for updates – as 'things change from minute to minute'. Bonington agreed, but told Harlin he would wait 'a few hours' before calling the weather centres again. He also took the opportunity to make his peace with Harlin over the premature amalgamation of the two teams. 'I sincerely hope that my negotiations while up there haven't ballsed you up too much. It's very difficult to see things up above and down below at the same time.'

Harlin forgave him. 'That's all right. I realise that you were forced into a decision which was about the only thing you could do. I think that strategically it should have waited for a day but we're entitled to balls things up – everything's fine.'

After the call, Harlin, Haston and Kor debated what they should do. They decided that Kor should descend to Kleine Scheidegg to recover from his exertions of the previous three days, returning with supplies as soon as the weather improved. After Kor had left, Haston and Harlin engaged in further discussions. Should they make a reconnaissance climb to the Spider? Or stay in the snow hole and conserve their energy? They decided to wait for the next radio call at 11.45 a.m., which should bring the most up-to-date forecast, but would probably spend the afternoon carrying supplies to the Spider.

One of the most striking aspects of this sequence of radio calls and discussions is what it reveals about Harlin's leadership – itself a topic of debate among his colleagues. Throughout the climb

Harlin had been juggling permutations and possibilities. He had been thrown off course by the arrival of the Germans and had endeavoured to second-guess both their intentions and the weather forecasts. Haston presented a positive view of his leadership in *In High Places*: 'He was like a general in a mountaineering hierarchy, planning, directing, conceiving new ideas.'

Yet Haston also complained that 'the simplest decision became incredibly complex', as Harlin considered it from every angle, sometimes testing his colleagues' patience. On one notorious occasion during the five-day snow-hole siege, Harlin asked me if Bonington had any advice. 'Yes,' Bonington replied. 'Stop buggering about and get on with the climb.' I rashly relayed that advice to Harlin, simultaneously gaining both his enmity and that of Bonington. Sometimes Bonington and Haston had taken matters into their own hands by overriding Harlin's deliberations in order to keep the climb moving. In the end, the team's improvisational abilities had produced a dynamic to match the German steamroller.

Now, at this critical moment, Harlin faltered once more. Instead of taking decisive action, he resumed his fixation on the weather that had dominated his thinking for so long. He showed no interest in what the Germans were doing and whether they might be taking advantage of the good weather to make progress on the face. It was almost as if he was still in denial over both their capabilities and their achievements. He may also have felt that his leadership had been challenged by the way both Bonington and Kor had joined forces with the Germans, resulting in key advances. During that morning's radio call Harlin mentioned the Germans just once, saying that when he did make the summit push he would 'offer that one or two of the Germans come with us'. He still appeared determined to hold to his original view of the climb, even though it required the spell of good weather that refused to arrive; and if any of the Germans wanted to join him on his summit push, that was up to them.

Haston's position is equally puzzling. So forceful at critical moments, he now appeared passive and unassertive. In his account, he talked of 'moping around' as he and Harlin were plagued by indecision over what to do. It appears that he deferred to Harlin when he was in full leadership mode, which matched the pattern of Haston's previous relations with more experienced climbing partners. The simple truth is that if either man had left the snow hole to find out what the Germans were doing they would have received a profound shock – and one that could have had a crucial bearing on what transpired.

At 8 a.m., while Harlin was discussing the weather forecasts with Kleine Scheidegg, Golikow and Strobel left their bivouac in the Spider and headed for the Fly. As Lehne wrote, they climbed as if they were on fire. He had expected them to take all day to reach the Fly, following a line out of the top-right corner of the Spider; they were there at 10 a.m. The climbing was far from easy, up narrow grooves in loose rock where it was difficult to place pitons. But this was ideal ground for Golikow – Katastrophen-Karle – who was ready to climb with minimal protection. Once at the Fly they pushed up the first cracks on the headwall, dislodging stones which forced Lehne to take cover. The Germans' support operation was in full swing and Votteler and Hupfauer arrived in the Spider with heavy loads.

It was all going far better than Lehne had hoped or anticipated. But Lehne was puzzled: where were the Americans? He had expected them to reach the Spider by 10 a.m. and asked Votteler and Hupfauer if they had seen them, adding: 'They should have been here long ago.' He was astonished when Hupfauer told him that Kor had headed back to Kleine Scheidegg without stopping to speak to the Germans. As for Haston and Harlin, Hupfauer added, 'We haven't seen them all morning.'

Lehne was baffled that the Americans were not climbing in such good weather. He also recalled that Harlin, as Bonington had told him, had agreed to meet him in order to discuss how the two teams might combine for the summit push. As Lehne saw it, the two teams were already working together, since Kor had climbed four crucial pitches with him and Golikow. Now, the Germans were so far ahead that the only way Harlin could catch them up was by agreeing that the two teams should formally combine. At around midday, as Lehne was pondering all this, Strobel arrived from the Fly to tell him that more ropes were needed for climbing the headwall. Strobel was clearly impatient – he was swearing, Lehne recorded – and Lehne decided that his discussion with Harlin would have to wait until the evening. He pulled on a rucksack and set off up the fixed ropes towards the Fly.

Down at the hotel, where we could see that the face was clear, we were equally puzzled that Harlin had decided not to climb. At around 11 a.m., showing more curiosity than Harlin or Haston, Burke decided to find out what the Germans were doing. He went on to the hotel terrace and peered through the telescope, angling it upwards until he reached the Spider, where he saw a climber together with a rope extending towards the Fly. He swung the telescope higher – and there in the Fly was a second climber. Burke called me to look and I too saw the climber, etched against the ice and moving slowly up the Fly.

Our immediate thought was that, if the Germans had reached the Fly so quickly, the climbing must be easier than anyone had predicted. Our second was that our team should be out there too. Bonington, Burke and I convened in my bedroom for the 11.45 a.m. radio call.

'Hello, John,' I began. 'The first piece of information we have for you is that there is a German in the Fly. Repeat, there is a German climber in the Fly.'

'Roger, understand,' Harlin replied.

Bonington took the radio and asked Harlin what he planned to do. Harlin explained that he and Haston had intended to look for a bivouac site in the Spider. However, he added, the news that 'someone is on the Fly perhaps might change things'. Still Harlin hesitated: he and Haston could perhaps climb to the Fly and go for the summit the next day. 'But we really need a lot of opinion and suggestions on this because it's a very difficult decision to make.'

It was Bonington who delivered the decisive opinion: Harlin and Haston should waste no time and go for the summit. The weather was still good and, if the latest forecasts proved wrong, 'then you're in a very, very good position for the final thrust'. If the weather turned against them, they could retreat to the Death Bivouac without having lost anything.

'Roger to that,' Harlin told him. 'Well, I guess we'll alter our plans fast.' In that moment, the decision was made. He and Haston would leave as soon as possible. He asked us to apologise to Kor for leaving without him – 'I think he'll understand' – and suggested that he try to join the second German team. He asked us to stand by for the next scheduled radio call at 3.45 p.m., but added: 'We're going to be working awfully hard. I don't know whether we'll be able to make that broadcast.'

I asked Harlin how he felt and he replied: 'Real great. OK, Pete, I gotta get going. Anything else? If not, Eiger out.'

The call ended with shouts of 'good luck' and I said: 'Scheidegg out.'

Some of the camp followers had joined the group in my room and there was both exuberance and relief that the summit push was on at last. There was a similar feeling in the snow hole as Haston and Harlin prepared to leave; the two men exchanged grins and Haston, who left the snow hole first, told Harlin: 'See you in the Spider.'

Haston later wrote: 'I felt I was on the way to the completion of my greatest dream.' Harlin's thoughts were imagined by his son, who wrote: 'He was poised to be in the first team to complete the greatest route of his generation, the most sought-after climb in the Alps, the route he had been trying to climb for three years, the one that meant more to him than all the rest put together.' Once in the Spider, 'a single day of fast climbing would transform his all-consuming dream into the greatest satisfaction he'd ever known'.

At around 1.30 p.m., having made fast progress up the Third Icefield, Haston reached the blue 7mm rope hanging from below the Spider to the top of the Central Pillar. For the first 100 feet from the top of the pillar to the lip of the overhang it was dangling free, offering one of the most disconcerting ascents of the route, where the climbers hung in midair on their Jumars, often spinning on the rope with the weight of their rucksacks. As Haston set off up the rope, he saw Harlin starting up the Third Icefield.

Haston concentrated on his ascent, pushing the Jumars upwards in rhythm, relaxing only when he reached the easier stretch below the Spider. He joined Hupfauer and Votteler on a ledge that had been carved into the ice at the foot of the Spider. Above, Lehne was moving up the rope to the Fly.

'It was a happy scene,' Haston wrote. He enjoyed the thought that he and the two Germans were casually chatting as mountaineering history was being enacted around them. He reckoned that Harlin was about thirty minutes behind him.

Chapter Fourteen

THE TELESCOPE

I remember the telescope, of course. I know, because I wrote it before, that I wanted to find out how far Harlin and Haston had climbed. It was 3.15 p.m., half an hour before the radio call that Harlin said he might not be able to make. The weather was holding and the face was clear. I also know that someone before me had been looking for climbers at the Death Bivouac, because that was where the telescope was focused.

If Haston and Harlin had left their snow cave as promptly as they had said, reflecting the new urgency that had overtaken them, they should be at or near the Spider. I swung the telescope upwards, following the line of ascent. I was close to the Spider when a figure, dressed in red, entered the frame. It was stretched out, falling, turning as it fell. It feels to me now as if it hung there for ever. In reality, it can have been in my sight for no more than a second before it disappeared at the bottom of the frame.

I wrote that I cried out: 'There's someone falling, there's a man falling!' I don't remember that now. Nor do I remember – as I wrote – that the figure disappeared behind a buttress, which may have been the Central Pillar. I do remember locating the foot of the buttress and seeing chunks of snow tumbling down; and seeing another climber standing a short distance above the Death Bivouac, as if transfixed by what he must have witnessed. Then the climber climbed back towards the Death Bivouac.

Of the events of the next hour, I can no longer be sure what I remember. But as I read my account in *Eiger Direct*, both images and feelings come to me. As I stood up from the telescope, three other journalists who had been on the far side of the terrace walked towards me: Guido Tonella; Rudi Rohr, from the Swiss tabloid *Blick*; and Hugo Kuranda. Tonella asked me what I had seen: could it have been an anorak or a rucksack; did it have limbs?

I told him I had seen a figure stretched out, falling.

Kuranda stooped briefly to look through the telescope, then walked away without a word. Rohr fetched Fritz von Almen, who had been looking at the face a short while before. Both he and Tonella had seen a climber on the fixed ropes below the Spider. He was not there now.

Bonington and Wendy were in their room on the fourth floor of the hotel, overlooking the terrace and the telescope. The window was open and I called up to him. When he appeared I called again: 'Chris, come down here.'

Bonington arrived on the terrace and I asked him to look through the telescope. As he did so, I whispered in his ear: 'I think someone's fallen, Chris. I'm pretty sure it was someone. I don't know who it was.'

Bonington stood and looked at me in puzzlement. We found a corner beyond the terrace and I told him what I had seen. He asked if it could have been a rucksack. Although I knew what I had seen, I conceded that it could have been. 'But I don't think it was.'

Von Almen was looking through the telescope, searching below the face. He had done this before. Soon he found pieces of equipment, scattered brightly against the snow some 150 metres below the Vorbau. At their centre was a dark, huddled shape. Bonington looked, too. He recognised a blue rucksack near the shape and knew that it was Harlin's.

Still we resisted certainty. I looked at the debris too, then swung the telescope back towards the Spider. Three climbers were grouped around the bivouac site: two were wearing red, one blue. It felt unreal looking at them, as they were clearly oblivious to what had happened a short distance below. I wanted the two in red to be Haston and Harlin, but then remembered that the Germans were also dressed in red.

Bonington clung to another hope. He was certain it was Harlin lying in the snow, but said he could just be still alive. 'We must get there quickly,' he said. He found Kor and told him what had happened. Kor looked through the telescope and thought that the shape in the snow could be a bivouac sack. Both men fetched their skis and prepared to set off. I suggested they wait until I called the face at 3.45 p.m. Harlin had said he might not able to take the call, but the two figures in red standing in the Spider – Harlin and Haston? or two of the Germans? – were certainly in a position to do so.

At precisely 3.45 I attempted the call. 'Scheidegg to Eiger, Scheidegg to Eiger, how do you read? How do you read? Over.'

There was no response, only the static hiss of radio silence. I knew, beyond all doubt, what it meant. Bonington and Kor set off on their skis, heading for the shape in the snow.

Two men had seen Harlin fall. I was one; the other was Rosenzopf, the climber I had seen standing, as if mesmerised, at the Death Bivouac. Rosenzopf was in no doubt that he had seen a climber falling, but he did not know who it was. That took some time to establish; and it was several hours before some climbers even knew that anyone had fallen.

Rosenzopf had left the snow hole at the Death Bivouac with a load of equipment an hour or so after Harlin; but for that margin he would have been the fifth man that day to tackle the long ascent above the Central Pillar. 'I was the next one up when he flew past me,' he said in 2013. 'I didn't know who it was.' His first guess was that it was Harlin, because he had been immediately ahead of him on the climb.

Rosenzopf returned to the snow hole where Schnaidt and Haag were preparing to leave. He told them: 'Someone just fell past me', but said he did not know who it was.

'We immediately asked him, "What was he wearing?"' Schnaidt recalled in 2014. 'He said he didn't see exactly. But he did see that the climber didn't have a helmet and that he had blond hair.'

That made it most likely that Harlin was the climber as he had blond hair. But somehow the Germans came to believe that it could be Votteler, even though he had darker hair than Harlin. 'We had the tentative suspicion that it was Roland who had fallen, or to whom something had happened,' Schnaidt said. 'What had really happened, we didn't know.'

The Germans at the Death Bivouac were desperate to talk to their colleagues higher up the face, but they could only communicate via the Stöckli. They radioed to report that someone had fallen – and that it was probably Votteler. Frey was in Stuttgart so they spoke to the Stöckli's proprietor, Fritz Bohren. Soon afterwards Frey heard from Kleine Scheidegg that someone had fallen and he called the Stöckli himself, but Bohren had no further news.

At 4.15 p.m., the prearranged time, Hupfauer called the Stöckli from the Fly. He and Lehne were ready to pass on the news that Strobel and Golikow were making good progress above the Fly. Bohren interrupted and told him that someone had fallen – either Harlin or Votteler.

Hupfauer pressed Bohren. 'I think it's most likely to be Donald,' Bohren told him.

Forty-eight years later, Hupfauer still felt the shock that hit him when he heard it was probably Votteler, his long-time climbing partner, who had died. 'If I tell you that it gives me the shivers through and through, right now as I think about it, then you know everything.'

Meanwhile, using the hotel telescope and a walkie-talkie, I was guiding Bonington and Kor towards the debris in the snow. At 4.30 p.m. they reached a buttress where they saw equipment scattered over the snow some 300 metres away. Bonington had a sudden feeling of relief, believing that the shape we had seen before was a rucksack that had burst open; Kor still thought it was a bivouac sac. Then Bonington saw something ominous higher up and they skied towards it. There was no longer any doubt: it was Harlin.

In 2014, Bonington remembered that Harlin's body lay spread-eagled in the snow. It was surprisingly intact, suggesting that he had fallen clear of the face for a long way and had perhaps landed in thick snow. Bonington later wrote in his autobiography that he felt for Harlin's heart, but in 2014 he did not remember that. He did recall seeing Harlin's body stretched out against the background of the Eiger, forming 'the most perfect representation' of the dangers of mountaineering. His voice choked as he added that he knew it was a photograph he could never take.

Throughout this time I had kept the radio link open. At 4.35 p.m. there was a burst of static, then Bonington spoke. His voice was breaking as he said: 'It's John. He's dead.' He and Kor sat down in the snow and cried.

I was sitting with von Almen in his office when I took the radio call. We had a bizarre conversation which unsettles me even now. I asked him to arrange for the Grindelwald guides to fetch Harlin's body. Von Almen refused and told me to instruct Bonington and Kor to carry the body to the railway track at Alpiglen themselves. I was aghast and told him: 'We must have guides.' He refused for a second time and insisted that I tell Bonington and Kor to carry down the body. With the greatest reluctance I called Bonington. Clearly distraught, Bonington said that he and Kor could not do it. I then told von Almen that I would call the chief Grindelwald guide, Hans Schwendener, myself. Von Almen shrugged and made the call. I have remained puzzled ever since by his attitude. As the Eiger's custodian, had he simply become blasé about death?

Throughout this time, Haston was waiting in increasing puzzlement for Harlin to join him at the Spider. He reckoned that Harlin had been half an hour behind him; an hour had elapsed. Maybe Harlin had stopped to talk to one of the Germans; maybe he had been slowed by the effects of bronchitis. After another hour Haston could suppress his fears no longer, and he sensed that Votteler was equally anxious. Hupfauer had departed for the Fly and Votteler was due to return to the Death Bivouac to ferry more supplies. For want of something to do, Haston decided to follow Hupfauer to the Fly. Votteler said he would try to find out why Harlin had been delayed, adding that he would pass on the information that Haston had moved up to the Fly.

'I abseiled down,' Votteler said in 2014. 'The first pitch was OK. But as I started the second pitch, I thought: "My god, this rope is slack." I pulled it up and there was just this stump of rope. So I went back up right away. I didn't know that Harlin had fallen – just that the rope had broken.'

When Haston reached the edge of the Fly he looked back and saw a climber on the final rope below. For a moment he thought it was Harlin and relief surged through him. Then he realised it was Votteler, who looked up at him and shook his head in an ominous manner.

Haston slid back down the rope, crashing into the ice of the Spider. As Votteler recalled in 2014, he told Haston: 'Down there, the rope has broken.' Haston replied: 'It can only have broken when John was on it.'

Like Bonington and Kor, Haston clung to the slenderest of hopes. Maybe the rope had broken as soon as Harlin put his weight on it and so he had not fallen; maybe he had fallen and survived.

There is now a discrepancy in the climbers' accounts. In the German version Hupfauer, still racked by the fear that it was Votteler who had fallen, looked down from the edge of the Fly in the hope of finding out who it was. He saw Votteler and his torment ended.

In Haston's account, Hupfauer had heard by radio that it was Harlin who had fallen. He shouted down to Haston: 'John's dead.'

'We didn't speak,' wrote Haston. 'There was nothing more to say. A broken rope, and gone was one of my greatest friends and one of Europe's best mountaineers.'

There was someone else we had to tell. As soon as we knew that a climber had fallen, we asked Wendy Bonington to head for Leysin. She took the next train to Grindelwald and would call for further news as soon as she reached Leysin. By chance, after Bonington and Kor had set off on their skis, Whillans called from Leysin to ask how the climb was going. I told him that we had seen someone fall but did not know yet who it was. Whillans and his wife Audrey set off for the Harlins' chalet. At 5 p.m. he called again.

'It's John,' I told him. 'He's dead.'

'You're absolutely sure?'

'Yes,' I said.

Whillans and Audrey arrived at the Harlins' chalet ten minutes later, shortly before Swiss radio stations began to report that Harlin had died.

John Harlin Jr, then nine years old, was playing with his sister and some friends in the house next door. Later, he remembered the mortified look on his mother's face when she came into the room where he was playing and he realised something was terribly wrong. He did not remember what she said, only his own feeling of bewilderment and the sound of people crying. Marilyn remembered him saying: 'I thought he'd make it this time.' He could not understand how his father could have fallen so far that it killed him, he could not believe he could have made such a costly mistake, and he wanted to know how it had happened. Andréa's first words, as Marilyn recalled them, were: 'Why did he go up that damn mountain?' For Marilyn, telling her children that their father had died, and seeing their eyes as she did so, was the hardest thing she ever did.

Bonington and Kor returned to Kleine Scheidegg around 6 p.m. Bonington's instinctive assumption was that the climb was over. Haston would come down, and he felt that the Germans should do likewise. At around this time Frey spoke to me from Zürich. He had learned that Harlin had died and told me that the German team would abandon the climb. When I told Frey that we were unable to talk to Haston, as Harlin had been carrying the team's radio, he told me to go to the Stöckli and use the Germans' radio. At 7 p.m. I spoke to Haag at the Death Bivouac. In our first confirmation of what had happened, Haag told me that the rope above the Central Pillar had broken. He told me that the Germans would arrange for us to speak to Haston, who was in the Spider. He also said that the German team would come down. At that moment, those of us in Kleine Scheidegg believed the climb was over.

What seemed so clear at Kleine Scheidegg was far less so to the climbers high on the mountain. After learning that Harlin had died, Haston ascended the ropes to the Fly to fetch his bivouac equipment. As he abseiled back down again, he was so distracted that the rope cut into the bare flesh of his neck. When he reached the Spider, Votteler applied a plaster to the wound. Since Votteler had no bivouac equipment, Haston passed him his down jacket. They had no food – Harlin had been carrying supplies for him and Haston – but they were able to brew some coffee.

Somehow, out of those shared moments, Haston moved towards the view that the climb should go on. His immediate reaction, like ours, had been that he should abandon the climb. But then, so he explained in *Eiger Direct*, he reasoned that to do so would invalidate all they had done and mean that it had been in vain. To continue to the summit would serve as Harlin's memorial. It is hardly surprising that Haston, so determined at crucial moments in the climb, should want to continue. All the qualities that have been ascribed to him, from his fortitude to his ruthlessness, would have contributed to that view. It was also unthinkable for Haston that he should be left behind if the Germans decided to continue.

Haston's inner dialogue was replicated among the Germans. In the Fly, Lehne had allowed Strobel and Golikow to continue up the easier ground below the final headwall. He wrote afterwards that he did not want 'to expose them to the depression which was affecting us', although it can also be deduced that he did not want them to stop them when they were climbing so well. Fifty metres or so above him Strobel was in his element. 'It was difficult terrain but it was like climbing in our Alb, crack climbing and so on,' he said in 2014. 'It was climbing that was intended for me.' Strobel was on a high. 'Tomorrow we will be on the summit!'

At dusk, elated at having made such good progress, Strobel and Golikow returned to the Fly, where Lehne told them that Harlin had fallen. Strobel remembered the fevered atmosphere: 'It was back and forth, radio calls, back and forth, give up the climb, what are we going to do? And so on. It was a big mess.'

Golikow, Votteler recalled, was profoundly affected, and told Lehne that he wanted to join Haston in the Spider. By then my request to speak to Haston had reached the Fly, and Golikow agreed to take the Germans' radio set with him. He departed in such a hurry that he left it behind. Lehne called him back. Golikow told Lehne he had forgotten his glasses and set off again without the radio set. Lehne called him back for a second time and stuffed the radio into his waistband. Golikow, he wrote, was out of it.

After Golikow had left, Lehne and Strobel continued to discuss what they should do. Strobel remembered feeling uncertain, particularly as Golikow, his climbing partner, had departed. But gradually the issue became clear. What would it mean, Lehne wrote, if after five weeks' struggle they gave up just a day from the summit? It would be senseless. They accepted that the convention on Himalayan expeditions was to turn back if a climber died, but this was different. To continue would accord greater respect to Harlin than to give up – and they would call it 'the John Harlin climb'.

At the Death Bivouac, a parallel debate was taking place: Haag, Schnaidt and Rosenzopf were equally inclined to continue. 'If we finished it off,' Schnaidt summarised in 2014, 'it would be more in accordance with John's wishes.' Haag accepted the drift of the argument, as he wrote later: 'At first we all wanted to go down. But gradually we became convinced that we should finish what we had started. It would be better for John if we achieved the *direttissima* in his name. If we went down we would leave nothing behind but an attempt.'

When Golikow arrived at the Spider with the Germans' radio, he put his arm round Haston's shoulder and swore angrily. Haston, Golikow and Votteler crawled into their tent sack and discussed what they should do: Votteler was for continuing, Golikow was less sure. At Kleine Scheidegg, Bonington, Kor and Burke gathered in my room, all of us assuming that the climb was over. At 8 p.m. we spoke to Haston and in the space of fifteen minutes he talked us round. To my everlasting regret, this is the one conversation we failed to record: my excuse is that it was the intensity of the occasion that led me to insert the microphone lead in the wrong slot. What I still recall is Haston's quiet persistence in overcoming our doubts. There is always something self-serving in arguing that a course of action is what a dead person would have wanted, which Haston did. But underlying our discussion were two key strands.

The first was expressed by Lehne, who asked in his book whether the rope above the Central Pillar had broken when Harlin climbed it as a result of a technical problem, or statistical probability, or sheer fate. Lehne did not supply an answer. But if the climbers abandoned the attempt it would mean accepting a defeat that had been beyond their control. To continue would mean they were ready to defy the odds.

Lehne had also said that to abandon the climb would be senseless. Lehne used the word *Sinnlosigkeit*, a key term in the writings of the German philosopher Martin Heidegger; its literal meaning is senselessness but is often translated as absurdity. Lehne was invoking the language of existentialism, made fashionable in the 1950s and 1960s by the writings of Albert Camus and Jean-Paul Sartre, who held that life was absurd and without meaning; and that the only way to invest it with meaning was by finding goals to fulfil, even if that appeared to be a paradox. By the same token, Lehne was implying, Harlin's death would acquire a meaning if the climbers continued their struggle to reach the summit. But he could not foresee – as he later admitted – just how extreme that struggle would prove to be.

The second became obvious during our conversation with Haston, as we faced the choice between the hideous emptiness we would be left with if the climb were abandoned; and the chance to fulfil the dream for which Harlin had died. The choice was stark; the decision was clear.

At some point during this turbulent day, I wrote a report for the *Daily Telegraph*. I can recall nothing about doing so, nor can I remember when I first notified the *Telegraph* that Harlin had fallen, or how anyone there responded. Nor could I remember telephoning Leni to tell her what had happened; but forty-eight years on, she vividly remembered me calling to say Harlin had died. I told her that what I had seen seemed to go on for ever, but can only have lasted a moment. I used the word 'cartwheeling' several times and was evidently in shock.

For my dealings with the *Telegraph*, all I have to go on is the front page of the issue of 23 March 1966, with its headline 'Climber Killed on Eiger'. There are two subheads: 'American falls 4000ft: stone cuts rope'; and 'Two teams decide to carry on'. The report begins with a classic summary paragraph: 'John Harlin, 30, the American leader of the Anglo-American team attempting the unclimbed "direct" route on the North Face of the Eiger, was killed in a 4,000ft fall from the face at 3.20p.m. today.' The second paragraph contains the assertion, supporting one of the subheads, that Rosenzopf had said that the rope was severed by a falling stone, and that this information had been radioed from the face by Haag.

Only in the sixth paragraph does the story move into the first person. I relate that at 3.20 p.m., as I was looking through the Kleine Scheidegg telescope, 'I saw a figure in red cartwheeling downwards. It fell too fast for me to follow it.' I then describe seeing snow knocked from the face near the Death Bivouac, and another climber – Rosenzopf – standing nearby. 'Five minutes later I saw a figure lying in the snow below the Face. Scattered around were a rucksack and clothing.'

I described how Bonington and Kor found the body and confirmed it was Harlin, and how Haston radioed from the face at 8 p.m.

to say that he and the Germans had decided they should continue the climb in Harlin's memory. A further dozen paragraphs were devoted to the day's events before the accident, the background to the climb, and Harlin's personal history.

I believe now that I wrote my initial report about Harlin's death once it had been confirmed by Bonington and Kor, and that I telephoned the *Telegraph* later with the news that the teams intended to continue with the climb. The detail about the rope being cut by stone puzzles me, as that was the theory first voiced the next day by Golikow when he examined the ropes. It did not appear in the Germans' dispatch from Kleine Scheidegg that evening, although who sent that is unclear, as Harri Frey was in Stuttgart. Frey in fact returned from Stuttgart overnight, catching the first train up from Grindelwald in the morning, and the next day a press agency reported him as saying that the rope had been broken where it had worn against a sharp edge of rock.

Reading my report again now, it strikes me as restrained and non-sensationalist. The *Telegraph*'s editors resisted any temptation to give my brief first-person account any greater prominence. The report was illustrated with two of Bonington's photographs: one is a portrait of Harlin, taken on the chill morning when we met them as they returned from their enforced five days at the Death Bivouac; the other shows Kor as he follows up Bonington's crucial lead pitch beside the Central Pillar. The whole presentation, I feel, does the *Telegraph* credit.

Hugo Kuranda felt no such restraints. At the moment of Harlin's death, it should be recalled, he was standing with two other journalists on the far side of the terrace from the telescope. After my involuntary cry of alarm, he strolled to the telescope, took a quick look and walked away again. From that brief look, presumably, he constructed the following account, which was published in the *Daily Mail* the next morning.

John Harlin, leader of the Anglo-American team of super-mountaineers, plunged 4,000ft to his death today down the Eiger North Wall, the Alps' greatest killer.

I was peering at Harlin, 30-year-old American, through a powerful telescope. It had just focused on his solitary figure in a bright red climbing suit with a huge blue rucksack on his back.

He was in a very steep gully on his way to the White Spider glacier, 11,620ft up.

Suddenly I saw the little figure throw up its arms. A split second later it sailed through the air, bouncing again and again against razor edged rocks, releasing a train of avalanches.

It seemed to me a horrible eternity before the body landed 4000ft lower down, on a snowfield at the foot of the North Wall. I was watching from the roof of the hotel on the 7000ft high pass at Kleine Scheidegg, Switzerland . . .

I was fully aware, once I read the story, that it was a work of fiction. I was at the telescope, not Kuranda, and he had not seen what he claimed to have seen, which did not happen anyway. For a long time, I felt that Kuranda's carelessness with the truth typified the ethos of a certain section of the British press. There was, in a way, something endearing about the readiness of some newspapers to print stories that were manifestly implausible. I no longer think that. As I began to write this book, and was required to reflect again on the moment I saw a man about to die, I came to view Kuranda's fabrication as a violation. Kuranda had stolen that moment and falsified it. Worse, he had appropriated and defiled Harlin's death.

Chapter Fifteen

THE DEVIL WAS OUT

The six climbers at the Spider and the Fly had uneasy nights. Following his conversation with Kleine Scheidegg the previous evening, Haston felt relieved that the decision to continue had been made. But he, Votteler and Golikow had their sleep interrupted by a succession of minor avalanches that they were powerless to avoid as they huddled in their tent sack. The night in the Spider, Haston wrote, 'was long and cold'.

In the Fly, where Lehne shared a sleeping bag with Strobel in the open and Hupfauer was on his own nearby, Lehne was preoccupied with whether their efforts of the previous weeks would at last pay off. He wrote graphically of their concerns. 'We found it impossible to sleep, not only because we were so uncomfortable, but also because our thoughts were in turmoil – and not least because we knew that the resolution of our struggles on this wall was about to be reached. Had we suspected how dramatic this end would be, we would have all decided to turn back.'

Lehne had hoped to make a prompt start up the fixed ropes in the morning. But his plan was disrupted by a new discussion in the aftermath of Harlin's death. This time the issue was not whether they should carry on with the climb, but how. The debate in fact became a furious row between two hitherto staunch friends and fellow climbers that threatened the unity of the team. It has never before been disclosed – Lehne did not mention it in his account of the climb, and even some of the team members were not aware of it.

The original German summit plan had been for the eight climbers to divide into two groups of four, with the stronger team going for the summit first. During the climb, the two groups had gradually coalesced. Lehne, Strobel, Haag and Golikow had moved ahead and had done all the leading. Hupfauer, Schnaidt, Rosenzopf and Votteler had become the support group, excavating bivouac sites and organising and hauling the equipment. Now, in the Fly, Strobel revived a version of the plan, which in part made a virtue of necessity. He pointed out that the lead climbers had frequently had to wait while the equipment was hauled up behind them, and proposed that the Germans should divide into two groups, each of which would make a separate dash for the summit. He elaborated on this in 2014, explaining that the two teams should remove some of the fixed ropes to use as climbing ropes, 'and climb to the summit Alpine-style while the weather was still good'.

Hupfauer was dismayed by what Strobel proposed. He felt that if the climbers divided into two separate teams it would violate the spirit that had proved so strong in holding them together to that point. It also seemed likely that he and Votteler would be placed in the second team, raising the question of whether there was enough equipment to go round: 'we would have been left with our pants down', Hupfauer said in 2014. There was, said Strobel, 'a real battle' between them – graphically adding: 'The devil was out.'

It fell to Lehne to arbitrate between the two. At first he sympathised with Strobel's case, which must have accorded with his own drive to reach the summit as soon as possible – and to be in the leading group. Then he saw Hupfauer's point of view. For the team to divide at that point would indeed fracture the collective basis which had taken it so far. Lehne did not have a radio to consult his co-leader, Haag, who was at the Death Bivouac. Alone, he decided that the climbers should see the climb through together. It was a decision of immense strength and integrity, and one foreshadowing the role as leader Lehne was assuming in the testing final stages of the climb.

The matter settled, Lehne set off up the fixed ropes at nine and an hour later was at the high-point reached by Golikow and Strobel the previous evening, which they reckoned was some 250 metres below the summit. Above rose an immensely steep recess in the headwall, known as a dièdre or dihedral. It was far steeper than the ground immediately above the Fly and presented a formidable challenge. The previous evening Strobel and Golikow had predicted that it would be easier than they had first thought, but Lehne still reckoned it would take a day to climb, at least. There was no time to be lost.

Lehne spent the next four hours balanced on the tiny stance at the foot of the headwall, becoming increasingly cold and even more frustrated as the day slipped away. Clouds were rolling in from the south-east, shrouding the Kleine Scheidegg ski runs and signalling the approach of bad weather. The delay stemmed from the activities in the Spider and the Fly, where the remaining climbers were organising and hauling the supplies required for the summit push. Haston had arrived in the Fly shortly before Lehne left. When Haston revealed he had no food, Hupfauer gave him some bread and chocolate and Strobel lit the Germans' stove for a brew. Meanwhile, Strobel was waiting for more ropes before he could follow Lehne. They took an age to arrive, and it was not until 2 p.m. that he finally joined Lehne at the stance.

As well as ropes, Strobel brought two items of news. When Haston returned to the Fly that morning, he had brought the radio set Golikow had taken down to him the previous night. Strobel had talked to Harri Frey at the Stöckli after Lehne left the Fly, and he now told Lehne what he had learned. The first item was that Bonington had asked the Germans to continue the climb. If that was indeed what Bonington had said, it endorsed the decision that Haston and the Germans had collectively made the previous evening. It also carried an important corollary, which Lehne identified: the two teams, German and American, would now be climbing together. On the day Harlin died, Lehne had spent the morning waiting for him to arrive in the Spider so that they could discuss whether and how the two teams could combine. Now, following his death, and without the question being explicitly debated, the two teams had joined. 'I was happy,' Lehne wrote.

The second piece of information was that the climbers at the Death Bivouac had decided to continue with the climb. That appeared to confirm the decision which had been reached the previous night. But here Strobel's news was out of date. By then, there had been further anguished discussion among the group at the Flatiron over whether they should go on. It turned partly on what they had learned about the state of the fixed ropes above the Flatiron. It also became clear that the Germans were no longer of the same mind in their response to Harlin's death.

That morning, during the operations to haul more equipment and supplies, Golikow descended from the Spider to the location where the broken rope had hung. He replaced it and continued down the line of ropes to the Death Bivouac, where he delivered some startling news. He told Haag and Schnaidt that in at least half a dozen places the fixed ropes above the Death Bivouac had been damaged, possibly by stonefall. Golikow argued forcefully that the ropes were too dangerous for any further use and should be taken down. From that it followed that the four Germans at the Death Bivouac, himself included, should withdraw from the attempt.

It looked like a sensible, pragmatic decision. But by Schnaidt's recollection in 2014, there was more to it than that. He remembers Golikow saying: 'It doesn't make any sense to continue. It's not worth it.'

Most of the Germans had felt that the way to expiate Harlin's death was to continue the climb. Golikow, emotional, instinctive, the first on the mountain to befriend Harlin's team, took the opposite view. His shock on hearing of Harlin's death had been clear in his bewildered behaviour at the Fly, as he attempted to take a radio set to Haston. Rosenzopf recalled in 2014 that Golikow was prone to making sudden, impulsive decisions and it looked as though he had done just that. Votteler said in 2014 that although he had already noticed that some of the fixed ropes were frayed, none were damaged to the point where the core was exposed.

Haag was of the same mind as Golikow and announced that he was also pulling out. He wrote that the state of the fixed ropes was merely the 'exterior impetus' for the decision to descend. The true reason was the 'inner need' of the climbers at the Death Bivouac to return. Haag, sociable, quick to make friends, so delighted to have met Harlin at Trento in November, had lost his will for the climb too, as his wife Barbara confirmed in 2014.

'Peter was deeply moved when John Harlin died. For Peter, the whole thing was finished ... It was like a dream for Peter and the moment John Harlin had the accident, the world collapsed for him. The undertaking became irrelevant and without value and he didn't want to achieve it any more.' In his letter to Barbara after the Trento festival, Haag had called the Eiger 'his great love' and his 'love in winter dress'. Now his love had been betrayed.

As for Rosenzopf and Schnaidt, the other two climbers at the Death Bivouac, they no longer had any choice in the matter. Schnaidt said in 2014 that he felt no personal disappointment. 'For me it was only important that our comrades get off the wall safe and sound.' The decision was made soon after midday – a full two hours before Strobel erroneously told Lehne that the Death Bivouac group intended to continue the climb.

I can be confident of the timing because of events at Kleine Scheidegg. At 9.30 that morning Kor left for the face, intending to join the Germans at the Death Bivouac and go with them to the summit. At 11 a.m. I spoke at a press conference that had been arranged by Harri Frey. I found myself in the spotlight, since I had seen Harlin fall. I mostly spoke in French and remember the cameras whirring as I attempted to make the crucial distinction between *au dessus*, meaning above, and *au dessous*, below, in relation to the Spider. At 11.45 a.m. I spoke to Kor. He was already at the First Band and told me that he hoped to be on the summit by the following night. I gave him the weather forecast, which predicted snow for the following day, and he reckoned he would be safe if they could reach the Summit Icefield before the snow arrived. I had sensed that Kor was uncertain whether he should continue and attempted to reassure him. 'We're really feeling this down here but if you and Dougal get to the top it's going to make all the difference,' I told him.

After the call I returned to the hotel lobby. Frey approached me and whispered that he needed to speak to me in absolute confidence. We found a table in a corner where Frey told me that Golikow had inspected the ropes below the Spider and had found they were damaged or frayed – even more so than at the place where the rope had broken. The Germans had therefore decided that those above the ropes should continue and those below should return to Kleine Scheidegg.

My immediate response was concern for Kor: what would happen if he started climbing the damaged ropes? Frey was due to call Haag at 2 p.m. and so I asked if Haag could intercept Kor and warn him about the ropes. Shortly before 2 p.m. I looked through the telescope and saw Kor approaching the Death Bivouac. I dashed to the hotel phone booth and called Frey, urging him to ensure that Haag spoke to Kor. I returned to the telescope and was relieved to see Kor disappearing into the German snow hole. (I later learned that he had intended to pay the Germans a social call anyway.)

Kor now wavered. When Haag told him that the Germans at the Death Bivouac were not continuing with the climb, he said he accepted their decision. Then he asked Haag if he would partner him to the Spider and go to the summit via the Exit Cracks. 'I just wanted to finish the thing,' Kor recalled. 'I was ready to grab one of the Germans and if there'd be too many people up there to finish it direct, I was going to use the Exit Cracks. I thought, "Layton, climb the thing and get it over with."'

Haag seemed interested, but then Golikow intervened again. He and Rosenzopf had left the Death Bivouac with two rucksacks for the group at the Spider: one contained food, the other equipment including the ropes that would be needed on the headwall. They had agreed to deliver them to the top of the Central Pillar, where they would be retrieved by Votteler. It was an extraordinary act of team loyalty as it meant ascending the ropes that Golikow had just condemned as too risky to use – although it may also confirm Haag's judgement that the supposed state of the ropes had been the 'exterior impulse' for Golikow's decision to withdraw from the climb. Once at the top of the Central Pillar, they linked up with Votteler who – most likely – was at the overhang thirty metres above them. After Golikow and Rosenzopf had secured the rucksacks, Votteler hauled them up. Then Golikow returned to the ice cave, this time bringing the damaged ropes with him.

That put paid to Kor's lingering hopes: continuing to the summit by whatever route was no longer an option. 'We were committed to going down,' Kor recalled. 'We had no choice.' But Kor was clearly ambivalent over whether he should carry on, to judge from his remarks to me afterwards. 'I didn't have any feeling for the climb any more. It's not worth someone's life – and when it's someone you know.'

In a call to Kleine Scheidegg at 3.45 p.m., Kor told us that he and the Germans at the Death Bivouac would descend the following morning, bringing the ropes with them. He spoke to Burke, who understood his disappointment. 'You've done really well, lad,' Burke told him. 'It's just hard luck. I'm sorry.'

Burke himself was about to be caught up in the drama of the final stages of the climb. That morning, he and Bonington had skied down to Grindelwald to carry out the chilling task of formally identifying Harlin's body. Back at Kleine Scheidegg, they made their preparations for Bonington's plan to photograph the climbers as they reached the summit. Their equipment included two 100-metre lengths of rope and two aluminium stakes to enable Bonington to abseil from the summit. Bonington had hired a helicopter from Hermann Geiger and it arrived from Sion at 4.15 p.m. He and Burke, equipped with three rucksacks, clambered aboard, watched by a group who included Marie-France Rivière and me. When the pilot asked where he should go, Rivière stepped in to interpret, pointing towards the Eiger and telling the pilot: '*Au sommet, s'il vous plaît.*'

'*Impossible,*' the pilot replied.

By now, clouds filled the great bowl of the face and were spilling across the West Flank. The summit was out of sight and the wind was rising. With a due shrug of the shoulders, the pilot lifted off. When he reached the lower part of the Eigergletscher, the glacier between the Eiger and the Mönch, he offered to drop Burke and Bonington there.

They were still 1500 metres below the summit of the Eiger, with dangerous ground to cover in between. Bonington gestured to the pilot to take them back to Kleine Scheidegg, where he and Burke abandoned one of the three rucksacks – which contained, among other items, one of the ropes, both aluminium stakes, one of their two walkie-talkie radios, and three of the four gas cartridges required for their stove. With his load lightened, the pilot took them further up the Eigergletscher, where he hovered a few metres above a 30-degree snow slope and gestured to them to jump. With hearts in mouths Bonington and Burke did so; and then, as the wind rose around them, they climbed up to the ridge that connects the Eiger and the Mönch. After a prolonged search for a location for a snow hole, they found one somewhere below the ridge on the mountain's southern flank. It took them three hours to excavate somewhere large enough to lie down and it was past midnight by the time they were able to attempt to sleep.

That afternoon, Lehne and Strobel had moved above their high-point at last. As Lehne watched, his limbs stiff with cold, trying to ignore the pangs of hunger and thirst, he was lost in admiration for Strobel's calm progress, moving economically and conserving his energy. Lehne judged him the finest climber among the two teams and considered that a stonemason could not have worked more precisely – an unconscious comparison with Kor, perhaps, since he was a stonemason and bricklayer. It took Strobel two hours to climb the first pitch and, by the time Lehne joined him at his stance beneath an overhang, the wind was increasing and snow was slithering down the headwall. Strobel started up the next pitch and appeared to be making good progress when Lehne heard the clatter of crampons and stonefall. The next instant Strobel was hanging on the rope a short distance above Lehne's head.

Strobel at first believed the fall had been his fault. 'I thought I was a complete idiot – I fell off my étriers for no reason before I clipped in the rope.' Only when he returned to his high-point did he discover that a tiny device known as a fifi hook, used to attach étriers to a piton eye, had broken. Spurred by his anger, he climbed another six metres before he and Lehne decided to call it a day. It was 6.30 p.m. and they had climbed just one and a half pitches above the Fly.

When Strobel and Lehne returned to the Fly, they found it transformed. Hupfauer and Haston had worked for most of the day to carve out a ledge where they could sit with their legs dangling over the edge. They were melting snow to make coffee when Strobel and Lehne arrived and told them about Strobel's fall. They gave an optimistic estimate of the next day's climbing, saying that they were close to the start of the Summit Icefield.

In a crucial call to the Stöckli, Haston told me the summit team was 'at the end of obvious difficulties'. He did not have time to elaborate, as the Germans had important business to transact. During the call Haag broke the news to Lehne that he and the other climbers at the Death Bivouac had decided not to continue. Lehne showed little reaction and appeared more interested in what Frey could tell him about the impending weather. It was not looking good. Frey reported that a storm and heavy snowfall were on the way and urged them to climb as fast as possible the next day. Lehne was accustomed to Frey putting the best gloss on things; if Frey said the forecast was bad, it meant very bad indeed – and they were in trouble. The phrase he used in his account was *im Schlamassel*, which is usually translated as in a mess or in a dog's breakfast. In today's vernacular, it could be rendered as 'in deep shit'.

After the call, Lehne informed the other climbers that all five of their colleagues at the Death Bivouac, including Kor, were pulling out. He added that the ropes above the Death Bivouac were in such a dangerous condition that they had been taken down. The implications were stark. Although a descent was not out of the question, it had just been rendered immensely more difficult. But, as Haston memorably wrote, 'There was no thought of retreat – the way out was up.' His words were echoed almost fifty years later by Strobel when he said: 'The retreat was cut off – we had to get out.'

Lehne displayed impressive serenity when he wrote of the 'wonderful calm, the peaceful confidence' that pervaded the bivouac. The hammering wind made it impossible to cook but that no longer mattered as they should be on the summit by noon the following day. Besides, he had full trust in his colleagues. Strobel was the best climber in either team. Haston was a superb ice-climber, who had not yet had the full chance to demonstrate his skills. Hupfauer, with them in the Fly, and Votteler, who was in the Spider, were calm and dependable. What could go wrong?

Among the five climbers, two were feeling less sanguine than the others. As Hupfauer explained in 2013, he and Votteler had accepted that they had been cast in a supporting role, hauling loads and – his personal forte – preparing bivouac sites. Now they found themselves thrust into the sharp end of the attempt, facing a climb up unknown ground in hideous conditions. 'I wasn't at all sure whether Donald and I could actually make it.'

On 24 March I woke soon after dawn. From my bedroom I could see angry clouds shrouding the Eiger and powder snow swirling around the hotel. At 6.30 a.m. a BBC radio news programme called to ask if the climbers would reach the summit that day. I told its listeners that, by and large, that was the plan. A German television crew laden with rucksacks appeared in the hotel lobby shortly afterwards. They had booked a helicopter to take them on to the West Flank, but Hermann Geiger called to say that flying in such atrocious conditions was out of the question.

High up on the mountain, Bonington and Burke were experiencing the full force of the storm. I radioed Bonington at 7.45 a.m. and passed on the message from Haston that the climbers were 'at the end of obvious difficulties'. Bonington took that to mean that the climbers could be arriving at the summit any time soon. After packing his cameras, he and Burke left their snow hole and set off for the summit. The wind was intense and they had to cut steps for most of the way, reaching the summit at midday. As they peered down the North Face, where the swirling cloud prevented them from seeing more than fifty metres, no climbers were in sight. Bonington noticed cigarette butts and orange peel among the rocks near the summit and thought for a moment that the climbers had been and gone. Then he examined the peel more closely and concluded that it had been there for some time (it was refuse from the Germans' reconnaissance climb more than two months before).

Bonington and Burke waited for thirty minutes, sheltering as best they could as the cold sliced into them. They descended some 150 metres down the West Flank to a point where they decided to excavate a new snow hole, putting them far closer to the summit than the first they had dug. Bonington said later that conditions that day were as bad as anything he had known in the Himalayas or Patagonia.

While I was ensconced in the warmth of the hotel at Kleine Scheidegg, and Bonington and Burke could retreat into their snow hole, those were the conditions the five climbers high on the face were contending with as they prepared to set out for the summit. When Haston looked out of his bivouac sack at first light he was greeted by swirling snow that reduced visibility to a few metres; Lehne emerged a short distance away looking like a ghost. As the wind increased the snow churned around them, driving into their faces no matter which way they turned, clinging to their eyelashes and filling their nostrils. Breakfast consisted of a few pieces of chocolate. Their stove refused to light and there were no hot drinks.

Lehne set off up the ice-encrusted rope above the Fly at 8 a.m. He had climbed only a short distance when the teeth of his Jumar clamps iced up and he was left poised on tiptoe on seventy-degree ice. He abseiled back to the Fly, unearthed a pocketknife from his clothing and dug the ice out of the clamps. He started up again with the knife between his teeth and found he had to stop every ten metres to repeat the process. By the time he reached the previous day's high-point, a pitch and a half above the start, his jaw muscles were cramping from the effort of gripping the knife. It was already ten o'clock but Lehne still reckoned that if the Summit Icefield really was only a short distance above, as they had reported the previous evening, they should be at the top by the end of the day. Lehne was expecting Strobel to follow him, but half an hour passed, then an hour, and there was no sign of him. The stance was narrow, powder snow poured down from above, and he tried to stave off the cold by moving his arms and legs.

At the prearranged time of 11 a.m. Lehne radioed the Stöckli. Frey took the call and told Lehne that Golikow had just returned from the face. They were worried about the climbers and Lehne found himself reassuring them. He said that they had climbed to within a few metres of the Summit Icefield the previous day; he had seen it during a brief clearing of the clouds and the angle looked easier than they expected. Lehne admitted to himself that this could be wishful thinking and, as he peered into the snow and cloud, seeing no more than twenty metres ahead, racked his memory of the terrain from the photograph the team had studied before the climb. 'I would have given a kingdom for a photo of the headwall,' he wrote.

Frey changed the subject and told Lehne that Haag and Schnaidt were in the act of removing all the ropes below the Death Bivouac as well as those above it. Lehne recalled that they had always agreed that they would clear the mountain of their equipment, but it made no sense to do it now. He was appalled. If their summit attempt failed, a retreat would be even more difficult: they would have to descend fully 1600 metres, most likely in a storm, without fixed ropes. Hearing Lehne's anger, Golikow took the radio from Frey.

'You're mad,' Lehne shouted. 'You should at least wait until we are on the Summit Icefield.'

Golikow attempted to calm him down. 'If anything goes wrong, we will come down from the top to help you.'

It was hardly a realistic proposition. After the call there was still no sign of Strobel and Lehne's disquiet increased. Growing ever colder, he shouted down the face, but there was no reply.

Back at the Fly there were problems. The climbers had planned for the lead pair to climb light, fixing ropes as they progressed, leaving the remaining three to organise the supplies. Haston had expected Strobel to follow Lehne up the rope while he hauled loads with Hupfauer and Votteler. But Strobel showed him an ugly black blister on one of his fingers, the result of frostbite after removing his gloves to climb. Strobel was afraid he could lose all his fingers if he carried on climbing with bare hands and asked if Haston would follow Lehne up the rope. Haston agreed – but having seen Lehne struggle to use Jumars, he said he wanted to take Hiebler clamps, reckoning they would give better purchase on the iced-up ropes. The Germans were still using them, along with Jumars, but none arrived in the next batch of equipment from the Spider and Haston set off up the rope with four Jumars and just one Hiebler.

Haston found ascending the rope as testing as Lehne: the Jumars kept slipping, leaving him dangling by the solitary Hiebler. At the top of the first pitch, to make progress easier, he removed his ruck-sack and hung it from a piton. It was a crucial decision that would have a significant bearing on events of the following day. He still found the going painfully slow and finally joined Lehne at his stance in the second pitch shortly after midday. Half the day had gone and the climbers had not covered a metre of new ground.

Haston took the lead, pushing on past the point where Strobel had fallen the previous day. He found it hideously difficult: a mix of rock and ice, with only shallow or friable cracks for pitons, compounded by the constant buffeting of the wind. Watching apprehensively from below, Lehne noted that it took Haston an hour to climb the last six metres to yet another meagre stance above an overhanging corner that slanted steeply to the right. Haston had hoped that they were now truly at the end of obvious difficulties, in keeping with the phrase that had raised so many hopes the previous day. But he glimpsed a chimney above his stance and the difficulties were all too obvious.

Down below them, a new disaster was unfolding. Hupfauer and Votteler were back in their role of organising supplies. Votteler was still in the Spider, where he had spent the whole of the previous day and night alone – consoling himself with the thought, he said, that he had a rope link to the climbers in the Fly. Now Hupfauer, who was in the Fly, shouted down to Votteler to send up the two rucksacks containing food and equipment that had been hauled from the Death Bivouac the day before. Votteler transported them over the awkward traverse from the Spider and attached them to the rope dangling from the Fly. Trying to lift both at once proved a mistake. As Hupfauer and Strobel hauled away, the rucksack containing the food jammed in a crack. 'We all pulled,' Strobel recalled in 2014. 'The pack ripped apart and fell down the face.'

The loss of the food supplies would place further demands on the climbers' diminishing stamina. But, as Strobel remarked in 2014, if they had lost the equipment instead it could have cost them the ascent – and left them in extreme peril. It was after the surviving rucksack reached the Fly that Strobel set off to join Lehne and Haston with 120 metres of rope. He reached the foot of the third pitch above the Fly to find that Haston was belaying Lehne, who had taken over in the lead.

Like Haston, Lehne could see no end to the difficulties, but he was still hoping they could make the summit that night. He passed the overhang above the stance and found himself at the foot of the chimney Haston had glimpsed, which rose vertically for some twelve metres. He removed his gloves and, without placing any pitons, climbed like a man possessed before being halted by an overhanging balcony of snow. He was now fifteen metres above the stance, there was no protection to limit a possible fall, and he could find no holds for his hands. He plunged his ice axe into the overhanging snow and clung to it but his legs began to tremble.

Feeling himself weakening and about to fall, Lehne decided to jump back to the foot of the pitch and hope for the best. He was preparing to do so when, as if by a miracle, the snow above him peeled away and crashed past him, driving his ice axe against his chest. He reached up and blindly hammered a piton into the place where he guessed the faultline continued. It went in for about three centimetres and he hauled himself up, the panic which threatened to overwhelm him ceding to the dreamy calm that came from knowing he had just had the narrowest of escapes.

Back on the stance, the snow Lehne had dislodged smashed past Haston and Strobel on its way down the face. Above them, Lehne climbed another twenty metres without protection before placing three more dubious pitons in what he described as 'no rock, just rubble of all calibres'. From there he pushed up a steep ice ramp that trended leftwards, with icy overhangs fringing it from above and sheer rock disappearing into the void below. He climbed a further stretch of ice-plated slabs and came out on top of a pillar of rock. The wind was blasting at even greater force and whenever he turned into it, shielding his face with his hand, ice crystals froze into his eyelashes and beard.

It was 3 p.m. – time for the next radio call to the Stöckli. Lehne clung to his holds and pulled out the aerial with his teeth. The radio croaked into life and, over the roar of the storm, he could just make out the voice of Frey asking where he was.

At that precise moment the clouds were briefly torn apart by the wind. Away to his left, Lehne recognised the Exit Cracks and reckoned that he was already higher than the point where the 1938 route emerged on to the Summit Icefield. Above him, tantalisingly close, was a sheet of pitted grey ice. Lehne yelled into the radio: 'We are at the foot of the Summit Icefield.'

Down in the Stöckli, desperately trying to make out Lehne's words, Frey thought that he had said he was at the foot of the final summit pyramid. He repeated that for Lehne to confirm.

'No, the Summit Icefield, the Summit Icefield,' Lehne screamed back, until finally Frey understood.

The call eased Lehne's feeling that he was utterly alone. Although he had not run out the full length of the rope, he felt a sudden urge to bring up Strobel and Haston. He hammered in three widely spaced and shaky pitons and then decided to use his last remaining wooden chock for extra security. He drove it in, untied himself from his rope, pulled in some slack and attached it to the pitons before running the rope out to the chock. Then he descended a short distance and leaned back on to the rope. The chock shot out of the crack, throwing Lehne backwards. He was already falling when he grabbed hold of the rope. His legs trembling from yet another narrow escape, he climbed back up and drove in the wooden chock again, belaying himself on one of the shaky pitons. This time the chock remained in place. Then he tugged on the rope to call up Haston and Strobel.

As Lehne watched impatiently, it took Haston half an hour to climb the last twenty metres to his stance. Lehne forgivingly greeted him with Golikow's catchphrase: 'It's a hard life.' Haston, ice framing his face and seemingly near exhaustion, smiled back.

By then they had climbed three pitches above the Fly, and Lehne was convinced that they were almost at the Summit Icefield. He offered Haston a choice. Should they continue up the leftwards ramp they were following? Or head straight up? Haston put the decision back to Lehne. 'If you want to go straight up, just carry on.'

Lehne climbed a short distance along the ramp and then headed rightwards and up. Firmly expecting to see the Summit Icefield, he was appalled to discover another forty metres of rock ahead. It brought the dread recognition that the summit was beyond their reach for the day – and that they would have to endure another bivouac. He fixed the rope and descended to join Strobel and Haston at the previous stance. When Lehne said that the Summit Icefield was out of reach, Strobel refused to believe him and insisted on looking for himself. 'Once on the icefield we could have got off even during the night,' he said in 2014. Lehne was annoyed in turn, as he felt they should be looking for somewhere to bivouac.

Strobel climbed twenty metres beyond Lehne's high-point but, as darkness finally enveloped him, he had to concede that Lehne was right. He climbed back down the rope hand over hand without protection. Back at the stance, Lehne interrogated Strobel about how far they still had to climb. 'No problem,' Strobel assured him. 'More ice, then twenty metres of rock and then we are on the Summit Icefield.'

There was definitely a problem over where they should bivouac. Haston had headed down to look for the rucksack containing his bivouac equipment. The only place Lehne and Strobel could find was the stance at the foot of the third pitch. It was an unenticing prospect, as there was nowhere to stand and they would have to spend the night sitting in slings. They hung their tent sack from a piton, but as they tried to pull it around them their crampons sliced into the fabric, so that snow poured in both through the holes and from above. They had abandoned their frozen sleeping bags that morning because they didn't think they would need them again. Lehne had last had a drink more than thirty-six hours before but whenever they tried to light their stove the wind snuffed it out.

Several times during the previous days Lehne had been gripped by a sudden desire to do something, anything, bringing a rush of adrenaline that drove him into action. Now, convinced once again that he was going to die, he decided to try to climb down to his colleagues in the Fly. Lehne described these episodes as a temporary madness and it is hard to disagree. He set off into the storm with little more than a feeble reflection from the snow to show him the way, firing a burst of energy that somehow overrode his thirst and hunger. He was spurred on when he glimpsed a ray of light that he guessed came from the Fly. But after making an exhausting abseil, then clawing his way to a piton at the back of the slanting rock corner of the second pitch, he felt unable to descend any further. That left him to make a despairing return to where Strobel was hanging in the tent sack. Lehne wrote later that he had no idea how long his foray had taken – 'one hour, two hours, more?' – and that he had the utmost respect for Haston, who had led that section the previous day.

Strobel had given up trying to light the stove. Their only sustenance for the entire day had been a handful of boiled sweets. They had just one left and Strobel offered it to Lehne. Lehne unwrapped it and put it into his mouth. But one of his fingers was bound with sticking plaster that came loose, and Lehne spat out both plaster and the sweet. Lehne searched through the snow and clothing in the bivvy bag, but it had gone. Lehne was distraught. 'Misery and damnation,' he wrote. 'I was in despair.'

The two men were now in an acute plight. Strobel was doubled over with stomach cramps, most likely caused by swallowing a large amount of Ronicol to try to ward off frostbite. Their feet and hands were becoming frozen. Lehne had no gloves and stuffed his hands inside his duvet trousers Whenever one of them tried to get comfortable, he pulled the other out of his position. It was impossible to sleep. Instead they kept up a defiant conversation, covering topics such as the romantic myth of the bivouac in a vein of gallows humour intended as an antidote to their surreal discomfort.

Lehne asked Strobel again about the climbing ahead. When Strobel replied that the Summit Icefield was only a short distance away, Lehne declared that as Strobel was the better ice-climber, he should have the honour of leading in the morning. Strobel objected that the front-points of one of his crampons had buckled forwards, rendering it all but useless. Lehne privately steeled himself to having to lead, but told Strobel they could decide in the morning. They continued their parodic bickering as they waited for the dawn. 'We just hung there and thought, "Hopefully the night will soon be over and we can finally get off,"' Strobel said in 2014.

The three climbers below were faring no better. Following the loss of the food rucksack, they had climbed the easier ground to the foot of the first pitch of the headwall, where they decided to hack out a bivouac site. By mid-afternoon they had fashioned a ledge wide enough for two when a new calamity struck. Somewhere above them a rock was dislodged – possibly by one of the lead climbers – which fell and smashed into Votteler's left shoulder. The pain was intense and Votteler passed out.

A photograph taken two days later shows a massive area of deep bruising, extending from Votteler's left shoulder down his left arm. If the rock had landed a few centimetres to the right, it would have crushed his skull. As it was, his left arm was rendered all but useless, and when Votteler regained consciousness he told Hupfauer he would not be able to go on. 'He looked terrible,' Hupfauer recalled in 2014. 'He said he was finished, he wanted to sit down and die.'

Hupfauer told Votteler he wasn't going to leave him. 'I told him to pull himself together and we could do this together.' Even forty-eight years on, when pressed for details, Hupfauer choked with emotion and was barely able to speak. 'It still upsets me,' he said.

'I was pretty well unable to move,' Votteler said in 2014. Hupfauer told him to keep raising and lowering his arm to prevent it from seizing up. 'Sigi certainly felt his responsibility,' Votteler said. 'We were a good bunch. No one would have left anyone alone. I don't know what would have happened if Sigi hadn't done that and my arm had gone stiff overnight. I would have had a problem for sure.'

None of this has been described before. Lehne does not mention it in his account – even though he must have seen Votteler's vivid red-blue bruising when he was photographed at the Stöckli. But then, as Votteler pointed out in 2014, he and Hupfauer were virtually written out of the German account of this part of the climb. He said, without undue rancour: 'Jörg never interviewed us about our experiences and contributions during the last two days. I cannot remember that we ever discussed this with him or even just talked about it. We were essentially lost from the story.'

Equally intriguing are the omissions in Haston's accounts. After reaching his rucksack, he related, he heard shouts and saw a red bivouac sack pinned to the ice some fifty metres below. He abseiled down and found Hupfauer and Votteler, 'looking remarkably cheerful' as they sat on the ledge they had carved into the ice. They had hacked out a second ledge a metre further down and that was where, after taking a can of hot soup from Hupfauer, Haston spent a wretched night. Secured by a network of slings, he had one leg on the ledge and the other hanging free. Although his sleeping bag was frozen and he was racked by shivering fits, he snatched some brief periods of sleep. He heard Votteler and Hupfauer shifting on their ledge above him as they, too, had a restless night.

What is notable is that, first, Haston does not mention Votteler's injury. Votteler confirmed in 2014 that he did not tell Haston about it – 'I didn't advertise myself' – and he and Hupfauer believed that Haston was too exhausted to notice it. They had an entirely different recollection of his arrival at the bivouac site. 'He was done in,'

Votteler said. 'He could hardly stand.' Hupfauer gave up his bivouac spot so that Haston could lie down, which meant that Hupfauer spent the night standing up secured by a piton. 'We laid him down and cooked for him, whatever he needed to survive,' Votteler said. Nothing like this appeared in Haston's version.

It is just about possible to reconcile the main points of these two accounts – but only just. Haston's is detailed and appeared, with minor variations, in both *Eiger Direct* and his book *The Eiger*. Votteler's recollections were endorsed by Hupfauer during our meetings, conversations and emails in 2013 and 2014. It could be objected that they were talking forty-eight years on, when memory is likely to prove fallible. Yet Lehne did include one confirmatory detail in the German *Eiger* book, which he must have gleaned from somewhere – namely, that Haston had been so exhausted that Hupfauer had given him his place on the bivouac ledge.

The best that can be said is that both parties – Haston; Hupfauer and Votteler – created their own realities out of an immensely stressful episode. Haston was manifestly exhausted, following his desperate efforts that Lehne had witnessed. Hupfauer and Votteler were nothing short of traumatised: Votteler by his injury, Hupfauer by the anguish of seeing his closest climbing partner in distress, a pain which had not been expunged forty-eight years later. As Haston fashioned his account, he may have excised how much he had needed the help of Hupfauer and Votteler, and possibly Votteler's plight too. Votteler may have found a new focus for his trauma in the sufferings of Haston, and that stayed with him as powerfully as his own ordeal. It was as if each of their brains had shut out the worst of their experiences to assist them to survive. Fifty years on, each account is valid as a testament both to the intensity of the three men's experiences, and to the distortions they are liable to as they attempt to impose meaning on what they endured.

Throughout this tempestuous day, the rest of us were struggling to learn what was happening on the mountain. Following my radio conversation with Bonington at 7.45 a.m., which had dispatched him to the summit in vain, I spoke to him again at 1.45 p.m. He told me that he and Burke had not seen the climbers, adding: 'It's pretty desperate up here – the wind's really savage.' Since I had no radio link with Haston, I trekked up to the Stöckli to see if the Germans had any news. They had locked themselves into their bunkroom and I had to hammer on the door before they would let me in. Frey had good news to impart, or so he thought. He had heard from the face at 12.30 p.m. that Haston and Lehne were a dozen metres below the Summit Icefield. That, in fact, represented no advance on the previous day, as Lehne – belayed by Haston – had only just started climbing again. Frey was unable to check further as the radios had stopped working. But Frey asked Lehne to press his transmitter button three times if he could hear Frey calling and we heard three crackles in response. At least Lehne was still alive.

Also in the bunkroom, newly arrived from the face, were Golikow and Rosenzopf – the first climbers to return since Harlin's fall. They shook my hand firmly in a gesture of sympathy. From a pocket, Golikow produced a crumpled package of tissue paper which he opened to reveal a short length of blue rope. One end had been neatly cut. At the other was a bouquet of shredded white strands formed by the kernel of the rope. It was the section of rope that had broken, sending Harlin to his death.

We would consider the rope more closely later, when we tried to determine why it had broken. For the moment my thoughts were on Bonington and his resolve to be at the summit to meet the climbers. I had left my radio set at the hotel and hurried down through the snow to be in time for the next call to the West Flank. When I reached Bonington I relayed the news from the Stöckli. 'I have big news, Chris,' I told him. 'They are on their way.' I told him that two hours earlier Haston had been 'forty feet below the traverse leading to the Summit Icefield'.

I was ready to discuss what this could mean in terms of the climbers reaching the summit, but Bonington – evidently anxious to lose no time – signed off with the words 'Right, out' and ended the call. For the second time that day, he and Burke climbed to the summit and for the second time saw no sign of any climbers. Once again, they could endure the tempest for no longer than half an hour before descending to the sanctuary of their snow hole.

Wendy Bonington had been with me during these calls, understandably anxious for news. We returned to the Stöckli, taking our radio with us. We arrived not long after Lehne, his radio working again, made his dramatic call saying that he was at the foot of the Summit Icefield – or so he believed. At 6.45 p.m. Wendy and I went outside and spoke to Bonington. Since it was almost dark, he was not inclined to make a third visit to the summit – especially as the Summit Icefield was 'a big place'. He asked us to radio instructions to the climbers telling them how to find the snow hole. He and Burke had cut steps from the summit, although he warned us that they were rapidly filling with snow. He would also fix their red-bladed shovel as a signpost outside, but even that would be difficult to see as they were in a total whiteout. Wendy and I were shivering in the searing cold. 'It's bloody shattering down here,' I told Chris. 'God knows what it must be like up there.'

'It's really grim,' Bonington replied. 'It's desperate.'

Up on the West Flank, Bonington and Burke discussed their options. They had been excavating their new snow hole so that it could accommodate the climbers when they finally arrived. But because they had expected the climbers to be on the summit that morning, they had left most of their food in their lower snow hole, and it was now beyond reach in the darkness and the blizzard. They were also appalled at the intensity of the storm and by what it could mean. They presumed that the five men on the face were unable to climb and so would be doing their best to shelter somewhere. If they were unable to move soon, they were in the utmost peril.

Bonington and Burke were in no position to help. They were equipped to take photographs, not to venture on to the face in a storm. Apart from half a bar of chocolate, they had no food and their energy was being sapped. They concluded that they should descend to Kleine Scheidegg at dawn and organise a rescue party. They would return to the summit with food and equipment as soon as possible, ready to abseil down to search for the climbers. With that plan in mind, they settled down in the snow hole for the night.

Bonington had managed to radio his decision to me at the Stöckli. I was still there at 9 p.m. when Lehne made a final call from the face. He said that he and Strobel were still looking for a bivouac site and had no idea where they were. The notion that they were nearly at the Summit Icefield, the mantra that had been repeated during the previous two days, no longer appeared to apply.

Chapter Sixteen

A MIRACLE AND A DREAM

Bonington and Burke awoke as the first light of the morning filtered into their snow hole. The roar of the wind sounded more intense than ever. Bonington, he wrote later, was convinced that the climbers on the face had little chance of survival in so savage a storm. But he and Burke were powerless to help them unless they descended to Kleine Scheidegg to collect more equipment and to raise a rescue party which, with luck, could be back on the West Flank by mid-afternoon. Bonington hoped that would not be too late.

Down at Kleine Scheidegg, I was as fearful as Bonington for the climbers. I was trying to calculate how long it would take him and Burke to descend to Kleine Scheidegg when there was a knock on my door. It was Toni Hiebeler, who told me that he, Golikow, Rosenzopf and Schnaidt were planning to climb the West Flank in a bid to help the climbers on the face. Hiebeler told me that Haag was unable to take part – he was suffering from an infected tooth – and asked if Kor would join them.

It was six o'clock, and my first thought was to contact Bonington. To my relief he responded to my radio call and I told him that a rescue party would be on the way. Bonington said that he and Burke would, in that case, stay put and dig out a snow hole large enough to accommodate both climbers and rescuers. I asked Bonington if there was anything he needed and he managed to say, 'Yes, we'd like ...' before his voice became a distorted crackle. Our radios had failed again. I remembered that Frey had communicated with Lehne by asking him to press his receiver button to indicate yes or no; I attempted that with Bonington and it worked. I tried to second-guess his needs by reciting a list of possible emergency items, asking him to signal three times for yes and twice for no. I learned that he needed gas cylinders, gloves and goggles; he did not need any more rope; and he managed to convey the information that he and Burke were planning to dig a new snow hole higher up the West Flank.

I found Kor in Bonington's bedroom. I asked if he wanted to join the rescue party but he told me that unless it was absolutely necessary he would prefer to attend Harlin's funeral, which was being held in Leysin that afternoon. He was looking for a shirt and found one among Bonington's clothing, although it hardly fitted him as it was far too small. He asked if I had a black tie and I fetched him the one I had borrowed from Harlin to wear at the funeral of Hilti von Allmen eight days before.

I went down to the hotel lobby where I met Haag, who was in search of a bolt set and some cooking pots for the rescue party. Kor supplied the bolt set but we could only find a battered kettle that lacked a lid. Haag had gas cylinders, I found some gloves in Bonington's room, and I bought some goggles in the ski shop next to the hotel. The rescue team had boarded the train to Eigergletscher and I passed the goggles through the window. As the train moved off I shouted to Hiebeler that Bonington and Burke planned to make a bivouac site near the summit.

By then Bonington and Burke were preparing to leave their snow hole. After battling to pull on their outer clothing, which had frozen solid, they headed up the West Flank, bracing themselves against the ferocity of the wind – it was measured at 120 kph that day by the weather station on the neighbouring Jungfrau. When they peered across at the North Face, they could see no signs of life, only swirling clouds of ice and snow. They found a potential site for a new snow hole and started to dig.

Later that morning, I trekked up to the Stöckli, fighting my way through the wind that seemed more fierce than ever. With my malfunctioning radio, I reckoned it was better to join forces with the Germans to pool whatever information we could obtain. Wendy Bonington and Joan Matthews came with me and we sat with Haag and Frey, going to the window from time to time to look at the clouds surging across the face. Frey was unable to contact Lehne but he spoke to Golikow, who told him that the rescue party was making slow progress up the deep snow on the West Flank. I tried repeatedly to call Bonington but could hear nothing. Later, I learned that he could hear me and was exasperated that I did not pass on any news. Although I justified myself by saying there was no news to give, I should have told him just that.

At 2.30 p.m. we still had no information from the face: where the climbers were, or whether they were even still alive, we had no idea. More in hope than expectation, I crossed to the window again and looked towards the face. Just as I did, the clouds round the headwall parted, revealing the entire face above the Spider. I called to the waiting group and we hurried out to the telescope on the Stöckli's terrace. I angled the telescope to look at the headwall and there were two climbers, one leading up what appeared to be the Summit Icefield while the other belayed him. Somewhere below them three more climbers were standing in a group.

Scarcely believing our eyes, we scrutinised them over the next five minutes before this magical vision vanished, enveloped in cloud once more. We hastened back into the warmth of the Stöckli, grinning, beaming and hugging, close to tears.

The night had exacted a heavy toll from the climbers. All awoke from fitful sleeps to find hands, feet and limbs immobile in the cold. Some would suffer permanent injuries. In his bivouac at the foot of the first pitch above the Fly, Haston's gloves and gaiters were frozen solid. As he attempted to tighten his crampon straps, one broke. It took him an hour, with numbed fingers, to find a spare strap in his rucksack and replace the one that was broken. It seemed unthinkable that they could climb in such hideous conditions; but, in Haston's epic phrase, the way out was up. Nearby, Hupfauer and Votteler forced themselves into action. Votteler was immensely apprehensive about his left arm: even after flexing it all night it was intensely painful and his left hand was unable to grip.

Two pitches above them, Lehne and Strobel were suffering too. It was fifty hours since they'd had anything to drink. Following the catastrophe of the last boiled sweet, there was nothing to eat. Like Haston, Lehne had numb fingers which made the task of stuffing the remnants of their bivouac sack into his rucksack a protracted trial. Strobel's gloves were shredded and he had black blisters on his fingers. Although he did not fully realise it yet, since he could no longer feel his feet, they were becoming frostbitten too. That was in part a consequence of the design of their boots, with their leather outer and an inner made of a plastic foam. The climbers had found that the foam became damp with sweat and condensation and proved impossible to dry, even when they tried to heat it over their stoves. 'As long as you were walking, moving, you could warm up the boot,' Strobel said in 2014. 'When you were standing, it froze.'

Lehne set off up the ropes into the storm, uncertain what lay ahead and still fearing that they might be forced to turn back. He reached Strobel's previous high-point and pushed on into the unknown, first up a steep ice gully and then over brittle slabs of

Strobel leads up the chimney system above the Death Bivouac on 10 March. The first pitch, an overhanging crack blocked by snow mushrooms, took him three hours.

Kor makes the key traverse, opening up the route, across the foot of the Central Pillar on 19 March.

Lehne, photographed by Kor, ascends the rope above the Central Pillar on
21 March, the day the two climbers opened the way to the Spider. Kor replaced
the fixed rope with a new 100-metre length of 7mm rope. It was this replacement
rope which broke.

Golikow watches Kor climbing above the Central Pillar on 20 March – the same pitch photographed from above as on facing page.

Haston arrives in the Spider at 2 p.m. on 22 March.

Strobel climbs the steep rock between the Spider and Fly on 23 March.

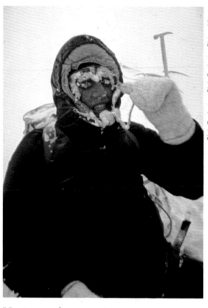

Lehne (left) and Strobel at the West Flank snow hole soon after reaching the summit on 25 March.

Haston at the summit.

Votteler, photographed by Hupfauer, ascends the last few metres to the summit.

Votteler (left) and Hupfauer at the summit, photographed by Golikow.

Funeral at Leysin, 25 March. Marilyn Harlin is centre left, Andréa to her right. Bev and Jan Clark are behind Andréa. Left of Marilyn is Konrad Kirch. Below Kirch is John Harlin Jr, standing with his grandparents, John and Sue Harlin.

The summit five during the descent by the West Flank, 26 March. From left: Lehne, Strobel, Votteler, Haston, Hupfauer.

The teams pose at Kleine Scheidegg on 26 March. From left: Frey, Votteler, Golikow, Bonington, Kor, Haag, Lehne, Schnaidt, Hupfauer, Rosenzopf, Strobel, Haston, Gillman, Burke.

The five surviving German climbers meet in Stuttgart, March 2014. From left: Hupfauer, Strobel, Votteler, Rosenzopf, Schnaidt.

Kor at the Valley of Fire, Nevada, in 2009.

Bonington near his home in the Lake District, in 2014.

Barbara Haag with daughter Christiane and granddaughter Laura in 2014.

John Harlin Jr at the Leysin cemetery in 2014.

Andréa Cilento (née Harlin) in Olympia, Washington, in 2014.

Marilyn Harlin at her home in Portland, Oregon, in 2014.

overlapping rock that reminded him of the shell of a turtle. So far he had placed just two pitons and he now faced a new problem caused by the drag of the rope. It was so severe that he had to stop climbing and abseil back to the foot of the pitch. Strobel had been waiting there for an hour and when Lehne saw him he resembled a pillar of ice, so covered with snow that he almost merged with his surroundings.

Strobel was horrified to see Lehne arrive, fearing that he had given up and they would have to descend. He was relieved when Lehne told him about the rope drag and proposed that they move up to Strobel's high-point. Rigging a belay proved all but impossible. They were unable to place bolts as every attempt at drilling just left a shallow hole in the friable limestone. It took Lehne an hour to place two widely spaced pitons through which he could run his rope. The climbing became even more precarious, culminating in a five-metre section without handholds where he was balancing only on the front-points of his crampons. He tried to move up by grasping a tiny flake of rock from underneath, but it broke away and he toppled backwards. As he struggled to stop himself falling a violent gust of wind slammed him back upright and he held on. Shortly afterwards he was at the top of the pitch.

Lehne described this pitch – 'the only possible way out of this place' – as the boldest of his entire climbing career. It could be added that his propensity for taking risks which marked his early career had proved its worth precisely when it was most needed. Later, Lehne concluded: 'There are possibly few climbs in the Alps where the leading climber has to take such high risk. Personally, I know none.'

Strobel joined Lehne at the stance. Ahead, stretching up into the murk, was a sheet of ice. It appeared ominously thin, but as Lehne moved up it the angle eased and the ice thickened. He drove in his last ice piton for protection and headed rightwards to a tiny arête, where he stopped and plunged his ice axe up to the hilt. He let out a yell of joy, an exultant discharge of energy and relief, that was snatched away by the wind. They had reached the Summit Icefield, the promised land that had seemed beyond them for so long.

Strobel followed Lehne to their next stance and Lehne pushed on, following the snow arête which gave way to a further stretch of rock crowned by a short, stubby pillar. They hammered in a piton and attached their last fixed rope. As he did so, Lehne realised he had not seen Haston, Votteler and Hupfauer all day and – as he later recorded – wondered if they had decided to go back down. It was a curious observation, a seeming repudiation of the collective spirit that had sustained the German team over the previous five weeks. But it allowed Lehne to savour the fact that he and Strobel were by themselves on the face and would be going to the summit alone – which, ironically, was what Strobel had proposed two days before.

The next pitch – the ninth above the Fly – led up a sixty-degree slope with a ten-centimetre crust of snow that had been pounded into place by the wind. Although the difficulties were eased, they could not relax as the wind was hammering from all sides, threatening to hurl them from the steps they were cutting, and flakes of ice were soaring past them, transported by the gale. At the top of the pitch Lehne told Strobel that his arms were cramping and asked him to take over the lead. They were uncertain where they would reach the crest of the icefield and assumed they would do so somewhere to the left of the summit, on the Mittellegi Ridge. Strobel was in difficulty with his crampons but the angle had relented sufficiently to allow him to take over. Still cutting steps, he headed on up.

Lehne was pondering where the summit was when the clouds momentarily cleared. Kleine Scheidegg appeared, then the Stöckli, and Lehne wondered if he and Strobel could be seen from there. He shouted in a fanciful bid to bridge the distance to the Stöckli – and, to his surprise, heard answering yells from closer at hand. He looked down and saw Hupfauer, Votteler and Haston several pitches below. He shouted back: 'We are going for the summit. Bonington will be there with 120 metres of rope. We will lower it down to you – wait for it.' News of Bonington's plan to take one or more ropes to the summit had clearly reached Lehne, most likely in a radio call – and Lehne's concern for the three following climbers marked a reassertion of the collective spirit that he had appeared to disavow a few moments before. He could not tell if the climbers below had heard him, and then the clouds closed in again.

Haston, Hupfauer and Votteler had left their bivouac site above the Fly not long after Lehne and Strobel set off two pitches above them. Haston led up the fixed rope on the first pitch but halfway up he sensed that his fingers were freezing. At the top of the pitch he removed his gloves and saw that his fingers resembled ten white wooden pegs. He swallowed a handful of Ronicol pills and waited, in intense pain, as blood permeated his fingers. Below him, Votteler was in difficulty as he attempted to ascend the rope using his right hand, while Hupfauer did his best to shepherd him up the rope. 'My left arm was useless,' Votteler said in 2014. 'It was a matter of up, up, up.'

Somewhere above, they presumed, Lehne and Strobel were making progress. That was confirmed when they made it to the point on the fifth pitch Lehne and Strobel had reached the previous evening. Haston was dismayed that they had taken all the ice-climbing equipment with them, not even leaving him an ice axe. In 2014 Hupfauer guessed that Lehne and Strobel had lost some of their own equipment, as they had taken his ice axe the previous day – leaving the three without one between them. Haston also saw that although they had left a fixed rope in place, it ended around twelve metres above him. Haston considered climbing the stretch solo but caution got the better of him, and he waited for Hupfauer and Votteler to arrive so that he could lead it on a rope. It was, he observed, not particularly difficult, but was made far more so without an ice axe.

Haston climbed the pitch and fixed the rope for Hupfauer and Votteler to follow. They had just joined him on the stance when, in the moment of revelation that had enthralled us at the Stöckli, the clouds cleared. They looked up towards the summit and saw Strobel and Lehne cutting their way up a sixty-degree ice slope. Haston judged that they were 'a rope-length' away, but that appeared to be wishful thinking: Strobel was most likely leading the tenth pitch above the Fly, putting him and Lehne some four pitches ahead and 100 metres below the summit. Haston did not hear Lehne's shout of encouragement, or his instruction that they should wait until Bonington lowered a rope from the summit.

Above them, Strobel reached the top of the tenth pitch and brought Lehne up. Strobel led on again, passing an awkward rock bulge and emerging on to another ice slope. Ahead, at last, he could see the end of the climb. Their fifty-metre rope proved just long enough. 'The rope was finished, I fell down and I was on the summit,' Strobel said in 2014.

Strobel's first thought was to bring up Lehne – which almost produced the ultimate disaster. Strobel drove his ice axe into the summit snow cone and wound the climbing rope around it as best he could with his frostbitten fingers. Below him Lehne, who had been waiting on the final stance for an hour, thought he heard Strobel call him up. That was a mistake – and neither the ice axe nor the belay was secure as Lehne set off. Strobel was straining against the pull of the rope, clinging to the shaft of his ice axe just a step or two away from the void, as he fought to support Lehne's weight.

The ice axe held. Lehne pulled over the final crest and found that they were just three metres to the right of the summit – thus fulfilling Comici's edict about a falling drop of water almost to the letter. He and Strobel embraced but were unable to smile as their faces were covered in ice. Deep down, Lehne wrote, they were in turmoil, ready to laugh and to cry. Lehne's attempts at celebration were cut short when he saw how poorly Strobel had secured his rope and realised just how close to calamity they had been.

Strobel also reflected on the narrow margin of their success. 'I have often wondered what would have happened if the rope hadn't lasted to the summit. We didn't have pitons left, nothing. It was a miracle – more than that, it was like a dream.'

Lehne drove his own ice axe into the snow and secured the rope for Haston, Hupfauer and Votteler. His immediate instinct was to head down from the summit to find shelter from the wind which was threatening to hurl them off the narrow summit ridge. But they were unsteady on their feet, the result, Lehne assumed, of attempting to walk on a horizontal plane after so long existing on the vertical. Then a figure loomed out of the swirling snow: it was Bonington.

He embraced both men and told them: 'Fantastic, wonderful, wonderful.' Bonington thought that Lehne looked surprisingly fit while Strobel was clearly suffering from frostbite and in trouble. Such was the emotion of the occasion, Lehne recorded, that no one could manage to utter a coherent sentence.

A short while before, Bonington had met Golikow about 150 metres below the summit on the West Flank. Bonington and Burke were still digging out their new snow cave but Golikow told him that the Germans had been excavating another one further down. Golikow also had news of the climbers. Frey had told him that we had seen the two groups, one apparently close to the summit, and Golikow had been determined to meet them – in 2014 Schnaidt recalled him insisting: 'I have to go up, I have to go up, no matter what.'

It has to be said that precisely who met who on the summit is yet another subject of conflicting accounts and possibly fallible memories. The version I gave in *Eiger Direct*, where Bonington meets Lehne and Strobel alone, is consistent with what Lehne wrote. But in *The Next Horizon*, Bonington wrote that he went to the summit with Golikow. After grabbing hold of Lehne and Strobel, 'we shook hands and thumped them on their backs on seeing them alive'. That is also what Strobel remembered in 2014. 'Jörg had just arrived, and then a figure came through the fog – it was Karl,' Strobel said. 'I will never forget that moment. We both cried.'

My account and Lehne's have the advantage of having been written closest to the time. But in adjudicating between the conflicting accounts, I prefer that of Bonington and, above all, Strobel's, because of the clarity of the image and the emotional truth it expresses. Almost fifty years on, I am willing to change my story.

There are several aphorisms which purport to instruct photographers on their craft. One holds that a good photographer needs to be in the right place at the right time. Another says that if your photographs aren't good enough, you're not close enough. By arriving at the summit moments after Lehne, Bonington fulfilled both criteria. But he – or his cameras – proved to be another victim of the cold.

Five minutes passed, as the embraces and congratulations continued, before Bonington attempted to take photographs. In 2014 Bonington had no recollection of what happened next, but this was described by Lehne. 'We posed for the summit photo but nothing happened. The mechanism was frozen.' Bonington had three cameras with him. After the first failed, he tried the second, then the third: all had frozen. There is a hint of Schadenfreude in Lehne's concluding remark: 'Tough luck, after he spent two days waiting for us in a snow hole on the West Flank.'

All was not lost. Bonington led Lehne and Strobel down to his snow hole where he unwrapped a fourth camera from his sleeping bag. In one of Bonington's photographs Lehne is kneeling in deep snow, his forehead, eyelashes, nose and mouth still crusted with ice, which also rims his balaclava, while a tangle of climbing iron-mongery dangles from his neck. Strobel is sitting beside him. He has removed his right glove to reveal a blackened hand; pain – or distress – is etched on his face. In a second photograph, Lehne is looking down at Strobel, who is looking up at him with the trace of a smile. They are the perfect documents to attest to the two men's suffering, endurance and comradeship; and to their deter-mination to give meaning to Harlin's death.

As Golikow led Lehne and Strobel to the new German snow cave, Haston, Hupfauer and Votteler were fighting for their lives. They spent an hour covering the next three pitches to the Summit Icefield, where the climbing became easier. But when they reached the top of the eighth pitch they were abruptly halted. They had reached the end of the fixed ropes and ahead stretched a fifty-metre pitch of bare sixty-degree ice. Lehne had judged it steep but straightforward, but he was equipped with an ice axe and func-tioning crampons. Haston had neither. His left crampon, which he had spent so long trying to secure that morning, had come adrift and was twisted at a forty-five degree angle; his right crampon was loose too. Worse still, Lehne's steps had been obliterated by snow which now drove into Haston's face, all but blinding him as it froze to his eyebrows and eyelids. With just one ice dagger to assist him, Haston set off, scraping the snow out of Lehne's steps with his hands and pulling himself on to each in turn.

Below him, Hupfauer and Votteler were watching in trepidation, as aware as Haston that they had only a poor belay and one slip by Haston could kill them all. 'He scraped his way up,' Votteler said in 2014. 'It was more than a masterpiece.' Above him, Haston could see the rope which by then Bonington had dropped, and thought that once he reached it he would be safe. But at the top of the pitch Haston saw that the rope was dangling some six metres to his left. He began edging his way leftwards, tentatively trusting himself to his unstable crampons, and then headed back. Without an ice axe it was hopeless.

Haston knew that Hupfauer and Votteler were waiting below and that it lay in his hands to get them off the face. There was just one answer – and a desperate one at that. If he could drive his ice dagger into the ice he could set up a tension traverse, just as Hinterstoisser had done thirty years before. Using a Hiebler clamp, he hammered the dagger into the ice; it penetrated barely an inch. He attached a sling, passed his rope through it and set off again, balancing on his crampon points as he worked his way towards the rope hanging down the next pitch.

'Point by point I edged across the icy slabs,' Haston wrote in *Eiger Direct*. 'There was no real point in worrying because it was out of my hands. Three lives on an inch of metal. A long last reach and there was the rope.' Haston attached his clamp and clung on. He wrote that it had been the longest thirty seconds of his life.

Haston tied off his rope so that Hupfauer and Votteler could follow and continued up the fixed rope. He heard voices and saw two figures looming through the cloud and the storm. Bonington, who had returned to the summit with Golikow, called down to him and Haston shouted back: 'Christ, is that you, Chris?'

This time Bonington got his summit picture. Haston, his face encrusted with snow, is lifting a mittened hand to acknowledge Bonington's camera; behind him, Lehne's ice axe is embedded in the summit cone. Haston wrote that his overwhelming feeling on reaching the summit was gratitude that Bonington and Golikow were there to meet him.

Bonington led Haston down to the snow hole, while Golikow waited for Hupfauer and Votteler. Hupfauer arrived half an hour later, followed after another half-hour by Votteler. He too collapsed when he reached the sanctuary of the summit ridge. 'The first thing I did was to fall flat on my face. We had been in the vertical the whole time, and all of a sudden I went "bang" and fell straight to the ground.'

There were more remarkable summit photos. Hupfauer had been carrying a Hasselblad camera throughout the climb. The shutter release jammed at the last but he extricated his Swiss Army knife and jammed in the corkscrew to give the release leverage. He photographed Votteler nearing the top of the rope, his head down as he strives to pull himself up the last few metres, the North Face disappearing into the murk below. When Votteler reached the top Hupfauer took a second shot that shows him kneeling on the summit cone. Then Golikow grabbed the camera and took two shots of Hupfauer and Votteler. In the first, Hupfauer is watching Votteler, who is stooped after removing his Hiebler clamp from the fixed rope. In the second, the two men, their faces encrusted with the familiar carapace of snow, have an arm around each other's shoulder and are leaning towards each other in an image of unity and support.

Hupfauer's reaction on reaching the summit, as he related in 2013, was simple: 'We had to get down.'

Votteler said: 'We had survived – nothing more.'

It was snowing heavily that afternoon in Leysin. The mourners who found a place in Leysin's Protestant church, with its angular wooden pews and its ornate curved oak ceiling, could shelter there, while those outside were gradually draped with snow. Kor arrived with Bev Clark, who had flown out with his wife from London and met him at Kleine Scheidegg. Harlin's father had travelled from Uganda, his mother from California. Harlin's first Eiger partner, Konrad Kirch, gave the eulogy, praising his qualities as both a mountaineer and a man of the broadest interests, an inspiring teacher who sought to promote peace and understanding. The German group at Kleine Scheidegg sent a telegram regretting that they were unable to attend as they were assisting the climbers on the face, together with a wreath inscribed: 'Goodbye John'.

John Harlin Jr remembered reading the inscription on the Germans' wreath as the mourners followed the hearse down a winding lane to the cemetery on a hillside on the edge of Leysin. He remembered the mountain guides from France and Switzerland in their climbing clothes and the snow falling as he stood beside his grandfather and watched his father's coffin being lowered into the grave. His sister Andréa was with her mother, one hand in a white hand warmer, the other bare. Forty-eight years later she remembered the snow, and 'flowers, flowers, flowers'.

Schnaidt had a down jacket in his rucksack, but such was the crush he was unable to take it out. It hardly mattered as the warmth of the climbers' bodies permeated the hole, although it also condensed and the moisture saturated their clothes. They brewed an exotic mix of hot drinks – tea, coffee, bouillon, Ovomaltine – until the stove puttered out and was jettisoned through the cave entrance. A bottle of schnapps was quickly emptied, cigarette smoke cloyed the air. 'No one felt like sleeping,' Haston wrote, 'so we talked the night away.'

The one person unable to enjoy the camaraderie was Toni Hiebeler, who had reached the snow hole in a state of exhaustion. He was so eager to shelter and rest that he was the first one inside, and was jammed against the rear wall by the squash of bodies. He vomited next to Strobel, who recalled in 2014 that he would have vomited too if his stomach had contained any food. During the night Hiebeler repeatedly called for the entrance to be opened so that he could breathe: 'Air, air, let in some air … I'll croak!' The Germans had lost patience with Hiebeler, feeling that he had come along for the ride and had done nothing to help. 'I cried, "Better you do",' Schnaidt recalled. 'Because he hadn't done anything. Nothing.'

The climbers did not linger in the morning. As light penetrated the snow hole at around 6 a.m., they made their preparations to leave. Bonington strapped on Haston's crampons and then Strobel's, and they hauled themselves out of the hole. They were assailed by wind and driven snow, leaving them uncertain whether they could make the descent safely. Haston knew that the West Flank could be dangerous, and the Germans were in further trouble as their saturated clothing froze solid the moment they emerged.

Fortune was on their side. A short distance below the hole the clouds cleared and they could see all the way down to Kleine Scheidegg. The depth of snow provided perfect conditions for glissading – sliding down long sections in a sitting position. There was still the risk of speeding over the edge of a buttress, but by then they were almost oblivious to danger. 'We didn't really care,' said Schnaidt. 'We were down in no time.'

Down at Kleine Scheidegg, I had known what to expect. The previous evening Haston had told me in a radio call: 'We'll be going hell for leather for Scheidegg in the morning.' I spotted them high on the West Flank from my bedroom at around 8 a.m. and took the train to Eigergletscher, where I found a throng of journalists who had stayed at the skiers' guesthouse overnight. I saw a line of climbers sweeping down the West Flank and headed up the slope to meet them. The climbers ploughed to a halt in a flurry of snow, Bonington and Burke in the lead. I had joined forces with a German television journalist, Heiner Hepper, and we handed out cans of beer. Burke ruffled my hair and Bonington paid me the ultimate compliment: 'Good old Pete – out in front as usual.' We congregated at the Eigergletscher station and then climbed aboard the train to Kleine Scheidegg. I appeared to be one of the few people with any money and bought the tickets for the entire Eiger team and numerous others besides.

I had booked a room for Haston at the hotel and he climbed into the bath, nursing his blistered hand. Bonington and Burke went to Bonington's room. Burke was anxious because his feet were wet, and he was relieved to find they were undamaged when he removed his boots. When Bonington took off his own boots he pointed out that the felt inners were bone-dry. But when he removed the inners he was horrified to see that three toes on his right foot were black with frostbite.

We found a doctor with experience of frostbite who applied cream to Bonington's and Haston's wounds and dressed them. The German summit climbers were worried about their injuries too. The German team descended from the Stöckli where the entire group of climbers and supporters, myself included, posed for a photograph. Then Lehne, Strobel and Votteler were taken away by Harri Frey to a hospital in Kirchheim, near Stuttgart. Chris and Wendy Bonington left soon afterwards, going to a hospital in

Interlaken in the hope of obtaining treatment for his frostbite. That evening Haston, Burke and I joined the four remaining Germans and their entourage at the Stöckli. We drank beer and passed a 'subdued but happy evening', so I recorded in *Eiger Direct*.

In the morning Haston and I drove to Leysin. Forty-eight years on I remember a widowed mother's concern for her children, Harlin's parents bemused in their grief, and two bewildered children. I also remember touching my own memories: of my father dying when I was eleven, of my mother bringing me up alone. I told John Jr and Andréa that I could sense what they were feeling. Much, much later, when I met John Jr again in the year 2000, he told me that this had given him some comfort. Kor, Burke and Bev Clark arrived that evening and we went out for dinner in Leysin, Marilyn's first meal in five days.

The next day Haston and I visited Harlin's grave. The colours of the flowers and the wreaths stood out against the greys and the greens of the cemetery. We stood before the grave without speaking or looking at each other, then walked briskly back to our car. We returned to Kleine Scheidegg that afternoon and the next day headed home.

The four German climbers who did not go to the summit – Haag, Rosenzopf, Golikow and Schnaidt – were soon back doing their day jobs. The most abrupt transition was Schnaidt's: the day after returning to his home in Rommelshausen he was back at the family carpentry business. 'They said, "Good, you are back. This needs to be done, that needs to be done." I had absolutely no time to think about what happened next.' Haag and his wife Barbara had other distractions, as their son Daniel was born in June.

Of the four climbers who had reached the summit, Hupfauer was the least injured. He stayed at home to recover, and after two weeks returned to his work as a tool-maker. The other three – Lehne, Strobel and Votteler – had lengthy stays at the hospital in

Kirchheim. It was staffed by nuns and had been recommended by a doctor at Kleine Scheidegg on the grounds that one of its consultants specialised in frostbite, although it turned out his experience largely dated from the Second World War, when he had treated German soldiers on the Eastern Front.

Lehne, who had frostbite in his right foot, was the least affected; the injuries to Strobel and Votteler were far worse. As Votteler recalled, their toes appeared to have been mummified. 'They were black and as hard as wood – we knocked our toes on the steel bedsteads and it drove the nuns crazy.'

They were first treated with a series of painful spinal injections of a vasodilator, a drug intended to improve the blood flow by expanding the arteries. Strobel remembered the enormous syringe that administered the anaesthetic – 'You had to sit up and got the injection rammed in. It was so brutal!'– and the hallucinatory after-effects. 'It was like you were in outer space. You didn't know whether you were dangling from a rope or were floating.' But after four weeks their doctors decided they had to amputate all their toes.

Votteler remembered trying to stand for the first time three weeks after the operation. 'When you get your feet into the vertical, the blood rushes down. I thought my feet were about to burst and I fell straight into the cupboard.' On one occasion, following yet another vasodilator injection, he passed out and appeared to stop breathing. A team of nurses rushed in and revived him, and he awoke to find himself in an oxygen tent. The Eiger team paid frequent visits, usually bringing alcohol – 'We could have stocked a restaurant with all the wine,' Strobel recalled – and sometimes staying the night. Schnaidt remembered feeling awkward when he coincided with Strobel's family, who had so strongly opposed him taking part in the climb. 'It was embarrassing.'

Votteler's spell in hospital at least gave his shoulder injury time to recover. He and Strobel were still at the hospital when an orthopaedist arrived to equip them with shortened boots that would enable them to continue climbing, and they sneaked away to try them out on the crags at the nearby Blautal. In 2014 both reckoned that their toes could have been saved with more expert treatment that was available at a specialist hospital in Innsbruck. When they were finally discharged, Strobel went back to work at his brother's company, where relations remained strained; Votteler returned to his work as a moulder at an iron foundry.

Lehne, who had lost the big toe of his right foot, was already back at Belser, where he and Haag were due to deliver the book they had contracted to write as a condition of Lehne taking part in the climb. Haag embarked on the project with his customary obsessional enthusiasm. He had mixed emotions about the climb, still troubled by Harlin's death and distressed by the suffering of Votteler and Strobel. Against that, Barbara recalled, he was immensely proud of the climbers' achievement and the part he had played. 'He enjoyed writing it, he was good at doing it, and he was very happy with what he wrote.' Although he and Lehne divided the climb between them, Lehne describing it from 15 March onwards, Barbara believed that Haag helped Lehne to write his section.

The book had a secondary purpose – namely, to respond to the deluge of criticism that the climb had received. Far more than in Britain or the US, mountaineering is a mainstream topic in the principal Alpine countries, and the tactics used on the climb had been the subject of intense scrutiny. As the climbers recognised, there was a valid debate to be had about the extent to which the two teams had modified their strategies, moving from a continuous climb to one resembling a Himalayan ascent, with the bonus of being able to return to Kleine Scheidegg for periods of rest and recupaertion. But the climbers were unprepared for the vituperative nature of some contributions to the debate.

A writer in the Munich *Abendzeitung* asked rhetorically whether the ascent had been 'a climb or a circus', and claimed that traditional Alpinists considered it an 'offence'. A columnist in the *Süddeutsche Zeitung*, the Munich newspaper that was among the largest circulation of all German dailies, satirised the ascent by claiming that the climbers had lived in luxury, with waiters arriving from Kleine Scheidegg to deliver plates of blue trout and flambéed calves' liver. The tabloid *Bild am Sonntag* wrote that the Eiger *Mordwand* – 'murder wall'– had become a location for luxury tourism, and published fanciful quotes from 'Swiss Alpinists' who supposedly claimed that the climbers were 'circus performers'. *Bild*'s vitriolic coverage mostly likely stemmed from pique that the rival magazine *Quick* had secured exclusive use of the Germans' photographs. But there were more troubling comments from Albert Eggler, president of the Swiss Alpine Club, who had claimed that the climbers were gladiators performing for money, and from the prominent Swiss Alpinist Michel Vaucher, who was quoted as saying that the true Direct was yet to be climbed.

Some of the climbers shrugged off the criticisms. 'There were so-called experts and they had to write something – just like nowadays,' said Votteler. But Haag proved far more vulnerable. 'The criticisms hurt Peter a lot,' said Barbara. 'Especially when it was said that they were risking their lives for money or fame.'

Among the Harlin team, Bonington was ready to concede that the climb had an element of theatre and melodrama. But Bonington considered that inevitable where the Eiger was concerned, and he judged that the controversial tactics had been largely forced on the climbers by the weather. Neither team had planned a long-drawn-out assault; nor did it serve as a dangerous precedent for Alpine climbing. 'Only a few people would deny that the Eiger Direct was a great climb,' he concluded. Haston responded with characteristic venom: climbers who themselves had not dared to make the attempt were 'coming out of their holes' to criticise. 'Was it envy? Insecurity? It left a sad impression on me that people could be so petty.'

Lehne himself gave a detailed reply to the criticisms in a long article for a climbing journal. The hype surrounding the climb was not of the climbers' asking; and while the media had profited from the climb, the climbers were still repaying their debts a year later. He addressed the complaint that the climbers had used too many pitons and bolts, known as technical aid; the German team had placed 190 rock pitons, eight bolts and twelve ice screws for 'direct aid', which he considered fair and reasonable for a route of around seventy-five pitches on a 1700-metre wall. (Harlin's team, taking advantage of Kor's expertise, had used no bolts for direct aid at all.) In comparison with some renowned direct routes, particularly in the Dolomites, theirs was 'an inspirational, natural line'. The climbers, he concluded, had wanted to do the *direttissima* because 'we were excited by the challenge, as we were aware of its magnificence ... A more rewarding goal? There was none for us.'

The book he and Haag wrote was a triumph. Their accounts combine the graphic and the poetic, and there was a lavish use of the climbers' superb photographs, matched by the high-quality reproduction and imaginative design. Lehne's account of the last three days of the climb fully rebutted any claims that this was a luxury tour, and Martin Hörrmann, the pastor who knew the climbers and had officiated at the Haags' wedding, addressed the criticisms directly in a powerful epilogue. The book, he contended, provided the evidence to judge the climb on its merits rather than on supposition and prejudice. Far from climbing for money, the climbers were entitled to seek financial support for their attempt. The book told the story of climbers playing at the limits and exercising the freedom that was so important to mountaineers. And the climb offered an antidote to the materialism of everyday lives.

Haag was immensely proud of the book. He told Barbara, 'Now we get famous and rich.' But despite the high production values, Belser swiftly lost interest in the book. What was more, the climbers received only minimal proceeds from their supposed royalty of one Deutschmark, to be shared between them. The climbers believed that was because of the costs Belser set against the sales revenue, which included hiring a special train to Kleine Scheidegg for a Belser executive during the final stages of the climb. It proved impossible to check these beliefs as Belser, today part of a publishing conglomerate, was unable to locate any records relating to the book; all were missing from the company archives, together with the photographs and diaries which the climbers had been required by their contract to supply in 1966. Haag did retain a profit-and-loss account in respect of Belser's syndication agreement with the climbers. It showed income of 16,794.43DM and costs of 16,432.54DM, resulting in a profit of just 361.89DM. Belser was entitled to 25 per cent of that, leaving 271.42DM for the climbers – divided eight ways, giving them around £9 each.

The climbers' responses ranged from resignation to outrage. Lehne wrote a spirited letter to his own boss, Hans Weitpert, proposing that the account be recast in a way that would produce 8,945.36DM for the climbers (around £300 each), but Belser refused to budge. Haag's optimism faded. 'At the end there was nothing, nearly nothing,' Barbara recalled.

In 1968, the entire Eiger team received an invitation from Karl Herrligkoffer to take part in a new expedition to Nanga Parbat. Strobel and Votteler both accepted, reckoning they could manage to climb in their shortened boots. The two who declined were Lehne – who had been on Herrligkoffer's expedition in 1961 – and Haag. 'It was a difficult choice for Peter because his friends were going,' recalled Barbara. But Haag had misgivings about Herrligkoffer's leadership, and was uneasy about leaving his family for so long.

Herrligkoffer appointed Schnaidt as his deputy leader and the expedition reached 7100 metres on Nanga Parbat's Rupal Face, 1000 metres below the summit. It came to an abrupt end when

Strobel fell as he tried to jump across a bergschrund above Camp
Two, suffering multiple fractures to his lower left leg. Hupfauer led
the rescue party which, in an immensely difficult carry, spent fourteen hours transporting Strobel to Camp One, from where a team of
Hunza porters carried him back to Base Camp. In his typically bom-
bastic style, Herrligkoffer later wrote that 'all the comrades achieved
a superhuman feat'. For Votteler, the rescue demonstrated a self-suf-
ficiency and team spirit that had persisted from the Eiger. 'It was
another example that our strategy from the Eiger worked,' he said in
2014. 'We were a group who were able to rescue themselves.'

Although Lehne did not go to Nanga Parbat, he had resumed
climbing at a high level. He was still climbing with his Eiger colleagues and in March 1968 – before the Nanga Parbat expedition –
he, Golikow and Strobel attempted the first winter ascent of the
North Face of the Droites above Chamonix. By then his marriage
was disintegrating, and he and his wife Gertraud were due to conclude their divorce on 1 August 1969. On 23 July – nine days
beforehand – he and Golikow set out to climb the Walker Spur on
the Grandes Jorasses. That night, after they had found a bivouac
site 200 metres above the start of the route, a thaw set in, unleash-
ing volleys of stones. Although they thought they were protected,
they were hit at 2.30 a.m. by some rocks that ricocheted into their
bivouac. Golikow's thigh was fractured and Lehne was hit in the
back, most likely suffering a fractured spine. Lehne was groaning
with pain and told Golikow he wanted to throw himself off the
bivouac ledge. Golikow, in intense pain himself, could do nothing
to help him. After half an hour Lehne murmured: '*Kalle, danke für
alles*' – Karl, thank you for everything. They were his last words.

In the morning two English climbers came to Golikow's aid and he
was helicoptered to safety. Lehne, thirty-three when he died, was
buried at Rosenheim one week later. For Haag, Barbara recalled,
Lehne's death was 'a catastrophe'. Hupfauer later remembered Lehne

saying that 'stonefall is never aimed at random' – a commentary, perhaps, on the fatalism that Lehne invoked to justify his risk-taking.

It took Golikow a year to recover from his injuries and he spent part of that time with his adoptive parents in Bremen. Once back in Stuttgart, he met a young kindergarten teacher named Adelheid Reiter. She loved his confidence, his humour, his teasing, his ebullience and willingness to take risks. In early 1972 they moved into an apartment in Stuttgart together and in the spring went camping in the Dolomites. On 10 August they became engaged, intending to get married in December. Those eight months together, said Adelheid in 2014, were 'a lovely time'.

By then Golikow had returned to climbing. On 2 September he and a nineteen-year-old student, Otto Uhl, set out to climb the North-east Face of the Piz Badile, hoping to make a one-day ascent. There was a good weather forecast and they carried minimal equipment. They made fast progress but that afternoon they were hit by a violent thunderstorm. Their progress slowed dramatically and by nightfall they were still two pitches below the summit ridge.

Sigi Hupfauer and a partner, Alois Ritter, were also attempting the route and were following a short distance behind. Unlike Golikow and Uhl, they were equipped for bad weather and were able to take shelter when the storm broke. One pitch above them, Golikow and Uhl were in mortal peril from hypothermia. Shortly before midnight Uhl fell from his bivouac site and was killed. In the morning Hupfauer and Ritter climbed up to Golikow and found him half-covered in snow, suffering from hypothermia and in deep shock from his partner's death. It took Hupfauer and Ritter almost six hours to escort him up the final two pitches, hauling him for much of the way.

They set off up the final ridge in the hope of reaching a bivouac shelter on the summit but Golikow was moving ever more slowly and then took a fall. He was semi-conscious and unable to help himself, presenting Hupfauer and Ritter with an agonising decision, as Hupfauer recalled. 'Should we leave him? If we stayed with him we would die.' They secured him with pitons and told him they would return with help in the morning, but it is doubtful whether Golikow could hear or understand them. They reached the shelter on the point of exhaustion. When climbers found Golikow in the morning he had died. His funeral was held in Stuttgart ten days later.

Although the view was that Golikow had finally taken one risk too many, Haag once again was badly affected by his death. 'It really hit him,' Barbara recalled. By then Haag was climbing less intensely, mixing serious routes with easier ones which he climbed with Barbara. In 1974 he injured his elbow when a piton came out during a climb in the Donautal – the Danube valley. He stepped down another level and mostly went on mountain holidays with Barbara, Daniel and their daughter Christiane, who was born in 1969. In 2014, Christiane particularly remembered a camping holiday in the Pyrenees in 1980. Her father delighted in using minimal equipment, and they slept in a tiny tent with no table or chairs. 'The camping had to be as primitive as possible.'

That winter Haag fell ill. The initial diagnosis was hepatitis, but then he was found to have a malignant cancer. After an operation to remove most of his stomach and part of his colon, he was given six months to live.

At first he was determined to fight the illness, and he went walking and did his best to stay active. 'But then he got really bad pain,' Barbara recalled. 'He didn't go to hospital and I gave him morphine injections. Then he heard that his liver was malignant. He was told it could be a matter of months and he just let go.'

From that moment Haag prepared for his death. He told Barbara that he was content that he had lived intensively and had done in forty years what others had done in eighty. He gave instructions for his funeral, which he wanted to be 'a celebration'. He asked his mother to wear a dirndl, a traditional German costume, and wanted other mourners to come in Swabian dress. He also wanted to say goodbye to his friends. 'He told everyone, "Come on, visit me for the last time,"' Christiane recalled.

The invitation caused consternation among Haag's musician friends. 'They couldn't cope with it,' said Christiane. The remaining five Eiger climbers all accepted. 'As a climber you are confronted with death and they knew how to handle it,' Christiane believed. The weather was warm on the day of their visit and they and Haag sat outside together. Schnaidt, who came with his wife Margret, squeezed Haag's emaciated arm and asked: 'Hey, there's not much left there – what's up?'

Haag appreciated the joke. 'He was quite cheerful, saying, "Let's drink some wine and eat some marzipan"' – recalling a popular item in the Eiger diet. 'At the end he said goodbye to everyone.'

Haag died two weeks later, on 30 September 1981. 'We were all there,' Christiane recalled. 'It was good for us to see it and to say goodbye. Since that time I am not afraid of death.'

In 2007, Christiane moved from Germany to London, and in 2014 was living in south-west London. She worked as an artist: painting, drawing and print-making in her studio and teaching art, mostly to children. Her father's piano, made by Krumm of Stuttgart, sat in her basement. Her daughter Laura, eighteen in 2014, planned to study costume or set design in Berlin or Vienna; her son Nikita, twenty-two, was studying audio-engineering in London. Her husband Norbert, who worked in market research, took up indoor climbing with Nikita, who appeared to have inherited a talent for climbing from his grandfather. 'He is in many respects like Peter,' Christiane said. 'Very sociable, makes friends everywhere, is very open-minded and doesn't like authority.'

Haag was forty-four when he died. By then, three of the five surviving climbers were in their forties and the remaining two were approaching that landmark. Some felt that the Eiger helped changed their life, or had forced them to make adjustments; for others, things continued as before.

After returning to the family business, Schnaidt qualified as a master carpenter; later, he taught carpentry at the school where he had obtained his master's certificate. He and Margret had two daughters, born in 1965 and 1966. In 1975, Margret took part in Herrligkoffer's latest expedition to Nanga Parbat, helping to carry out his programme of physiological research. The expedition failed in an attempt on a new route on the Rupal Face, but Margret was in a team of four who made the first ascent of a neighbouring 6000-metre peak, Toshe. After Nanga Parbat, the Schnaidts made further mountain and adventure trips, including visits to South America, Nepal and Tien Shan. In the 1990s they took up cycling, making increasingly ambitious journeys around Europe. Margret was initially reluctant but soon found she enjoyed it: 'It was good for our knees and backs.' By 2013 they had four grandchildren, including one who worked as a snowboard and sports-climbing instructor. Looking back on the Eiger, Schnaidt felt that it did not instigate any fundamental change in his life. 'The meaning for me is more incidental – I was there and I went along with it.'

Having returned to tool-making after the Eiger, Hupfauer later qualified for a master's certificate. He and Gaby married in 1967, and they had a daughter, Silke, in 1971. He became a certified mountain guide and used this to boost his income during the 1970s, when the German economy was struggling. He also began to take part in expeditions to the 8000-metre peaks. He climbed Manaslu in 1973; Everest in 1978, in a post-monsoon expedition led by Herrligkoffer; Shishapangma in 1980, as part of the first non-Chinese team to climb the mountain; and Hidden Peak in 1982.

In 1986, he and Gaby decided to attempt Broad Peak, twelfth

highest of the fourteen 8000-metre peaks, together. Although they had met through climbing, Gaby had struggled for acceptance in mountaineering circles. The youth section of the German Alpine Club did not allow girls to join. As an adult, she still encountered chauvinist attitudes, some men apparently feeling that if women succeeded on a climb 'it was because men pulled them up.' Even so, she was content to depend on Sigi. 'He was my mountain star, my idol. I learned everything about the mountains from him. I would never have put the same trust or confidence in anyone else.'

When Gaby first saw Broad Peak she felt overawed; standing on the summit with Sigi 'was incredible, a fantastic experience'. They were already planning their next target, Gasherbrum II, during their descent. 'It was like a child, it happened nine months later.' After Hupfauer climbed Nanga Parbat without Gaby in 1988, he and Gaby climbed Cho Oyo in 1990, making them the first couple to climb three 8000-metre peaks. Silke became the manager at a local climbing wall and they have one grandson. For Hupfauer, the Eiger 'was a starting point and gave me the confidence to continue climbing at a high level. I did not have the highest profile but it helped me turn my sport and hobby into a part-time profession' – which helped him, he added, to boost 'my rather poor pension'.

Strobel left his brother's construction company after a year. 'After the Eiger, things no longer worked with my brother. It was too complicated.' He began work at a sports shop and later trained as a mountaineering guide, leading ski tours including the renowned Haute Route, which he led thirty-eight times. At first he found it difficult to climb and ski with his shortened feet, but then met an orthopaedist who designed an insole that solved the problems: 'then everything was possible'. Strobel returned to serious climbing with a younger partner, Rainer Schlump, tackling a range of top-level routes including the Central Pillar of Frêney and the Walker. At sixty-seven, with a new partner, Björn Buchner, he climbed the Lotus Flower Wall, a classic route in northern Canada. 'It worked out after all.' Most recently he took up cycling, like the Schnaidts. Strobel was married, then divorced, and has one daughter. He looks back on the Eiger as 'a great experience, for me at any rate. We had a lot of luck and a lot of misfortune.'

Rosenzopf also resumed his day job as an engineering technician. After the Nanga Parbat expedition of 1968 he worked for the Daimler company, first on the development of gas turbines for helicopters, then on heavy-duty industrial turbines. He was mostly based in Stuttgart and retired in 2000, at the age of sixty-two, after the company moved its headquarters. He was married in 1981, when he was forty-one, but had no children, and later he and his wife separated. He continued mountaineering after the Eiger and, in 1988, he and a group of friends climbed Pik Lenin, a 7000-metre peak in the Pamirs, his highest summit. He remained active in the Alps until he retired, when he took up walking at lower levels. The Eiger, he said in 2014, was a 'high point' of his life that had opened the way to travel and expeditions. 'If we hadn't all been to the Eiger, this would not have happened.'

Votteler became 'a kind of nomad', working in a succession of jobs in metal processing, ending up as general manager in a recycling plant. He found adjusting to his shortened feet 'a really painful time', but continued climbing after the Nanga Parbat expedition, his biggest prize an ascent of Denali, then widely known as Mount McKinley, the highest mountain in North America. He also took up long-distance running, completing some fifty marathons. 'Even without toes,' he said, 'everything was possible.' He was married in 1970 and he and his wife had twins – a son and a daughter – in 1976 and, later, two grandchildren. After he stopped climbing he took up mountain biking – 'so I am still going to the mountains quite often'. His wife died in January 2010 and his four Eiger colleagues and Barbara Haag attended the funeral. Looking back,

Votteler said in 2014, the Eiger was a 'detail' of his life. 'It is not so significant that I would still live off it. There were many other more exciting and more pleasant memories.'

Throughout the years since the Eiger Direct, the surviving climbers met each other on a number of occasions – not only funerals. Some were prompted by the Eiger. In 1986, Rosenzopf, Schnaidt and Votteler celebrated the twentieth anniversary of the Direct by going to Alaska to climb Denali. 'We all made the summit,' Votteler drily recorded. 'It was freezing.' Most attended a celebration in Grindelwald for the fiftieth anniversary of the original first ascent in 1988; Strobel made a speech on behalf of the Direct team, and Gaby Hupfauer attended for Sigi, who was at Nanga Parbat. Also there were Lehne's wife Gertraud and their two children, Marina, who was twenty-eight, and Klaus-Peter, twenty-seven. It was their last contact with the Eiger climbers, Marina told us in 2014, when she was living and working as a physician in Rosenheim. She added that she had barely known her father, as her parents had separated when she was very young. 'When he lived he didn't exist and when he died he didn't exist. But now I would like to have got to know him. From all that I have read and heard, he must have been a great guy.'

In 1991, Hupfauer, Rosenzopf and the Schnaidts met in the Swabian Alb, the climbing area south and east of Stuttgart, to celebrate the twenty-fifth anniversary of the Direct, together with Fritz Bohren, the proprietor of the Stöckli, and his wife. The Schnaidts and Strobel would usually meet every three months at a gathering of the Esslingen mountain rescue on the Alb, where they swapped reminiscences and sang mountaineers' songs; Barbara Haag sometimes came too. Even so, the five had not gathered in the same place at the same time for some thirty years. It was our hope that they would do so when we asked if we could meet them while conducting our research for this book.

*

Haston and I returned to London on 29 March. Press photographers were waiting at Heathrow; as they saw two men with rucksacks emerge through the arrival gates they were evidently unsure which one to photograph, and I pointed at Haston. He came to stay with us at our home in Clapham, as did Kor. The most urgent need for both Haston and Bonington was to obtain treatment for their frost-bite. They were offered help by Dr Mike Ward, who had been the doctor on the British 1953 Everest expedition and had developed an expertise in high-altitude medicine. Ward arranged for them to be treated at the London Hospital in Whitechapel, which was equipped with a hyperbaric oxygen chamber: a cylinder where oxygen could be pumped to twice the normal atmospheric amount, which sup-posedly spurred the growth of the damaged tissues and also reduced the risk of infection. Haston spent many hours in the chamber over a period of weeks, as did Bonington. Haston emerged with withered fingers and no fingernails, but both he and Bonington were spared amputations and made full recoveries. Ward judged that the treat-ment 'appeared to accelerate recovery while inhibiting infection', although the effectiveness of the chambers has never been conclu-sively proved. A few weeks later, we heard from Lehne that he had lost part of his foot, and that Votteler and Strobel had lost all their toes. After I wrote to Golikow, he replied telling me that his team-mates were bearing their fate 'with remarkable calm'.

During the journey home Haston and I had decided to write a book about the climb, and we signed a contract with the publish-ers Collins. Haston drafted the climbing sections, while I covered events off the mountain and then combined the two into a third-person account. We switched to Haston's first-person voice for the final stages of the climb and the book was illustrated with a selec-tion of Bonington's hard-won photographs. It was published in the US with the title *Direttissima* and also appeared in France and Japan – but not Germany. We learned later that Belser was aggrieved that we had not collaborated with them to produce a combined account. Neither Haston nor I had any inkling of this and it remained a mystery where the proposal had come from.

That summer Haston returned to Leysin. From then on we met intermittently, which included the televised ascent of the Old Man of Hoy, the spectacular sea stack in the Orkneys that was the subject of another BBC outside broadcast in July 1967. Haston appeared ill at ease in his role as star climber, unable to deliver repartee for the audience with the facility of media hands such as Ian NcNaught-Davis or Tom Patey, who had made the first ascent with Bonington and Rusty Baillie the year before. Haston wrote a sour note in his journal, delivering acerbic comments on his fellow climbers: Joe Brown was 'so like Whillans, but not even so entertaining. One discerns the plumber perhaps.' He called Brown 'insular' and complained that he had never 'pushed to the limits'.

In November 1967, Haston and I took part in an expedition to Patagonia, together with Mick Burke, Martin Boysen and Pete Crew. The four climbers were attempting Cerro Torre, the bewitching granite spire that soars more than 3000 metres feet above the Patagonian ice cap and had not yet had an undisputed first ascent. Haston and I had secured backing from the *Sunday Times*, for whom I was writing as a freelance. We had lunch with the news editor at Simpson's-in-the-Strand, and when Haston produced a photograph of Cerro Torre the news editor instantly attached the headline: 'The worst mountain in the world' – and the deal was done.

The expedition was not a success. The notorious Patagonia storms besieged the mountain for weeks at a time, pinning us down at our base camp below the Cerro Torre glacier. I was startled that Haston appeared to have taken against me. He did his best to exclude me from the nightly card sessions of bridge and made it plain he considered that I was there under sufferance. Burke confessed afterwards that he was appalled at the way Haston had behaved towards me.

Boysen later wrote that he felt the bad blood between us stemmed from clashes over writing *Eiger Direct*. That was not true as far as I was concerned, although I later learned from Bev Clark that Haston did not like the book he had helped to write. I was intensely relieved when the expedition ended, even though I was sorry that it had failed.

That summer, 1968, I wrote an article about the death of Dave Condict, the school friend who introduced me to climbing, who was killed in an accident above Chamonix. Haston wrote to me, accusing me of indulging in sentimentality and of being ignorant of the values of climbing. It marked the end of our relationship which had begun, for me, with the feeling that we valued and enjoyed other's company. During the Eiger Direct we had discussed philosophy, or what we could remember of it from our university courses. Even at the Cerro Torre base camp, despite our differences, we managed to debate the respective merits of Graham Greene and Günter Grass. His letter signalled that he was terminating our relationship and we had only occasional glancing encounters after that.

By then Haston was based in Leysin, where Clark had asked him to become Harlin's replacement as director of the International School of Mountaineering. Haston was the star name that helped lure clients to Leysin, but the school remained an improvisational affair, with erratic organisation and variable tutors. The clients learned to accommodate nights of hard drinking at the Club Vag, where Haston usually set the pace. In 1969, Haston, improbably, got married. He had known Annie Ferris, a nurse, since 1966, and although he provided her with a mix of glamour and hedonism, even she was unsure why he proposed to her.

In 1970, Haston joined a British expedition attempting the unclimbed South Face of Annapurna, the tenth highest peak. As leader, Bonington had no qualms about selecting Haston, remembering his fierce determination on the Eiger. Bonington always considered Haston a true friend, although he also observed

Haston's ability to form relationships that would prove useful to him. 'He was a single-minded powerhouse who was going to get to the top of the mountain, and he saw in me the person who was going to get it organised,' he said in 2014. Once at Annapurna, Haston identified Whillans as the best potential partner: 'He saw in Don the ideal partner and the best person for going to the top.' Haston's confidence was another key strength – 'he always took it for granted that he would be making the summit' – but, unlike Whillans, 'he never got up the nose of his fellow climbers'. He and Whillans reached the summit on 27 May, an ascent that stands as a landmark in mountaineering. It was the first time an expedition had climbed one of the major faces of the 8000-metre peaks; and, as an ascent of a challenging and pioneering new route, it had parallels with the Eiger Direct ascent of four years before.

In 1971, Haston made his first visit to Everest, as part of an international expedition that hoped to climb the mountain's South-west Face. Following Annapurna, this was considered the next great Himalayan challenge, with climbers determined to establish a new route rather than follow the tried and tested South Col route of 1953. Haston and Whillans reached the expedition's high-point, 450 metres below the summit, but the attempt ended in bitterness and acrimony. Haston returned in 1972 with an expedition, led by Bonington, which failed in a new attempt on the South-west Face. In 1974, Haston was back at the Eiger when he assisted in the filming of *The Eiger Sanction*, directed by and starring Clint Eastwood. The film was based on the bestselling novel of the same name and served to reinforce the mountain's legendary status in the popular imagination.

Haston made his third attempt on the South-west Face in 1975. The expedition was once again led by Bonington, who partnered Haston with Doug Scott, an irreverent figure whose hippy appearance belied a resolute determination that matched Haston's. Those qualities were required when they made their summit bid on 24 September. After problems with their oxygen equipment, which they calmly dismantled to remove a blockage caused by ice, they reached the summit as the sun was dipping beneath the clouds smothering the neighbouring peaks. They survived an open bivouac, without food, sleeping equipment or supplementary oxygen, just 100 metres below the summit – the highest bivouac ever made at that time. Tragically, Mick Burke died two days later, probably in a fall through a cornice or at the Hillary Step as he descended from the summit. Haston and Scott, as well as accomplishing a formidable new route, took the prize of becoming the first British climbers to reach the summit – the pair who succeeded in 1953 were from New Zealand and Nepal. They returned as heroes.

From this point the certainty which was one of Haston's greatest mountaineering assets appeared to bring a measure of calm and maturity into his personal life. By then his improbable marriage had collapsed, with both he and Annie having affairs and drinking heavily. Haston now set up home in Leysin with an elfin young woman of Italian descent, Ariane Giobellina. She saw in Haston the positive aspects of characteristics others may have read as faults. 'I think he was extremely sensitive, but he did not show it,' she said in 2014. 'He could appear arrogant but I think that was protection. But he wouldn't spend time with people he didn't respect. He wouldn't pretend or be polite. He was very self-confident and he knew exactly what he wanted.' She had been seeing Haston, intermittently, for several years and was aware of his libertine reputation, but considered that he was changing. 'He was more content, not so wild.' Others saw in Haston an unaccustomed domesticity and a readiness to exchange pleasantries with friends and even neighbours.

Haston was still director of the Leysin mountaineering school. He began preparing plans which included conducting climbing courses in Canada. He was also keen to continue writing; after his two nonfiction books – *The Eiger* and his autobiography, *In High Places* – he embarked on a novel, which he wrote in longhand and was typed by Ariane. The characters were mountaineers and were barely disguised versions of some of his friends and contemporaries, with a hero – Scotland's most successful mountaineer, who was also a rebellious figure – who was clearly based on himself. The novel included a scene in which a character outruns an avalanche that he triggers while skiing off-piste below a peak near Leysin called La Riondaz. Haston finished writing the novel in January 1977.

Haston, although never expert, had always enjoyed skiing, and was ready to take the risk of going off-piste for the sake of the solitude and the edge of excitement it brought. On 17 January, the day after completing his novel, he went skiing – off-piste – below La Riondaz. He was caught in an avalanche and choked to death when his scarf was pulled around his neck by the weight of snow. He was thirty-six.

It looked like a death prophesied in his novel, which was published in 1979 under the title *Calculated Risk*. If that seemed far-fetched, the novel included a character who speculated that the Haston figure would always seek to test himself against a series of risks and asked: 'Would he ever be satisfied? Could it ever end peacefully for him?' Haston had provided the answer. Following a funeral attended by many of his climbing colleagues, including Bonington and Scott, as well as both Annie Haston and Ariane, he was buried a short distance from Harlin in the cemetery at Leysin.

After the Eiger, Layton Kor came to London and stayed at our home for a time. We remember him as courteous and appreciative, if a little bemused at finding himself in a household with two boisterous infants – Danny was then twenty-one months, Seth three months. He returned to Leysin intent on fulfilling his dream of climbing some of the classic routes that had inspired his interest in Alpinism. He climbed two major routes on the Cima Grande and another on the Cima Ovest, put up some new routes around Leysin, made a second visit to the Dolomites and did a major 1000-metre winter route with Yvon Chouinard on the North Face of Les Courtes above Chamonix. Back in the US he made the first winter ascent, via a new route, of The Diamond on Longs Peak in Colorado. In June 1967, he and the climber/photographer Galen Rowell climbed the Salathé Wall, one of the great test pieces in Yosemite.

It looks like an impressive roster of climbs, suggesting a climber at the peak of his form. But something had changed. As Kor told me in an interview in 2010, he remained preoccupied with Harlin's death throughout that period. 'It takes a long time to get over things like that. It's a terrible emotional blow and it doesn't go away ... It's at the back of your mind all the time.' During their climb in Yosemite, Rowell saw in Kor an 'obvious pain ... he had seen a different world, one of finality and agony, and it had changed him'. Other partners recalled him discussing the meaning of life and death during climbs. The mountaineering author and journalist Cam Burns, who taped extensive conversations with Kor for a biography he is writing, confirmed that Harlin's death had prompted Kor to ponder 'the nature of life itself'.

Some friends felt that Kor's quest for answers reflected the restlessness he had displayed during the Eiger Direct, with the frenetic bursts of energy and adrenaline rushes on the face, punctuated by the urge to return to the contrasting world of Kleine Scheidegg. Improbable as it might appear, Kor found the answers he was seeking in religion. Having suffered from breathing difficulties, he attended a clinic in San Antonio, Texas, that offered alternative medicine therapy, including fasting. He shared a room with a Jehovah's Witness and met two other members of the sect who were having treatment. Kor, who had previously shown no interest in religion, was impressed by what he described as 'their sensible, non-emotional approach to the subject'. Once back in Colorado he contacted the local congregation and was attracted by the seeming simplicity and clarity of the Jehovah's Witnesses' beliefs, their diagnoses of the world's problems and their prescriptions for a spiritual life. He was baptised as a Jehovah's Witness in 1968.

In 1969 Kor got married. He met his wife as a delightfully convoluted consequence of the Eiger Direct. Joy Heron was an English nurse and climber, and had been Haston's girlfriend in 1966; she visited him at the London Hospital while he was being treated for frostbite and once met Kor there. The day before she was due to join Haston in Leysin, she received a letter from him dumping her in favour of Annie Ferris. Once she arrived in Leysin, Yvon Chouinard invited her to return to the US with him; she went climbing with him there and found work as a nurse in San Francisco. She met up with Mick Burke, who took her to visit Kor in Boulder. She and Kor went climbing and he introduced her to the Jehovah's Witnesses. Joy had been raised as a Quaker and some of Kor's friends hoped that she would reconvert him but the reverse occurred. They were married in Seattle on 21 June and had two children: a daughter, Julia, born in 1972 and a son, Jaime, in 1973.

The ideology of the Jehovah's Witnesses required Kor to reform his life in a number of ways. He gave up marijuana and for a time adopted a less manic style of driving. He joined in the movement's proselytising activities, calling door to door in Boulder to try to win converts. The movement frowned on climbing, as Kor would be exposing himself to physical harm and putting himself and his family at risk; he was also supposed to break off his relationships with friends from before his conversion. But Kor found the call of climbing too strong to resist. He continued in semi-secrecy on some deserted cliffs at Clear Creek Canyon, near Golden, recruiting partners outside the local climbing community. One former friend who later managed to lure him on to a climb found him far less driven and willing to share the leads. The restlessness had eased; religion, the friend commented, had made him 'a different person' and the competitive urge had gone.

Kor continued to work as a bricklayer and stonemason and for a time, when he was living in Glenwood Springs, installed fireplaces in the homes of the super-rich in nearby Aspen. He spent two years in Arizona, working in construction and indulging in a new passion for diving at the Gulf of California. In general, he took no pleasure from his work and, so his family later told Burns, 'all he wanted to do was to go climbing and read the Bible'.

By the 1980s the secret was out and articles began to appear about his climbing activities. The local Jehovah's Witnesses took a tolerant view and some even went climbing with him. The sect sanctioned the publication of a book about Kor, *Beyond the Vertical*, on the grounds that it was an inspirational story of a hedonist's conversion to the true faith.

Around 1990, Kor's first marriage came to an end. He spent several years in the Philippines and returned to Colorado with his second wife, Karen; later, they had a son named Arlan.

In 2005, Kor fell ill and was diagnosed as having kidney failure. He was recommended to have dialysis but Kor had no medical insurance, nor did he meet the criteria for subsidised healthcare, although he received other welfare payments. Mountaineering friends helped to raise funds by launching an internet appeal and raffling climbing equipment and services, much of it donated. By 2009, he and his family were living in a trailer in Kingman, Arizona. Two climbing friends, Joanne and George Urioste, met him there and Joanne went climbing with Kor several times. In 2015, she recalled that he had exercised with light weights to try to retain some strength in his emaciated body; and that he was desperately fatigued as he made his way to the crags. 'A twenty-minute approach would turn into an hour of struggle. But once on the rock he flowed.'

When I telephoned Kor in 2010, around the time I began to consider writing this book, he was friendly and willing to delve into his memories of the Eiger. When I asked for his principal recollections, Harlin's death apart, he told me: 'It was kind of cold and uncomfortable up there at times. At others there were beautiful views. It was such a contrast between there and Kleine Scheidegg, eating good food and having a good life.' He described his climbing with Lehne and Golikow, then added: 'What I remember most is going up and down the fixed ropes. It was hard work but I enjoyed everything. I had a good time up there except I didn't like being cold.' When I asked him to sum up his thoughts, he told me: 'It was a wonderful adventure many years ago.'

In September 2011 Kor and his wife Karen visited the Uriostes at their home in Las Vegas. Kor insisted on laying bricks to repair a dilapidated flower box, working through the day despite 100-degree heat to ensure the job was completed. In the autumn of 2012, Joanne fractured first her ankle and then her collarbone in successive accidents. During her rehabilitation, she recalled, Kor was 'awesome – calling me to cheer me up and alleviate the boredom. He talked a lot about gourmet food, especially the delicacies he remembered from Europe.'

At around that time, Kor developed prostate cancer, which compounded his kidney problems. On 22 April 2013, Karen called Joanne to tell her that Kor had suffered a haemorrhage and was being taken to a hospice in Kingman. To Joanne's surprise, Kor came on the phone and told her he would appreciate some crusty French bread and brie.

The Uriostes arrived at the hospice the next morning, 23 April. A distressed Karen and their son Arlan were by Kor's side. Kor's mouth was so dry that he was unable to eat the bread and cheese, but they gave him sips of lemon soda and applied balm to his cracked lips and massaged his legs and arms, which were cramping.

Then Karen told them that Kor was refusing to have a blood transfusion. 'I was floored,' Joanne recalled. Kor required dialysis but, as a result of his haemorrhage, he did not have enough blood – and without dialysis, the toxic wastes from metabolism in his blood were likely to prove fatal. Joanne had not known that Jehovah's Witnesses were forbidden to have blood transfusions – or that Kor was still strictly adhering to the Jehovah's Witnesses doctrines. 'I had to witness a sort of suicide.'

Two Jehovah's Witnesses came into the room, apparently to check that Kor was observing the rules. Early that evening Joanne kissed Kor's cheek and said goodbye. At 10 p.m., after they had returned to Las Vegas, Arlan Kor telephoned to say that his father had died. Although Kor was suffering severe chest pains, he refused morphine so that he could remain awake and in contact with his wife and son until the end.

Just as I made the phone call that led Chris Bonington to withdraw as a full climbing member of Harlin's Eiger team, I also made a radio call which signified that his ambition to become an adventure photojournalist had moved to the next stage. Around mid-point in the Eiger Direct, Bonington was at the Death Bivouac when I radioed a proposal from John Anstey at the *Weekend Telegraph* for him to photograph an ascent of a volcano in Ecuador named Sangay. Bonington accepted at once.

After returning from the Eiger, Bonington stayed in London for six weeks, much of that time spent at the London Hospital while he was treated for his frostbite. He made a full recovery and, ten days after being discharged, he was riding in a mule train in the depths of an Ecuadorian jungle as it searched for a path to the volcano. The writer on Anstey's assignment was an Old Etonian named Sebastian Snow, one of the gentleman adventurers who beat a path to Anstey's door with ever more improbable proposals. Before they set off to climb Sangay, Bonington learned that Snow had never worn crampons or used an ice axe before. Bonington made three attempts to climb the volcano and obtain the money shot Anstey had stipulated; namely, the volcano's fiery inner core. He never quite succeeded but Anstey declared himself satisfied with the results.

Bonington's subsequent assignments included hunting caribou with Eskimos in the Canadian Arctic in the depths of winter; visiting the remote Hunza community in Kashmir with a writer who pulled out of the trip halfway through; and attempting to descend the Blue Nile from its source in inflatable boats, during which Bonington was shot at by bandits and nearly drowned. Although he completed his assignments honourably, Bonington was uneasy at the moments when he felt out of control of events. While in Ecuador he had also been compelled to face the hideous news that Conrad, the Boningtons' first son, had drowned in an accident.

From 1970 Bonington's career took a new trajectory, one that saw him establish himself as an accomplished expedition leader, a widely respected figure in the higher echelons of mountaineering and for many the public face of the sport. Although this had the appearance of a pre-planned strategy, Bonington insisted that it owed more to chance. In 1968 he and Wendy moved to the Manchester suburb of Bowdon, where they became part of a community of talented mountaineers who played bridge and squash together and sent their children to the same schools – the Boningtons' son Daniel was born in 1967, Rupert in 1969. They also talked of going to the Himalayas, and when they saw a photograph of the unclimbed South Face of Annapurna they decided that should be their goal. Bonington became the leader after Mike Ward, the Everest doctor, turned them down. 'Someone had to do something so I took the initiative,' Bonington said in 2014. It was, he added, 'a career change by default'.

On the two major expeditions, Annapurna in 1970 and Everest in 1975, Bonington proved himself a capable and empathetic leader who was also ready to make tough decisions – as shown in his choice of the summit teams, when Haston was selected on both occasions. Ironically for someone whose early career had been beset by financial uncertainty, he found he had a talent for persuading financial institutions to part with their money, most spectacularly when Barclays Bank stumped up £100,000 to sponsor the Everest expedition and even promised to meet any cost overruns.

For a while Bonington continued to pursue pioneering routes on major peaks. In 1978 he led an expedition – sponsored by the London Rubber Company, manufacturers of the Durex contraceptive – to the unclimbed West Face of K2, the second highest mountain; in 1982, sponsored by the financial and trading group Jardine Matheson, he returned to Everest to attempt its greatest remaining challenge, the immensely long North-east Ridge. Both failed, and both ended in the deaths of close friends. On K2, Nick Estcourt was engulfed by an avalanche; on Everest, Joe Tasker and Pete Boardman died, probably of exhaustion and altitude sickness, at the trio of pinnacles that comprised the crux of the route. These were additions to the tally of friends who died during his expeditions, beginning with Ian Clough on Annapurna in 1970 and Mick Burke on Everest in 1975. His own closest call and most harrowing experience was probably on the Ogre in 1977, when he fractured his ribs and damaged his lungs in a long fall sustained while assisting Doug Scott, who had broken both legs in an earlier fall. Bonington dealt with these deaths and his own narrow escapes by saying that they were an inevitable part of an activity that offered immense rewards, and that fate and luck played a major part in determining who survived.

Bonington reached the summit of Everest in 1985, as a member of a Norwegian expedition climbing the standard South Col route. Thereafter he scaled down his aspirations to lesser but still worthwhile peaks, usually with smaller, more intimate expeditions, continuing to do so through the 2000s, when he reached the age of seventy. At the same time he moved into the senior levels of the sport, first as president of the British Mountaineering Council, then president of the Alpine Club. He became active in environmental and charity work: president of the Council for National Parks, president of the leprosy charity Lepra, assisting charities and organisations that included support for the Sherpas of Nepal and victims of spinal injury, outdoor activities for the disabled and the protection of the English landscape. He was awarded a CBE in 1976 and became Sir Chris Bonington in 1996. He was appointed Deputy Lieutenant of Cumbria in 2004 and Chancellor of Lancaster University in 2005.

He wrote numerous books: the man who agonised over writing a short article for the *Weekend Telegraph* and was a year late delivering his first volume of autobiography developed into a fluent, empathetic and assured writer. He joined the roster of motivational and after-dinner speakers, earning five-figure sums for presenting talks under rubrics such as 'Delivering the Vision', 'Empowering' and 'Synergy in Teamwork'. Throughout this period he remained rooted in the mountaineering community and was approachable and generous with his help.

We met intermittently over the decades; he was always friendly and I liked to think that some bond persisted from the Eiger Direct. In April 2014, Leni and I visited him at his home, a converted shepherd's cottage near Caldbeck in the northern Lake District, where the Boningtons had lived since 1974. It was a difficult time, as Wendy had been taken ill with motor neurone disease. She was unable to speak, but could communicate by writing; when we asked about the Eiger Direct, her dominant memory was of getting lost while trying to find Zürich airport with her first consignment of Chris's film.

Bonington had another distraction that day – namely, that he was expected at a lunchtime reception for Prince Charles, who was meeting members of the Northern Fells Group, a rural revival group, in Caldbeck. Among his memories from 1966, Bonington considered his lead up the ice pitch beside the Central Pillar 'the hairiest thing I have ever done'. He remembered Harlin's body spread-eagled in the snow, and the photograph of his body framed against the Eiger that he could never take. He did not remember the radio discussion with Haston about whether to continue, or his cameras freezing at the summit. He did remember seeing his blackened toes when he removed his boots after returning from the West Flank.

Bonington was firm in his belief that criticism of the route was misplaced. But he felt that Harlin would have been hard-pressed to complete the climb in an Alpine-style push even if his ten-day spell of clear weather had arrived, and so would have had to modify his original tactics anyway. He conceded that the critics had a point in identifying the surreal nature of the support operations, with Kleine Scheidegg so temptingly close at hand; but all that added to the 'wonderful sense of theatre' that prevailed, with Kleine Scheidegg offering a 'dress circle' view for spectators and resting climbers alike. He offered a comparison from the Second World War, when ground troops spent their time in acute discomfort and danger whereas fighter pilots would have a short burst of intense danger before returning to ground-level comforts. 'In a way, the jump between Kleine Scheidegg and the face was much the same.'

Even so, he stood by the quality of the climbing and the achievement it represented. 'It was incredibly challenging and probably some of the hardest climbing done in the Alps to that time. Being involved was absolutely fantastic. There's never been anything like it for me, before or since.'

Bonington had to break off to meet Prince Charles, selecting a discreet tie for the occasion. When he returned, he and I went for a short walk on the fells above his home: he needed to stay fit, he explained, as he had agreed that a charity raffle could offer 'A Walk with Chris Bonington' as a prize.

Before we left, Bonington told us that he hoped Wendy would live long enough to attend the family celebrations for his eightieth birthday in five months' time. Sadly, she did not. She died, aged seventy-six, in July, and so her family assembled at her funeral instead. They included their son Joe (he had changed his name from Daniel) and his wife Jude, who came from Australia; their second son Rupert and his wife Ann; and their four grandchildren. In a moving eulogy, Bonington said that Wendy 'was the rock of my life who enabled me to achieve what I have. She was my wonderful lover and my best and closest friend.'

Chapter Eighteen

THE SHADOW

John Harlin once told Marilyn that she would make a pretty widow as she looked good in black. She took him at his word by wearing the dress he was referring to – one that could be stuffed into a rucksack – at his funeral. If it appears that his was a death they had both foretold, it should not be surprising in light of the fears she had lived with throughout their eleven years of marriage. She told Bonington, replying to a letter of condolence, how much she missed him – but she could not afford regrets, given how far her life had been enriched by their time together. Almost fifty years on, she wrote that even though Harlin had immersed himself in danger, his death still came as an unexpected shock – and one that 'hit and still hits at gut level'.

Marilyn also listed some of the mistakes 'made by friends when dealing with widows'. These included asking what they planned to do, telling them they will remarry, avoiding subjects likely to make them cry, and even suggesting that their husband was so flawed that they are better off on their own. She contrasted these with the help and support she had received: a university professor wrote asking how he could help her get back into the academic world;

friends took John Jr on a holiday to Greece, where they taught him to use his father's camera. She was especially moved when Karl Golikow came to Leysin and afterwards, in a note of thanks, told him: 'Your thoughtful visit meant a great deal to me.' She listed the ways he had given 'special attention to John', which included giving up the climb and visiting his grave, and described them as 'kindnesses John would have appreciated'.

The person who most emphatically did not help was Haston, and what transpired between them left her with an anger that persisted throughout her life. The first disagreement concerned the Leysin climbing school. Marilyn objected to Haston taking it over when he returned to Leysin that summer. But, in Bev Clark's view, 'the school as a physical entity did not exist – there wasn't a physical thing to take over'; and because Haston had established himself in Leysin, 'he became the logical person to run the school'. Even so, Haston rejected Marilyn's attempts to preserve anything of what she saw as Harlin's inspirational legacy in running the school. In a climactic, expletive-filled row, he told her that – as a result of the five days they had spent together at the Death Bivouac – he knew her husband better than she did. He cited that as justification when he appropriated Harlin's climbing equipment from the Chalet Pollux. As John Jr later saw it, Harlin and Haston had become so close on the mountain that, for Haston, 'they were the partnership, not the family. So he took the equipment – anything that dad had was his.'

Worst of all for Marilyn was an admission from Haston that left her with the feeling that Harlin's death could have been avoided. During one of their encounters at the chalet, the question arose of why the rope Harlin was ascending had broken. Haston, she vividly recalled, told her that he had noticed that the rope was fraying but did not think it would break. Her reaction had been one of shock and disbelief, and that was still apparent when she replayed

that conversation to me in Portland, Oregon in 2000, the first time
I'd met her since the Eiger. She told me again the next time we met,
when Leni and I visited her in June 2014. Haston, she recalled, had
come to the chalet in Leysin with a group of climbers. Although she
could not remember who they were, she could still visualise the
moment Haston spoke to her. 'I can see his face right there and I
can see mine right here.'

The question of why the rope had broken was an urgent preoccupation for all climbers, not only those who had taken part in the
Eiger Direct. It was a 100-metre length of 7mm rope and, it should
be recalled, had been fixed on the pitch above the Central Pillar by
Layton Kor on 21 March. There has been speculation over whether
it was part of a consignment of ropes donated to Harlin by the
long-established Swiss company Mammut. It was not. I still have
the invoice from the Max Eiselin equipment shop in Lucerne which
shows that it was among a batch of equipment he supplied on 12
March. It is listed, with no maker's name, as '1 Seil 100m' and cost
180 Swiss francs. On 12 September 1966, Eiselin wrote to Marilyn
expressing his 'deepest sympathies' for Harlin's death, adding the
following paragraph:

'I regret very much that owing to a sad fact the accident happened with a rope which John Harlin has bought in my shop.
However this would have happened with any other rope too.'

However self-serving Eiselin's apology might appear, the quality
of the rope was not as important as the use to which it had been
put – namely, its repeated ascent by climbers carrying heavy loads.
What was more, their entire weight had been applied to a section
where the rope hung over an angled slab of rock. The climbers
were following a technique pioneered in big-wall climbing in the
US; but, as Bonington observed in 2014, 'conditions in Yosemite
could not have been more different from the Alps in winter'. He
offered an explanation for what had happened by saying that the

climbers 'were using the stuff that was available' and knew no better; and that the competition between the two teams 'did not allow enough time to reflect'. In short, however, ascending a 7mm rope on Jumars was 'absolute madness'.

Following Harlin's death, and a similar accident in the US, climbers rapidly revised the technique. First, no one would ascend ropes less than 8mm thick; second, they used static ropes which did not have the enormous stretch that so alarmed the Eiger climbers and also increased the loading on the most vulnerable points.

As for Haston's apparent mea culpa, his confession to Marilyn that he had noticed that the rope was fraying but had not warned anyone, others were inclined to read it differently. Larry Ware exonerated Haston on the grounds that he must have judged that the rope was truly not likely to break – otherwise 'he would have done something about it'. Nor did Ware detect any sense of culpability on Haston's part. Some who knew Haston believed he was troubled by the Glencoe accident throughout his life, and Ariane Giobellina told us he had taken her to see the accident site. Ware, too, remembered Haston being 'deeply affected' by the Glencoe road accident but, by contrast, never saw any intimation of guilt, any sense of 'because of me this happened', when Haston talked about the Eiger Direct.

In their discussions about life following the Eiger Direct, the Harlins had intended to remain in Leysin and had been on the point of buying a large chalet with apartments for rent to boost their income. Now Marilyn began planning for a return to the US. On the day Harlin died, her father started to construct a cabin at his farm in Olympia to provide her and the children with somewhere to stay. In May, Marilyn sent Andréa ahead to the farm. In June, shortly before his tenth birthday, she took John Jr to the Matterhorn, in part-fulfilment of a promise Harlin had made that he and his son would climb the mountain together one day. (Harlin had added the typically ambitious rider that he wanted his son to be the youngest person ever to make the climb.) They hiked below the North Face, sleeping in a deserted grain shed, and John Jr used his father's camera to photograph flowers and rock formations.

John Jr wrote later that he could not fathom how his mother managed all her responsibilities, but they did mean that she could immerse herself in her work and organising her family's affairs. She continued her teaching and took her students on field trips to Greece and France. She viewed the 8mm movie film Harlin had been shooting during the climb and sent it to the eminent director D.A. Pennebaker in the hope that he could make a documentary, but word came back that the individual sequences were too short. She began collaborating on a biography of Harlin with Jim Ullman, writing him countless letters and providing introductions to his friends.

She and Ullman split the proceeds fifty-fifty, which included $5000 each from the publisher's advance; the book, *Straight Up*, was published in 1968. Her finances were in fact in good order, not least because she had been the family's principal breadwinner. She received $14,000 from an insurance policy her father had set up when John Jr was born: her father had presciently listed 'climbing' among Harlin's activities, leading Harlin to joke – to her distress – that she would be making money out of his death. The AAC president Carlton Fuller sent a personal cheque for $1000 and the climber Jim McCarthy, acting in his guise as lawyer, obtained $1000 from a magazine that reproduced family photographs without permission.

In July, John Jr joined Andréa at their grandparents' farm in Olympia. For Andréa, the time she spent there alone was to become the focus of a deep unhappiness that pervaded her life. By contrast John Jr, who had bonded with his grandfather during the family's visit in the summer of 1964, later recalled a 'fresh and magical new world'. He learned to hunt and fish, drove a tractor and acquired woodworking and farming skills. He remembered his grandfather's stories of the family's forebears and the rain drumming on the roof above his bedroom.

After winding up her family and professional matters in Leysin, Marilyn came to Olympia in the autumn. She spent the next four years doing graduate studies in marine biology at the University of Washington in Seattle. At first, she commuted the sixty miles from Olympia, then she bought a house for the family in Seattle; they also spent a year living on San Juan Island, offshore from Seattle, where she was working at a marine laboratory. In 1971 she obtained her doctorate and that autumn the family moved to New England, where she had been appointed as assistant professor specialising in marine algae, otherwise known as seaweed, in the botany department at the University of Rhode Island. She was the first woman to be appointed to any of its science departments, and at first had to struggle against an entrenched chauvinist professor; she outlasted him and, by the time she retired in 2000, half of the academic staff in her department were women.

Marilyn, who became a full professor at URI in 1983, had a well-regarded academic career, conducting research, undertaking sabbatical visits to universities in Canada and Australia, and inspiring successive generations of students. She was troubled with occasional bouts of illness that included epilepsy, migraines, muscle tension and difficulties with memory – a seeming set of psychosomatic problems that first occurred in Leysin and which she attributed to 'packing emotions into my muscles'. She twice came close to remarrying, but concluded that her independence was more important than 'merging a life with someone else'. Nor did she want to attempt to replicate life with her former husband. 'I did not want the marriage I had before, exciting and rewarding as it was.'

When Marilyn retired, she returned to the north-west US,

buying a distinctive eighty-year-old house with a pitched roof in Portland, which offered a retreat bringing her 'peace, privacy and joy'. A further attraction was that the house faced Laurelhurst Park, a 'wonderland' of trees that included sequoia and redwood. She became chair of the Friends of Laurelhurst Park, a volunteer group that helped install a breathtaking range of original and native plants, shrubs and trees, from Oregon grape to wild rose, vine maples to magnolias. She joined the local Unitarian church and in the summer of 2005 spent two weeks touring partner churches and historic sites in Hungary, Romania and the Czech Republic. Shortly after returning home she was visited by her son, who broke the news that he was about to climb the North Face of the Eiger.

Just as it had his father, the Eiger was to preoccupy John Harlin Jr for much of his life. At the time of his father's death, he was already imbued with a love of the wild which he inherited from his father and was strengthened by his stays with his grandfather. When he was being bullied at school, he found an escape by immersing himself in books that he borrowed from the school library, and he was especially affected by the fictionalised story of a researcher who spent a year following and studying a wolf pack in the Canadian Arctic. In 1969, shortly before he was thirteen, a graduate student friend of Marilyn invited him to join a Seattle mountaineering group on a visit to Alaska that summer. It was, he wrote, 'one of the happiest days of my life'.

Once in Alaska, he thrilled at climbing a 3000-metre peak, spotting signs of wolves and throwing a frisbee across the Arctic Divide, the watershed between the Arctic Ocean and the Pacific. He returned to Alaska for hiking and kayaking trips during the following two summers and, after the family moved to Rhode Island, went skiing in New Hampshire. During vacations he found work logging and delivering boats. In 1976, at the age of twenty, he enrolled at the University of California in Santa Barbara, majoring in environmental biology. He joined the mountaineering association and his first rock climb, at Tahquitz Rock near Los Angeles, brought the transcendental pleasures others have described: the delicate moves, the controlled fears, the adrenaline rushes. He felt like a lost child who had 'returned to home's soft embrace'.

Those experiences and pleasures set a template for his life. After graduating in 1979, he had a succession of outdoor jobs, including forestry and guiding. He became an expert climber, mountaineer and skier, travelling widely with the same relish for new places and experiences as his father. He became an accomplished writer, with his father's emotional intelligence and literacy. He was a respected editor, first of *Summit* magazine and then the *American Alpine Journal*. He chaired and judged mountain literature and film awards. It was a life and career, one feels entitled to say, of which his father would be proud.

Yet his father was casting a shadow that he could not escape. At first, following his death, the Harlin family had dealt with his absence by pretending he was away on an expedition. Like his mother, John Jr filled his life with so much activity that he scarcely had time to notice that his father's expedition never seemed to come to an end. But before long he had to contend with being John Harlin, son of the famous climber, instead of John Harlin in his own right. He also came to harness himself to his father's ambitions and first resolved that he would climb the Eiger Direct to the finish, accomplishing the task on his father's behalf. He next abruptly forswore his plans and pledged not to climb the Eiger. Then he gradually revised his goal, sensing that he would not achieve peace until he fulfilled it. What remained constant was a determination not to reveal his plans to his mother until he finally had to.

His first aim after graduating, he told us in 2014, was to spend

two years in which he intended 'to get climbing out of my system –
I was going to climb Dad's routes, finish the Eiger Direct and climb
routes of my own at the highest level'. His girlfriend, an artist and
painter named Adele Hammond, was studying in France for a year
and he planned to spend time with her, allowing him to climb in
the Alps and perhaps attempt the Eiger.

But first he made a trip to the Canadian Rockies, where he and
a partner climbed a challenging route on Mount Robson, the highest peak in the range. They were descending separately and were
within a few metres of safety when his partner missed a handhold
and fell 150 metres to his death. After finding his battered body,
John Jr spent a wretched night in a climbing cabin, where he wrote
in the logbook that, after losing his father and seeing his partner
die, he considered climbing was 'a bit too serious a game'. When he
called his mother he was deeply troubled by her reaction, and concluded that he could not subject her to the risk of him dying in a
similar accident. 'I felt I didn't have the right to put her through
that,' he later remarked. He renounced any plans to climb in the
Alps, the Eiger included, and pledged to climb only on rock. In the
spring of 1980, he went to Grindelwald with Adele and saw the
Eiger for the first time since 1966. He wrote that he felt like a religious devotee at a shrine. Although he renewed his vow not to
climb it, he could not help wondering: 'How would I do up there?
How would it feel?'

He and Adele were married in 1981. In 1982, he started delivering lectures on the Eiger Direct, incorporating his father's movie
footage and recordings of his radio calls. He found that he would
choke when he heard his father's words to me during his last radio
call: 'We're going to be working awfully hard; I don't know
whether we'll be able to make that broadcast.' He began receiving
letters from students his father had inspired; when they asked if he
intended to climb the Eiger, he assured them he did not. In 1990,

he took part in a group ascent of the Matterhorn organised by the Swiss tourist authority, Swiss Tourism. Since he was provided with a guide, he did not count this as real Alpine climbing and, in any case, considered that he was fulfilling his father's promise that they would climb the Matterhorn one day, even if he could no longer be the youngest person to do so. He was dismayed when a magazine published an article about him that was headlined: 'Yes, he was my father'. In 1994, he climbed Mount Waddington in British Columbia and, when he won his partner's praise, he imagined it was coming from his father. He still felt he was being measured against his father's accomplishments – not least by himself. He was in thrall to the demands and aspirations of a father who showed his dismay when he did poorly in an international ski race and when he lost a fight with a school bully in Leysin.

By then, he and Adele were living in a farmhouse they had bought and expansively refurbished in Hood River, Oregon. In 1996, a month before he turned forty, he and Adele had a daughter, Siena. Until then he had done his best to balance his responsibilities to his wife with his desire to climb, sometimes agonising over his decisions and hoping that he was being fair to both of them – and implicitly showing greater responsibility and restraint than his father had. Now the urge to climb the Eiger took hold again, as if fatherhood had exposed a totemic need to resolve his conflicting feelings towards his own father. In 1999, the family went to Europe and they visited Leysin to show Siena her grandfather's grave. Adele and Siena returned to the US while he geared himself up for an attempt on the Matterhorn, followed by the Eiger. He was in floods of tears when they said goodbye at Lausanne train station, overwhelmed by feelings of ambivalence and guilt. He accepted that it would be 'unforgivable' if he left his family bereaved, as his father had done; and yet he yielded to the 'irresistible' drive to climb.

After he and a partner traversed the Matterhorn – ascending on the Italian side, descending on the Swiss side – he arrived at the Eiger with a new pledge: he would only make an attempt if conditions were perfect. He spent a day peering at the North Face from Kleine Scheidegg, doing his best to divide the route into a series of manageable sections. Poor weather ruled out an attempt and when he left he tried to persuade himself that he had freed himself from his urge. Since he now knew that he could climb the face, he no longer needed to do so. The ploy failed. He returned to the Alps in 2003 and 2004, and was drawn back to the Eiger each time, but was relieved when it remained out of condition.

Then came the culminating temptation. In 2005, he was invited to take part in a film sponsored by Swiss Tourism that would entail climbing the North Face of the Eiger by the classic 1938 route. Before then, he had hoped to climb the Eiger without telling his wife or his mother until afterwards. Since the climb was to be filmed in IMAX format and would be a highly public event, he would have to come clean. When he confessed to Adele, she accepted his argument that undertaking the climb for a film made it as safe as could be. When he drove to Seattle and told Marilyn, she was 'not amused' and told him she didn't like the plan 'one little bit'. When he argued that no one had died during any of the production company's previous projects, she responded with the one word: 'Yet'.

It was clear that Marilyn remained troubled over her husband's death and its aftermath. Two years earlier, she had shaken uncontrollably when a film producer asked to interview her for a documentary about the Club Vag in Leysin, leaving her wondering who she was angry with. Was it her husband, for the nights he had spent drinking and carousing at the club, returning and going to bed just as she was getting up to go to work? Or was it Haston, for doing nothing about the fraying rope? She had declined to be interviewed and her anxieties now returned. But the next day she told John Jr that since he was determined to climb the Eiger, she would give him her support.

The climb was predicted to take three days. John Jr had two partners, the German climbers Robert Jasper and his wife Daniela. Jasper could be seen as a climber from a new age. In the four decades since the Eiger Direct, two dozen or more new routes had been put up on the face as climbers took advantage of advances in equipment and technique to climb at ever higher levels of skill and audacity. Jasper, thirty-seven in 2005, had climbed a dozen different routes on the face, and John Jr concluded that he would be hard-pushed to find a safer partner.

John Jr had presumed that during the climb he would be preoccupied with his father, as if he were following in his ghostly footsteps. In fact, he told us in 2014, 'I was fixed in the moment,' concentrating on the practicalities of the climb but also thinking about Siena. When he looked across to the Central Pillar and saw where the rope had broken, he imagined his father's final thoughts and wondered if – echoing his reflections on death – he was 'savouring the vivid moment of truth'. Otherwise he was in his own world, 'not Dad's'.

Adele and Siena were watching from Kleine Scheidegg, and Adele was at the telescope when he took a short, two-metre fall. Although he was unharmed she walked away, unable to look any more. When he reached the Summit Icefield on the third day, he looked across at the headwall where Haston and the Germans had fought for their lives while he was watching his father's coffin being lowered into his grave. But nothing could mar his swelling euphoria, or his delight at being reunited with Adele and Siena after the climb. Marilyn was staying with friends in Rhode Island when the call came that the climb was over and her son was safe. She duly recorded in her memoir: 'No one was killed.'

Although John Jr succeeded, and although he had truthfully promised his mother he would never attempt the Eiger Direct, the climb did not deliver the closure he had sought. That only came when he wrote a book about his father, their lives, and his own ascent of the Eiger. He had proposed a book which would incorporate his father's writing some time before, but his agent told him that he needed to climb the Eiger to complete the story. He learned far more about his father while researching the book, particularly among the voluminous letters which were held – against the family's wishes – in the Ullman Archives at Princeton University. Much of what he knew, or thought he knew, about his father had been at second or even third hand. Letters and memoranda from his mother, sometimes embarrassingly frank, told him about his father's dark side, from his womanising to the fantasies he spun about himself. They also revealed details about his own reaction to his father's death which he had obliterated. 'Writing the book was the real reconciliation, not the climb,' he told us in 2014.

The book, *The Eiger Obsession*, was published in 2007. His mother observed that when he staged readings from the book, 'he kept choking on his tears, at long last grieving openly'. It was widely acclaimed and won the award for the best book of climbing history at the Banff Mountain Festival. One of the judges, Ed Douglas, praised it as 'a judicious and moving memoir of a famous father and his son's journey from beneath his shadow'.

The IMAX film that included the Eiger climb, *The Alps,* was premiered at the Smithsonian Natural History Museum in Washington, DC, in March 2007. The sponsors made it a red-carpet event and the guests, who stayed at the Willard hotel on Pennsylvania Avenue, included both Marilyn and Andréa, together with her six-year-old daughter Cassia. Although it appeared to be a cause for celebration, it was in fact a rare family reunion. The sad truth was that Andréa had never come to terms with her father's death and had also directed an unrelenting anger towards her mother, causing a rift that remains unhealed.

Andréa was eight when her father died. In the dynamics of the family, John Jr was closer to his mother, Andréa to her father. Marilyn and John Jr were the rational, analytic and scientific pair; Andréa and her father tended to the artistic, emotional and instinctive. Harlin had predicted that if their marriage broke down, John Jr would go with Marilyn, Andréa with him. When we asked Andréa in 2014 what she remembered of her father, she described how he had helped her to colour a drawing of a musical instrument – a viola, she thought, or a double bass. 'I had a purple crayon and he showed me how to make an outline and fill it in.' She remembered playing miniature golf with him, but also recalled her jealousy when he took her brother skiing and climbing: in physical activities, 'he got all the attention and I felt like a lost child'. She remembered sitting on her father's lap as he brushed her hair and called her his princess. 'I remember him being funny and I remember feeling wanted by him.' Above all, she remembers the aroma of wet wool. 'I remember him being away more than being home. He was gone a lot and I would come home and smell sweaty socks and that meant he was at home.'

Two months after her father's death, Andréa went to stay with her mother's parents at Olympia – and here, her perceptions and memories differed strikingly from those of her mother and brother. John Jr recalled that Marilyn was finding it hard to cope with Andréa's demands, but both he and Marilyn believed that she had enjoyed her stay in Olympia in 1965 and was keen to return there. Andréa, by contrast, always insisted that she had been reluctant to go there after her father died. For her, it was a time of irredeemable loneliness, made worse by missing her brother and their dog and cat. 'It was an eternity.' Above all, she remembered her anguish on seeing her grandparents' photograph of Marilyn and the two children. 'I just cried and cried and cried. I felt like I just cut my heart out.' All of this became overlaid with the belief that her mother had rejected her. 'I felt it was a deliberate way of getting rid of me.' This conviction has persisted through her entire adult life, compounding the grief for her father that has gone unassuaged.

Andréa was thirteen when the family moved to Rhode Island, separating her from her friends in Seattle. 'Every time we got settled and developed a little community, boom, we are gone again.' She felt isolated at her new school – and, crucially, was clinging to a set of fantasies about her father. He hadn't died on the Eiger; he had rowed with her mother; he had walked out of the home and the marriage; it was all her mother's fault; the funeral had been a charade or pretence; one day he might even return. 'It is amazing when I think about it now,' she said. 'I thought my mother was making it up – maybe he has left us and she is telling us a story.' Her imaginings 'helped keep that feeling alive that he would come back one day'. Only when she was fifteen or sixteen did she finally conclude that he was dead and would never return.

By then Andréa was at mid-point in a troubled adolescence. Soon after the move to Rhode Island, Andréa went to stay in Seattle, where Marilyn hoped she would be happier among her former friends. Not long afterwards she ran away, leaving Marilyn frantic with anxiety before she reappeared in Rhode Island. From that point she traversed the full gamut of teenage problems, punctuated by further disappearances. In 1975 she enrolled at the University of Rhode Island, where she majored in plant science, although she dropped out in her final year. In 1978, when she was twenty, she got married. Her husband, Gene Cilento, was a fellow plant science student and a talented ice hockey player; they met when she was working as a waitress and he was employed in a nearby fishing dock. She was astonished to see a picture on the wall at his home of the Dents du Midi, reminding her of the view from the Chalet Pollux in Leysin. 'I was just like, "Okay I love you." I felt it was fate.' They married two months later.

Cilento came from a large family of Italian descent, offering her tactile and expressive qualities that she felt her own family lacked. At first they travelled widely across the US but stopped when they had children: 'Once we had kids I wanted to stay put.' They began by living in a trailer on a hillside at Summit Lake, Washington – fifteen miles from Olympia. Through the years they extended it into an airy and spacious family home, with a veranda providing a vista of the pine forests surrounding the lake. They had four children: two daughters and two sons, one of whom they adopted in Thailand. Gene became an occupational therapist, specialising in problems of the hand, working for the public school system in the state of Washington.

For a long time, Andréa had a framed copy of a magazine article about her father on the wall, and she kept a box of clippings about him in her room. By Marilyn's account, she was thrilled to be invited to the premiere of *The Alps* and considered it 'the best time of her life'. She was 'composed, interacted well ... and was mentally clear when she gave an interview to Associated Press'. She told her mother she regretted that they had been estranged and, having been appalled when she learned that her brother intended to climb the Eiger, 'now forgave him the climb after she learned from the book why he had to do it'.

Andréa recalled the film premiere in broader brush strokes, which included the pleasure for her daughter Cassia of staying in a luxury hotel in Washington and placing orders on room service: 'We had a lot of fun.' She also remembered telling Cassia about her grandfather. In her memoir, Marilyn printed a photograph of the family in Washington that shows her with an arm around Andréa's shoulder, but the reunion did not bring the reconciliation she had hoped for. She and Andréa met only rarely afterwards, although Marilyn did her best to maintain contact with her grandchildren. Although Andréa saw more of her brother, she felt apart from him too. Their relationship, she said in 2014, 'is not what I wish it would have been ... We took completely different directions. We did have a great love for each other and I wish it was better.'

The family estrangement remained a matter of profound regret for Marilyn. She treasured a piece of embroidery Andréa made for her, a wall hanging of seashore plants and animals, which displayed her 'bright and creative' personality and showed 'some wish to connect' at the time she stitched it. The question can be asked whether her father's death was the sole cause of Andréa's distress; or whether other aspects of her background and the family dynamics were contributing factors. It is a moot point. Andréa believed that her anger following her father's death was 'a form of protection and I wish I had been able to figure that out'. Did she think that she and her mother could ever be reconciled? Her answer was a blunt, 'No.' But she asked us to be judicious in describing her feelings towards her mother. 'I don't want her to feel pain over what I feel.'

Four months after returning from the Eiger and resuming work at the *Weekend Telegraph*, I was sacked. During the last week of the climb, I had led the *Telegraph*'s front page three times in four days. Following my report of Harlin's death, my accounts of the last two days of the climb had been the main news story on 25 and 26 March, and I felt immodestly pleased with my efforts. The *Telegraph* evidently agreed, as shortly before I left Kleine Scheidegg I received an effusive telex, known in the trade as a herogram, from Anstey, congratulating me on my work.

Soon after my return, Anstey stopped talking to me. For some reason, I found that I had been cast in the role of office scapegoat, and received typed notes from Anstey levelling accusations at me that were either entirely unjust or related to problems that were nothing to do with me. Similar tales of Anstey's behaviour were to become legion. Arbitrary sackings, victimisation, sexual harassment became the currency of conversation among *Telegraph* veterans who had worked for him before he retired in 1986 (he died of lung cancer two years later). Although the bullying I experienced was minor in comparison, he delivered a characteristic ploy just as Leni and I were about to leave for a holiday in Switzerland, where Bev Clark was lending us his apartment in Leysin. On the morning of our departure, a letter marked 'Special Delivery' arrived from Anstey giving me the sack. This too, I later learned, was typical of the man. Having read the signals, I was lining up freelance work at the rival *Sunday Times Magazine*, so I replied telling Anstey that I quit. He was determined to have the last word and wrote again to insist that he had sacked me before I resigned. When I returned to the office to work out my notice I found that Anstey's herogram had disappeared from my desk, as had the copy that was kept in the magazine's telex file.

At that stage, in the summer of 1966, I was twenty-four, had a wife and two young children to support and a mortgage to pay. I was also jobless. I had a cushion in the form of payments from *Eiger Direct*. The man who came to my rescue was Peter Crookston, the features editor at the *Sunday Times Magazine*, who liked my work and offered me a freelance contract. That began a long relationship with the *Sunday Times* that included a spell on its staff under Harold Evans, one of journalism's greatest editors. Evans encouraged his journalists to tell things as they saw them and published the results irrespective of whom they might upset. I worked as a reporter and feature writer and spent five years on the *Sunday Times*'s renowned investigative unit, the Insight team. I covered the conflict in Northern Ireland, reported frequently from the Middle East, and was assigned to Washington during the Falklands War.

I count myself fortunate to have been part of one of the great adventures of journalism which came to an end, for me, when Rupert Murdoch took over the *Sunday Times* and it lost credibility as it began to reflect his political and commercial interests. I left the staff and resumed life as a freelance, although I continued to write for the *Sunday Times Magazine* until 2011.

As for Leni, when our children were old enough to go to school, she began a career as a teacher and lecturer in the public education sector. After falling foul of educational politics once too often, she left teaching for journalism and we formed a writing partnership that produced numerous articles published under our shared byline. We wrote books together, including *The Wildest Dream*, the biography of our Everest hero George Mallory, which won the Boardman Tasker award for mountain writing in 2000.

Our children became adults and took up careers in teaching and counselling; in time, we had four grandchildren, who became the light of our lives. As for climbing, I gave up rock climbing at a serious level and devoted my outdoor energies to hill walking, above all in Scotland in summer and winter. I succumbed to the lure of the Munros, and climbed many of them with Danny and Seth. I climbed the final peak in 1997, and in 2010 added the last of the new peaks on the Scottish Mountaineering Club's revised list. I had the supreme pleasure of climbing a Munro, Meall nan Tarmachan, with our youngest grandson, Jacob, when I was sixty-seven and he was six.

By then, the idea of retelling the story of the Eiger Direct was nagging at me. I wanted to provide a new account which did full justice to the dimensions of the drama and the achievements and perceptions of both teams. I also wanted to understand what I had seen when I looked through the telescope and saw Harlin framed there fractionally after the rope broke. I had preserved that image without examining it, and had also sealed my mind against the way it had been violated by Hugo Kuranda's invention.

In 1982, I watched a reconstruction of Harlin's fall in a remarkable film by the intrepid climber and filmmaker Leo Dickinson. Dickinson had enlisted a sky diver to simulate the fall by jumping from a helicopter and releasing a parachute after he passed the location where Harlin fell. Dickinson added the soundtrack of my last radio call to Harlin and I was profoundly shaken by the sequence – emerging from the viewing theatre, Dickinson told me, pale and unsteady. I suspect that afterwards I locked these feelings away, only retrieving them when I began writing this book and was surprised by my anger at Kuranda's act of despoliation.

There were other clues that something within me was urging me to write the book. I began to suffer nightmares about trying to meet deadlines. Some were connected to writing and journalism, others to aspects of everyday life such as catching trains or planes, and I would usually wake just as the deadline was about to elapse and I knew I would miss it. The deadlines conveyed a new impetus in real life when I realised that the fiftieth anniversary of the climb was approaching and if I did not start writing soon it would be too late.

I made my first research visit to Germany in October 2013. Jochen Hemmleb and I met three of the surviving German climbers – Sigi Hupfauer, Günter Schnaidt and Rolf Rosenzopf – at Hupfauer's home in the village of Pfaffenhofen, set in well-ordered farmland twenty miles from Ulm. They were welcoming and I was flattered that they remembered me from 1966. They were a little guarded as we began to talk, and Hupfauer explained that some of the climbers remained wary of the media, having been shaken by the criticism they received after the climb. Strobel was particularly reluctant to take part in media projects and Votteler was ambivalent too: he had referred to the climb as 'that old thing' when Hupfauer approached him on our behalf. But the three we met answered all our questions over the best part of a day, with a break for a Swabian lunch which included pretzels, Weisswurst – a white sausage – and hoppy beer. Hupfauer was the most talkative and expressive; Schnaidt looked back on events with affectionate good humour; and Rosenzopf, although the most reserved, made some telling interventions.

We returned for a second meeting in February 2014, this time at the home of Günter and Margret Schnaidt in a suburb of Stuttgart. Between the two visits, Hupfauer had been working on Strobel and Votteler. At his suggestion, we sent a letter asking Strobel if he would meet us, listing the questions we wanted to ask. Schnaidt handed our letter to Strobel at their mountaineers' singing group.

On the day before the meeting, Hupfauer had reported that Votteler was still unsure whether to come. When we arrived at the Schnaidts', we were relieved to find him there, but it was still unclear whether Strobel would take part. Then he arrived, a tall, upright figure with receding white hair and a distinguished grey moustache. Fulfilling our hopes, it was the first time all five Eiger climbers had met at the same time for thirty years, and the banter and jokes were soon flowing. I thought I was reasonably fluent in German, having spent five years learning it at school but, as the climbers relaxed, their Swabian dialect became all but impenetrable. Strobel and Votteler were soon talking without inhibition, and both appeared pleased at the opportunity to relate events and experiences concerning the final stages of the climb which, in Votteler's case, had been largely ignored in the German book about the climb. We were struck by Votteler's enduring sense of humour and his wry understatement when describing both the trials of the final stages of the climb and his long hospital stay. We were also impressed by the desire of Strobel – still the most hardcore climber of the team – that we should understand the technical qualities of the climb. He especially wanted to convey the importance of the Harlin team's decision to use the rope he had fixed on the dangerous pitch above the Second Band on 8 March. For it was then, Strobel said, that 'rivals became friends'. There was an equivalent spirit about the gathering of the climbers, easy in each other's company even though it was so long since they had all been together, enjoying the banter and the bonhomie, relaxing in their comradeship, their solidarity and their nostalgia.

We also sensed that the more traumatic aspects of the final stages of the climb were finally being addressed. That applied, we felt, to Votteler's injury from stonefall and Hupfauer's fears that they might not make it off the face alive. We also realised that the two who had been uncertain whether to meet us were the two who had lost all their toes to frostbite. That helped to make sense of Strobel's recurring complaints in the Belser book about how long the climb was taking, a theme that was reinforced in an intriguing manner in the course of our meeting. During a break, Strobel handed us a sealed envelope, which we opened at our hotel that evening. It contained a typed five-page reply to our questions and was rich in illuminating detail. The most dramatic concerned the argument after Harlin's death over whether the Germans should divide into two teams, as Strobel recommended, with the faster going to the summit first. Strobel described how Lehne had wavered before deciding that the team should stick together, as Hupfauer wanted, and had captured the intensity of the occasion with the vivid phrase: 'The devil was out.'

We felt that Strobel's account clarified some further issues. It helped explain why he had been reluctant to talk about the climb, as he appeared still to be angry with his colleagues that the final ascent had been delayed. If he had reached the summit after one bivouac instead of two, his toes might have been saved. That interpretation appeared to be confirmed when Strobel spoke to Jochen a few days later, asking us not to reveal details of the row in case it upset his team-mates. 'My friendship with Sigi would be over.'

That left us in a quandary over how much we could write about an incident, never before revealed, that said so much about the problems and pressures facing the climbers during their fight to survive. Our dilemma was resolved when we raised it with Hupfauer. He was content for us to write about the argument, as he had thrashed it out with Strobel two years before and there were no hard feelings between them. He was also delighted that our project had brought the climbers together. The next time we talked to Strobel he was pleased the row was out in the open. We therefore included it as a testament to the depths of the climbers' ordeal, to the quality of Lehne's leadership as he faced his lonely decision, and to the enduring strength of the group of climbers almost fifty years on.

In March 2014, Leni and I went to Kleine Scheidegg. It was our first return visit since the summer of 1966, when we had taken the train from Grindelwald, only to find the North Face covered by cloud. This time we were granted dazzling sunshine, enabling us to pick out every detail of the face. During our meeting with Andreas von Almen, when he talked about the restoration of the hotel, he recalled one extraordinary detail from the day Harlin died. In 1966, when he was eight, his parents ran the Hotel Jungfrau in nearby Wengernalp. On the afternoon of 22 March he and his mother were skiing beneath the North Face of the Eiger when they saw a small avalanche ahead of them. 'It was nothing dangerous, and then we saw a rucksack gliding down about fifty metres away from us, and we saw a piece of rope too.' His mother told him the ruck-sack must have been dropped by the climbers who were attempting the face by a new direct route. That evening he learned of Harlin's death – and later realised that Harlin had fallen just a few minutes before at the very spot he and his mother had passed, and that his body must have come to rest somewhere out of sight below.

The weather that had been so kind to us at Kleine Scheidegg broke the next morning as we drove to Leysin, where John Harlin Jr was spending time setting up environmental and personal devel-opment projects at the American School. When he took us to the Leysin cemetery it was snowing, just as it had done on the day of his father's funeral. In Switzerland graves are 'turned over' after forty years, meaning that they are recycled, and the headstone to his father's grave had been removed. A short distance away, Haston's grave was intact but it had never had a headstone. We met John Jr again in June, on our trip to Oregon and Washington, when we also visited his sister and his mother. Marilyn, who was about to turn eighty, was as lively and witty as I had remembered, and took both pride and pleasure in showing us the garden she had created at her house, with its rich range of native plants, and in taking us on a walk around Laurelhurst Park.

Once we started writing, our book took six months to complete. The narrative was complicated, drawing on the experiences and perceptions of more than a dozen key characters, and using sources in several different languages. As always, Leni and I discussed the shape it was taking and the meaning it held. As we did, the moment of Harlin's death, the moment I had witnessed, assumed ever greater importance. I was reluctant to elevate my role too far, as the fact that I happened to have seen it was of minor significance compared with its impact on the Harlins themselves. Yet it seemed to offer a key to one possible reading of the narrative.

The protagonist, John Harlin, was driven by ambition to climb the Eiger Direct. He was both a richly talented and a flawed character, one who attracted friends and enemies. He struggled to balance his ambition with the other aspects of his life, most importantly his love for his wife and children, but it would not be quelled. After falling out with a number of prospective partners he assembled his team. A rival team appeared, equally intent on making the first ascent. But Harlin was reluctant to take it seriously and dismissed its prospects. When the climb started, Harlin faced a series of tests as leader. Here too he displayed both talents and faults. He had provided the inspiration and the impetus for the climb, but proved indecisive at crucial moments. His rivals were demonstrating that they were a force to be reckoned with, yet still Harlin sought to downplay their chances. When they proposed that the two teams join forces, Harlin turned them down for fear this would devalue the prize of the first ascent.

After a month on the face, the two teams were poised to go for the summit. But still Harlin hesitated, and his rivals took the lead. Harlin hastened to catch them up, but died in the attempt. His ambition had exceeded his ability to fulfil it and had brought him down. His death was memorialised when the rival teams combined to complete the ascent, which they named 'the John Harlin climb'.

The narrative has an alluring shape. Yet in one key respect it is open to question. Five people had previously ascended the rope that broke; four of them that same day. So did Harlin die because he had prevaricated that morning? Or was his death pure chance, the outcome of a lethal game of existential roulette, just as it was pure chance that I happened to be watching at the moment he lost the game? Was the flaw in his character? Or in the rope?

We are tempted to say: Dear reader, you decide. Or perhaps we should end by citing the view imparted to us by his son. He too had reflected on the narrative construct his father's life and death appear to fit, that of a character who dies in pursuit of a dream, and felt that it made a perfect story. And having long pondered his father's character and his death, he concluded: 'I don't see him as an idol but I do see him as someone admirable. He had his flaws but they were part of his personality, not his whole personality, and helped to make him the man he was.'

ROUTE DESCRIPTION

In 1966, after the climb, Dougal Haston wrote a technical description of the Direct Route. It provides his estimate of the length and gradings of the seventy-three pitches of the ascent, together with the angle of the ice pitches. The Scottish ice gradings are still in use, but now go up to grade XII to reflect their increased technical difficulty. Haston's rock gradings refer to the Alpine standard in use at the time. The highest grade now stands at XI/XII, but it has been largely replaced in Europe by a French system ranging from 1 to 9. The A gradings refer to aid climbing and run from A0 to A5. Under the gradings of the time, the 1966 route would be summarised as V+ (one pitch VI), A3, 70–80° (one pitch 90°). Using 2015 gradings, if the rock pitches are climbed free, climbers would classify the route ED+, M8, 7a. ED stands for *Extrêmement Difficile*, a modern overall grading for Alpine climbs.

During the climb, Harlin's team usually described distances in feet, while the German team used metres. For the sake of consistency, we have used metric measurements throughout the text, apart from in direct quotes. We have however preserved Haston's use of feet in his route description.

For pure ice, Scottish gradings of (I–V) are used. For mixed rock and ice, standard gradings (I–VI). Go across snowfields to prominent couloir to left of first pillar and almost directly below Eigerwand station. Start in couloir.

1	Climb a steep ice pitch (70°) (IV)	*100ft*
2	Go left on snowfield 30ft, then up ice (70°–80°) for 70ft to snowfield (IV)	*100ft*
3–8	Follow snowfield 50° to foot of next steep section	*ca 100ft*
9	Go up narrow couloir to the left of rock buttress ice (75°), then traverse right on poorly iced slabs to stance on snowfield (III sup.)	*100ft*
10	Climb steep ice (75°–85°), trending first slightly left then straight up to bolt belay (IV sup.)	*120ft*
11	Move left 70° for 20ft, then climb iced corner (90°) for 30ft to Icefield (IV sup.)	*50ft*
12–13	Up Icefield 50°	*200ft*
14–16	Continue on steeper Icefield (60°) with small steep steps (III) for three rope-lengths to beneath gallery window [first bivouac cave]	*400ft*

End of first section/Vorbau

17	Go up to the right of the station window to a bolt stance. Belay in slings (A3)	*80ft*
18	Go straight up for 50ft, then traverse 20ft right into a diedre, climb this for 50ft then come 20ft right to beneath a smooth bulge. Climb the bulge to another sling stance (A3)	*120ft*
19	Climb a very strenuous overhang above the stance, then more easily to sling stance at top of First Band (A3)	*100ft*
20	Climb steep ice (70°) with a few bulges (IV sup.)	*60ft*

21	Continue on this ice (70°) with odd bulges to stance on slab (IV sup.)	*120ft*
22	Go straight up on difficult mixed ground to a snowfield (V–V sup.)	*40ft*
23	Climb the snowfield for a rope-length. Second bivouac cave	*100ft*
24–25	Climb First Icefield	*300ft*
26	Traverse right at top, then back left to poor crack which leads to prominent gully system on Second Band	*140ft*
27	Climb crack (V)	*40ft*
28	Traverse right on snow	*100ft*
29	Climb the gully above – poor snow with ice steps (III)	*120ft*
30	Go up the chimney with rotten snow on left of stance (V sup., VI – crux of Band)	*50ft*
31	Traverse left on steep ice to top of Band. Third bivouac cave (III sup., IV)	*100ft*
32	Climb steep ice above arête at top of Band to stance beneath lower left end of Flatiron (IV)	*140ft*
33–34	Traverse right under base of Flatiron	*250ft*
35–38	Go up Second Icefield on right of Flatiron. Mainly snow with occasional steep ice steps	*300ft*
39–40	Traverse 200ft right on snow and ice	*200ft*
41	Climb V crack on ordinary route to ice pitch. Belay above	*100ft*
42–43	Go up rotten ice to top of Flatiron	*160ft*
44–45	Traverse left to crest of Flatiron. Death Bivouac	*300ft*
46	Go round corner from Death Bivouac on mixed ground, then straight up Third Icefield on hard water-ice (60°) to ice-peg belay (III)	*140ft*
47	Continue to top of Third Icefield	*100ft*

48	Climb mixed ground to crest of arête leading to Central Pillar (V sup.)	*100ft*
49	Go up crest to stance on right side of Central Pillar (III)	*100ft*
50	Traverse left on aid to bolt and belay on sling stance at left end of Central Pillar (A3 sustained)	*100ft*
51	Climb thin ice groove of sustained difficulty to bolt belay (IV sup.)	*100ft*
52	Go up ice trough to top of Central Pillar (IV)	*80ft*
53	Go along the narrow neck which connects the Central Pillar to the main face for 30ft. Climb crack system above, starting in a roof to sling and bolt stance (A2 sustained)	*140ft*
54	Go straight up above the stance on mixed artificial and free climbing (A2, V)	*100ft*
55	Traverse right into ice grooves and climb these to the foot of the arête at the bottom of the Spider (III)	*100ft*
56–7	Go up the Spider to the start of a traverse line leading out of the right side	*200ft*
58–60	Traverse rightwards on mixed ground for three pitches to the Fly	*300ft*
61	Go up Fly to top left corner	*100 ft*
62–4	Three pitches on mixed, loose ground to foot of prominent chimney system (IV and V sustained)	*300ft*
65–6	Climb the chimmey in two pitches to an awkward stance (V, V sup. Steps of A1)	*200ft*
67	Go up behind stance to overhang, then traverse right to stance at the foot of chimney (V, V sup. Steps of A1)	*130ft*

68 Climb the chimney for 40ft, then move diagonally
left on icy slabs to poor stance at the foot of a
leftward sloping diagonal fault (V sup.) *130ft*

69 Follow the fault to its end on mixed ground (V) *80ft*

70 Move back right and up for 100ft on icy slabs
(V sup.) *100ft*

71–2 Up Summit Icefield on water-ice *300ft*

73 Go left from stance round rock bulge and straight
up to the summit *150ft*

ACKNOWLEDGEMENTS

Our research was aided and enriched by the invaluable assistance we received from a wide range of people. We have already acknowledged the help generously provided by the principal figures involved, and we now thank them again: Marilyn Harlin, John Harlin III and Andréa Cilento; Sigi Hupfauer, Rolf Rosenzopf, Günter Schnaidt, Günther Strobel and Roland Votteler; and Sir Chris Bonington. We are especially grateful, too, to Barbara Haag and her daughter Christiane; and to Peter Lehne and Marina Lehne. We also thank the other participants and observers we were able to interview, in person and/or by email: Andreas von Almen, Rusty Baillie, Cam Burns, Bev Clark, John Cleare, Ariane Giobellina, Gaby Hupfauer, Konrad Kirch, Alex Low, Hans-Mayer Hasselwander, Jim McCarthy, Margret Schnaidt, Joanne Urioste, Larry Ware, Adelheid Widmaier (née Reiter).

We were provided with further advice, help and information by the following: Sandy Allan, Gerhard Baur, Lothar Brandler, Julian Browne, Daniela Ceccin, Yvon Chouinard, Joanna Croston, Leo Dickinson, Ed Douglas, Norman Dyhrenfurth, Jon and Dorothy Evans, Mick Fowler, Lindsay Griffin, Celia Haddon, Graham Harrison, Dietrich Hasse, Tom Hornbein, Hermann Huber, Tadeusz Hudowski, Ned Kelly, Gudrun Lawlor, Hilde Löw, Calista Lucy, Anderl Mannhardt, Martina Mehta, Brian Moynahan, Dal Norris,

Martin Oelbermann, Mike Parsons, Federica Pellegatti, Rainer Rettner, Mary Rose, Audrey Salkeld, Katie Sauter, Chic Scott, Luca Signorelli, Christine Thel, Simon Thompson, Dick Turnbull, Stephen Venables, Eric Vola, Ed Webster, Bill Wesbrooks.

We are particularly grateful to Tad Hudowski at the Alpine Club library; and to Mike Parsons and Mary Rose for their article 'Eiger Direct 1966, Another Bare-knuckle Fight', which compares the equipment used on the 1938 first ascent and the 1966 Direct.

We record once again our gratitude to our partner, Jochen Hemmleb, for his assiduous help, advice and expertise in researching and shaping this book. We wish to give special thanks to our grandson, Blake Gillman, for his insightful comments on our manuscript; and at Simon & Schuster we thank Ian Marshall, Charlotte Coulthard, Lorraine Jerram and Lewis Csizmazia.

BIBLIOGRAPHY
AND SOURCES

Achey, Jeff; Chelton, Dudley and Godfrey, Bob, *Climb! The Stock of Rock Climbing in Colorado* (Mountaineers, 2002)

Ament, Pat, *Royal Robbins: Spirit of the Age* (Stackpole, 1998)

Anker, Daniel (ed.), *Eiger: the Vertical Arena* (Mountaineers, 2000)

Arrigoni, Gabriele, *Arrampicando ho Conosciuto: Ricordi d'Alpinismo di Roberto Sorgato* (Club Alpino Italiano, 2000)

Bonington, Chris, *I Chose to Climb* (Gollancz, 1966)

Bonington, Chris, *The Next Horizon* (Gollancz, 1973)

Bonington, Chris, *The Everest Years* (Hodder and Stoughton, 1986)

Boysen, Martin, *Hanging On* (Vertebrate, 2014)

Breuer, Thomas M., *Eiger im Detail* (Self-published, 1963)

Burns, Cameron M., *Layton Kor* (work in progress)

Coffey, Maria, *Where the Mountain Casts its Shadow* (St Martin's Press, 2003)

Comici, Emilio, *Alpinismo Eroico* (Vivaldi, 1995)

Connor, Jeff, *Dougal Haston: the Philosophy of Risk* (Canongate, 2002)

Curran, Jim, *High Achiever: the Life and Climbs of Chris Bonington* (Constable, 1999)

Desmaison, René, *Professionel du Vide* (Arthaud, 1979)

Desmaison, René, *Les Forces de la Montagne* (Hoëbeke, 2005)

Douglas, Ed, *Tenzing: Hero of Everest* (National Geographic Society, 2003)

Gillman, Peter and Haston, Dougal, *Eiger Direct* (Collins, 1966)

Gillman, Peter, *In Balance* (Hodder and Stoughton, 1989)

Gillman, Peter and Leni, *The Wildest Dream* (Headline, 2000)

Grammiger, Ludwig, *Das gerettete Leben* (Rother, 1986)

Hansen, Peter H., *The Summits of Modern Man: Mountaineering after the Enlightenment* (Harvard, 2003)

Harlin, John, *The Eiger Obsession* (Simon & Schuster, 2007)

Harlin, Marilyn Miler, *Making Waves: Memoir of a Marine Botanist* (FriesenPress, 2014)

Harrer, Heinrich, *The White Spider* (Rupert Hart-Davis, 1959)

Harrer, Heinrich, *Das Buch vom Eiger* (Pinguin, 1988)

Haston, Dougal, *In High Places* (Cassell, 1972)

Haston, Dougal, *The Eiger* (Cassell, 1974)

Haston, Dougal, *Calculated Risk* (Diadem, 1979)

Hiebeler, Toni, *North Face in Winter* (Barrie and Rockcliffe, 1962)

Hiebeler, Toni, *Eigerwand – Der Tod klettert mit* (Limpert, 1963)

Hiebeler, Toni, *Eigerwand – Von der Erstbesteigung bis heute* (Bertelsmann, 1976)

Jones, Chris, *Climbing in North America* (Mountaineers, 1997)

Kor, Layton, *Beyond the Vertical* (Falcon Guides, 2013)

Lehne, Jörg and Haag, Peter, *Eiger: Kampf um die Direttissima* (Belser, 1966)

Mailänder, Nicholas, *Hart am Trauf* (Panico, 2003)

Nugent, Frank, *In Search of Peaks, Passes and Glaciers: Irish Alpine Pioneers* (Collins Press, 2013)

Rettner, Rainer, *Eiger: Triumphe und Tragödien* (AS, 2008)

Rettner, Rainer, *Wettlauf um die grossen Nordwände* (AS, 2010)

Roth, Arthur, *Eiger: Wall of Death* (Gollancz, 1982)

Rubi, Rudolf, *Der Eiger* (Paul Haupt, 1959)

Thompson, Simon, *Unjustifiable Risk? The Story of British Climbing* (Cicerone, 2010)

Ullman, James Ramsey, *Man of Everest* (Harrap, 1955)

Ullman, James Ramsey, *Straight Up: the Life and Death of John Harlin* (Doubleday, 1968)

Zeper, Nereo, *Ladro di Montagne: Ignazio Piussi* (Muzzio, 1997).

Journals

Alpinismus
Alpinist – issues 40 and 41, The Eiger Contradiction
The Alpine Journal
The American Alpine Journal
Mountain
Article: 'Eiger Direct 1966: Another Bare-knuckle Fight', Parsons, Mike
and Rose, Mary (to be published)

Other documentary sources include a voluminous collection of letters and
other documents generously provided by John Harlin III; letters and documents kindly lent to us by Barbara Haag; files at the library of the Deutscher
Alpenverein in Munich; and contemporary newspapers and journals.

A vital source was, of course, our interviews with the participants and
observers we have quoted or whose information we have used in the
text. We have listed these in our Acknowledgements section.

INDEX